NAPOLEON'S
LAST CAMPAIGN
IN GERMANY

BY THE SAME AUTHOR

NAPOLEON'S CAMPAIGN IN POLAND, 1806–1807

NAPOLEON'S CONQUEST OF PRUSSIA, 1806. With an Introduction by Lord Roberts

NAPOLEON AND THE ARCHDUKE CHARLES, 1809

SIMON BOLIVAR: El Libertador

NAPOLEON'S LAST CAMPAIGN IN GERMANY 1813
BY F. LORAINE PETRE
WITH SEVENTEEN MAPS & PLANS

The Naval & Military Press Ltd

Published by

The Naval & Military Press Ltd
Unit 10 Ridgewood Industrial Park,
Uckfield, East Sussex,
TN22 5QE England

Tel: +44 (0) 1825 749494
Fax: +44 (0) 1825 765701

www.naval-military-press.com
www.nmarchive.com

In reprinting in facsimile from the original, any imperfections are inevitably reproduced and the quality may fall short of modern type and cartographic standards.

AUTHOR'S PREFACE

THE author's first two volumes, on Napoloen's campaigns of 1806 and 1807, dealt with the Emperor at the culminating point of his military genius. In the third, the campaign of 1809, signs of decline had already begun to appear, and the great master neglected the relentless pursuit of the enemy's main army which had hitherto been the guiding principle in all his wars.

In the campaign of 1813, described in the present volume, it is only at times that the flame of his genius burns with its old vigour. Time after time he seems to lose sight of the real objective, and to hanker after secondary objectives and the occupation of mere geographical points, the attainment of which would inevitably have followed on success in the true objective, the decisive defeat of the enemy's main army.

Over Napoleon's opponents a change in the opposite direction showed signs of approach. They had learnt something from their great enemy, though they still too often hesitated and were lost. Yet now the hesitation was not, as heretofore, all on their side, and the picture of Napoleon sitting at Düben in doubt and uncertainty is one which could never have been imagined of the conqueror of Ulm, of Austerlitz, or of Jena.

The whole character of the war against Napoleon had changed. He found himself no longer opposed to dynasties, but rather to whole peoples, encouraged by the examples of Spain and Russia to rise *en masse* against the tyranny of the oppressor.

One consequence of this was a vast increase in the

numerical strength of the armies which opposed him, and a complete change in their spirit and enthusiasm. War assumed more the character of that of our own day. It became, not the war of one hired army against another, but of nations against nations. Leipzig was justly called "The battle of the Nations," and in the numbers engaged we must wait for the war of to-morrow to see it largely exceeded.

At the same time, it would be wrong to draw too close a comparison between 1813 and war in the twentieth century. The immense improvements in range and accuracy of weapons necessitate the operation of modern armies on fields many times greater, even in proportion to their numbers, than those on which Napoleon fought in 1813. This was brought very vividly before the author's eyes in the manœuvres of the 4th French division, from which he has just returned. The general idea was the advance of Napoleon, in 1814, to the battle of Craonne, and on to that of Laon. The troops engaged, representing Napoleon's army, were about one-third of his numbers; yet they covered a front two or three miles broader than he did.

Another point which gives special interest to the study of the campaign of 1813 is the breakdown, under the new conditions, of Napoleon's centralised system of command. He was compelled, at least in the campaign of the autumn, to wage war with armies, not with an army of moderate dimensions always controllable by himself alone, as had been the case in his earlier campaigns. His marshals, who had served him well when they were only required to command units of the army which the Emperor controlled in person, showed themselves unfitted, as some of them had already done in Spain, for semi-independent command. When the leading strings to which they had hitherto been accustomed were perforce relaxed, Oudinot, Macdonald, and Ney in succession showed themselves incapable of walking alone. Marmont, at least, had the wisdom to foresee the result when he wrote, "I fear greatly lest on the day on which your Majesty has gained a victory, and believe you

AUTHOR'S PREFACE

have won a decisive battle, you may learn that you have lost two." It was but a few days after this was written that Napoleon, flushed with victory at Dresden, learnt that Macdonald had been disastrously beaten on the Katzbach, that Oudinot had been checked at Gross Beeren, and Vandamme destroyed at Kulm.

All the maps and plans for this volume have been drawn by the author. The contours in the plans of Lützen, Bautzen, Dresden, and Leipzig are taken from modern surveys, whilst the villages, woods, etc., are filled in from old maps representing them as they were in 1813.

The contours in the plans of the Katzbach, Gross Beeren, and Dennewitz are only rough conversions from old "hâchured" maps.

F. L. P.

5th October 1912.

CONTENTS

	PAGE
AUTHOR'S PREFACE	v

CHAPTER I
AFTER RUSSIA 3

CHAPTER II
THE NEW GRAND ARMY OF 1813 9

CHAPTER III

THE ALLIED ARMIES	21
(1) The Prussian Army	21
(2) The Russian Army	26
(3) The Austrian Army	27
(4) Swedish Army	28
(5) Anglo-German Troops	28
(6) Mecklenburg Contingent	29
(7) The Allied Commanders	30

CHAPTER IV
OPERATIONS BETWEEN NAPOLEON'S DEPARTURE FROM AND HIS RETURN TO THE ARMY 32

CHAPTER V
NAPOLEON'S CONCENTRATION ON THE SAALE . . . 47

CHAPTER VI
THE BATTLE OF LÜTZEN OR GROSS GÖRSCHEN . . . 66

CHAPTER VII

FROM LÜTZEN TO BAUTZEN 91

CHAPTER VIII

THE PRELIMINARIES OF BAUTZEN 106

CHAPTER IX

THE BATTLE OF BAUTZEN 116
    The Battle of the 21st May 125

CHAPTER X

FROM BAUTZEN TO THE ARMISTICE 142

CHAPTER XI

DURING THE ARMISTICE. PREPARATIONS AND PLANS OF CAMPAIGN 160

CHAPTER XII

FROM THE END OF THE ARMISTICE TO THE BATTLE OF DRESDEN . 185

CHAPTER XIII

THE BATTLE OF DRESDEN 200
    (*a*) The 26th August 200
    (*b*) The Battle of the 27th August 214

CHAPTER XIV

FROM DRESDEN TO KULM 227

CHAPTER XV

THE KATZBACH AND GROSS BEEREN 250

CONTENTS

CHAPTER XVI

	PAGE
THE SECOND ADVANCE AGAINST BLÜCHER, AND NEY'S DEFEAT AT DENNEWITZ	265

CHAPTER XVII

FROM THE 6TH SEPTEMBER TO THE END OF THE MONTH	279

CHAPTER XVIII

NAPOLEON'S QUEST OF BERNADOTTE AND BLÜCHER	297

CHAPTER XIX

THE BATTLES ROUND LEIPZIG ON THE 16TH OCTOBER	324
(1) Wachau	331
(2) Lindenau	339
(3) Möckern	341

CHAPTER XX

THE BATTLE OF LEIPZIG—18TH OCTOBER	352

CHAPTER XXI

THE STORMING OF LEIPZIG	373

CHAPTER XXII

THE PURSUIT AFTER LEIPZIG AND THE BATTLE OF HANAU	386
The Battle of Hanau	388
INDEX	395

MAPS AND PLANS
(AT END OF VOLUME)

SHEET I.

GENERAL MAP OF THEATRE OF WAR.

INSETS: (a) NAPOLEON'S MARCH TO THE SAALE IN APRIL 1813.
(b) POSITIONS OF BOTH SIDES ON 30TH APRIL 1813.
(c) DIAGRAM OF GENERAL POSITIONS, 7TH OCTOBER 1813.
(d) DIAGRAM OF GENERAL POSITIONS, 12TH OCTOBER 1813.

SHEET II.

(a) THE BATTLE OF LÜTZEN.
(b) THE BATTLE ON THE KATZBACK.
(c) THE BATTLE OF GROSS BEEREN.
(d) THE BATTLE OF DENNEWITZ.

SHEET III.

THE BATTLE OF BAUTZEN.

INSETS: (a) THE FRENCH MARCH FROM LÜTZEN TO BAUTZEN, AND POSITIONS, EVENING OF 19TH MAY.
(b) DIAGRAM OF GENERAL POSITION OF BOTH SIDES AT THE RE-OPENING OF HOSTILITIES IN MIDDLE OF AUGUST.

SHEET IV.

(a) THE BATTLE OF DRESDEN.
(b) COUNTRY SOUTH OF DRESDEN—BATTLE OF KULM.
(c) PRUSSIAN PASSAGE OF THE ELBE ON THE 3RD OCTOBER, AND ACTION AT WARTENBURG.
(d) THE BATTLES ABOUT LEIPZIG, 16TH-18TH OCTOBER.
(e) THE BATTLE OF HANAU.

NAPOLEON'S
LAST CAMPAIGN
IN GERMANY

NAPOLEON'S LAST CAMPAIGN IN GERMANY

CHAPTER I

AFTER RUSSIA

THE amount of ground to be covered in describing Napoleon's Saxon campaign of 1813 compels economy of space in regard to events between the Emperor's departure from the remains of his army of 1812 and his reappearance, in April, at the head of the new Grand Army of 1813. Still, some account, however brief, of the military and political situation, consequent on the great disaster to his arms in Russia, is necessary to the understanding of the events of 1813.

On the 5th December 1812 the defeated Emperor set out from Smorgoni on his weary journey across Europe to Paris, leaving to Murat the command of the miserable remnants of over 600,000 men who had crossed the Niemen at one time or another in the last six months. His departure has been criticised as a disgraceful abandonment of the troops who had sacrificed so much for him. That view of his conduct can only be based on ideas of chivalry which he certainly never entertained. His vast ambition had as its goal an empire such as the world had hitherto never known. In 1812 he had suffered his first great defeat, but his ambition still remained, and he was resolved on another effort to recover the power and prestige which, for the moment, he seemed to have forfeited in Europe. The question whether he should remain with his army or return to France was, from his point of view, entirely one of expediency. However much we may condemn his projects, it seems impossible to deny that, holding to them as he still did, he took the wisest course in hurrying back to France. If he did not altogether realise the magnitude of his disaster at the moment, he certainly knew that, for the next campaign, he would require a fresh army, which he alone was capable of creating, and the organisation of which demanded his presence at his capital. Moreover, he knew that his position in France was threatened in his absence by plots, and that only the magic of his personal presence could ensure its maintenance.

Had he elected to remain with what was left of the army of Russia, he could have done nothing either to save it, or to alleviate the miseries of its inevitable retreat. Napoleon's journey across Europe was certainly not a dignified one. As far as Dresden he travelled in a sleigh, with infinite precautions to conceal his movements from the numerous bands of disaffected persons in Germany, who, had they known that the hated tyrant was passing through their midst almost without escort, might well have made an end of him. After a short halt, during which he endeavoured to reassure his ally the King of Saxony, and wrote to the King of Prussia and the Austrian Emperor demanding a fresh auxiliary contingent, he left Dresden in a carriage. He reached Paris on the 19th December, and at once set to work to organise his new army, a matter which will be dealt with presently.

The political results of the Russian disaster were immense, though the terror of the Emperor's name still sufficed to keep the greater part of Europe outwardly submissive. Russia, of course, was openly at war with France, though even in that country there were two parties; one headed by Kutusow, the Russian commander-in-chief, was by no means inclined, now that the invader had been driven from Russian soil, to follow him westwards, or to fight battles for the liberation of Germans and others who, willingly or unwillingly, had formed a large part of Napoleon's army of invasion. The Tsar Alexander, on the other hand, was quite inclined to play the part of Liberator of Europe, but found himself unable, during Kutusow's last days, to drag the old general in his train.

Prussia and Austria had both supplied contingents to Napoleon's army of Russia, both really under compulsion. In both countries Napoleon was hated as the tyrant who had torn from each a large portion of its former possessions. In Prussia especially, he and the French soldiery had rendered themselves odious, and the country had long been preparing for, and looking forward to, the day of reckoning. But the king, Frederick William, stood in mortal terror of the conqueror of Jena, and was perpetually haunted by visions of the complete destruction of Prussia as an independent power.

As it happened, the only parts of Napoleon's army of 1812 which escaped comparatively uninjured from the great "débâcle" were the right wing, of which the principal constituent was the Austrian contingent of about 30,000 men, and the left, of which the Prussian contingent, under Yorck, formed the greater portion. Napoleon, when he left Smorgoni, and for some time even after he reached Paris, thought, or professed to think, that he could still rely on these two contingents, and even wrote from Dresden demanding an increased contingent both from Prussia and from his father-in-law the Austrian Emperor. The Prussians were the first to fail him. Yorck had been kept informed of the real state of affairs in the French centre when Macdonald, the commander of the whole French left wing, had been purposely kept in ignorance. Yorck's information was derived from the Russians in Riga.

When, at last, Murat and Berthier found it necessary to enlighten Macdonald, and to recall him from Riga behind the Niemen, there was only just time for him to escape with his mixed division of Poles, Bavarians, and Westphalians. Yorck had managed to get separated with his

Prussians from Macdonald, and though, as General von Cämmerer remarks,[1] there was no military necessity for his doing so, he concluded with his Russian opponent the famous convention of Tauroggen on the 30th December. By it the Prussians were nominally neutralised; in fact, they practically passed over to the enemy, though, for the present, they took no active part against their late allies. Yorck concluded this convention with the rope round his neck; for the French would probably have shot him if he had fallen into their hands, whilst Frederick William's dread of Napoleon induced him to disavow and publicly condemn the action of his general. Yorck's action was of supreme importance, for it was the first overt act of revolt against the tyranny of Napoleon, the signal for the gradual uprising of all Germany against the oppressor.

On the other wing of the French army, Schwarzenberg, the commander of the Austrian contingent, characteristically acted with less boldness and openness than the Prussian. He would put nothing in writing; nevertheless he presently came to a verbal understanding with his Russian opponent Miloradowich, under which the Austrians were to retire, not on Kalisch as ordered by the French commander, but on Cracow. The French general, Reynier, who commanded a mixed corps of Saxons and French under Schwarzenberg, was left to shift for himself, and to retire on Kalisch, whilst Poniatowski, with his 8000 or 9000 Poles, had to accompany Schwarzenberg to Gallicia. He took no part in the spring campaign, and it was only during the armistice in the summer that he was allowed to march back through Austria to rejoin Napoleon's army in Saxony.

Austria now assumed a position of armed neutrality, posing as the mediator between Napoleon and his Russian and, later, his Prussian adversaries.

Another prospective adversary of Napoleon was his former marshal, Bernadotte, now Crown Prince and Regent of Sweden. His conduct as a marshal of France had never been marked by straightness, and during the years 1812-

[1] *Die Befreiungskriege*, 1813-1815, p. 6.

1814 he appears in a peculiarly unfavourable light. In 1812 he had desired to filch Norway from Denmark, a project which Napoleon refused to countenance, the result being that Bernadotte turned for help to the Emperor's enemies, especially when Napoleon occupied Swedish Pomerania in January 1812. In April 1812 a treaty was concluded with the Tsar Alexander, under which Sweden was to be compensated for the loss of Finland by the transfer to her of Norway. Though Bernadotte concluded another treaty with Great Britain in March 1813, and shortly afterwards landed in Swedish Pomerania with 12,000 Swedes, it was not till the reopening of the campaign in August that he was at last induced to take an active part in the war against Napoleon. The crookedness and selfishness of his conduct will appear in the course of this history.

All Germany was seething with the spirit of revolt against French tyranny. Austria endeavoured to form a group of states to join her as armed neutrals, but, for the present, only had some success with Saxony, whose king was, however, soon wheeled into line on Napoleon's appearance at his capital in May 1813. The French Emperor, therefore, in the early months of 1813 found himself actively opposed by Russia; Prussia was clearly contemplating a junction with the Russians. Sweden, as represented by Bernadotte, was only waiting to enter the lists against him until the Crown Prince could make what he considered a satisfactory bargain with Napoleon's enemies. England, of course, was still at war with Napoleon, and gradually pressing forward against his rear, thereby detaining in Spain a large army, which otherwise he might have used in Germany. He still maintained his hold on the Rhenish Confederation, though he did so only through force, and the whole population was hostile at heart. It was the same in his brother Jerome's kingdom of Westphalia.

Austria was, for the present, neutral, but her conduct was more than suspicious, and it was impossible to say when she might openly join the side of Napoleon's enemies. Italy and Naples were, for the present, safe, and Denmark was being forced, by Bernadotte's schemes for robbing her of Norway, into active alliance with France.

Napoleon's prestige in Germany had been terribly shaken by the Russian disaster, and nothing short of a decisive victory over the Russians, and the Prussians when they decided on hostilities, could restore it. Such a victory might yet right all, might ensure the continued fidelity of the states of the Rhenish Confederation, and might compel Austria to return to her French alliance. The result to Russia of such a victory would be to drive her back to the position she held previously to the late campaign. As for Prussia, a defeat such as Napoleon hoped to inflict on her and the Russians, must inevitably mean the end of her independent existence, at least during Napoleon's life-time, and the dethronement of Frederick William.

CHAPTER II

THE NEW GRAND ARMY OF 1813[1]

FOR his contemplated campaign in Germany Napoleon required practically an entirely new army. It was not a case of a reorganisation of the army of Russia, for that once great force had almost ceased to exist. On the right wing, when Schwarzenberg and his Austrians retired on Cracow, there was nothing left but Reynier's weak corps; for Poniatowski and his Poles were for the present interned in Gallicia. Of the left wing there remained, after the defection of Yorck at Tauroggen, only one weak corps of 7000 or 8000 men.

It was in the centre that the destruction had been most complete. Davout's corps had crossed the Niemen in June 1812 with a strength of 66,345 officers and men; on the 13th January 1813 it counted only 2281. On the 21st December 1812 there remained of the 50,000 men of the Guard only 500 fit for service, and 800 sick and cripples, of whom 200 were permanently disabled by amputations necessitated by frostbite or wounds.

The I., II., III., and IV. corps had, in June 1812, a strength of over 125,000 men; on the 1st February 1813 their united strength was reported as 6400 combatants. There were a certain number of reinforcements in Germany which had never reached Russia, two divisions on the march from Italy, and the garrisons of the German fortresses, but it is hardly an exaggeration to say that the army of 1812 had ceased to exist.

---

[1] This chapter is based largely on Camille Rousset's *La Grande Armée de 1813*, and *Die Französische Armée*, etc., published in Berlin in 1889.

The Emperor's task, looking to the tremendous sacrifices he had already required from France and his allies, was Herculean, but he faced it undauntedly, and his success in conjuring up, as if by magic, a fresh army is perhaps one of his most remarkable achievements.

He had certain elements for his task in France, in Germany, in Spain, and in Italy.

In September 1812, when the calls on the conscription of 1812 had been practically exhausted, Napoleon had obtained a Senatus Consultum decreeing the levy of 120,000 conscripts of 1813, a number which he subsequently raised to 137,000 by assigning an extra 17,000 to complete the so-called "cohorts." The greater part of this levy had reached the depôts when the Emperor got back to Paris in December, but the men were naturally not ready for service.

The force readiest to hand consisted of the "cohorts." This body had been instituted, in March 1812, when Napoleon, about to leave France for the farther end or Europe, desired to leave behind him to protect the country something so nearly akin to the regular army that, in case of need, it might take its place in it.

By a Senatus Consultum of the 13th March 1812, the National Guard was organised in three "bans."

(1) Those men of from 20 to 26 years of age, of the classes of the six years 1807-1812, who had never been called up to active service.

(2) Men of sound physique aged from 26 to 40 years.

(3) Similar men of between 40 and 60.

The decree ended with a demand for 100 "cohorts" (reduced next day to 84) from the six classes of the first ban.

These cohorts, which were not for service beyond the limits of France, were organised by Departments in the different headquarters of military divisions. Each cohort consisted of 6 companies of 140 men, a depôt company, and an artillery company of 100 men. The officers were taken either from retired officers and men of the regular army, or from men of the National Guard who had served with the active army. Each cohort should have had a strength of 1080 officers and men, which would give about 91,000 for the 84. As a matter of fact, the strength was about 78,000.

After the Russian disaster the cohorts were induced, often by the exercise of considerable pressure, to volunteer for foreign service. A Senatus Consultum of the 11th January 1813 finally transferred them bodily from the National Guard to the active army. They were organised in regiments of 4 battalions. The number of cohorts having now been raised to 88, there were 22 regiments. Their strength, at 6 line companies and 1 depot company per battalion, should be 86,240. Once this strength was attained, future recruits would be available for other corps. The artillery companies (1 to each battalion) were reduced to 1 per regiment, the rest being formed into 3 regiments of artillery "à la suite de l'armée."

In addition to disposing of the cohorts, the Senatus Consultum of the 11th January authorised a supplementary levy of 100,000 on the classes of 1809-1812. This was commonly known as the "levy of the four classes." Also a call of 150,000 was made, nearly two years in advance, on the conscription of 1814. The levy of the "four classes" was called up at once; the other 150,000 were not demanded till February, as it would, Napoleon said, be inconvenient to arm too many conscripts at once.

The Emperor, at the same time, induced the Departments and large towns to come forward with an offer of some 15,000 to 20,000 men, mounted and equipped.

The Municipal Guard of Paris had two battalions of a total strength of 1050 men. These were sent to Erfurt to form the nucleus of a new regiment. In the same way, 4000 men raised by contributions from the Municipal Guards of capitals of Departments were amalgamated to form the new 37th light infantry. In the ports there were 12 battalions of marine artillery standing idle owing to British supremacy at sea. These the Emperor split into

24 battalions which, according to him, made up 16,000 men. He raised them to a nominal strength of 20,000 by the addition of 2000 from the levy of the "four classes," and 2000 from the conscription of 1814. The actual strength was, however, only 12,080, of whom the marines were 8000.

Yet another Senatus Consultum, of the 3rd April, authorised the following levies : (1) 80,000 men of 1807-1812 from the 1st ban of the National Guard, that is, from the source which had already supplied the cohorts; (2) 90,000 from the conscription of 1814; these were to be replaced from the Garde Nationale Sédentaire of the South and West; (3) 10,000 mounted Guards of Honour. These last were so-called volunteers, young men of well-to-do families, whose real position was indicated by the soubriquet of "the hostages," given to them in the army.

To sum up, the military elements which the Emperor sought to utilise in the first part of 1813 were :—

(1) Old Soldiers of the Paris and other Municipal Guards who had served before . . .	5,000
(2) Artillerymen of the Marines, averaging 23 years of age	8,000
(3) The cohorts, aged 20 to 26 years . .	78,000
(4) Conscripts of the 1st ban of 20 to 26 years	80,000
(5) Conscripts of the "four classes," 20 to 24 years	100,000
(6) Guards of Honour, and horsemen "offered" by Departments, 20 to 25 years . .	25,000
(7) Levy of September 1812, on the conscription of 1813, 19 to 20 years . . .	120,000
(8) Conscripts of 1814, 18 to 19 years . .	240,000
Total . .	656,000

With the later levies of August 1813 (30,000) and October (240,000) we need not concern ourselves, as they took no part in the campaign in Saxony.

The 5000 at the head of the above list were old soldiers who had seen service; the marine artillery had no experience

THE NEW GRAND ARMY OF 1813

of land warfare or infantry manœuvres; the rest were conscripts of various degrees of efficiency, but all without experience of war. Of them St Cyr[1] says: "For some time past, and more than formerly, one had noticed that our young men were very delicate and unformed when they attained the age for conscription; those who were two years younger were weak to a degree which was painful to behold." Marmont, on the other hand, speaking of the cohorts, says[2] that, though the officers were often too old, and generally indifferent, the soldiers were admirable. He adds that the four-battalion regiment drawn from the Departments was magnificent, as were the fifteen battalions of marine artillerymen whom he commanded. There was, as might be expected, a great dearth of officers, and various devices had to be resorted to to fill up the vacancies. When the remains of the Grand Army were formed into four weak divisions, the superfluous "cadres" were sent back to help with the new levies. Many young and inexperienced cadets from the military colleges were utilised. These were generally sent to the older regiments, where less leading was required. On the other hand, there was among the officers of the younger battalions a strong leaven of sergeants and corporals promoted to lieutenancies, men of long experience of war, though perhaps not likely to make really good officers. Many officers were drawn from the army in Spain, which was over-supplied in this respect.

The Emperor decided on the following method of re-organising his infantry:—

(1) The 36 regiments which had formed the first four corps in Russia were to be reconstituted with four battalions each. For these more than 100 "cadres de bataillon," over 2000 officers, were required.

(2) There were in France (besides depôt battalions) 100 battalions of regiments serving in Spain, Illyria, etc. These, being merely "cadres," were completed from the recruits of 1813, and were grouped in twos or threes to form "regiments de ligne" or "regiments provisoires," according

[1] *Hist. Mil.*, iv. p. 53.   [2] *Mém.*, v. p. 7.

as the battalions belonged to the same or to different regiments.

(3) The cohorts, as already mentioned, formed 22 regiments.

(4) The marine artillery formed 4 regiments of marine infantry.

(5) The 5000 veterans of the Municipal Guards formed 2 regiments (6 battalions).

(6) Two old regiments in Italy (9 battalions) were transferred for service in Germany.

Of these elements the following corps were provisionally constituted:—

(1) The Corps of Observation of the Elbe (afterwards the V. corps), General Lauriston; 3 divisions (48 battalions). To assemble at Magdeburg between 15th February and 15th March. These were all cohorts.

(2) The 1st Corps of Observation of the Rhine (later the III. corps), Marshal Ney; 4 divisions (60 battalions). To assemble about Mayence during March.

(3) The 2nd Corps of Observation of the Rhine (later the VI. Corps), Marshal Marmont; 4 divisions (50 battalions). Three divisions to assemble about Mayence at the end of March and beginning of April. The fourth was not ready till the end of May.

(4) The Corps of Observation of Italy, General Bertrand; 4 divisions (54 battalions). These later became the IV. and XII. Corps.

(5) The I. Corps; 4 divisions (64 battalions).

(6) The II. Corps; 4 divisions (48 battalions).

(7) Durutte's division of the VII. corps, to which 2 Saxon divisions were to be added.

(8) The Guard. One division of the Old Guard to be formed of what had returned from Russia, added to 3000 old soldiers drawn from Spain. Three divisions of Young Guard to assemble at Mayence. These were conscripts, differing in no respect from those who formed regiments of the line.

(9) Two corps of reserve to be formed at Mayence. They were not ready till the end of August.

THE NEW GRAND ARMY OF 1813

The cavalry was still more difficult to constitute than the infantry. About 9000 or 10,000 had wandered back from Russia. For the rest, conscripts had to be taken. As far as possible, men were chosen who had some acquaintance with horses. It was decided

(1) To reconstitute the Guard cavalry entirely.

(2) To reorganise the 52 regiments of the late Grand Army in two corps under Latour-Maubourg and Sebastiani, altogether three heavy and four light divisions. "Cadres" were to be completed from the regiments in Spain.

(3) A third corps, under Arrighi, was to be formed about the nucleus of one squadron supplied by each of the regiments in Spain.

It is not within the scope of this work to enter into all the complicated details of the reorganisation of the French army. Those who are curious on the subject will find full details in the works referred to at the commencement of this chapter.

But something must necessarily be said regarding the military value of the troops with which the great Emperor conducted this his last campaign in Germany.

Colonel Lanrezac, on the whole, passes a more favourable judgment on the army than do Camille Rousset and the author of *Die französische Armée*. He states the numbers of infantry present, according to a return of the 20th April, at 210,000, of whom 175,000 were French and 35,000 Allies. Of the 175,000 French not more than 75,000 were conscripts of 1813; the rest were men of earlier years, for the recruits of the 1814 conscription had not yet joined. Even the 1813 men had four months' service, and averaged 20 years of age. The weaklings and malingerers had dropped out on the way to the front. On the other hand, Camille Rousset tells of one detachment of 600 which had to leave 100 in hospital in Brussels, and another of 950 at La Rochelle, which had 300 in hospital and an excessive mortality. In the west of France it became necessary to hunt up the "réfractaires" with mobile columns, and the commander of one of these reported that he was afraid to use his young recruits for this purpose. He would, he said, rather have 100 old soldiers than 600 conscripts of 1813, such as filled most of his companies. They had never had a musket in their hands before quitting the depôts, and were unfit for the necessary marches. The training seems to have been less than elementary at the depôts. There was an order which required that no conscript be sent forward till he had fired at least six blank and two ball cartridges! Yet commandants of depôts who tried to insist on this very rudimentary fire training often found themselves censured for delaying their conscripts. Camille Rousset gives the following as a common type of report on inspection: "Some of the men are of rather weak appearance. The battalion has no idea of manœuvring; but nine-tenths of the men can manage and load their arms passably."

There was the wildest confusion in the depôts, where it seems to have been tacitly agreed that infantry depôts were equally liable to be drawn on for other arms. In the confusion training was neglected. It often happened that where there were four series of battalions to be reformed the fourth was ready first. There were bitter complaints of the state in which the "détachements de marche" reached the regiments. From Osnabruck General Lambardière writes, on the 15th April: "These battalions arrive very fatigued; every day I supply them with special carriage for the weak and lame. . . . All these battalions are French; I must say that the young soldiers show courage and good-will. Every possible moment is utilised in teaching them to load their arms and bring them to the shoulder."

When the conscripts of 1813 required to complete the 1st battalions began to run short, the Emperor said the deficiency could be supplied from conscripts of 1814, provided only the "big and strong" were picked out. The adjectives could only be applied to the conscripts selected in relation to the weaklings, who were distinctly small and weak. So poor were they in physique that the Minister of Police protests against their being drilled in the Champs

Elysées during the hour of promenade, on account of the scoffing and jeering they gave rise to. Besides all this, there was a shortage of muskets, so much so that Napoleon even suggested arming the 1814 levies with foreign ones of the same calibre as the French, though he insisted on ample reserves of French weapons being kept at Strasburg, Mayence, and Wesel for issue to troops on their way to Germany.

Camille Rousset insists on the deficiency of officers, but Colonel Lanrezac shows, on the other hand, that the III. corps, on the 15th April, had the high average of one officer to every 31 men, whilst even less favoured corps had one to every 40. The real difficulty, he says, was that there were no reserves of officers to supply the waste of war. As long as the numbers of the men went on diminishing proportionally the matter was not so important. The rub came when, in the second half of the campaign, reinforcements in men were poured up, without a corresponding number of officers.

Of the whole corps of officers, perhaps, the central portion was the best. The commanders of corps, of divisions, of brigades, of regiments, and, perhaps, even of battalions, were, almost without exception, still the old experienced leaders of many years of war. But the Emperor's system of command, whilst excellent for the training of tacticians, was fatal to the development of strategical initiative. His corps commanders were not encouraged to look upon themselves as responsible in any way for strategy. That, they considered, was the Emperor's province alone, and, with the possible exceptions of Davout and Masséna, they were incapable of exercising an independent command on a large scale. Spain had already laid bare the deficiencies of several of them in this respect. So long as Napoleon had but one army in the field, and that of dimensions which he could manage alone, the strategical deficiencies of his immediate subordinates mattered comparatively little. But when he himself was commanding a vast host in Russia, and at the same time carrying on, through one of his marshals, a deadly struggle in Spain, he had to recognise that his curbing of initiative in his lieutenants must be fatal. As regards his war in Germany in 1813, Eugène's mistakes on the Oder and the Elbe were one instance of the want of good independent commanders, though certainly Eugène was a particularly bad example, and something better might have been expected from Davout, Soult, or Gouvion St Cyr.

When the Emperor once more gathered the reins in Germany into his own hands, in April 1813, he was again operating with a single army of dimensions within his own power of control, and the marshals slipped back into their old position of mere instruments of the great leader. In the second half of the war it was different. The numbers of the army were too great to be directly commanded by a single man, even by a Napoleon. Moreover, the strategical position necessitated something more like the modern system of a war of armies, each commanded by a subordinate capable of acting independently, without having the great director always at his elbow.

The marshals, or some of them at least, were aware of their deficiencies, as is evidenced by Marmont's famous prophecy, which was realised almost as soon as uttered. In August 1813, that marshal, criticising the Emperor's plans,[1] wrote: "I fear much lest, on the day when Your Majesty has won a victory and believe you have gained a decisive battle, you may learn that you have lost two." A few days later came the news of Macdonald's defeat on the Katzbach, and Oudinot's at Gross Beeren, which had almost coincided in time with the Emperor's own victory at Dresden. His power, his throne, everything depended on himself alone. As Count Yorck von Wartenburg says: "All his actions were connected with his own personality, and based upon it alone; so, when this became weak, there was no longer anything in his army or state that could support or sustain him."[2] Europe freed herself from the

[1] What a change from the old days is evidenced by the mere fact of Napoleon's inviting his marshals to offer an opinion on his own plan of campaign!

[2] *Napoleon as a General* (English translation), vol. ii. p. 270.

THE NEW GRAND ARMY OF 1813 19

tyranny of the Corsican by the uprising of her peoples, and at enormous expense in blood and treasure. All that would have been saved had a stray bullet taken the charmed life of the conqueror; for his empire must have collapsed at once with his own disappearance from the scene.

The same causes resulted in an absence of capacity in the personnel of his headquarters staff. He, like Frederick the Great, was his own chief of the staff, he managed everything, and Berthier was but a glorified head-clerk. The organisation of the General Staff was what it had been in the days of the Revolution. The Emperor only awoke to its deficiencies as an instrument for the governance of the vast armies he was now leading when, on the 2nd July 1812, he wrote: "The general staff is organised in such a manner that nothing is foreseen."[1] It was good enough for the management of *an* army; but, "the war of armies requires staffs of the first rank, staffs constituted of chosen men, educated in the higher knowledge of war, united by a community of doctrine, and amongst whom initiative has been carefully developed."[2] That description is utterly inapplicable to the staff of which Berthier was the nominal head.

Perhaps the worst part of the army of 1813 was its cavalry. In the first part of the war, up to Lützen, it numbered but 15,000, mostly old soldiers, 11,000 French and 4000 allies. It was opposed to a far more numerous cavalry of generally excellent quality, against which it was almost impotent. Later, it was greatly increased in numbers, but the recruits were of very inferior quality and training. On the other hand, the artillery was very good and numerous, though the draught horses were rather young.

On the whole, we may well accept Lanrezac's estimate of the army of 1813. "Certainly, the new troops were not the equals in value of the bands destroyed in Russia, and, moreover, their constitution exposed them to a rapid exhaustion; nevertheless, they were good. . . . Anyhow,

[1] *Corr.* 18,884.   [2] Lanrezac, *La Manœuvre de Lutzen*, p. 31.

the army with which Napoleon opened the campaign . . . was a good instrument of war; however, it had in itself serious germs of weakness."[1] The estimate is supported not only by the opinion of contemporaries like Odeleben,[2] certainly not prejudiced in favour of the French, but still more by its actual achievements in the victories of Lützen, Bautzen, Dresden, and even the gallant but unsuccessful fighting at Kulm and Leipzig.

In one department especially, the attack or defence of localities, of woods or villages, the French infantry ever displayed that capacity which, in the French soldier, seems to be an inborn instinct.

Of the Emperor himself what shall we say? Perhaps it will be best to show as we go along the evidences of the decline of his personality, and of his failures to be true to his own principles, which alternated with flashes of the old genius and decision.

As for his marshals and generals, most of them were long since tired of war, by which they had been enriched. Now they looked for a period of peace in which to enjoy their wealth. The prevalence of such a spirit augured ill for success.

[1] Lanrezac, *La Manœuvre de Lutzen*, pp. 28 and 29.
[2] "The good military bearing which predominated in this new army, sprung, as it were, from the earth, and assembled by the wave of a wand, was truly admirable; and, if one felt horror at the excesses of the French soldiers, the military spirit, the activity in marches, and the bravery of the young troops so rapidly formed and opposed to experienced soldiers, excited no less astonishment."
—Odeleben, *Campagne de* 1813 (French translation), vol. i. p. 62.

CHAPTER III

THE ALLIED ARMIES

(1) THE PRUSSIAN ARMY[1]

BY the Treaty of Tilsit in 1807, Prussia's army was limited to 42,000 men of all arms, the proportion of the arms being also fixed. Napoleon had carried 20,000 men, nearly half of the whole army, to Russia with him in 1812, and we already know what had become of that, thanks to Yorck's defection from the cause of the French. Including what Yorck had left, there remained a standing army of about 33,000 men. This "old" army was extremely good, with young and well-instructed officers. So good was it that Von Boyen, writing in 1838,[2] described the infantry as the best he had ever seen. The cavalry was also good, though the horses of some regiments were rather old. It consisted of 2 Guard and 18 line regiments,[3] which, at 600 men per regiment, made 12,000, in 80 squadrons of 150 each.

The artillery comprised three brigades, each of three horse and 12 foot companies. Total 6000 men, in 21 batteries, with 168 guns. There were six companies of engineers (pioneers). In 1813 the strength was raised by calling up reservists, so that there were 36,846 infantry, and the total strength of the army was about 56,000. Moreover, artillery had been collected to such an extent that there were available, even in the spring of 1813, 236

---

[1] This section is mainly based on Friederich's *Der Herbstfeldzug* 1813, vol. i. chap. ii.
[2] *Erinnerungen*, iii. p. 35.
[3] Seven heavy and thirteen light.

guns. This army was the nucleus round which the new formations were collected.

In 1810 Scharnhorst had started his "Krumper"[1] system, under which each company or squadron, at fixed intervals, discharged a given number of trained soldiers, and took in an equal number of fresh men for training. By thus constantly passing men through the ranks, Napoleon's restrictions were evaded, and it became possible to nearly double the 42,000 by calling up the men who had been trained. So when the king issued his order of the 1st February 1813, calling up the reserves and "Krumpers," 52 reserve battalions could be formed. Several of these took part in the spring campaign; others were only called to the army at a later period. By these means the army received eventually a reinforcement of 42 battalions— 33,642 men.

At first these regiments of "Krumpers" and reservists left much to be desired, but, by appointing to them ex-officers of regiments which had been disbanded in 1807, they were worked up to a state of efficiency equal to that of the rest of the army.

It must be noted that the lesson of 1806-7 was taken to heart in Prussia, and the whole military system was radically reformed. It was sought to induce the obedience of the soldier not, as in the old days, by force alone, but chiefly by an appeal to his patriotism. Corporal punishment was abolished, save for dishonourable offences, and the military man, from being the lowest in the social scale, as he was in 1806, was raised to a position of respect, and had come to be looked upon as the eventual saviour of his country from French tyranny.

Though artillery had been collected, there was a great shortage of uniforms. Many of them were of the simplest character. Black or grey cloth jackets with various coloured facings were worn over trousers of the poorest cloth. Some

---

[1] Krumpen=to shrink. According to a memorandum by the king, printed in Von Boyen's *Memoirs* (ii. p. 345), the total effective strength of the army on the 24th July 1810 was only 22,392.

THE ALLIED ARMIES

regiments even had old English uniforms. The muskets were of four or five different patterns.[1] To facilitate the supply of ammunition and prevent confusion, advantage was taken of the cessation of hostilities in June-August 1813 to effect exchanges of weapons, so that each regiment might be, as far as possible, armed with muskets of the same calibre.

The next body to be raised consisted of "Volunteer Jägers," young men of independent means, of from 17 to 24 years, equipped and armed at their own expense, or at that of the neighbourhood. They were those who did not already belong to the army, and had no sufficient cause for exemption. As the decree of the 3rd February dealing with them was supplemented by another of the 9th, limiting the causes of exemption and prescribing penalties for failure to join, it seems clear that these were volunteers only in name.[2] Their numbers are uncertain, but they probably never exceeded 5000 infantry, 3000 cavalry, and 500 artillery and engineers. Their moral was probably greater than their military value, though, later, they formed good schools for the training of officers and under-officers, in supplying whom there was considerable difficulty.

A few "free corps" were established as follows:—

Lützow's—3 battalions, 5 squadrons, 8 guns.

Von Reiche's Jäger battalion.

Hellwig's—3 squadrons, one Jäger detachment.

The "Schill" free corps—2 squadrons of hussars.

The Elbe regiment—2 battalions raised from the provinces torn from Prussia in 1807.

These free corps consisted largely of foreigners, were of very varied constitution, not always either well led or well

---

[1] Two Prussian, one Austrian, one English, and, later on, the French muskets captured in the field.

[2] On this subject there is a significant note in Colonel Lanrezac's book, p. 36: "What happened in France in 1792, and in Prussia in 1813, proves that, however great the patriotic feeling of the nation, voluntary enlistment furnishes in time of war but a small number of defenders. Without a law compelling to military service all citizens of a certain age, only insignificant results are obtained."

disciplined, and, altogether, not so important as they might have been.

More was still required for an army which had to struggle for the very existence of the Fatherland.

A decree of the king established the "landwehr," based on the model of that of Austria of 1809. This decree, signed on the 9th February 1813, but only brought into force on the 17th March, required universal service. No preparations for this had been possible during the years succeeding 1807. As the impoverished state of Prussian finances precluded much assistance from the State, the expense of equipment had to fall on the men themselves, or their villages. The consequence was that the men had miserable clothing, which was ruined by the first heavy rain. They had caps which protected them neither against the weather nor against blows; they had shoes which, being unprovided with gaiters, were often drawn off by the mud through which the men had to march—and wretched linen trousers. At first, the front rank was often armed with pikes or scythes, and it was only as French muskets were taken from the battlefields that the men were armed with yet another pattern of firearm. There was a great dearth of officers, as most of the half-pay officers still fit for service were required for the reserve battalions. All sorts of officials, many of them very unsuitable as military officers, joined, and it was only later on that men of some experience were got from the "Volunteer Jägers," etc.

Naturally, the landwehr, as a whole, was at first of no great military value, though their initial worth was in some corps (Yorck's and Bülow's especially) enhanced by long marches and still more by early successes.

The landwehr infantry numbered about 100,000 at their highest strength, and the cavalry about 11,500. The latter were, on the whole, proportionately better than the infantry, but their horses, drawn from the fields and other sources, were a very mixed lot. Friederich says that once a body of this cavalry began to give way no power on earth, saving an insurmountable physical barrier, could stop them.

THE ALLIED ARMIES

The whole strength of the Prussian army in August 1813, after the armistice, may be summarised thus in round numbers:—

Infantry.

Regular, exclusive of garrison and depot battalions	72,000
Landwehr, garrison and depot battalions, "free" corps, Volunteer Jägers, and Landwehr reserve	156,000
	228,000

Cavalry.

Regular, excluding depot squadrons . . .	12,600
Landwehr, Volunteer Jägers, etc. . . .	18,500
	31,100
Artillery (376 guns) and engineers . . .	13,000

This total of 272,000 later rose to about 300,000, which represents about 6 per cent. on the then population of Prussia.

Of the 272,000 there were actually in the field at the close of the armistice in August about 192,500, inclusive of 30,500 (mostly landwehr) blockading Küstrin, Stettin, Danzig, and Glogau. Prussian writers justly claim that their country supplied the backbone of the uprising which overthrew Napoleon. The greatest actual numbers of troops in 1813 were furnished by Russia, but looking to the general quality of the troops, and the spirit of patriotism and enthusiasm which pervaded them, the slightly smaller Prussian forces were of distinctly greater value. It must always be remembered that they were fighting for hearth and home, whilst the Russians had already saved their own country in 1812, and in 1813 and 1814 were fighting, not so much for their own safety, as for the liberation of Germany and Europe from the yoke of Napoleon.

(2) THE RUSSIAN ARMY

There is a good deal of uncertainty as to the actual numbers of the half-disciplined troops, such as Cossacks and Bashkirs. Though very inferior in quality from a military point of view, these half savages had created such alarm amongst the French that they were far from being a negligible quantity.

The Russian officers were still, as they had been in 1807, very ill-educated and rough, except those drawn from the nobility for the Guard and a few crack cavalry regiments.

The Russian soldier of the regular army was what he was in 1807, and what he still is, a fighter of the utmost bravery and obstinacy, without education or much intelligence.

In the beginning of February 1813 the total strength of the Russian army pursuing the French did not exceed 70,000 infantry, 30,000 cavalry and Cossacks, 10,000 artillery and engineers—110,000 in all. Most of the infantry regiments were reduced to a single battalion of about 350 men; the cavalry regiments had only 4 squadrons (instead of 8) of 100 men each.

A "ukase," of the 5th February 1813, prescribed the formation of a reserve army of 163 battalions, 92 squadrons, 37 batteries, to assemble about Bialystock. Its formation was much retarded by want of "cadres" and material. Between March and August 1813, it furnished to the active army 68,000 infantry, 14,000 cavalry, and 5 batteries. At the close of the armistice the Russian army in Germany and the reserves in Poland numbered about 296,000 men.

The corps, both of infantry and cavalry, were so split and mixed that Lanrezac quotes the saying of an unnamed eye-witness that "the generals did not know what troops to command, and, similarly, the troops knew not which chief to obey."[1]

---

[1] *La Manœuvre de Lutzen*, p. 39.

THE ALLIED ARMIES

(3) THE AUSTRIAN ARMY

Austria was neutral till the close of the armistice in August 1813, but it will be convenient to deal here with the army which she then brought into the field. After the campaign of 1809, the strength of the Austrian army was fixed at 150,000 men. The war had brought her almost to the verge of bankruptcy, the strictest economy was required, and it was practised largely at the expense of the army, especially of the Austrian (as distinguished from the Hungarian) portion. It was kept on the lowest peace footing, and the rest of the men received an extremely short annual training. Differences with his brother the Emperor had, unfortunately for Austria, resulted in the disappearance from her councils of her best leader and organiser, the Archduke Charles. Schwarzenberg's auxiliary force in the Russian campaign of 1812 numbered about 29,000 men and 7000 horses. After his return, Austria was quite unable to put a respectable force in the field to join the Russians and Prussians. Therefore, she was compelled to go no further than playing a neutral part, and pretending to serve as mediator between Napoleon and the allies, whilst she was reorganising her army. When, at last, she openly joined the allies, in August 1813, her armed strength was as follows:—

	Battns.	Squadns.	Guns.	Men.
(a) In Bohemia	107	117	290	127,345
(b) Between the Enns and the Traun, opposed to Wrede's Bavarians on the Inn				30,079
(c) In Upper Austria (Hiller)				36,557
			Total Field Army,	193,981
In garrison at Prag, Königgratz, and Josefstadt				27,544
			Total,	221,525

Besides these, a reserve army, strength not known, was organising at Vienna and elsewhere. There was no corps organisation, the army being divided into 12 infantry divisions, with 3 divisions and 1 brigade of cavalry.

As a consequence of the conditions above mentioned, two-thirds of this army consisted of recruits with scarcely three months' service.

Information regarding the military value of the Austrian army is not so plentiful as in the case of Prussia. The corps of 1812, however, appears to have been excellent, whilst the reserves and recruits were perhaps not far behind the corresponding elements of the Prussian army.

The cavalry was generally good, the artillery less so.

(4) Swedish Army

Bernadotte, Crown Prince of Sweden, ex-Marshal of France, does not cut an admirable figure in any way in 1813. His political conduct was crooked in the extreme, and as for his Swedish contingent, his main object seems to have been to expose them to as little fighting as possible.[1] The army consisted partly of Swedes, partly of Germans recruited in Pomerania and the island of Rügen. In discipline, equipment, and clothing they left nothing to be desired. They, too, only appeared in the north after the armistice, when their strength was :—

	Battns.	Squadns.	Guns.	Men.
(a) In Brandenburg	33	27	54	23,449
(b) In Mecklenburg with Walmoden	6	5	8	3,814
	39	32	62	27,263

(5) Anglo-German Troops

Most of these were Germans, or a mixture of all nations. The only really British troops were :—

[1] Friederich refers to an English caricature representing the Crown Prince leading back his army in the guise of a flock of sheep and saying to the old king, "Here am I with the sheep you entrusted to me. Behold! I have not lost one of them."

THE ALLIED ARMIES

1 [1] regiment of hussars—5 squadrons.
2 horse artillery batteries with 12 guns, and—
28 rocket apparatus. These Congreve rockets, then a new invention, created much alarm amongst the French at Leipzig.

The strength of this Anglo-German contingent was about 9000 men.

There were also 6 English battalions (3459 men) in garrison at Stralsund.

(6) MECKLENBURG CONTINGENT

Four battalions, 4 squadrons, 2 guns, 6149 men.

Of these only the Guard Grenadier battalions were old troops. The rest were recruits.

To sum up the field forces[2] of the allies, about the beginning of the autumn campaign they stood as follows :—

	Battns.	Squadns.	Cossack Regts.	Guns.	Men.
Prussian Field Army	185½	174	—	362	161,764
Russian ,,	212	228	68	639	184,123
Austrian ,,	107	117	—	290	127,345
Swedish ,,	39	32	—	62	23,449
Anglo-German Contingent	9	17	—	26	9,283
Mecklenburg ,,	4	4	—	2	6,149
	556½	572	68	1381	512,113

Adding to these the Russian and Prussian blockading corps, reserves in second line, the garrison of Stralsund, the Austrian armies on the Italian and Bavarian fronts, etc., the allies had some 860,000 troops.

[1] This is Friederich's statement. It seems doubtful if it is correct as regards the hussar regiment. The present-day O Battery, R.H.A., has claimed to be the representative of Captain Bogue's rocket battery, but here too it appears that the claim to direct descent has not been made out. The author is indebted for this information to the author of the *History of the British Army.*

[2] Exclusive of blockading troops before the fortresses and of the Austrian and Russian reserve armies.

(7) THE ALLIED COMMANDERS

Napoleon's great advantage over the allies, at periods when he began to find himself with inferior numbers, consisted in the absolute unity of his command. The final decision always rested with him alone. The disadvantages of his system in depriving him of men trained to semi-independent command have already been noted.

The allies, on the other hand, had no unity of command whatever. No one could know with whom the final decision lay. Even when the Russians were alone there was some difficulty, so long as Kutusow lived: for he was strongly opposed to embarking on chivalrous adventures for the benefit of the rest of Europe. So great had been his services to Russia that, until his death, even his master, the Tsar, felt bound to defer to some extent to his views.

Then Prussia joined in the war against Napoleon, and the difficulties at once increased; for it became necessary to consider the new ally, and the opinions of her generals, amongst whom were men of the highest military capacity, such as Clausewitz,[1] Scharnhorst, Gneisenau, Müffling, and others, like Blücher and Yorck, who, if they were not great commanders, had at least very decided opinions, and still more decided wills. Then came Austria, the views of whose leaders had again to be consulted, and who, on at least one occasion, insisted on changes in the allied plans. Bernadotte introduced a further complication, for he wanted to be commander-in-chief of the allied armies, a position which it was impossible to confer on him.

Of the allied sovereigns, the Tsar generally succeeded in taking the most influential position. He was surrounded by a multitude of advisers, Toll, Barclay de Tolly, Wittgenstein, to whom were added, later, Jomini and Moreau. Knesebeck, Borstell, Von Boyen, Scharnhorst, Gneisenau, Clausewitz, Schwarzenberg, Radetzky, and Müffling all had

---

[1] Clausewitz was still in the Russian service which he had entered in 1812, but he had been a Prussian officer and may fairly be classed as such. He returned to the Prussian service in 1815.

their say in the perpetual councils of war which discussed and tinkered with the allies' plans. To such a pitch did dissensions come that when the Tsar, before Leipzig, was unable to gain over Schwarzenberg to his views, he took the extreme course of telling the Austrian (and allied) commander-in-chief that he might keep his Austrians between the Pleisse and the Elster, but that the Russians and Prussians, being the affair of the Tsar and the King of Prussia, should be brought over to the right bank of the Pleisse. After the battle of Lützen there were dissensions between the Russians and the Prussians, each blaming the other for the defeat.

Then the divergent interests of the Russians, desiring to preserve their direct communication with Poland, and of the Prussians, thinking of directly covering their capital and the Mark, nearly led to a separation which would certainly have been fatal to Prussia.

Even when a commander-in-chief had been appointed to succeed Kutusow, his position became almost intolerable; for Wittgenstein, who was selected, constantly found the Tsar consulting Toll and others without reference to him, and passing important orders over his head.

Many of these difficulties will appear in their proper place in the course of this history. They are only briefly referred to here in order to indicate generally the extremely divided state of the allied command, and the many obstacles to the co-operation of armies with such divergent interests as those of the allies. One expedient adopted was the intermixture of the various forces, so that Bernadotte, Blücher, and Schwarzenberg each commanded troops of two or more nations. By thus mixing them up in separate commands it was hoped to remove the temptation to any one nation to act on its own account.[1]

---

[1] This chapter certainly anticipates much; but the author has thought it better to collect in two preliminary chapters a general view of the organisation of the armies of both sides, rather than to recur again and again to the same subject as each new force comes on the scene.

CHAPTER IV

OPERATIONS BETWEEN NAPOLEON'S DEPARTURE FROM AND HIS RETURN TO THE ARMY

WHEN Napoleon left Smorgoni for France he entrusted the supreme command to Murat, with instructions which it was impossible for him, or any one else, to carry out. With the wretched rabble which was all that represented the main body of the army, it was out of the question either to wait at Wilna or to make a stand on the Niemen. The King of Naples could but continue the retreat as best he might. On the 19th December, the day of Napoleon's arrival in Paris, the few thousands of stragglers, and the few hundreds of the Guard, reached Königsberg. They had not been pursued by Tchichagow's Russians beyond the Niemen, but, on the 1st January 1813, the news of Yorck's defection at Tauroggen warned Murat that he must continue his retreat across the Vistula. Leaving in Danzig the remains of Macdonald's corps and Heudelet's "division de marche," which he met coming forward in East Prussia, he reached Posen on the 16th January. There he gave over the chief command to Eugène Beauharnais, and betook himself to his kingdom of Naples.

Eugène's position was a difficult one, far too difficult for a commander of his very limited capacity. With the remains of the Guard, the I., II., III., IV., and VI. (Bavarian) corps, he had some 12,000 worn-out troops. As the mixed division of Macdonald's corps, and Heudelet's "division de marche," the only troops still worth anything, had been thrown by Murat into Danzig, the unfortunate Viceroy would have had practically no army at all, but for some 10,000 men of various nationalities gathered from "regiments de marche."

As for the Prussians, Yorck, as we know, was with the Russians, busily reorganising and recruiting his corps about Königsberg. Bülow, in Pomerania, was organising another corps, nominally in response to Napoleon's call for a fresh contingent. Blücher was doing the same in Silesia. Both were merely waiting for their king to summon up courage to declare against Napoleon.

When Eugène took over command, he found himself with the prospect of a fortnight's breathing space in which to reorganise his forces. If the French army had been almost annihilated in the retreat from Russia, their pursuers had also suffered severely, and were far from being in a condition to carry on an active winter campaign. Wittgenstein, on their right, crossed the Vistula on the 13th January with 30,000 men; but he found himself at once compelled to send the greater part of his force to watch Danzig, in which there was a garrison of 30,000, of whom two-thirds were serviceable troops. He stopped, therefore, at Stargard to await the arrival of the other Russian corps on his left. Tchichagow was marching slowly on Thorn with 20,000 men; Kutusow was moving with 30,000 on Plock, and Miloradowich was very slowly pushing back Schwarzenberg, Reynier, and Poniatowski on Warsaw. There was little chance of the Russians being abreast of one another on the Vistula till after the end of January. As the ruins of the infantry of the I., II., III., and IV. corps were unfit for employment in the field, Eugène sent them respectively to garrison Stettin, Küstrin, Spandau, and Glogau. The "cadres" set free by this arrangement were sent back to Erfurt for use in organising new units.

Eugène was now left with a few of these men whom he kept back, the remains of the Guard, two fresh battalions of Young Guard called up from Stettin, and the "détachments de marche" already mentioned—some 12,000 in all. These he organised as four weak divisions. He had not more than 2000 cavalry, a very mixed lot.

With these small forces he took post at Posen, pushing out his Bavarians to Gnesen in order to keep in touch with Thorn and Warsaw. He soon found that he could expect little help either on his right or his left. Schwarzenberg, as already mentioned, had arranged to go off to Gallicia, and Bülow refused to take Eugène's orders.

Behind him the Viceroy had Lagrange's division of the XI. corps, guarding Berlin and Spandau. Between the 20th and 25th January, Grenier's division (18,000 men) reached Berlin from Italy. There it was split into two divisions which, joined to that of Lagrange, constituted the XI. corps, under the command of Gouvion St Cyr. It was intended to call it up to Posen, but, as Grenier's men required rest, and Lagrange's had partly to be called in from the fortresses it would require some time before they could move. Moreover, Eugène considered the whole corps not too much to keep order in Berlin and the Mark. He, being on the spot, judged the danger of Prussian disaffection more accurately than his stepfather the Emperor, who still pretended to believe in the permanence of the Prussian alliance. A fresh danger now threatened Eugène, for Wittgenstein, though unable to advance beyond Stargard, had organised his Cossacks as the "free corps" of Czernitchew, Benkendorf, and Tettenborn. These columns, of 1500 or 1600 men and a couple of guns each, pushed far and wide through Pomerania, raising the country, cutting off French detachments, and penetrating as far as the lower Oder. Meanwhile Tchichagow reached Thorn on the 28th January, and Bromberg on the 8th February, on which date Kutusow and Miloradowich arrived respectively at Plock and Warsaw.

On the 10th and 11th February, Eugène's advanced troops were attacked and driven in. On the following day he prepared to retreat, and on the 18th he was at Frankfort-on-Oder, where he learned that, two days earlier, the Cossacks of the free corps, crossing the river above and below Küstrin, had harried the country almost to the gates of Berlin.

EUGÈNE'S OPERATIONS

Here also he found waiting for him St Cyr with the 35th and 36th divisions.[1]

Meanwhile, Reynier (VII. corps), who had incautiously halted at Kalisch, had been surprised from Plock, had suffered heavily, and been compelled to retreat on Glogau, which he reached, on the 19th February, with only 9000 men.

The general position on that day was this—

Eugène was at Frankfort with 30,000 men.[2]

Reynier at Glogau with 9000.

Augereau at Berlin with 6000 or 7000.

Lauriston at Magdeburg with two divisions of the V. corps, waiting for the other two to come up.

Morand[3] had 2000 Saxons in Swedish Pomerania.

The garrisons of the fortresses on the Oder were, Stettin, 9000; Küstrin and Glogau, 4000 each.

Spandau was held by 3000 men.

As for Poniatowski, Schwarzenberg had carried him and his 8000 or 9000 Poles off to Gallicia, and included him in his own armistice with the Russians.

Regarding the enemy, it is true that the 5000 Cossacks of the three Free corps were beating up the country in Eugène's rear, and that they actually got into Berlin for a short time on the 20th February; but, after all, this was a mere raid, which could not meet with any permanent success, seeing that its supports were still far east of the Oder. Wittgenstein had, on the 18th February, only 19,000 men (exclusive of the Free corps) available for active operations, and was still 150 miles from the Oder in Pomerania. Kutusow with 40,000 men was at Kalisch; Sacken with 20,000 was watching Schwarzenberg towards Gallicia.

Prussia had not yet declared war. Yorck was two or three marches behind Wittgenstein, Bülow at Colberg, and

---

[1] The two into which Grenier's division had been split.

[2] 12,000 whom he had brought with him from Posen, and 18,000 of St Cyr's two divisions.

[3] Not Count Morand, the commander of a division at Auerstadt in 1806. He still commanded a division of the corps marching from Italy.

Blücher at Breslau. So long as Berlin and a large part of Prussia was in the hands of the French, Frederick William was not in the least likely to risk a declaration of war.

Under these circumstances, there was no immediate necessity whatever for Eugène to retire behind the Oder. But he now came under the influence of Augereau, who was extremely nervous about an insurrection in Berlin. Even if that had occurred, Eugène might well have dealt with it by posting himself half-way between Berlin and the Oder, 20 miles from each. Thence he could have controlled Berlin, and, at the same time, have defended the line of the Oder.

Napoleon's view of the situation is stated in a subsequent letter to Eugène,[1] where he says, "an experienced general who had established a camp east of Küstrin would have given time to the Corps of Observation of the Elbe (Lauriston's V. corps) to reach Berlin; or, at any rate, if such a general had camped in front of Berlin he could not have been attacked, except by the extensive dispositions which he would have forced the enemy to make." Napoleon himself would certainly have defended the Oder from the eastern bank. Later on, on the 15th March,[2] he wrote: "If, . . . instead of retiring on Frankfort, you had concentrated in front of Küstrin, the enemy would have thought twice before throwing anything on to the left bank. You would have gained at least twenty days, and given time for the Corps of Observation of the Elbe to occupy Berlin."

But Augereau's fears prevailed, especially as St Cyr was ill and unable to urge the view, which he afterwards expressed,[3] that the line of the Oder should have been defended, though he was for a defence on the left bank.

On the 22nd February Eugène retired once more to Köpenick a short way south-east of Berlin. He had been alarmed once more by the destruction, on the 21st, of a

---

[1] *Corr.* 19,688 of 9th March.   [2] *Corr.* 19,721.
[3] *Hist. Mil.*, iv. pp. 6-9. On the next page St Cyr says he found Augereau nervously keeping his troops in the streets of Berlin. St Cyr promptly sent them back to barracks.

regiment of Italian chasseurs by Cossacks. Even now, he took half measures and, instead of keeping his force united, left 4000 of Gérard's division at Frankfort, where such a paltry force was useless. Rechberg's Bavarians were at Krossen, and a battalion of the Guard at Furstenwalde maintained communication between these two outposts and the main body.

Frederick William of Prussia [1] at last made up his mind to join the crusade against Napoleon, and signed (28th February) the Convention of Kalisch, allying himself with the Russians. Had that agreement been made public there and then, Yorck and Bülow could have joined Wittgenstein, and Blücher could have brought his forces to the Russian left. But the King of Prussia, trembling for the fate of Berlin, refused to publish his decision, or to sanction active measures by Prussian troops, before the Russians were in secure possession of his capital. Kutusow, the Russian commander, on the other hand, refused to move forward without Prussian co-operation. The deadlock was solved by a compromise. Frederick William directed his troops to follow the Russians to the Oder, but to avoid active hostilities until war was declared.

It was not till the 15th March that the French ambassador in Prussia got wind of the Convention of Kalisch. Prussia's declaration of war only reached Paris on the 27th.

The allied sovereigns, under the impression that the French were in no position to offer resistance, decided on a very widely extended advance to the Elbe, on which river they proposed to concentrate towards their left, so as to be in touch with Austria, whose adhesion to the side against Napoleon was hoped for, and believed to be imminent.

Kutusow was to be in supreme command. Wittgenstein, with the right wing (19,000 Russians and 30,000 Prussians under Yorck and Bülow), was to cross the Oder between Küstrin and Stettin. Blücher, on the left, with the corps of Winzingerode (14,000, mostly Russian cavalry) and his

---

[1] He had left Berlin on the 22nd February on the pretext that he was going to Breslau to raise the fresh contingent for Napoleon.

own 27,000 Prussians, was to advance from Silesia on Dresden; Kutusow, with the reserve (Miloradowich and the Russian Guard) of 30,000, to follow three or four marches behind the left wing. Altogether there were 120,000 men in three groups, separated by distances which forbade any hope of mutual support. What a chance for a capable French leader, and what advantage Napoleon himself would have taken of it!

But Eugène was certainly not even a capable general, and, as soon as Wittgenstein crossed the Oder, on the 1st March, half-way between Küstrin and Stettin, he fell back to the west side of Berlin. What Napoleon thought of this move is best shown in the words of his letter of the 9th March to his stepson.[1]

"Nothing could be less military than the course you have taken in posting your headquarters at Schönberg, in rear of Berlin; it was quite clear that that was to call up the enemy. If, on the contrary, you had taken a position in front of Berlin .... the enemy would have had to believe you wished to fight a battle. Then he would not have passed the Oder till he had assembled 60,000 or 80,000 men with the serious intention of capturing Berlin; but he was still far from being able to do that. . . . You could have gained twenty days, which would have been very advantageous from a political, as well as from a military point of view .... But from the day on which your headquarters were placed behind Berlin it was tantamount to saying that you did not wish to keep that city; you have thus abandoned an attitude which it is the art of war to know how to preserve."

The enemy clearly thought little of Eugène after his successive retreats, and ventured to advance on Berlin with 7000 cavalry and Cossacks (inclusive of the Free corps) and 5000 infantry, whilst Wittgenstein's main body was still (4th March) full five days' march short of Berlin. It was before this puny force that Eugène's 30,000 men fell back. The Viceroy was making for Wittenberg, leaving to their

[1] *Corr.* 19,688.

EUGÈNE'S OPERATIONS

fate Gérard at Frankfort and Rechberg at Krossen. The former succeeded in cutting his way through to Wittenberg, whilst Rechberg got away by Güben and Luckau to Torgau. Admission to that fortress was refused to him by Thielmann, commanding the Saxon garrison, and he was therefore compelled to make for Meissen.

Eugène continued his retreat till he had placed practically the whole of his army behind the Elbe. Under his orders of the 10th March, his forces were thus disposed. In the centre, astride of the Elbe at Wittenberg, Grenier commanded the 35th and 36th divisions of the XI. corps, 18,000 men.

The right wing, commanded by Davout, comprised the remains of Reynier's (VII.) corps, which had retreated from Glogau, the 31st division, with which had been amalgamated the divisions of Girard and Gérard, and the 1st brigade of the 1st division—17,000 men in all. With these Davout had to hold Dresden and defend the Elbe from Königstein to Torgau. At the last-named place was Thielmann, with 5000 or 6000 Saxon levies. He refused to admit either side, though his sympathies were clearly with the allies.

The left wing consisted of about 35,000 men of the V. corps under Lauriston at Magdeburg.

Headquarters and Roguet's Guard division (3000 men) were at Leipzig.

Victor, with 12,000 men of the 4th division and the 2nd brigade of the 1st, was organising behind the Saale at Bernburg.

Carra St Cyr was at Hamburg, where his 1000 men, in the midst of a hostile population, were in a very critical position. Morand, with 2000 Saxons, had been forgotten, and, on hearing by chance of the evacuation of Berlin, had started for Hamburg. It was very doubtful if he would be able to escape.

Eugène, with the choice of defending either the upper or the lower Elbe (for he could not defend the whole), had elected the former, the effect of which would be to leave open to the enemy the 32nd military division, which was French territory, and to expose Holland and Hamburg. He understood that his rôle was that of an army covering the assembly of Napoleon's new army in the valley of the Main, and it seemed to him that he must hold Dresden, and cover *directly* the roads from the Main to the Elbe. He had not yet received the Emperor's letter of the 9th March, already quoted,[1] censuring his arrangements for the defence of the line of the Oder from the rear. Not only did he propose to defend the Elbe in a similar manner, but he also committed the fatal blunder of spreading his forces in a cordon of 150 miles in length, with no reserves to speak of. On the 15th March, Napoleon hearing of these dispositions wrote condemning them absolutely.[2] They were, he said, well calculated to stop the passage of light troops; but what was to happen if the enemy passed in mass, as he could easily do when and where he pleased? The only way to defend a river line was to place large forces in the bridge heads beyond the river, where they would be ready to take the offensive as soon as the enemy should commence his passage:—

"Nothing is more dangerous than to attempt seriously to defend a river by lining the bank opposite (to the enemy); for once the enemy has surprised the passage, and he always does surprise it, he finds the army in a very extended defensive position, and prevents its rallying."

But already Napoleon had written on the 2nd March and again on the 9th. In the letter of the 2nd[3] he had told Eugène exactly what to do if he retreated from Berlin, a measure which, in the letter of the 9th,[4] when he had heard of it, he condemned as unnecessary as matters then stood. The main body of the available forces should be collected in front of Magdeburg, only a small portion being spread along the river to prevent the passage of light troops. If circumstances forced the army to abandon Magdeburg, it

---

[1] *Supra*, pp. 36, 38.   [2] *Corr.* 19,721.
[3] The letter was addressed to Lauriston in cypher, in which form he was to pass it on to Eugène, if he had a cypher arranged with the Viceroy, which the Emperor had not. Lauriston had no such cypher, and the orders only reached Eugène on the 9th. Lanrezac, p. 61. See also *Corr.* 19,640 to Lauriston.
[4] *Corr.* 19,688.

should have its line of operations on Wesel, not on Mayence. In fact, Napoleon preferred to defend the lower rather than the upper Elbe, whilst Eugène, by retreating on Wittenberg, exposed (as the writer believed) Magdeburg itself, as well as Hamburg, Holland, etc. That was not quite so, seeing that Eugène had 35,000 men at Magdeburg. No doubt, as Col. Lanrezac says, the Emperor's reproaches were, strictly speaking, deserved; but it must be admitted that the task imposed on the Viceroy was a very difficult one, especially when it is remembered that a large portion of his troops had deteriorated in consequence of a long retreat unrelieved by any success, and that he was very inferior to the enemy in cavalry. Moreover, Napoleon, according to his custom, persistently over-valued Eugène's strength, and undervalued that of the enemy. He does not blame himself for not taking the obvious measure of putting at the head of his covering troops, not a young and inexperienced general like his stepson, but a man like Davout or Gouvion St Cyr, both of whom were available. The former had so often, especially in 1806 and 1809, proved his worth that it seems inexplicable that the Emperor should not have chosen him on this occasion, or, later on, for the task of the command in Silesia, which was given to the honest but by no means brilliant Macdonald. Eugène did not in the least understand what the Emperor contemplated, and it is not much to be wondered at that he did not. One thing he *did* know was that Napoleon was, in his instructions and censures, misrepresenting the actual condition of affairs. He had told Eugène that the enemy had not as many troops as he had. That was wrong, for they had 120,000 good troops, whilst Eugène could not put more than 80,000 in line, when he had deducted the Saxons in Torgau, who would not move, and the divisions of Durutte and Rechberg, which would have to be sent to the rear to reorganise. Of the 80,000 men, 12,000 (the 1st and 4th divisions) were not yet properly organised.

Accepting his own false assumptions on these points, what Napoleon now required to be done was this :—

Eugène was to take post with 65,000 men east of Magdeburg, in a position guarded by works at such a distance that he could manœuvre between them. Behind his right rear would be Victor on the left bank, guarding the Elbe as far as Torgau. From Torgau to Bohemia the river had to be watched by Reynier with 12,000 men (he really only had 6000). Davout would be on Eugène's left rear, about opposite the infall of the Plauen canal. Both Victor and Davout, whilst depriving the enemy of the chance of using boats on the river, were to maintain means of passage for themselves, in case they were required to cross and operate against the flank of a general attack on Eugène. In consequence of these arrangements, the enemy would be compelled, if he attempted to pass the Elbe, to do so three marches at least above or below Magdeburg, and would certainly not dare to do so both above and below, with two bodies separated by six or seven marches, and with Eugène in the middle of them.

As for Dresden, Napoleon admitted the importance which Eugène attached to it, but said it was useless to attempt to defend it with Reynier's force, if the enemy marched against it in strength. All Reynier could then do would be to fall back successively behind the Mulde and the Saale, whilst Eugène faced south, with his left on the Elbe and his right on the Harz Mountains.

The last thing the Emperor desired, if Eugène was driven from the Elbe line, was to have him falling back on the new army towards Mayence. His retreat should be towards the lower Rhine. If the enemy were rash enough to follow him in that direction, the Emperor, advancing from the Main, would be in a position analogous to that before Jena; only, thanks to the possession of Magdeburg, his strategic position would be much better than it was in 1806. His new army would not be ready before the middle of April; therefore he wanted the enemy, if he succeeded in passing the Elbe, to be drawn away from, not towards, Mayence and the Main. That was why he prescribed Eugène's line of operations on the lower Rhine.

But Napoleon thought the allies might very well be kept beyond the Elbe for a considerable time by the arrangements he ordered. If they were to cross towards Dresden, he held that a threat of advance by Eugène on Berlin would very soon compel them to return to the right bank, and he was convinced that, if they did attempt a passage, it would be above Magdeburg, not below it. Also, he held that they would not dare to cross at all without watching Eugène with at least 80,000 men, a force he rightly held them incapable of finding in addition to an equal force thrown over the river, and exposed to be attacked by Eugène rapidly falling back to the left bank through Magdeburg. Moreover, they could not cross between Dessau and Magdeburg, owing to Victor's position. Consequently, they would have to force the lines of the Mulde and the Saale, on which they could be delayed by Victor and Reynier whilst Eugène came up.

Eugène's task did not include the fighting of a great battle. He must carry it out by manœuvring, not by fighting.

The Emperor reckoned without his host when he calculated that a threat of advance on Berlin by Eugène would fetch the allies back to the right bank. They had lost all fear of the French after their long retreat, and they were quite prepared to treat Eugène's army as an almost negligible quantity.

Notwithstanding all that was said in the letter of 9th March, it was only on the 18th that the Viceroy made up his mind to take post east of Magdeburg. It was a difficult operation to concentrate his dispersed army.

Davout left Dresden on the 17th March, after blowing up an arch of the bridge there, leaving behind only 6000 or 7000 men under Durutte.[1] When he was within a march of Leipzig (21st March), the 35th and 36th divisions and Roguet's Guard division marched from Wittenberg and

---

[1] Reynier had fallen ill. Davout's destruction of the bridge was censured by Napoleon as calculated both to invite an advance of the enemy and to exasperate the inhabitants (*Corr.* 19,767). The latter effect it certainly had.

Leipzig on Magdeburg, leaving Victor along the left bank of the Elbe. On the 23rd March a division of the V. corps moved to Möckern, a short way east of Magdeburg, so as to draw the enemy away from Wittenberg; but the main body of the corps still remained on the left bank.

Meanwhile, Carra St Cyr had lost Hamburg to Tettenborn, and had later lost 2000 men under Morand, who were destroyed or captured as they advanced on Lüneburg, unsupported by the other 3000 whom Carra St Cyr took back to keep Bremen in order. On the other flank, Durutte, reduced to 3000 men owing to the departure of his Saxons for Torgau, was forced to leave Dresden, where Blücher passed the Elbe with light troops on the 27th March.

At this time there was a good deal of hesitation at the headquarters of the allies. Wittgenstein was, on the 20th March, still at Berlin with his main body, with advanced troops towards Magdeburg and the Elbe. Blücher, in the south, was moving slowly towards Dresden, with the head of his main body no farther forward than Liegnitz, though his partisans and cavalry were already on the Elbe. The army of reserve was still far behind at Glogau and Kalisch. Kutusow and Scharnhorst viewed matters in very different lights. The latter, and the Prussians generally, wanted to push rapidly on; the Russian did not believe much in the value of his Prussian allies, and insisted on holding back till he had reorganised his own army. The Tsar would have gone with the Prussians but could not induce Kutusow to concur.

Kutusow's plan was for Wittgenstein to leave a few thousands to mask Magdeburg, whilst, with his main body, he marched to join Blücher by the right bank of the Elbe. When the two had joined forces, they could cross the Elbe and march on Leipzig. Wittgenstein objected that that would mean exposing Berlin, and he proposed moving to the south-east of Magdeburg, whence he could cover Berlin indirectly. At the same time he would throw a bridge at Rosslau. He would thus, whilst still covering Berlin, be ready, when Blücher was on a level with him,

EUGÈNE'S OPERATIONS

to cross the Elbe. He thought a rapid movement of his advanced guard on to the lower Saale, the heads of Blücher's corps being already on the Pleisse, would effectually stop any idea of an advance on Berlin by Eugène. At the same time, a raid was to be carried out by Czernitchew crossing the Elbe below Magdeburg at Havelburg, and trying to penetrate into Hanover and Westphalia. Eugène, a prey to various, generally unfounded, rumours of hostile operations on the lower Elbe, still kept his main body on the left bank, and even withdrew the division of the V. corps which he had advanced to Möckern. At last, on the 31st March, he learnt that Wittgenstein had left Berlin and appeared to contemplate passing the Elbe at Rosslau. Then the Viceroy decided to carry out the Emperor's orders, by taking his main body across the river, leaving Victor to guard the lower Saale, and twelve battalions to watch the Elbe towards Tangermunde, below Magdeburg. The latter were to be supported, in case of a passage below Magdeburg, by Davout with 11,000 men. Eugène still could not make up his mind to take over a large enough force. He had about 50,000 men, including 4000 cavalry and 180 guns.

We do not propose to describe in detail the combats known by the name of Möckern, which took place on the 3rd, 4th, and 5th April, between Eugène's forces and those of Wittgenstein. The Viceroy, obsessed by the fear of losing his communications with Magdeburg, wasted a large portion of his troops in guarding posts which could have been held safely by much smaller forces. His heart was not in the operation, and he was within a hair's breadth of being beaten when night brought the combat of the 5th April to a close. An incorrect report that Wittgenstein was passing the Elbe at Rosslau gave Eugène the desired excuse for taking his whole force back to the left bank next day.

His action had done no good. He had only drawn against himself a portion of Wittgenstein's force, instead of the main body, and his ill-success enabled the allies, with some show of truth, to vaunt a great victory. If they had not gained that, they were, at least, able to produce a favourable moral effect in Germany. As for Wittgenstein, he crossed the Elbe without difficulty on the 10th April, that is exactly at the juncture, which he had intended all along, when Blücher had reached Leipzig.

After his failure at Möckern, the Viceroy decided to take post on the lower Saale, for the defence of the strip of country between that river and the Harz mountains. From the 6th to the 21st April nothing of much importance happened on this part of the theatre of war. Thielmann in Torgau would give it over neither to one side nor the other, but he seems to have incited the allies to an attack on Wittenberg. He would probably have gone over to them himself, had he been sure that his officers would support him.

The attack on Wittenberg failed, thanks to Lapoype, who commanded the French troops there.

The allies were waiting for the rest of their army, since they had available at present only about 70,000 men. The Russian Guard, having only left Kalisch on the 7th April, could not be at Leipzig till the 27th or 28th. Kutusow was still obstructive. Miloradowich was following Blücher. Barclay de Tolly, with 14,000 men, was besieging Thorn. He was set free to march to the front by the surrender of the fortress on the 18th April. Spandau yielded three days later.

The allies, meanwhile, busied themselves repairing the bridge at Dresden, constructing two more there, and others at Meissen and at Mühlberg. The King of Saxony was trying to play the neutral, and it was under his orders that Thielmann held Torgau against both sides.

On the 19th April, the allies, alarmed by a report that Napoleon was advancing from the Main to join the Viceroy, began to concentrate. It was, in fact, not till the 21st April that the advanced guard of Napoleon's army began to appear at Erfurt.

CHAPTER V

NAPOLEON'S CONCENTRATION ON THE SAALE

NAPOLEON had lost in Russia, in killed, wounded, sick, and prisoners, half a million of men. Yorck's corps of Prussians, and Schwarzenberg's Austrians, had deserted him, and the latter had carried off Poniatowski's Poles. Such disasters would have crushed most men; on Napoleon they had no such effect. His ambitions of Empire, and his hopes of recovering his position of the beginning of 1812, were as high as ever, and his active brain was as busy as ever in evolving great schemes.

His first project for the coming campaign, says Count Yorck,[1] "need not fear comparison with his best, either in point of boldness or of brilliancy." It is explained in "Notes for the Viceroy of Italy," dated the 11th March.[2] After estimating various distances in marches, the Emperor says that the principal objective of the army appears to be to come as soon as possible to the rescue of Danzig. He assumes Eugène's army concentrated at Magdeburg, Havelberg, and Wittenberg. From the two latter it is only three marches to Berlin. The army of the Main, which was in process of assembly when he wrote, he assumed to be concentrated at Würzburg, Erfurt, and Leipzig. It would be a natural movement, which could easily be concealed from the enemy, to march the army of the Elbe, followed by that of the Main, via Havelberg to Stettin. Arrived there, the army would have passed the Oder and gained ten days, without the enemy (whom Napoleon assumed to be at Dresden, Glogau, and Warsaw) being able to arrange

---

[1] *Napoleon as a General*, ii. p. 242. [2] *Corr.* 19,697.

himself so as to cover Danzig. He continues: "After having made all demonstrations to induce the belief that I wish to march on Dresden and into Silesia, my intention will probably be (under cover of the Thuringian mountains and the Elbe) to march by Havelberg, reaching Stettin by forced marches, with 300,000 men, and to continue the march of the army on Danzig, where I could arrive in fifteen days; and on the twentieth day of movement, after the army had passed the Elbe, I should have relieved that town, and should be master of Marienburg, of the Island of Nogat, and of all the bridges of the lower Vistula. So much for the offensive."

He regretted that Magdeburg with its fortress was not at Werben, but, as that could not be helped, he was anxious to have, if possible, a fortified passage of the Elbe at Werben, or somewhere in that direction. It would not be possible to take the offensive decidedly before the beginning of May. This project at once strikes one as a deviation from the Emperor's general principle of making his objective the enemy's army. But, if he went direct for that army, there was always the danger that it would fall back straight before him, and that, with his great deficiency in cavalry, he would not be able to bring it to a decisive action. On the other hand, as Colonel Lanrezac remarks, a "coup de théâtre" of the kind contemplated would go much farther to re-establish the Emperor's lost prestige than merely driving the enemy straight back on Warsaw. Moreover, in his march through the north of Germany, Napoleon would have Prussia at his mercy, and it must be remembered that on the date of his note he knew nothing of the Convention of Kalisch, and was not to receive Prussia's declaration of war for more than a fortnight. By relieving the fortresses of the Oder and the Vistula he would be able to draw in the veterans of their garrisons. Finally, he would be in a position as he advanced (unless the Russians retreated with great expedition) to fall from the north on their communications with Poland, and fight a new Jena with his front towards France. As he still held all the

NAPOLEON'S CONCENTRATION ON THE SAALE 49

permanent fortified passages of the Elbe and the Oder, the Russians would be dependent for their retreat on temporary bridges.

The scheme was never carried out, though we shall find the Emperor recurring to modifications of it later on. The reasons for its abandonment are not difficult to infer. To begin upon, at the commencement of May, when the offensive movement was contemplated, Napoleon had hardly more than two-thirds of the 300,000 men with whom he proposed to reach Stettin, to say nothing of a force left to "fix" the enemy towards Dresden during his movement by Havelberg. For such a scheme as his he would require a great superiority of numbers. Moreover, great mobility and endurance were requisite for the forced marches extending over many days. Could these be expected from the young troops now being raised? Again, long before the beginning of May, Prussia had joined the Russians.

The Emperor talks of its being easy to conceal his movement from the enemy. But, with his inferiority in cavalry, and with the widespread hostility to the French all over Germany, that was hardly probable.

Lastly, before May arrived, it had become necessary to wheel into line the King of Saxony, who was coquetting with the Austrian scheme of armed neutrality. Bavaria and other States of the Rhenish Confederation were also not above suspicion.

Let us now turn from the scheme which did not come off to the newer one which was actually executed. The Emperor's first objective now was to defeat the enemy's army, drive it across the Elbe, and re-establish himself in Saxony.

About the beginning of April he had the following forces assembling in or near the valley of the Main:—

(1) III. corps (Ney), 40,000 men,[1] about Schweinfurt and Würzburg.

---

[1] Strengths are given in round figures. The corps were not yet completed. See Map I. (inset *a*).

D

(2) VI. corps (Marmont), 25,000 men, about Hanau.

(3) Guard (Mortier and Bessières), 16,000 men, Mayence.

(4) Corps of Observation of Italy (Bertrand), 40,000 men, marching from the Tyrol on Bamberg, where its head was due about the 15th April. It was echeloned by brigades over a length of ten marches.

(5) Bavarian division (Raglowich), 8000 men, Baireuth.

(6) Baden-Hessian division (Marchand), 8000 men, Würzburg.

(7) Wurtemberg division (Franquemont), 7000 men, Mergentheim.

Altogether between 140,000 and 150,000 men.

The new scheme, if less ambitious than that for the relief of Danzig, might yet lead to great results, if all went well for Napoleon.

He had very little exact information as to the positions and movements of the enemy, but he did know for certain that their headquarters were still at Kalisch on the 22nd March, that they would probably not move thence before the 1st April, and that, consequently, the Russians and Prussians could not be in full force on the left bank of the Saale before the end of April. But, like Moltke in 1870, he had to contemplate the possibility of their risking an advance without waiting for their full force. In that case, they might cross the Saale so early as the 20th April. He, on the other hand, would not be ready to advance from the Main before the 15th, and could not reckon on assembling his corps on the Saale before the last days of April. In order to conform to his own principle that "all unions of corps d'armée should be effected in rear and far from the enemy," he must choose a point well to the west of that river. He selected Erfurt as the point of assembly for all but Bertrand's group. The enemy could not pass the Saale by the 20th with more than about 70,000 men, so, even without Bertrand, he would still have a large superiority.

In the event of this premature advance by the enemy, Eugène's army of the Elbe would take post behind the Wipper, with its left on the lower Saale, and its right on the Harz Mountains. Seeing that Napoleon held all the fortified passages of the Elbe,[1] and also that, for political reasons, the allies would not be willing to move far away from Austria, it was certain they would pass the Elbe above Torgau. If, after passing it, they advanced westwards they would be threatened in right flank by Eugène's army, very little inferior to them in numbers, in the position above named, whilst in front they would have at first 50,000 of the army of the Main, with another 40,000 arriving very shortly. The Elbe army would thus be covering, indirectly from a flank position, that of the Main. Such a system of defence was preferable to a directly covering position, since, in the latter case, Eugène, falling back before a superior enemy, would have done so on the heads of Napoleon's own columns, and, not to speak of difficulties of supply, etc., would have produced a very bad moral effect in the new army. Moreover, the enemy would not hesitate to attack him if he were directly in front of the army of the Main. It would be a very different matter for them to attack him when their own left flank was threatened by Napoleon's advance.

However, as it was not at all likely that the allies would venture to advance before the arrival of the Russian Guard, Napoleon calculated that they were not likely to be north of the latitude of Leipzig, by which town he proposed to debouch in full force, drawing to his assistance the army of the Elbe.

There were two possibilities with regard to the allies. In the first place they might, and, with their superior opportunities for acquiring information, it was probable they would realise the true direction of his movement. In that event, if they resolved not to retreat but to meet him, he would be able to attack with double their strength, he was almost certain of victory, and it was possible he might be able to ruin them by driving them into the Elbe.

But that was not what he most desired. He hoped that, having in their mind the manœuvre of Jena, and noting the

[1] Torgau was held by the Saxons, but Napoleon was not aware that Thielmann held it against both sides. Anyhow, it was not open to the allies.

advance of the corps from Italy, which was marching by the line Bamberg-Coburg-Saalfeld-Naumburg, they might be induced by demonstrations to move towards the upper Saale. In that case he would move rapidly with his left on Dresden, sweeping away the detachments which he might meet, and severing the enemy's communications. That would be precisely the manœuvre of Jena, carried out from the north instead of from the south, with the French left, instead of the right, in advance.

Supposing the allies marched against Eugène, the Viceroy would fall back slowly, and the allied movement would be almost immediately arrested by the threat of Napoleon's forces from Erfurt against their left flank. If they persisted in advancing they would very soon find themselves hemmed in between Eugène, Napoleon, and the Elbe about Magdeburg. Seeing that they would not be more than half the combined French strength, their position would be almost desperate.

Orders of the 28th and 29th March required the III. corps (Ney), VI. (Marmont), and the Guard to be, on the 18th April, on the road to Erfurt, the first by the road Schweinfurt-Meiningen, the two latter by that through Hanau, Fulda, and Eisenach. The Bavarian division from Baireuth would watch the Franconian forest towards Hof and Schleiz; the Badeners at Coburg, with an advanced guard at Gräfenthal, would watch towards Saalfeld. On the same date the corps of Italy would have its two leading divisions at Bamberg, ready to start next day towards Saalfeld.

On the 9th April the Emperor heard of the occupation of Dresden by the allies; a day or two later he knew that Eugène's operations beyond the Elbe had failed, and that he was posting the army of the Elbe behind the Wipper.

Napoleon at once pressed on the march of his own columns. The following passages from his letter of the 12th April to Bertrand[1] explain his views:—

"The Prince of the Moskowa (Ney) will have informed you that it is my intention to refuse my right . . . thus

[1] *Corr.* 19,852.

NAPOLEON'S CONCENTRATION ON THE SAALE 53

making a movement the converse of that which I made in the campaign of Jena, so that if the enemy penetrate to Baireuth, I can arrive before him at Dresden, and cut him from Prussia. . . . The Duke of Istria (Bessières), having under his orders the Duke of Ragusa (Marmont), 40,000 infantry and 10,000 cavalry, is moving on Eisenach, where he will arrive the 18th or 20th. The Prince of Moskowa is moving on Erfurt, where he also will arrive on the 20th; he has under his orders 60,000 men, including the allies, and some thousands of horses. . . . As I suppose your cavalry and your two divisions will be at Bamberg on the 16th, you will support the movement of the Prince of Moskowa by moving with these two divisions and your cavalry on Coburg. This movement is the most natural, since it is the shortest, and at Coburg you will be distant only two long marches from Meiningen, three from Erfurt, and three from Jena, and thus you could always manœuvre on the Saale. Thus, if affairs turn out so that the Prince of the Moskowa moves on Erfurt, your position at Coburg will place you on his right, and thence you can move, according to circumstances, on Jena, Erfurt, or Meiningen. . . . The enemy is far from suspecting the considerable number of forces which are advancing on the Saale. If we were lucky enough for the enemy to make a strong advance on Baireuth, he would soon be recalled to Dresden. . . . You can . . . direct the march of your 2nd and 3rd divisions on Würzburg."

The French were thus, on the 12th April, in three masses:—

(a) Army of the Elbe, 60,000 to 65,000[1] men, behind the Wipper.

(b) The III., VI., and Guard corps, the Baden and Wurtemberg divisions, 105,000 to 110,000 men, moving from the Main by Schweinfurt and by Fulda to Erfurt.

(c) The corps of Italy and the Bavarian division marching by Bamberg on Coburg.

This last group was intended as a bait to draw the enemy,

[1] Exclusive of 18,000 or 20,000 under Davout on the lower Elbe.

if possible, towards the upper Saale. Bertrand would avoid compromising himself, and, if seriously threatened, would avoid action, either by drawing nearer to the other corps on his left, or, if it so happened that transverse communications rendered this difficult, he could always fall back towards Coburg, or even farther south. Till he should be seriously threatened he would follow the line Coburg-Saalfeld-Jena, always keeping on the left bank of the Saale. The army of the Elbe held fast for the present about Aschersleben, whilst that of the Main and the Corps of Observation of Italy were moving towards the Saale; but, though not attacked, it was not unmolested; for the enemy's cavalry gained several small successes which, though not important in themselves, were calculated to create alarm in Eugène's army. One detatchment, under the son of Blücher, reached Weimar and was joined there by a Saxon battalion, which passed over to the enemy. Helwig, with 150 cavalry, made a successful attack on the greatly superior rearguard of Rechberg, capturing two guns and 100 men. Next day the same detachment dispersed a Westphalian regiment, thereby creating a quite disproportionate alarm in the mind of the commander of the Westphalian division, who magnified this single squadron into a strong force of all arms. These raids even created some excitement at Ney's headquarters, which had reached Erfurt.

Napoleon, leaving Paris at 4 A.M. on the 15th, was in Mayence forty hours later, and remained there till the 24th, considering that there was no urgency for his appearance at the front. There he made some changes in the organisation of his army. The "Corps of Observation of Italy" was split up into the IV. corps, consisting of Morand's French, Peyri's Italian, and Franquemont's Wurtemberg division, under Bertrand, whilst a XII. corps, under Oudinot, was formed of Pacthod's and Lorencez's divisions and Raglowich's Bavarians. The latter had been acting somewhat suspiciously, falling back on Baireuth, instead of holding the heights of Ebersdorf as ordered by Napoleon. When called to account by Bertrand, Raglowich pleaded orders of the King of Bavaria, and it was not till the 22nd April that that sovereign directed him to obey Bertrand. The incident pointed to hesitation on the king's part in his allegiance to Napoleon.

Marchand's Baden-Hessian division was placed by the Emperor under Ney's orders as part of the III. corps, which now had five divisions.

The armies of the Main and the Elbe now, on the 25th April, comprised the following corps : [1]—

ARMY OF THE MAIN

III. corps (Ney), 8th, 9th, 10th, 11th, and 39th (Baden-Hessian) divisions	45,000
VI. corps (Marmont), 20th, 21st, 22nd, 23rd (not yet formed) divisions	25,000
IV. corps (Bertrand), 12th, 15th (Italian), 38th (Wurtemberg) divisions	30,000
XII. corps (Oudinot), 13th, 14th, 29th (Bavarian) divisions	25,000
Guard (Dumoustier), infantry. Partly Young, partly Old Guard	11,000
Guard, cavalry	4,000
Total	140,000

ARMY OF THE ELBE

XI. corps (Macdonald), 31st, 35th, 36th, divisions	22,000
V. corps (Lauriston), 16th, 17th, 18th, 19th divisions	22,000
Guard (Roguet)	3,500
32nd division (Durutte)	4,500
4th division (Victor)	6,000
1st cavalry corps (Latour-Maubourg)	4,000
	62,000
Grand total, both armies	202,000

[1] Lanrezac, p. 116. Figures and organisation based on present states in Ministère de la Guerre.

Their positions were as follows, from left to right:—

Army of the Elbe, headquarters at Hoym, with Victor south of Bernburg, on the left bank of the Saale; the rest about Hoym and Aschersleben.

III. corps at and behind Weimar.

Guard, at and behind Erfurt.

VI. corps behind the Guard, from near Gotha to Vach.

Baden division about Ilmenau.

Wurtemberg division, between Königshofen and Hildburghausen.

IV. corps, Coburg.

XII. corps, Anspach and Nürnberg, with the Bavarian division at Baireuth and Munchberg (detachment).

On the 22nd, Napoleon had despatched the following orders for the 25th:—

(*a*) The army of the Main to advance on Jena and Naumburg.

(*b*) Army of the Elbe to move up the Saale, occupying Halle and Merseburg.

(*c*) Corps of Italy, if circumstances permitted, to march by Saalfeld on Jena by the left bank of the Saale.

In a letter to Eugène, of the 22nd, Berthier says:—

" The intention of the Emperor is to guard the whole of the Saale, in order to prevent the enemy from detaching any party on the left bank of that river." Napoleon was so conscious of his inferiority in cavalry that he was obliged to use the river as a screen for his movements.

On the 24th April, Napoleon left Mayence, reaching Erfurt in the afternoon of the next day.

The assembly of the armies on the Saale was effected without fighting, except at Halle, where an attack by Lauriston was beaten off by the Prussian general Kleist. Eugène, for reasons not apparent, moved very slowly, and Bertrand was delayed by the difficulties of the road throu the mountains from Coburg to Saalfeld.

By the 30th April, a considerable part of the army was

NAPOLEON'S CONCENTRATION ON THE SAALE 57

on the right bank of the Saale, the positions on the evening of that day being as follows :—

Army of the Elbe :—
Headquarters, V. corps, and Guard at Merseburg (left bank). Four battalions at Halle, which Kleist had evacuated when Merseburg was occupied by the French.

XI. corps, on right bank in front of Merseburg, with the 1st cavalry corps in front of it.

Durutte's (32nd) division, behind at Schäfstadt.

Victor (4th division). Headquarters at Bernburg, with troops spread along the Saale from Barby to Wettin.

Westphalian division, assembling at Sondershausen.

Army of the Main:—
Imperial headquarters, Guard cavalry division, the Old Guard portion of Dumoustier's Guard division,[1] Weissenfels. Young Guard, Naumburg.

III. corps. Headquarters and four divisions east of Weissenfels. Marchand's division, Stössen.

VI. corps. Headquarters and two divisions, Naumburg. Friederichs' division, Kösen.

IV. corps. Headquarters and Morand's division, Dornburg, with three battalions at Camburg.

Peyri's division, Jena.

Franquemont's division, Burgau, Kahla, and Rudolstadt.

XII. corps echeloned between Saalfeld and Coburg.

The assembly of the army was not yet complete, for the XII. corps and the Wurtemberg division of the IV. were still two days' march away from the main body.

Let us now see what the allies had been doing whilst the army of the Main was marching to the Saale.

Miloradowich, passing the Elbe at Dresden, between the 16th and the 19th April, marched to join Blücher, who had been in cantonments about Altenburg since the 14th. The

[1] Roguet's and Dumoustier's divisions after this became Old and Young Guard respectively by transfer of troops. Each had been partly Old and partly Young Guard so far.

Russian Guard, with which were the Tsar and the King of Prussia, only reached Dresden on the 24th.

Hitherto, the influence of Kutusow had prevailed in the councils of the allies, and, as we know, he distrusted the value of the Prussian troops, whom he judged by the recollection of 1806. He was now lying on his death-bed at Bunzlau. He died on the 28th April, and henceforward the command fell into the hands of men who, unlike their great opponent, were incapable of forming a positive decision, uninfluenced by the opinions or advice of others.

The Tsar had, before Kutusow's death, decided that the command should be given to Wittgenstein. But there were grave difficulties in the way of his appointment, for he was only 44 years of age, many years the junior of Blücher, Tormassow, and Miloradowich, and junior to the two latter in the Russian army. He was, according to Clausewitz, full of good will, activity, and enterprise, and Napoleon himself was aware of his reputation for boldness.

Blücher, never inclined to overrate his own strategical ability, or to push himself forward as a candidate for supreme command, was willing to serve under Wittgenstein; but with the two Russians it was different. Consequently, when Wittgenstein received his written appointment on the 27th April, though it styled him "Commander-in-chief of the combined army of the allied powers," it only gave him "chief command of all troops under General of Cavalry Blücher, and General Adjutant Winzingerode," making no mention of Tormassow's and Miloradowich's commands. To these two generals orders were conveyed by the Tsar over the head of Wittgenstein, who, throughout his period of command, found himself in the difficult position of having orders thus passed, sometimes without his knowledge, by the Tsar, who had successfully arrogated to himself the leading position. Wittgenstein's relations with Blücher were cordial, partially owing to the esteem in which the latter's Chief of Staff, Scharnhorst, was held at Russian headquarters by Wolkonski, Toll, d'Auvray (Chief of Staff to Wittgenstein), and other advisers of the Tsar.

NAPOLEON'S CONCENTRATION ON THE SAALE

Up to 25th April Alexander's military advisers had their attention fixed on Leipzig and Altenburg as the front line for Wittgenstein's and Blücher's forces, whilst Miloradowich should advance to Zwickau, and Tormassow to Chemnitz. They believed that several weeks must elapse before Napoleon could make his attack, and they believed that, if he attacked earlier than the end of May, he would advance with his right, refusing his left, that is, he would move forward with the army of the Main. In that case, Toll, who had been studying the writings of Jomini, advocated an advance from Altenburg with the allied left, against Napoleon's communications on the Leipzig-Naumburg road. Toll was with Blücher and Scharnhorst at Altenburg on the 25th; the information gathered there convinced him that the decision was nearer at hand than had hitherto been believed. He therefore posted off to Dresden, only to find the Tsar had gone to visit his sister at Teplitz. As time pressed, Wolkonski, Alexander's Chief of Staff, assumed the responsibility of ordering Tormassow to march at once from Dresden in two columns, which were to reach Rosswein and Freiberg on the 28th, Frohberg and Kohren on the 30th.[1]

On the 26th April the allied positions were these:—

Wittgenstein's command.—Bülow, in the north, with main body between Cöthen and Rosslau, and advanced troops on the lower Saale. Yorck at Zorbig, half-way between Halle and Dessau, with two advanced guards at Wettin (Zilinski) and Halle (Kleist). Berg at Landsberg.

Blücher's command.—Winzingerode, main body between Leipzig and Borna. Prussian infantry in the triangle Borna-Altenburg-Mittweida. Russian cavalry pushed forward on Weissenfels, Merseburg, and west of Altenburg. Under orders from Blücher, reconnaissances in strength were made on Dornburg, Camburg, and Naumburg.

On the 27th April, Berg was called into Leipzig, Yorck to Schkeuditz, and Wittgenstein took post at Lindenau, the

[1] See Map I.

western suburb of Leipzig. Zilinski having to retire from Wettin before the advance of the army of the Elbe, burned the boat bridge there and fell back on Leipzig.

To the south of Blücher, Miloradowich was at Chemnitz on the 24th with a cavalry brigade at Zwickau.

On the 26th, Wittgenstein issued an order expressing his intentions clearly, though he rather confused matters by a subsequent "instruction" of the 27th. In the order of the 26th he wrote: " I desire to assemble all available troops at Leipzig, so that, in union with the forces of Generals Blücher and Winzingerode, I may, if the enemy assumes the offensive by Weissenfels, offer battle at Lützen."

His staff next drew up an impracticable scheme aiming at meeting all possible combinations. The most notable point about it was that it kept steadily in view the idea of fighting a battle. It was severely criticised by Scharnhorst, whose proposal was to withdraw to Brandis (midway between Leipzig and Wurzen) if Napoleon appeared to be moving on Leipzig, though he was willing to wait a little in the present stations to see if the Emperor proposed to threaten the allies' left flank by an advance on Pegau.

Clausewitz, on the other hand, had advocated a defensive position between the Freiberg Mulde and the Elbe. Toll, on hearing these different views, expressed his own that Napoleon meant to push forward between Leipzig and Altenburg, so as to separate Blücher from Wittgenstein. Therefore, he proposed collecting all the allied forces about Altenburg. If Napoleon advanced on Altenburg, the allies would hold a good position in which to meet him, and also cover their line of operations through Dresden. If, on the other hand, the French moved towards Leipzig, they would be threatened in right flank from Altenburg, and might be driven on the Elbe between Wittenberg and Magdeburg. At Altenburg the allies would have behind them a bridge over the Elbe at Mühlberg, another at Meissen, and three more at Dresden. To the Leipzig position Toll objected that Napoleon, manœuvring against the allies' left, might cut them from their line of operations and drive them on Rosslau, where they had only one bridge. Meanwhile, Wittgenstein's "instruction" of the 27th reached the Tsar on the 29th. Alexander would have nothing to do with a battle east of Leipzig on the Partha, and sent Wolkonski to stop the idea. By the time Wolkonski reached Wittgenstein, the enemy had appeared in Weissenfels and Naumburg, and Wittgenstein at once accepted Toll's proposal for an assembly between Leipzig and Altenburg, with the idea of moving forward from that position towards Lützen, to attack the French right flank from the south.

On the 28th April, Kleist had repulsed Lauriston's attack on Halle, and was contemplating a counter attack. Yorck remained at Schkeuditz, but sent a detachment to replace the Russian cavalry in Merseburg. Berg remained west of Leipzig.

On the 29th there were two small fights. In the first place, Yorck's detachment was driven out of Merseburg, the result of which was to compel Kleist to evacuate Halle during the ensuing night. The other fight was at Weissenfels, between Souham's division of Ney's corps and the cavalry of Lanskoi, ending in the repulse of the latter by the French infantry.

Wittgenstein reached on this evening a position south of Lützen, where he was protected by Lanskoi's cavalry.

The allied movements on the 30th April were as follows:—

Berg from Leipzig to Zwenkau.
Yorck from Schkeuditz to in front of Berg at Zwenkau.
Kleist from Schkeuditz to Lindenau.
Blücher's corps assembled at Borna.
Main army (Tormassow) reached Frohberg and Kohren.
Miloradowich remained at Penig, though Toll says he was "invited" to march to Altenburg.

As has been already noted, Napoleon had not completed the concentration of his army on the evening of the 30th April, for the XII. corps and the Wurtemberg division were still two days' march off. He had, however, immediately at hand about 145,000 men, and though he, as usual now, somewhat underestimated the enemy's forces, they certainly had not above two-thirds of that number. With such numbers, and with Napoleon in personal command, there could not be much doubt of the result of a battle. Something decisive was of the utmost importance to Napoleon, in order to restore his prestige, so badly shattered by the events of 1812, and to bind once more to their allegiance Austria and the Princes of the Rhenish Confederation. The Emperor's information regarding the allies was, owing to his want of cavalry and the hostility of the country, very meagre. He believed them to be scattered from Dessau to Zwickau with their main body about Altenburg.

If he delayed his decisive movements, the enemy, recognising his vast numerical superiority, might lose heart and slip away across the Elbe again, to lead him away on a long stern chase in which, with his weakness in cavalry, he would be powerless to force a decision. Once the enemy realised fully that his object was to pass round their right and force them to a battle with reversed front, they would take fright and retreat. After all, the four divisions which were spread along the upper Saale might help his movement by drawing the enemy's attention in that direction. These reasons, and the necessity for gaining space beyond the Saale, are doubtless, as Colonel Lanrezac thinks, what prompted Napoleon to push on on the 1st May, without waiting for the complete concentration of his army. His orders for that day required the Elbe army to advance from Merseburg to Schladebach; III. corps and cavalry of the Guard, from Weissenfels on Lützen; VI. corps to support the III. with two divisions, the third being left at Naumburg; IV. and XII. corps to close as quickly as possible towards Naumburg.

The march of the corps from Weissenfels and Naumburg would take them on to an open plain eminently favourable for cavalry, in which Napoleon was so very weak that his

NAPOLEON'S CONCENTRATION ON THE SAALE 63

troops were compelled to march in mass, so as to be ready at any moment to receive the enemy's cavalry. Winzingerode's cavalry, which attempted to interfere with the passage of the Rippach brook, was beaten off, but the French suffered a heavy loss by the death of Bessières, who was killed at this spot by a round shot. The infantry divisions drove off several Russian cavalry charges, and Ney reported to the Emperor that his young troops had done magnificently.[1] In the evening of the 1st May the French had attained the following positions :—

The army of the Elbe had the XI. corps at Quesitz and Markranstädt; the V. behind Günthersdorf; 1st cavalry corps between Schladebach and Oetzsch. A regiment was detached at Halle, and Durutte's division guarded the passage of the Saale at Merseburg. Napoleon, with the cavalry of the Guard, was at Lützen.

The army of the Main was thus distributed :—

Infantry of the Guard (2 divisions), Weissenfels.

III. corps. Headquarters, Kaja. Souham's division in the four villages Gross and Klein Görschen, Kaja, and Rahna, about three miles south of Lützen.

Girard's division in Starsiedel, west of Souham.

Brennier's and Ricard's divisions somewhere about Lützen, exact position not certain, and Marchand's towards Lützen.

VI. corps. Headquarters, Rippach. Bonnet's division on the heights east of Rippach.

Compans', west of the Rippach brook.

Friederichs', Naumburg.

IV. corps. Headquarters, Stössen; also Morand's division, with advanced guard at Pretzsch.

Peyri's division, Gross Gestewitz.

Wurtemberg division, Jena.

XII. corps, from Kahla back to behind Saalfeld.

---

[1] A great deal of fuss was made about this trifling affair, not because there was anything remarkable in the repulse of the cavalry, but because the Emperor was desirous of inspiriting and flattering his new troops.

St Cyr (iv. p. 34) thinks there was a great deal of unnecessary forming of squares at this time in Napoleon's army. He believes neither in the necessity for nor the efficacy of squares.

There was no fresh information about the enemy, and the French army now consisted of a "corps de demonstration" (IV. and XII. corps), which it was hoped might draw the enemy, in part at least, up the Saale. The rest of the army formed the "masse de manœuvre," assembled in an area of about 19 miles by 9, from Markranstädt to Stössen, ready either to march on Leipzig, or to receive an attack by the enemy, whether from Leipzig, from Pegau, or from Zeitz.

During this 1st May the allies moved thus:[1]—

Blücher from Borna to Rötha.

Main army (Tormassow) assembled at Borna.

Miloradowich to Altenburg.

Winzingerode's corps, after the repulse of its cavalry already noted, bivouacked a mile or two west of Zwenkau, thus forming the advanced guard of the army.

The day's fighting had demonstrated clearly that Napoleon was marching towards Leipzig, but two unfortunate failures of the cavalry misled the allied headquarters. In the first place, the Russian cavalry failed to report that there was a whole French division in the four villages about Kaja, and another at Starsiedel. Secondly, the Prussian cavalry reported that there were French troops of all arms in the villages just beyond Droysig, that is some six miles to the south-east of Stössen, whereas Bertrand certainly had not spread half that distance from the latter village.

The consequence of this exaggerated report was the creation of apprehension of an attack on the allied left towards Zeitz, whilst the failure to report Souham's presence about Kaja led to the belief that there was only a weak flank guard there. The numbers and positions of the allies available for battle on the 2nd May are thus given by Von Cämmerer in his larger history of the spring campaign.

[1] For positions of both sides see Map I. (inset *b*).

NAPOLEON'S CONCENTRATION ON THE SAALE

I. Russians

	Infantry	Cavalry	Cossacks	Artillery, etc.	Guns
Berg (Zwenkau)	6,200	400	500	900	60
Kleist (Lindenau)[1]	1,800	560	800	200	32
Winzingerode (Schkorlop)	6,400	4,000	2,700	1,350	90
Tormassow (Lobstedt)	9,600	5,200	—	1,700	136
Miloradowich (Altenburg)	5,000	1,740	1,000	1,130	86
	29,000	11,900	5,000	5,280	404

II. Prussians

	Infantry	Cavalry	Cossacks	Artillery, etc.	Guns
Blücher (Rotha)	18,500	5,500	—	1,480	92
Yorck (Zwenkau)	6,540	1,300	—	700	40
Kleist (Lindenau)[1]	2,200	440	—	200	16
	27,240	7,240	—	2,380	148
Grand Total	56,240	19,140	5,000	7,660	552

In all 88,040 men, of whom 24,140 were cavalry (including Cossacks) and 552 guns.[2]

To these Napoleon could easily oppose 140,000 men and 372 guns, but only 7500 of these would be cavalry. The great superiority of the allies in both cavalry and artillery naturally made them desire a battle in open country, where these arms would tell most, and where the French would lose the advantage of their superiority in village or wood fighting.

[1] Kleist's force was made up partly of Russians from the corps formerly commanded by Wittgenstein, partly of Prussians from Yorck's corps. Hence he appears under both I. and II.

[2] Danilewski (p. 75, German translation) says there were 69,125 (35,775 Russians and 33,350 Prussians) at Lützen. Apparently he omits Kleist (6200) and Miloradowich (8870), neither of whom was engaged in the main battle.

CHAPTER VI

THE BATTLE OF LÜTZEN OR GROSS GÖRSCHEN [1]

IT appears to have been assumed at the allied headquarters that Napoleon's corps were spread out in a long column marching from Weissenfels by Lützen to Leipzig, and that his right flank was guarded only by a weak detachment at Kaja. The assumption was rather a rash one, when it is remembered that Napoleon himself was commanding. The assumed weakness of the flank guard was, as already mentioned, based on the failure of the Russian cavalry to report.

Wittgenstein's plan was to attack by surprise this long column on its right flank,[2] to destroy the detachment at Kaja, to advance thence on Lützen, breaking Napoleon's line, and driving all that had passed Lützen northwards of their line of operations on to the marshes of the Elster below Leipzig.

Wittgenstein's orders for the 2nd May were not formally issued till nearly midnight of the 1st-2nd, though it would appear they had been partially communicated at an earlier hour, since Blücher began his march so early as 11 P.M.[3] on the 1st. Briefly, they were as follows :—

1. Blücher was to reach the Elster by 5 A.M. in two columns, the right at Storkwitz, due east of Werben, the left at Karsdorf, just north of Pegau. By 6 A.M. his right column was to be across the Flossgraben, near Werben, his left having already crossed half an hour earlier.

---

[1] See Maps II. (*a*) and IV. (*d*).

[2] Jomini (*Vie de Nap.*, iv. p. 278) says Wittgenstein expected to come on his rear.

[3] Danilewski (p. 75) has a story that Blücher started late as the orders were delivered to a sleepy staff officer, who put them unread under his pillow.

THE BATTLE OF LÜTZEN   67

2. Yorck and Berg were to follow respectively Blücher's left and right columns.

3. The Russian heavy artillery was attached to Blücher.

4. Winzingerode was to leave three battalions and a company of light artillery to guard the defile of Zwenkau, and to watch the Elster between that place and Leipzig. The rest of his corps was to cover Blücher's right.

5. The Russian Guard was to be at 7 A.M. at Pegau and Storkwitz, as reserve, holding the defiles at Stöntzsch, Karsdorf, and Storkwitz.

6. After crossing the Flossgraben, Blücher was to bear leftwards in first line, seeking, as soon as possible, to gain with his left the insignificant Grüna brook which flows from Gross Grimma to Dehlitz, and sending cavalry and artillery to hold the heights beyond the brook. His right was to be kept refused on the Flossgraben, and an advance was to be made with the left leading, between the Rippach stream and the Flossgraben. The second line to follow the 1st.

7. Kleist, at Lindenau and Leipzig, was only to act when he heard the main body of the army engaged far to his left. If he found himself attacked by very superior forces, he would retreat through Leipzig on Wurzen.

8. Miloradowich to advance towards Zeitz.

9. In the event of an attack in force by the enemy from Weissenfels on Blücher's left, the Russian Guard would move to the left from Stöntzsch, and attack the French right.

10. The aim of all manœuvres was to reach the enemy's right flank.[1]

These orders have met with very severe criticism from both French and Prussian writers. They are enormously long, extending to about 1100 words, and they give all sorts of instructions regarding the tactics of all arms, conduct of skirmishes, and other matters which should find no place in general orders. Yet they entirely omit all reference to the order of march of the columns before reaching and in passing the Elster, the result of which

[1] Orders given *in extenso* by Lanrezac in Appendix.

was crossing of columns and consequent delay. Practically no independence was left to corps commanders in the battle, which, as Colonel Lanrezac remarks, Wittgenstein seemed to think could be arranged in advance like a ballet.

The orders to Blücher to push his left along the Rippach, whilst keeping his right on the Flossgraben, would eventually result in his having a front of two-and-a-half miles, just about double what his force, under the conditions of 1813, was capable of covering.

General von Caemmerer points out that, looking to the actual positions of the allies on the evening of the 1st May, the best way to pass the Elster would have been this: Yorck and Berg direct on Hohenlohe village, Blücher at Storkwitz, Russian Guard at Pegau. As Blücher's was the longest column, it could have been shortened by sending the Prussian cavalry by Pegau. It was necessary, no doubt, to hold the defiles in rear in view of the probability of eventual retreat, but, looking to the enemy's weakness in cavalry, the guards were unnecessarily strong on a day when every available man was required on the battlefield.

It was, the same authority holds, unnecessary to send Miloradowich's whole corps towards Zeitz to guard against the supposed French advance from Stössen. His cavalry would have sufficed, and his infantry could have been used for the battle. Colonel Lanrezac suggests that he should have gone to Predel, where he would have been able to protect the allied left against the supposed danger, or to have joined in the battle when that danger was found to be illusory. Victory in the main battle would have settled the question of the flank attack. For some unexplained reason, Miloradowich marched so slowly that he was quite unable to take any active part.

The consequences of the failure to give proper orders for the march east of the Elster were that it was after 9 A.M. when Yorck was able to begin passing, and that he crossed Röder, who was delayed thereby till 10.30. It was only after Röder had passed that the Russian Guard, which

THE BATTLE OF LÜTZEN

had been waiting at Groitzsch since 7 A.M., could begin to move. It could not have cleared Pegau before 2 or 2.30 P.M.

Here we must give some description of the battlefield, which is contained in the space between the Rippach brook and the Flossgraben. The latter is a small channel flowing north-eastwards to Hohenlohe, where it sweeps round to the north-west to the Weissenfels-Leipzig road, north-east of Lützen. As a watercourse it is utterly insignificant, and is no real obstruction to the passage of infantry. But it flows generally between steep banks, which render it unpassable by cavalry and artillery, except at the bridges. Moreover, it was in most parts lined by trees and shrubs, which increased the difficulty for those arms. The Elster, on the other hand, which flows from south to north about a mile east of the Flossgraben, is a stream generally unfordable, and passable only at the bridges, even for infantry.

From Pegau through Stöntzsch towards Lützen is almost a dead level as far as the Flossgraben, after which there is a fairly sharp rise in the road for half-a-mile or so. Then there is another stretch of nearly a mile of practically level road to the height now known as the "Monarchen Hügel." From that point there is a steady, though slight, descent of about $1\frac{1}{4}$ miles to Gross Görschen, whence the road again descends very slowly all the way to Lützen. Looking southwards from Gross Görschen, one can see the edge of the plateau which begins at the Monarchen Hügel, but it would be impossible to see troops even 100 yards beyond that edge. The whole battlefield can be described as an undulating, perfectly open plain, but the contours described above must be remembered, for they caused all movements of the allies on either side of the Flossgraben as far down as Sitteln to be completely screened from the French in the quadrangle formed by the four villages, Gross and Klein Görschen, Rahna, and Kaja.

On the western portion of the field the ground is somewhat more cut up as it falls to the valley of the Grüna brook, but, generally speaking, it is a splendid country for the operations of a powerful cavalry such as the allies had. To the (French) right of the quadrangle of villages, about a mile distant is the village of Starsiedel, whilst to the left, rather closer but beyond the Flossgraben, is the village of Eisdorf. It is not possible from the space between the four villages to see Starsiedel. Only the upper part of its church spire appears over the intervening height.

The villages were generally enclosed by gardens, hedges, or earthen banks; the houses, though solidly built, were thatched, and easily set on fire.

From the Monarchen Hügel,[1] there is an extensive view over Lützen, and the level plain on which, in 1632, Gustavus Adolphus met his death in the hour of victory. At 10 A.M. the allies' outposts and a staff officer or two, who had ridden as far forward as the Monarchen Hügel, could see clouds of dust rising from the Leipzig road as the French troops marched. Müffling had already ridden somewhat nearer the quadrangle of villages, and reported that there appeared to be about 2000 men there, quite unsuspicious of danger, and with no outposts. It was not till 11 A.M. that Wittgenstein arrived at the Monarchen Hügel. A prisoner had stated that the troops in Gross Görschen belonged to Souham's division. As for the allies, the corps of Blücher, Yorck, Berg, and Winzingerode were on the plateau, but there was no chance of the Russian Guard being in line before 3 P.M. The men, after many hours of marching or standing under arms, were very fatigued, and it was decided to give them some rest before beginning the action.

Leaving them there, we must return to the French headquarters. It was for long accepted, partly on the strength of Napoleon's own bulletin,[2] that he did not expect a battle on the 2nd May, and that he was taken by surprise by the offensive of the allies west of the Elster. There was cer-

[1] There are several heights called by this name on the battlefields of 1813. The name was subsequently given to record the fact that the heights were where the allied monarchs took their post. It seems convenient to refer to these spots by a name which, of course, they had not acquired before the battle.

[2] *Corr.* 19,951.

THE BATTLE OF LÜTZEN

tainly, as we shall see, a tactical surprise of Souham, but there was no strategical surprise of the Emperor.

He was, on the evening of the 1st May, informed of an assembly of hostile forces towards Zwenkau, and his orders during the night and early morning clearly show that he hoped, and believed it possible, that the allies would cross the Elster to attack him. If they did not, but elected to wait for him east of that river, he intended to "fix" them on the Elster with part of his army, whilst with the rest he crossed the river at Leipzig, turned their right, and, as he hoped, destroyed them. If they were rash enough to cross to the left bank and attack, they would be playing his game; for, holding them with his centre, he would be able to close in upon them on both wings. His evening orders were :—

1. Mortier, with the Guard, to reach Lützen early.

2. Marmont (VI. corps) to call up the division left at Naumburg, to take post on the right bank of the Rippach, releasing Marchand's battalions which were there, and reconnoitring towards Pegau, whither the enemy had retired.

3. Bertrand (IV. corps) to march on Starsiedel with, at any rate, Morand's division, and, if possible, Peyri's, the Wurtemberg division moving up to Naumburg.

4. Oudinot to make for Naumburg.

At 4 A.M. Napoleon issued orders for Eugène's army [1]— Lauriston (V. corps) to march on Leipzig, Macdonald (XI corps) on Markranstädt, whence he was to send reconnaissances on Leipzig and Zwenkau, the latter to act with one which Ney was ordered to send in the same direction. Ney was also ordered to send a strong reconnaissance on Pegau, and to assemble all his five divisions on Kaja. Ney was to be informed of the direction to be taken by Lauriston, Marmont, and Bertrand, and that the last-named was due at Kaja about 3 P.M. Under these orders, which von Cämmerer commends as an example for all time in their brevity and simplicity, an attack from the direction of

[1] *Corr.* 19,942.

Pegau or Zwenkau would be held by Ney's 45,000 men in front, whilst Marmont, Bertrand, Macdonald, and Lauriston manœuvred against the flanks and rear of the allies, the Guard, as usual, was general reserve. In less than three hours from the commencement of the attack Ney would be supported by another 50,000 men. In at most six or seven hours 140,000 men would be on the field. The movements were promptly commenced on the morning of the 2nd May, with two all-important exceptions, due to the negligence of Ney. In the first place, he left his divisions as they were, that is to say, Souham in the quadrilateral of the four villages, with no other division nearer him than Lützen, except Girard's in Starsiedel.

The second, even more important, fault of Ney was his omission to send out the two strong reconnaissances on Pegau and Zwenkau. Had they been sent, there was nothing whatever to prevent both of them reaching positions whence the whole movement of the allies would have been clearly visible. The one on Pegau would have had a splendid view from a point two miles in front of Gross Görschen as soon as it approached the farther edge of the level plateau beyond the Monarchen Hügel.

The hours passed and Napoleon, hearing nothing from Ney's direction, began to believe that, after all, the allies were not going to be rash enough to attack him west of the Elster. If that was so, it was certainly not to be thought of that he should stand idle all day waiting for an attack which now would probably not come off. The day must be utilised for the advancement of his manœuvre against the enemy on the east of the Elster. At the same time, he must not risk anything if, after all, there should be an attack from Pegau or Zwenkau. Between 8 and 10 A.M. Napoleon issued a fresh series of orders:—

Lauriston was to proceed with his attack on Leipzig.

Macdonald to advance beyond Markranstädt, so as to be able to march either on Leipzig or on Zwenkau.

Ney to remain at Kaja.

Marmont to advance towards Pegau.

THE BATTLE OF LÜTZEN 73

Bertrand to reach Taucha, or, at least, to have his three divisions echelonned from Taucha to Stössen.

The Guard to remain at Lützen.

The result of these movements would have placed the troops thus on the evening of the 2nd:—

Marmont would be in front of Pegau, with Ney and the Guard behind him at Kaja and Lützen, and Bertrand on his right rear. Oudinot, still on the march from Jena to Naumburg. Lauriston would have secured the passages of the Elster and the Pleisse at Leipzig, and Macdonald would be between Markranstädt and the Elster, still in a position to lend a hand either at Leipzig or to Ney and Marmont.

If the allies' attack was not made on the 2nd, all would have been in readiness for the turning movement by Leipzig next day, whilst Marmont, supported by Bertrand,[1] held the enemy in front, and the XII. corps was marching from Naumburg. Ney had been told to report the position of his divisions and the result of his reconnaissances. It is not clear if compliance with the former order was insisted on, but, as regards the latter, Napoleon seems to have been satisfied with a general statement to the effect that there was nothing new, and that the enemy only showed the ordinary service (of cavalry outposts and patrols). This was about 10 A.M., and Ney was with him; at least they rode off together somewhere about 11 A.M. to Markranstädt. It certainly seems curious that Napoleon should be so easily satisfied, when a word of inquiry from Ney should have elicited the facts that the three divisions near Lützen had not been started off to Kaja, or even ordered there, and that nothing which could possibly be called a "strong reconnaissance" had been sent either towards Pegau or towards Zwenkau.[2]

---

[1] V. Caemmerer asks whether, if the allies had not fought at Lützen, Napoleon would have sent Ney to Pegau or to Leipzig. Surely he would have sent him to Leipzig, leaving Marmont, Bertrand, and perhaps the first arrivals of Oudinot's troops to fix the enemy at Pegau.

[2] This point, which strikes the author as of some importance, is not noticed by Col. Lanrezac. It certainly looks as if the Emperor was unusually confiding in his belief in Ney's careful execution of orders.

The first episode in the battle commenced at about 10 A.M. at Lindenau. Kleist, it will be remembered, had orders not to begin fighting till he heard the main body of the army heavily engaged on his left towards Lützen. But at 10 A.M. he had to defend himself against Lauriston, who had left Günthersdorf, midway between Leipzig and Merseburg, at 8 A.M. Leaving two battalions to watch the passage of the Luppe south of Schkeuditz, the French commander pushed forward towards Lindenau, where Kleist was drawn up in front of the causeway leading to Leipzig. Lauriston had but 100 cavalry, which was useless against the 1800 of his adversary. However, he drove off Kleist's cavalry with artillery fire. Then he sent his left division (Maison) to outflank the enemy by way of Leutzsch. Kleist, soon recognising that he was largely outnumbered, gave orders for retreat. He was hurried up by the French passing the Elster by a ford. In Leipzig itself there was some fighting between the rearmost Prussian battalion and Lauriston, but Kleist got safely away and took post at Paunsdorf, three miles east of Leipzig, whence he fell back towards Wurzen. Whilst Lauriston was actually passing through Leipzig, he received the Viceroy's orders to keep back most of his corps, as Ney was engaged south of Lützen. It was noon when Napoleon, reviewing the XI. corps at Markranstädt, and watching the course of Lauriston's fight with his glass, suddenly heard a furious cannonade from the direction of Gross-Görschen. Instantly he realised that the allies' attack on the west bank of the Elster, which he had begun to believe was not after all coming off, was commencing at this late hour. He must then have realised that the reconnaissances ordered on Zwenkau and Pegau had either not been made at all, or had been so in an utterly futile fashion. Still, if Ney had, as ordered, assembled his five divisions at Kaja, there was ample, with 45,000 men, to hold the enemy till the other corps came up. But, as we know, Ney had not moved a man, and still had three divisions about Lützen, two to three miles behind the advanced divisions of Souham in the quadrilateral of the four villages, and Girard at Starsiedel.

THE BATTLE OF LÜTZEN 75

The Emperor's orders were issued at once as follows—

III. corps to hold its position, which Napoleon evidently still believed to be at Kaja, at all costs.

VI. corps to prolong the right of the III.

IV. corps to advance against the enemy's left flank.

XI. corps and 1st cavalry corps to move against his right.

V. corps to hold Leipzig with one division, and to echelon the other two on Markranstädt, ready to move on Kaja.[1]

We now return to Wittgenstein on the plateau, $1\frac{1}{4}$ miles on the road from Gross Görschen to Pegau.

Shortly before noon, Blücher rode up to Wittgenstein. Notwithstanding his grizzled locks and his seventy-one years, the old Prussian had lost nothing of his youthful fire or of his intense hatred of Napoleon and the French as he saluted and asked permission to begin the battle. "With God's help" answered Wittgenstein in German.[2] Blücher at once sent his Prussians over the brow, pouring down the gentle slope leading to Gross Görschen, the nearest of the four villages in the midst of which Souham was bivouacking. As yet he had not even occupied Gross Görschen, and it was only now at the last moment that he sent a brigade into it, and hurriedly arranged the rest of his 12,000 men in rear of it. Till the dark lines of Prussians showed on the skyline of the Monarchen Hügel the French had been cooking in blissful ignorance of the fact that a large part of the enemy's army was within two miles of them.

Only a visit to the spot can bring out clearly the absolute inefficiency of the French outpost work which had enabled the enemy to effect this surprise. Had Wittgenstein allowed Blücher's men to go forward in mass with the bayonet, it is

---

[1] General von Caemmerer thinks the orders regarding the XI. corps and the 1st cavalry corps must have been delayed, as they could, if started at once, have reached Eisdorf by 3.30 or 4 P.M. at latest, whereas it was only between 6 and 7 P.M. that Napoleon ordered the decisive attack by the XI. corps. The author was unable to find, in the historical section of the French general staff, any evidence of the precise hour at which the orders were received.

[2] Danilewski, p. 76.

scarcely possible to doubt that they would have driven Souham out of the quadrilateral of villages on to the plain of Lützen, the advantages of which for the greatly superior cavalry of the allies were obvious. But he, in turn, had been surprised to find a whole French division where he had expected only a weak force of at most 2000 men as reported by Müffling. Arrived within 800 yards of Gross Görschen, he stopped the infantry and engaged during forty minutes in a bombardment, to which the French were only able to reply with two batteries. These were soon silenced by the superiority in numbers of Wittgenstein's guns.

Then Klüx's brigade, the left of Blücher's corps, rushed on Gross Görschen, which they took with very little loss. Souham, who had got his men in order beyond the village, now made a vigorous counter attack. It is true he could not recapture Gross Görschen, but his attack gained time, and stayed the advance of the Prussian brigade, which was now in strength very much below its opponents, from whom it had already taken many prisoners and two disabled guns. Farther to the allied left, Dolffs' Prussian cavalry, followed by Winzingerode's Russian cavalry, had moved forward on Starsiedel, which was held by Girard's French division. The latter was as completely surprised as Souham had been. The men were still bivouacking, and the artillery teams had been sent off for forage and water. A bold charge by the great force of allied cavalry would probably have carried them away, but, instead of that, the allies opened with their artillery, to which there was no reply. Covered by the village, Girard was able to resist the partial attacks which were made, and to hold on till he was relieved by the arrival of Marmont.

That marshal, when he received Napoleon's order from Markranstädt, was already an hour on his march from Rippach to Starsiedel. When he reached that village he was marching in six large squares of a brigade each. His arrival enabled Girard to leave the defence of Starsiedel to him, and to march to the aid of Souham in the four villages. Such was the position about 1 P.M. when Blücher, seeing

THE BATTLE OF LÜTZEN

Klüx's brigade almost exhausted, sent Ziethen to support him on his right towards Klein Görschen. The two brigades stormed forward furiously, driving Souham's men out of Rahna and Klein Görschen, back on to Kaja. Ney had now rejoined his corps. He had galloped off from Markranstädt as soon as he received Napoleon's orders issued in consequence of the cannonade which he heard. The marshal was probably tormented by the thought of the consequences of his own neglect to reconnoitre. On the way to Kaja he passed Marchand, whom he ordered forward to Eisdorf. Brennier's and Ricard's divisions he found now close up to Kaja, in which village Girard had arrived from Starsiedel, French artillery was assembling south-west of Kaja, and preparing to sweep the space between the four villages. Souham was slowly falling back on Kaja before the victorious Prussians.

Leaving Ricard as reserve, Ney put himself at the head of Brennier's division, and led it forward with those of Girard and Souham. The Prussians, unable to stand against these much greater numbers, were driven again from Rahna and Klein Görschen, and Ney continued his advance on Gross Görschen. Met by a storm of artillery fire, the marshal was unable to recapture the village.

Then the tide turned once more as Blücher sent in a third brigade (Röder's). The three brigades of Prussians again advanced from Gross Görschen with such fury that Ney's men were, for the second time, driven out of Rahna and Klein Görschen and forced back on Kaja.

Whilst these events were in progress in the four villages, Marmont had begun to debouch from Starsiedel with Compans' and Bonnet's divisions, keeping Friederichs' in reserve. As he did so he was charged by Dolffs' cavalry, and though the infantry held firm, Marmont decided to confine himself to defending Starsiedel.

Wittgenstein, with a view to relieving the pressure in the village quadrilateral, had marched Berg from the right across the front of Yorck's corps with orders to attack Starsiedel. But as Berg was moving he witnessed Ney's recapture of

Rahna and Klein Görschen. This decided him to stop south-west of Rahna.

It was 2.30 P.M. The Prussians, having taken Rahna and Klein Görschen for the second time, one of their battalions, with which was the King of Prussia, actually got into Kaja. Napoleon had galloped up from Markranstädt to find affairs in this parlous condition. His presence at once worked a marvellous change. From all sides rang out the cry of "Vive l'Empereur!" "Hardly a wounded man passed before Bonaparte without saluting him with the accustomed 'vivat.' Even those who had lost a limb, who in a few hours would be the prey of death, rendered him this homage."[1]

Yet the Emperor found grave cause for anxiety. As he rode up he had met many fugitives from the battlefield making for the rear. He saw that three of Ney's five divisions had been badly shaken. As he reached Kaja he received an urgent demand from Marmont for reinforcements at Starsiedel. "Tell your marshal," was the reply, "that he is mistaken; he has nothing against him, the battle turns about Kaja." Ney's corps had almost been driven from the village quadrilateral on to the plain of Lützen. That must be prevented at all costs until the Viceroy, on the one hand, Bertrand, on the other, could close in on the enemy's flanks and rear. That could not be for some time yet.

The Guard reached Kaja almost simultaneously with the Emperor, but it was not to be employed yet without absolute necessity. Napoleon knew that the enemy must have reserves approaching, and that the battle was not "ripe" for his own final thrust with the Guard.

On the side of the allies, the Russian reserves (the two divisions of grenadiers and the Guard) were not yet up. They had been stopped by Wolkonski who, when he saw the early successes of the Prussians, had sent Danilewski to tell the Guard there was no hurry, as all was going well.[2]

---
[1] Odeleben, i. p. 51 (French translation).
[2] Danilewski, p. 77 (German translation).

THE BATTLE OF LÜTZEN

He apparently wished to reserve them for the personal orders of the Tsar, who had now practically superseded the unfortunate Wittgenstein in the command. The latter, who had already heard of the approach of Macdonald against his right, and Bertrand against his left, was much hampered in providing a force to oppose them.

Blücher, meanwhile, had been wounded and succeeded in command of the Prussians by Yorck. Should Yorck's whole corps be now thrown in to support Blücher's? Wittgenstein, with both his flanks threatened, dared not do it before the Russian reserves arrived, and they were not on the Monarchen Hügel till nearly 4 P.M.

Towards 3 P.M. Napoleon ordered Mouton (Lobau) to take Ricard's division forward through Kaja. On the way he was joined by all that were fit to move of Souham's, Girard's, and Brennier's men. Kaja was cleared of the enemy, and the French once more stormed Klein Görschen and Rahna in the face of a desperate defence by the Prussians. The French attack was supported by a battery between Kaja and Starsiedel. The villages and the space between them presented a dreadful picture. They were a veritable shambles, for the fighting had been for hours of the most desperate description. The Prussians, inspired by a hatred of their foe bred of years of oppression, fought with a bitterness which had been unknown in their earlier wars against the French. Perhaps the most graphic description is that quoted by von Caemmerer from the diary of a Prussian Guard Jäger battalion : "The field between Klein and Gross Görschen resembled a bivouac where whole battalions had lain down."

Shortly before 4 P.M., the Russian reserves at last came on the field south of the villages, and Wittgenstein sent forward two out of Yorck's three brigades. Hünerbein's went to the right on Klein Görschen, Horn's to the left on Rahna, Steinmetz's was still kept in reserve. These reinforcements, added to Blücher's men, once more drove back the French. Klein Görschen and Rahna were taken for the third time by the Prussians, who again pushed forward into Kaja.

80 NAPOLEON'S LAST CAMPAIGN IN GERMANY

Napoleon had all along been exposing himself freely, urging on and encouraging his men, and personally leading them forward. "This is probably the day of all his career," says Marmont,[1] "on which Napoleon incurred the most personal danger on the battlefield. . . . He exposed himself constantly, leading back to the charge the defeated troops of the III. corps." With the Prussians in Kaja, he felt himself compelled to send in Lanusse's brigade of Young Guard. Some of Ney's battalions were already beginning to break up, and the situation was desperate. Charging with the bayonet, Lanusse's men, joined by those of Ney's divisions, cleared Kaja of Prussians. There the Guard brigade halted, leaving the pursuit to Ney's people. The awful struggle was renewed as the French again stormed Klein Görschen and Rahna, and again failed to break into Gross Görschen. This phase of the battle, since Yorck's two brigades joined in it, had lasted an hour and a half. The details of it are impossible of description. Death and wounds had wrought havoc among men and officers alike. On the French side, Girard and Gouré[2] were killed; Brennier and several of the brigade commanders were wounded; Ney had his horse killed under him. Here it was that the allies suffered an irreparable loss by the wounding of Scharnhorst, the re-organiser of the Prussian army.[3]

By 5.30 P.M. the Prussians had regained the upper hand, and driven Ney's men back out of Klein Görschen and Rahna, so that Yorck's and Blücher's corps stretched across the space between the villages, with their right on the Flossgraben in front of Klein Görschen, their left on the Lützen road north of Rahna. The latter village was held by Berg.

There remained less than two hours of daylight in which to decide this sanguinary battle, which was now very nearly "ripe" for Napoleon's deciding stroke. His corps were

---

[1] *Mém.*, v. p. 26.
[2] Ney's chief of staff. He was succeeded by Jomini.
[3] He died, as a result of his wounds, at Prag, on the 28th June.

THE BATTLE OF LÜTZEN

closing in, Macdonald on the right flank of the allies, Bertrand on their left.

Napoleon had been failed by Bertrand, who, at 1 P.M., had his leading division (Morand's) behind Taucha, less than four miles from the battlefield. Yet, instead of marching to the cannon at once, he must needs halt and "await orders," on the ground that, Miloradowich's advanced guard having reached Zeitz, Napoleon might wish him to operate in that direction. But Zeitz was too far off for Miloradorwich to be able to interfere in the battle, especially as his main body only reached it at 5 P.M. It was only on reiterated orders that Bertrand moved forward again after 3 P.M. To oppose his advance, Wittgenstein deputed the cavalry of the Russian Guard (Gallitzin), and that of Winzingerode, the latter being behind Dolffs. When he did that, the Russian reserve infantry was still not up, so he dared not send in Winzingerode's infantry under Prince Eugen of Wurtemberg.

About 5.30 P.M. Morand's division had advanced through Pobles to a point south of Starsiedel. Peyri's Italians (of Bertrand's corps) were still not over the Grünabach.

About the same time, Marchand's division of Ney's corps had at last reached the right bank of the Flossgraben north of Klein Görschen, and Macdonald was approaching Eisdorf. To meet these Winzingerode's infantry was now used. Prince Eugen advanced with one of his brigades through Klein Görschen, whilst St Priest with the other occupied Eisdorf, into which Wittgenstein had already sent two Prussian battalions. He was intended to make a flank attack on Ney's left from beyond the Flossgraben, whilst Eugen joined the frontal attack towards Kaja.

But St Priest found himself threatened in Eisdorf by Macdonald's advance, and Eugen had to deal with Marchand. St Priest at once reported the situation, whereupon Wittgenstein sent the 2nd Russian grenadier division, under Konownitzin, to support him south of Eisdorf.

Marchand now threatened the right flank of the advance on Kaja, but Eugen's men found a good defence in the trees and bushes along the Flossgraben. Here they managed to check Marchand's right brigade, and to drive out his left, which had momentarily got into Klein Görschen. Now, however, Charpentier's division of Macdonald's corps had driven St Priest from Eisdorf, whilst Fressinet with the 31st division had occupied Kitzen.

Wittgenstein had built up a strong defensive line from Gross Görschen to Hohenlohe, composed of St Priest's brigade and the Russian grenadiers, behind which were numerous cavalry and the Russian Guard infantry in support. Against this line the Viceroy of Italy did not feel himself strong enough to advance. The time was 6.30; Napoleon's final advance with the Guard was just commencing.

About 6 P.M. the Emperor had decided that, if he was to win the battle before dark, the time for his decisive blow had arrived.

He ordered Drouot to form a battery of 80 guns[1] south-west of Kaja to sweep the space between the four villages. Between this battery and Kaja the Young Guard was drawn up in four columns, each of four battalions, in line, one behind the other. Behind the Young Guard was the Old, behind them the Guard cavalry. At 6.30 all was ready, and, with the words, "La garde au feu," Napoleon ordered the advance.

The left column of the Young Guard marched on Klein Görschen, the right on Rahna, the two in the centre on Gross Görschen. As the Guard advanced under cover of a tremendous storm of artillery fire from Drouot's battery, they were joined by all the remains of Ney's five divisions. Marmont, too, sent Bonnet's division, followed by Compans', against Rahna from Starsiedel. The village, attacked in front by the right column of the Guard and in flank by Bonnet, was taken. The same fate befell Klein Görschen under the attack of the left column in front, and of Charpentier from Eisdorf. Blücher's and Yorck's men were driven back to Gross Görschen and beyond, though part of

[1] 58 of the Guard and 22 of other corps.

THE BATTLE OF LÜTZEN

the village was still held by them when, shortly after 7 P.M., the fall of night put a stop to the battle.

The ghastly scene was illuminated by the light of the burning villages, all four of which were blazing furiously. Beyond the north side of Gross Görschen the French made no further attempt to advance. South of the village the allies sought to assemble. Blücher's corps gathered southwest of Gross Görschen, covered by Steinmetz's brigade, which had stood all day in reserve. Yorck's other brigades, and the infantry of Eugen of Wurtemberg were south of the village on Blücher's right, the Russian guard infantry behind Eugen. Berg's corps fell back fighting before Marmont on the road to Pegau, while the cavalry on the allied left, which had kept up the fight with Morand's division of Bertrand's corps in a somewhat half-hearted way, retired in the same direction.

Even after dark the fighting was not quite over; shortly before 9 P.M. a desperate charge was executed by nine Prussian squadrons against Bonnet's infantry. The infantry was carried away in part by the fury of the charge. Marmont himself, on foot in the midst of it, unable on account of half healed wounds to mount quickly, narrowly escaped death or capture. His staff was fired on by their own men who took them for the enemy. The Prussian cavalry pushed on almost up to the square in which was the Emperor, before they were compelled to retire. If this charge did not do any very great material damage, it at least produced a very considerable moral effect, convincing the French, as it did, that the allies had still plenty of fight left in them. Moreover, it prevented them from taking the rest they so badly needed.

When the Tsar and the King of Prussia left the field about 9 P.M. they could hardly be convinced that the battle was lost. When, however, news came in that Kleist had evacuated Leipzig, thereby leaving the French in possession of the nearest road to their rear, they were compelled to admit that no course but immediate retreat was open to them.

84   NAPOLEON'S LAST CAMPAIGN IN GERMANY

Napoleon at Lützen had won a battle, but he had certainly not gained the decisive victory which was so necessary to him to restore his lost prestige in Europe. On the evening of the battle, according to Marmont,[1] the Emperor said to Duroc, " I am once more master of Europe."   That was a great over-estimate of the result of the battle, and if Napoleon did not in his inmost soul know it at that moment, he must very soon have realised it. The allies were beaten, but they hardly knew it, and in one way at least they had gained an advantage. The Prussians had fought splendidly, and had shown to others and to themselves that they were able to fight the French on equal terms. Even Napoleon contemptuously admitted the improvement since 1806, when he remarked, " Ces animaux ont appris quelque chose." Nesselrode, writing to Vienna, expressed the idea in more courteous terms: " The Prussian troops have covered themselves with glory; they have become once more the Prussians of Frederick."[2]   Up to 3 P.M. they had generally been fighting against double their numbers, and had more than held their own.

Gneisenau said of Wittgenstein's scheme that it was good in conception but spoilt by faults of execution. That seems too favourable an estimate. Wittgenstein who, thanks to his large superiority in cavalry, was much better informed generally of his enemy's movements than was Napoleon, decided to fight on the strength of an entire misconception of the situation. He assumed that the French corps were spread out in a long procession extending from Naumburg, or even Jena, to Leipzig, and that their right, about Lützen, was protected only by a weak flank guard opposite to him. With an opponent like Napoleon, such an assumption was unwarranted. As we have seen, the Emperor intended to cover his march with the whole of Ney's 45,000 men, backed by the guard at Lützen, and with Marmont and Bertrand coming up from Weissenfels. If Wittgenstein had succeeded in assembling his army, as he intended, by 7 A.M.,

[1] *Mém.*, v. p. 25.
[2] Friederich, *Die Befreiungskriege*, 1813-1815, i. p. 244.

THE BATTLE OF LÜTZEN

Napoleon would have had time to bring against his flanks Marmont and part of Bertrand's corps, Macdonald's corps, two of Lauristons divisions, and Latour-Maubourg's cavalry. In all, including Ney, he would have about 140,000 men, against whom Wittgenstein would have had only about 70,000, after deducting Kleist and Miloradowich, who were out of range of the main battle. All that Wittgenstein could hope to do with his inferior numbers was to surprise Ney, inflict a severe blow on him, and then get back beyond the Elster as he found himself threatened with envelopment by the other French corps.

His orders for the assembly were, as has already been said, very defective. Whilst dealing with many things which should find no place in general orders, they entirely failed to prescribe a proper order of march to the crossing of the Elster. The consequences were much delay, owing to the crossing of columns, and the infliction of much unnecessary fatigue on his troops. The army was not on the battlefield till at least four hours later than the hour prescribed. Yet, curiously enough, this delay perhaps saved the allies from the decisive defeat which Napoleon hoped to inflict on them. With two hours more of daylight it seems almost certain that, instead of gaining an indecisive victory, Napoleon would have been able to drive the allies into the Elster and almost completely to destroy them.

He might still have done so, but for the failure of his subordinates. The blame must fall chiefly on Ney, who failed either to assemble his corps at Kaja, or to make the reconnaissances on Pegau and Zwenkau ordered by Napoleon at 4 A.M. Looking to the delay which actually occurred on the allies' side, it is easy to picture the scene which would have met the eyes of a French reconnaissance pushed forward from Kaja at dawn. As it reached the top of the slope leading down to the Flossgraben on the road to Pegau, it would have seen the whole of the enemy's army moving to cross the Elster, and Napoleon would have had no doubt of Wittgenstein's intentions. There was nothing on the plateau to prevent a mixed force from moving to this point. As Col. Lanrezac remarks, Ney had only about 1000 cavalry, but he could have perfectly well made up for this by sending a force of all arms, for the distance to be traversed was short. The appearance of this force (say the strength of a brigade) would not necessarily have alarmed Wittgenstein, or made him hesitate to carry out his plan. Had it been sent out by, say, 6 A.M., Napoleon would have known for certain by 8 that he was to have the hoped-for battle. Macdonald and Marmont would have been hurried up at their best speed, Lauriston would probably have been ordered to observe Leipzig with one division, whilst the other two pressed forward on Pegau. Bertrand, too, would have been urged on from the opposite direction, and Ney's whole corps, with the Guard behind it, would have strongly occupied a line having its left supported by the four villages, its right in Starsiedel.

As it was, Ney's, or Souham's, idea of a reconnaissance in force seems to have been the sending of a few patrols half-way up the slope to the Monarchen Hügel, where they could see just as much and no more than they could see from Gross Görschen itself. When Wittgenstein at last caught Souham asleep at Gross Görschen, he lost his chance, owing to his hesitation and his successive attacks, first with only one brigade, then with two, then with three. His initial bombardment of Gross Görschen probably did not do very much harm, and gave Souham time to repair his fault to some extent. The shock of the discovery that the "weak flank guard" was a strong division seems to have upset the Russian's balance. The shock would have been much greater if, instead of one division in the village quadrilateral and one at Starsiedel, he had found five divisions there, as there would have been had Ney carried out Napoleon's orders. Marmont would have been approaching, as he actually was, and the Guard would have been up from Lützen in an hour. Marmont and Ney alone had 70,000 men, and, when he commenced his attack, Wittgenstein had only about 56,000 within reach.

At Starsiedel there was the same fault of hesitation in

THE BATTLE OF LÜTZEN 87

attack, which gave time to Girard to get his men into order, and for Marmont to come up and release Girard to support Souham.

Had Wittgenstein sent the whole of Blücher's corps against Gross Görschen at once, and Yorck against Starsiedel, he would still have had Berg and Eugen of Wurtemberg, with Winzingerode's infantry, in reserve, whilst the Russian Guard was coming up. Instead of that, he dribbled in Blücher's and Yorck's brigades one at a time, whilst, owing to Berg's stoppage, he never had any infantry at all against Marmont at Starsiedel.

Bertrand was another corps commander who failed Napoleon. He wasted two hours waiting for orders at a distance of only $3\frac{3}{4}$ miles from where he heard the battle raging. Colonel Lanrezac has pointed out that there might possibly have been something to be said for him if he had been sent on a special mission, though even then he probably ought to have marched to the sound of the guns. But his orders were to advance against the enemy's left flank, and he certainly had no business to halt, merely because a Russian advance guard had appeared at Zeitz, 10 miles from the battlefield. At most, he might have left a brigade to watch in that direction. Another general who is blamed by the French writer is Lauriston. He was ordered to leave only one division in Leipzig, though he had no distinct orders to march against the enemy's right. Still, a corps commander of the modern French or German school would probably have marched without orders, or at least started in anticipation of them, and sent urgent demands for them. According to Berthezène, Napoleon, next day, expressed to an aide-de-camp of Lauriston his opinion of that general's inaction in terms more forcible than polite. "What were you doing yesterday," said the Emperor, "when we were fighting here? You were warming your behinds in the sun!"[1] Still Napoleon himself cannot escape blame for not having sent definite orders. Nor is it clear why Macdonald and Latour-Maubourg were

[1] Lanrezac, p. 166 note.

so late in arriving, seeing that it is only about six miles as the crow flies from Markranstädt to Eisdorf, and in the open country they could march straight. As yet no evidence is available in support of Von Cämmerer's suggestion that their orders were delayed. Again, Marchand must have received Ney's order from him personally about 12.30. Yet he was not up till after 4 P.M. In his case it appears that he was hampered by Russian cavalry and Cossacks, who, however, could not have been any very serious obstruction to a whole division. He had only about three miles to cover, and took nearly four hours to do it.

On the side of the allies it was no doubt necessary to keep Kleist at Leipzig to watch the French advance in that direction, though the force he had was too insignificant to offer any serious resistance, and probably one-fourth of it would have served the purpose as well.

Miloradowich's absence from the battle was a much more serious matter. For the direction of his march Wittgenstein was responsible. The reason for its slowness is not apparent. The object in directing him on Zeitz was to meet an attack of the enemy on the allied left in that direction, which was supposed to be possible in consequence of the erroneous report by Prussian cavalry as to Bertrand's position.

Zeitz is 10 miles from Pegau, and it was practically certain that, when he arrived there, Miloradowich would be too late to make his influence felt in the main battle. We have already mentioned the suggestion that Miloradowich should have marched on Predel. He would have heard before he reached Predel that there was no danger to the left. He might have reached Predel by 1 P.M., though he probably would not have done so, considering the slowness with which he actually marched. Even if he had only reached Predel at the hour at which he reached Zeitz (4 P.M.) he would, with only five miles to march, have been able to join in the battle by 6 P.M. But he would probably have got news of the groundlessness of the fear of a French advance on Zeitz in time to enable him to turn to

THE BATTLE OF LÜTZEN

his right towards the battlefield long before he reached Predel.

The French cavalry did nothing on this day. Latour-Maubourg with the 1st cavalry corps was with Macdonald, according to whom [1] both he and Latour-Maubourg wanted the latter to charge the allies' right. This was prevented by the Viceroy, who dared not risk heavy loss to the weak cavalry.

Nor did the allied commanders do much with their cavalry, though it, and still more their great preponderance of artillery, prevented Marmont from debouching from Starsiedel, in support of Souham, till the final attack in the evening. It seems as if Marmont might, under the circumstances, have displayed a little more enterprise.

The losses on both sides in this sanguinary battle were enormous, though probably those of the allies were not much more than half of those of the French.

Von Cämmerer gives the losses of the two Prussian corps of Yorck and Blücher as 8400 out of a total of 33,000, whilst Eugen of Wurtemburg lost 1600 out of 6000, rather over 25 per cent. in each case.

Allowing for the losses of the other troops engaged, regarding which he appears to have had less reliable statistics, he takes the total loss at 11,500, of whom nearly 10,000 were killed and wounded. In trophies they lost nothing but two dismounted guns.

The French losses he estimated at 22,000, including 800 prisoners carried off by the allies. He puts the loss of Ney's corps alone at 15,000 men. They lost also five guns. Lanrezac, on the other hand, gives the French losses as 18,000, of whom 12,000 belonged to the III. corps. He states, however, that, when the French crossed the Elbe a few days later, their army was weaker by 35,000 men than when it crossed the Saale, owing to the great number of stragglers and deserters. The Prussian writer appears to have made an allowance for this cause in estimating the losses at Lützen.

[1] *Mém.*, p. 197.

The enormous leakage in stragglers, deserters, and marauders is attributed by Lanrezac to two causes—

1. The extraordinary exertions which Napoleon demanded from his men.

2. The bad organisation of his administrative services, which almost compelled the soldier to maraud, in order to live.

For the former he finds a defence in the decisive advantages obtained in many cases by almost superhuman activity. For the failure of the Emperor, after twenty years' experience of war, to organise his supplies on a better system he sees none.

CHAPTER VII

FROM LÜTZEN TO BAUTZEN[1]

WHILST the battle of Lützen was in progress, Bülow, finding Halle only weakly held, had attacked it with 6000 or 7000 men, and driven the four French battalions from it back on to Durutte's division at Merseburg. This action had no influence on Napoleon's battle, the result of which compelled Bülow to withdraw in the direction of Berlin, by Rosslau.

At 11 P.M. Napoleon ordered Lauriston to withdraw the one division he had in Leipzig, and to be ready to commence the pursuit on the 3rd May with his own corps and Latour-Maubourg's cavalry. When Lauriston evacuated Leipzig, Kleist sent some Cossacks into it before he received orders for his own retirement. When it was clear to the allied commanders that immediate retreat behind the Elbe was their only possible course, orders were issued for it to be made in three columns. The Russians were to retire on Dresden by Frohburg and Rochlitz. The Prussians and part of Winzingerode's cavalry took the road by Borna and Colditz to Meissen. Miloradowich and Eugen of Wurtemberg covered the retreat. Kleist was to go by Wurzen to the Elbe at Mühlberg, where there was a bridge of boats.

It was 3 A.M. on the 3rd May when Napoleon, assured that the enemy was retreating, issued orders for the pursuit. Ney's corps had been so shattered in the battle that it was left for the moment to recuperate at Lützen. The rest of the army crossed the Elster at Zwenkau, Pegau, Predel, and

[1] See Map III. (inset *a*).

Ostrau. Except for a small affair with Eugen and another with Miloradowich, the French met with no opposition, but they were so exhausted that they made little progress during the 3rd. Macdonald with the XI. corps and the 1st cavalry corps only reached Podelwitz, five miles beyond Pegau, with Lauriston on his left at Peres. Marmont halted at Löbnitz on Macdonald's right rear. Bertrand found the bridge at Predel destroyed, and was delayed also by Miloradowich, so got no farther than Ostrau. Napoleon, with headquarters and the Guard, passed the night of the 3rd-4th at Pegau. Oudinot, who had not received his orders in time to change direction to his right, was spread along the line Jena-Naumburg. The allies were in two masses at Borna and Frohburg with their main army. The Emperor was still uncertain as to the exact direction of the allies' retreat; he learnt more during the night, and decided to advance with his main army direct on Dresden, cutting off what he could of stragglers and convoys. At the same time he constituted an auxiliary army under the command of Ney. It consisted of Ney's own corps (III.), the VII. (at present only Durutte's division at Merseburg, but destined to have added to it the Saxons in Torgau), Victor's provisional II. corps, and the provisional corps of Sebastiani, consisting of the 2nd cavalry corps (2500), and Puthod's division of the V. corps. Puthod was no longer required on the lower Elbe, for Vandamme was now coming up below Magdeburg, and he, with Davout, sufficed to guard that portion of the river, and even to retake Hamburg.

Ney was to relieve Torgau and Wittenberg, and cross to the right bank of the Elbe as soon as he was joined by Sebastiani from Bernburg. He would then have about 60,000 infantry and 4000 cavalry, with 129 guns, including the Saxons at Torgau. The Emperor, on the other hand, would have, including Oudinot, 120,000 infantry, 11,500 cavalry, and 386 guns. He was without a bridge train, and, as he expected the allies to defend the Elbe at Dresden, he looked to Ney's advance from Torgau on their right to compel them to drop the river line. During the 4th May, Napoleon's columns reached without adventure the following points :—

Right—
IV. corps, Frohburg. The XII. was far behind on the march from Naumburg to Zeitz.

Centre—
1st cavalry corps and XI. corps as advanced guard under the Viceroy, Lausigk. Behind these the VI. corps and Guard, with Imperial headquarters, Flössberg and Borna.

Left—
V. corps, Stockheim. This column was now directed on Wurzen. Napoleon, hearing of a strong Prussian column (it was in reality only Kleist) marching on Mühlberg, had directed Lauriston to move leftwards, so as to be able, if necessary, to support Ney, who was now marching on Torgau.

During the 5th May, whilst Lauriston was marching as above, Napoleon's other two columns continued their advance on Dresden.

When Eugène debouched with the XI. corps from the Colditz forest, about 11 A.M., he found Steinmetz's brigade drawn up to dispute the passage of the Mulde. Into the details of the action which ensued we need not enter. Steinmetz, naturally, was compelled to retreat, and was followed to in front of Hartha, where he again took position. His retreat had endangered the communications of Miloradowich, who, finding himself not pressed, was crossing the Mulde at Rochlitz in a somewhat leisurely fashion. Seeing his danger, he sent all available forces to the assistance of Steinmetz, who was thus enabled to show front again at Hartha, but both retired to Waldheim behind the Zschoppau. The Viceroy did not carry his main body beyond Hartha, though he had outposts as far as the Zschoppau. During the day he reported having seen on his left a hostile force, alleged to be Kleist on his way to Mühlberg. Other information showed that the main body of the allies was making for Meissen and Dresden. Under these circumstances,

Lauriston's march on Wurzen was no longer necessary, and he was ordered to proceed, by forced marches of from 17 to 20 miles, towards Dresden.

In the evening of the 5th May the French army reached the following points :—

XI. corps and 1st cavalry corps, Hartha and beyond.

VI. corps, close behind XI.

Guard and headquarters, Colditz.

IV. corps, which had by its slowness left Miloradowich to cross the Mulde unmolested, Rochlitz.

XII. corps, Altenburg and behind.

Napoleon was not satisfied with Eugène's action. They were, he said, now in a hilly country, where the enemy's cavalry was comparatively useless, and the Viceroy should have succeeded in taking at least 2000 or 3000 prisoners.[1]

In the very early hours of the 6th, Napoleon wrote[2] to Ney expressing his anxiety to hear that the marshal was at Torgau, and had relieved Wittenberg. He now had information that the Prussians and Russians were marching in separate columns, and he deduced from this fact, and from various rumours of dissensions in the enemy's camp, that, as soon as they had crossed the Elbe, the allies would separate definitely, the Russians sticking to their own line of communications by Bautzen, Görlitz, and Breslau with Warsaw, whilst the Prussians went more to the north, with a view to covering their capital. If they knew that Ney was at Torgau, within 90 miles of Berlin, it was probable that the news would help to decide the Prussians in favour of covering Berlin. If this separation occurred, Napoleon's scheme was to contain the Russians with a small force, whilst he himself, with a force double the 60,000 or 70,000 available Prussians, fell upon and destroyed them.

When one looks to the way in which he cherished the hope of this division of the enemy's forces, one cannot help suspecting that the wish was father to the thought. Had he been in their position himself, he would certainly not have thought of directly covering Berlin, when, by holding

[1] *Corr.* 19,971. [2] *Corr.* 19,972.

together on the Dresden-Breslau line, he would indirectly do so. Moreover, Berlin was after all only a geographical point, though its capture by the French would certainly have had a considerable moral and political effect. On the other hand, he probably knew how anxious the Prussian king was to prevent a reoccupation of his capital by the French, and that the Russians were equally averse to any abandonment of their direct line of communications. That, perhaps, to some extent justified his assumption that the allies, of whose abilities he entertained a very poor opinion, would be induced by their divergent interests to separate.

An "ordre du jour" of the 6th May[1] shows clearly the state of indiscipline existing at this time in the French army. It complains of the straggling, and blames commanders for not keeping a special rearguard to pick up these men. Another thing reprobated is the soldiers' habit of unloading their muskets by firing them off, instead of drawing the charge, thereby creating alarms. For doing this the penalty was to be imprisonment and degradation, or, if anyone was killed or injured by the discharge, death.

Further details of the allies' retreat and the French pursuit to Dresden are unnecessary. The most notable point in it is the way in which Miloradowich conducted his rearguard. He constantly halted to take up a position, compelling his opponents to deploy and take measures to turn him. With admirable judgment, he always selected the latest safe moment to retire, only to take up another defensive position farther on. He would have been less successful had Bertrand, on the French right, kept in advance, but that general marched so slowly that he was generally not even on a level with the centre and left, instead of being well in advance of them.

On the 7th May the main body of the Russians, marching by Wilsdruf, passed the Elbe at Dresden. On the same day the main Prussian army crossed at Meissen, whilst Kleist's detachment crossed at Mühlberg. Miloradowich, who retired through Nossen and Wilsdruf, crossed the river on

[1] Foucart, i. 59.

the 8th at Dresden, where the span of the stone bridge, which Davout had blown up on the 20th March, had been temporarily restored by the Russians, and was now once more broken. The Russians had also fired their raft and boat bridges at Dresden, but the work was badly done, and the French were able to rescue many of the boats. On the 8th May all the allies were on the right bank of the Elbe, whilst Napoleon's army stood thus:—

XI. corps, 1st cavalry corps and headquarters, Dresden.
VI. corps, behind Dresden.
IV. corps, Potzschappel to Tharandt.
XII. corps, Oederan and behind.
V. corps (Lauriston), Meissen.

The French march from Lützen to Dresden had averaged only $12\frac{1}{2}$ miles a day.

Leaving Napoleon for the moment at Dresden, we return to Ney.

On the 4th May he was at Leipzig with his own III. corps and Durutte's division, which for the present represented the VII. corps, of which, when complete, Reynier was to have the command. Bülow had gone back to Rosslau on hearing of the result of Lützen, and, though his cavalry were all over the space between the Saale and the Mulde, they could be disregarded, for they must retire as Victor debouched from Bernburg. Ney started on the 5th May for Torgau via Eilenburg, sending two divisions of the III. corps to relieve Wittenberg. On the 7th May Reynier, with Durutte's division, arrived before Torgau, only to find himself in a very awkward position. Thielmann, the Saxon commander, refused admission to the French, pleading his own sovereign's order. The King of Saxony, who had been trying hard to play the neutral, as he had tried for a time in 1806, had gone off with two regiments of Guard cavalry to Prague. As soon as Napoleon heard, on the 8th, of Thielmann's attitude, he took very summary measures for dealing with his ally.

M. de Serra, the Emperor's minister at Dresden, was directed to represent that Metternich had stated that

FROM LÜTZEN TO BAUTZEN

Austria had nothing to do with Saxony or her king. The latter was given six hours in which to answer Napoleon's demands, which were:—

1. Thielmann to be at once ordered to leave Torgau and unite his troops to the VI. corps under Reynier.

2. The king to send his cavalry back to Dresden at once.

3. He was also to write a letter to the Emperor, admitting that his engagements of past years still subsisted, and expressing his intention of fulfilling them.

If the king failed to comply with these demands within the time allowed, he was to be informed that "I (Napoleon) declare him a felon, outside my protection, and that, in consequence, he has ceased to reign." This business was to be carried out by De Serra if he was at Prague; if not, Baron de Montesquieu, the bearer of the letter, was to do so. To anticipate somewhat, the king surrendered at once, and, on the 12th May, was back in person at Dresden, once more under the thumb of Napoleon. Orders were despatched to Thielmann, who yielded to them, but himself went off to join the allies.

Though Napoleon might not feel much doubt as to the success of his peremptory orders to the King of Saxony, seeing they were issued from that monarch's capital, still he could not afford to risk anything by waiting for the reply. Therefore, he sent orders to Ney to concentrate the III. corps and Durutte's division to the south of Torgau, and collect materials for the construction of a bridge at Belgern, half a day's march above the fortress. Lauriston, leaving a detachment at Meissen, could once more bear to the left, to a point half-way between Meissen and Torgau, whence he could join Ney if required.

Accordingly, Ney, on the 11th May, was ready to cross the Elbe with 60,000 men. He would have had to go without Sebastiani, who only reached Bernburg on the 12th. Napoleon, reaching Dresden on the 8th, had at once begun making preparations for a passage of his own army. With the Russians still holding the Neustadt, the part of Dresden on the right bank of the Elbe, it was not possible to repair the broken arch of the stone bridge. Therefore, the Emperor proposed to cross at Briesnitz, a short way below Dresden. Here the river makes a sharp bend to the south-west and then back again, the apex of the bend being at Briesnitz. At the apex and below it the left bank commands the right, but this is not so above Briesnitz, where both banks are low, about level with one another. Still, guns on the left bank can sweep the opposite peninsula. At Briesnitz Napoleon placed his bridge, sweeping the peninsula with 60 guns, partly on the heights, partly on the plains where the public slaughterhouse now stands. He also had 20 guns on the Brühlsche Terrasse close to the stone bridge. Two battalions first got across on rafts to protect the head of the new bridge. The Russians attempted to drive them out of their retrenchments, bringing up 60 guns for the purpose. But Napoleon, using 80 guns, compelled them to desist. The bridging operations at Briesnitz began at 7 A.M. on the 9th. The French guns on the Brühlsche Terrasse also drove the Russians in the Neustadt from the water's edge, enabling 300 French voltigeurs to cross in boats and effect a lodgment in a large building at the farther end of the stone bridge. Protected by them and the guns, the repair of the broken arch was hurried on and completed by the morning of the 11th May. It was a difficult task, owing to the great height of the trestle work which had to be erected, but the time in which it was completed was only a fraction of what it had taken the Russians in March.

All difficulties of the passage were solved for Napoleon by the fact that the allies made no serious resistance. By the evening of the 11th May, 70,000 French had crossed at Dresden.

Ney also crossed on the same day with the III., V., and and VII. corps, about 45,000 men. He passed, not by the temporary bridge at Belgern, but at Torgau, where, under orders of the King of Saxony, the gates were thrown open to the French, and the Saxon division (9000 infantry, 250

FROM LÜTZEN TO BAUTZEN

cavalry, and three batteries) was added to the VII. corps of Reynier.

Meanwhile, there had been much hesitation on the part of the allied commanders, and a succession of different plans. The interests of the Prussians, and their desire to cover their capital and the Mark, led them to favour a movement to the north, whilst the Russians were anxious to cover their direct line of communication with Warsaw by Bautzen, Görlitz, and Breslau. All were agreed that a stand should be made somewhere west of the Oder; for the spirit of the army demanded it, and moreover, if another battle were not fought, Austria and the German princes would naturally be led to believe in the decisiveness of the French victory at Lützen, a view which Napoleon was endeavouring to impress upon them. But where were the allies to fight? It was here that the many commanders differed.

At first, Wittgenstein was in favour of taking up a position between Herzberg and Luckau, whence he could fall with all his forces on the enemy as he passed the Elbe. Then, on the 8th May, he issued orders for the defence of the river itself, the Russians above Meissen, the Prussians below it, Kleist holding the passage at Mühlberg. In consequence of these orders the Russian main body took post at Radeburg, the Prussians at Grossenhain. Then came Miloradowich's failure to prevent Napoleon's passage at Briesnitz. He had received no support, and headquarters appear to have given up, as beyond their power, the idea of preventing the French passage. Wittgenstein was now in favour of a retirement northwards, in conformity with the desire of the Prussians to cover Berlin and the Mark. That was peremptorily stopped by the Tsar, who would not hear of abandoning the Russian communications. On the 10th, Wittgenstein believed Napoleon to be concentrating towards his left for a march on Berlin, the threats at Dresden being only a ruse to divert attention in that direction. That determined the allied commander to withdraw and await developments, with the Russians at Bischofswerda and the Prussians at Königsbrück. If strongly attacked here, he proposed to retire behind Bautzen, whilst, if Napoleon moved from Wittenberg and Belgern on Berlin, the allies would attack his right flank.

The offensive idea in this last plan was abandoned on receipt of news that the French were moving towards Bautzen, Königsbrück, and Reichenberg with three corps, and that Napoleon in person was in Dresden. On the 12th orders issued for assembly in a position beyond Bautzen, which the Russian Chief Engineer was sent on to fortify.[1] All these movements led Napoleon to cherish the hope that the Russians and Prussians were about to separate. He certainly would not have separated had he himself been in command; for a position such as Wittgenstein proposed to take on the 10th would cover Berlin indirectly better than a direct covering force could do. In this case Napoleon probably allowed the wish to be father to the thought, as he now so often did.

The allies now retreated concentrically on Bautzen, with Miloradowitch acting again as rearguard. The latter, supported by Eugen of Wurtemberg, fought a sharp rearguard action with Macdonald on the 11th at Weissig, and then fell back on Schmiedefeld. Kleist was attacked by Bertrand the same day near Königsbrück and forced back on Kamenz. Miloradowich again fought at Schmiedefeld on the 12th, whilst the allied main body got across the Spree at Bautzen. It was only in the evening that the Russian rearguard fell back, fighting at every step, nearly to Bautzen. Not till the 15th was the left bank of the Spree entirely evacuated by the allies.

Barclay de Tolly, with 13,500 men, set free by the capitulation of Thorn, was about to join them.

Here we must return to Napoleon at Dresden, busily preparing for his further advance. Reinforcements were coming up, among them a division of Young Guard, four battalions of Old Guard, and two cavalry "divisions de

---

[1] For the above account of the allied plans, see Friederich, *Die Befreiungskriege*, 1813-1815, i. pp. 250-255.

marche." The Saxons, now again at the Emperor's disposal, were distributed, the infantry division to the VII. corps, the four cavalry regiments to the 1st cavalry corps.

On the 15th May the French army comprised the following corps :—

I. Ney's Army

	Battalions.	Squadrons.	Batteries.	Men (about).
III. corps (Ney)	66	8	12	30,000
V. corps (Lauriston) (including Puthod)	44	—	12	27,000
VII. corps (Reynier)	16	1	—	9,500
II. corps (Victor)	22	—	2	13,000
Light cavalry division (Châtel) of 1st cavalry corps attached to V. corps	—	8 or 9	—	1,800
2nd cavalry corps	—	15 to 20	—	3,000
	148	32 to 38	26	84,300

II. Main Army (Napoleon)

IV. corps (Bertrand)	34	4	7	25,000
VI. corps (Marmont)	39	4	10	22,000
XI. corps (Macdonald)	31	2	8	17,000
XII. corps (Oudinot)	33	—	7	24,000
Old Guard (1 division)	6 or 7	— }	14	4,000
Young guard (2 divisions)	25 to 30	— }		15,000
Guard cavalry	—	20	3	4,000
1st cavalry corps (less light division) (Latour-Maubourg)	—	45 to 50	4	8,000
Total	168 to 174	75 to 80	53	119,000
Grand total	216 to 222	107 to 118	79	203,300[1]

To these the allies could not oppose more than about 110,000, inclusive of Barclay's corps and that of Bülow, the latter covering Berlin.

Napoleon now formally dissolved what had hitherto been the army of the Elbe under the Viceroy of Italy. He had had enough of his stepson's incapacity, and sent him

[1] Lanrezac, pp. 185-186.

off at a moment's notice to take command of the army which the Emperor was organising in Northern Italy for the purpose of detaining a part of the Austrian army on its southern frontier, in the event of that power joining the allies.[1]

Dresden was henceforward to be the great advanced depôt for Napoleon's operations in Germany. Durosnel was appointed governor with a garrison of about 6000 men, including the depôts of the IV., VI., VII., XI., and XII. corps. For the II., III., and V. corps depôts were established at Torgau. Cavalry depôts at Leipzig and Dresden.

The rearward communications of the army were laid down as the following:[2]—

1. Main line. Mayence, Frankfort, Fulda, Erfurt, Weimar. From this point the line bifurcated, one branch going to Dresden by Jena and Altenburg, the other by Naumburg and Leipzig.

2. From Leipzig a branch to Wittenberg.

3. From Augsburg by Nürnberg, Bamberg, Schleiz, Gera, Altenburg.

The route from Augsburg by Würzburg was abolished, though it would have been better than the last-named route which subsequent experience showed was too far east. The activity of the allies' partisans extended far west of the Elbe.

Three marches might have been saved by carrying a line from Erfurt direct to Altenburg, in addition to the one by Leipzig.

The stages on these routes averaged about 15 miles, with a day's rest in every six or seven. To guard against surprise by partisans, detachments on the march were to comprise at least 500 combatants.

In order to have a bridge head at Dresden, the enceinte of the Neustadt, on the right bank of the Elbe, was repaired and palisaded.

At Briesnitz there was a bridge of rafts and another of

---

[1] *Corr.* 19,998.   [2] Lanrezac, p. 188.

FROM LÜTZEN TO BAUTZEN

boats, whilst in Dresden itself there was the stone bridge. Later on the Emperor also had two boat or raft bridges, one above and one below the stone bridge. Also, during the armistice, the partially demolished enceinte of the Altstadt was repaired, and five forts were built outside the suburbs.

The general position of Napoleon's armies on the 11th May was this :—

1. At Dresden, on both sides of the Elbe, 119,000 men under his personal command.

2. At Torgau, also on both banks, Ney with 84,000.

3. On the lower Elbe, under Davout, Vandamme's provisional corps of about 30,000 which, for the present at any rate, need only be mentioned, as it had its own separate theatre of operations far removed from the main theatre.

The Emperor's design was to have Ney's army posted by the 16th as follows :—

III. corps and headquarters, Luckau, with advanced guard Lübben.

V. corps Dobrilugk.

VII. corps Dahme.

II. corps and 2nd cavalry corps, Schönwald.

In those positions it would be the "bataillon carré" posted about three good marches from Berlin, and half a march farther from Napoleon's own army. It would be ready to march in any direction.[1]

On the 13th May Napoleon was still in doubt as to the direction or directions taken by the allies. On that day he wrote to Ney :[2]—

"I do not see clearly what the Prussians have done; it is certain the Russians are retiring on Breslau: but the Prussians; are they retiring on that town, as it is said, or have they thrown themselves towards Berlin to defend their capital, as seems natural? That is what I shall learn

[1] As usual in these days, the Emperor exaggerated its numbers, representing it as 100,000 instead of 84,000. *Corr.* 20,006, to Ney, 13th May.

[2] *Corr.* 20,006.

exactly from the information I expect to-night. You must feel that, with the considerable forces you have, it is not a case for remaining quiet. To unblock Glogau, to occupy Berlin (so as to put the Prince of Eckmühl in a position to re-occupy Hamburg and advance with his five divisions into Pomerania) and to gain possession of Breslau myself, those are the three important objects which I propose to myself, and which I should wish to accomplish within the month. In the position which I am going to make you take, we shall always be united, able to move right or left with the maximum masses possible, according to information received."

When Napoleon writes that it seems natural that the Prussians should leave the Russians and move towards Berlin, he certainly did not mean that he would have done so himself had he been in their place, but that it was what he would naturally expect from his past experience of their strategical capacity, and their known anxiety lest the capital should again fall into his hands.

Again, it was not, strictly speaking, correct to say that he and Ney were united, since they were more than three marches apart. But, looking to the facts that they were not separated by any serious obstacle or difficult country, and that, whilst Ney's army was numerically not much inferior to the combined Russians and Prussians, whilst Napoleon's own was superior to them, there could be no doubt that the allies could not prevent a close union whenever it should please the Emperor to decide on it.

On the 11th May Napoleon still had the Guard and Oudinot in Dresden, on the left bank of the Elbe. The IV., VI., and XI. corps were across the river, gaining space for manœuvre. The XI. corps and a division of cavalry acting as advanced guard got forward on that day to Weissig. On the 12th it had pushed Miloradowich's rearguard beyond Bischofswerda, though the Russian general had again displayed his capacity as a rearguard commander in the same way as he had done between Lützen and Dresden

We have already mentioned the rearguard actions fought by Miloradowich against Macdonald, whose reports clearly exaggerate the strength of the enemy opposed to him. Marmont at first went northwards as far as Reichenberg, with Beaumont, commanding a Westphalian cavalry brigade and three battalions, scouting towards Grossenhain. On the 13th, Marmont, leaving Beaumont at Moritzburg, turned eastwards to Radeberg on the byroad to Bischofswerda.

The Emperor was now convinced that both Russians and Prussians were retreating by Bautzen. He was inclined to think they would not stand and fight there, notwithstanding reports that they were fortifying a position.

On the 15th, Macdonald advancing from Bischofswerda, again collided at Gödau with Miloradowich's rearguard, which he drove across the Spree, and himself took post on the heights on the near side. The VI. corps was now close up behind him, the IV. at Kloster-Marienstern, halfway between Gödau and Kamenz. The XII. closed up also. From his position Macdonald could clearly see the camps of the enemy beyond Bautzen, where it was now pretty clear he meant to stand fast.

CHAPTER VIII

THE PRELIMINARIES OF BAUTZEN

ONCE he was convinced that the enemy intended fighting at Bautzen, Napoleon hastened the assembly of his armies for the battle he so greatly desired. He had failed to gain a decisive victory at Lützen with numbers far larger than his opponent. He now hoped to unite against him a force very nearly double the combined Russians and Prussians.

His orders were for the XI., VI., and IV. corps to take position facing Bautzen, the XI. on the right, and the IV. on the left. The XII. in front of Bischofswerda, would be the reserve for this first line of 64,000 men, and would send three mobile columns of 1200 to 1500 men each to clear the woods between the Dresden - Bautzen road and the Austrian frontier, which was only some ten miles south of Bautzen. Napoleon would thus have nearly 90,000 men covering directly the advance of the Guard from Dresden, and indirectly that of Ney's army from the north.

The left flank was to be cleared by Mortier with the 1st cavalry corps, Beaumont's detachment, and a division of Young Guard, thus assuring communication with Ney. Beaumont's mission was to clear out the enemy's raiders towards Grossenhain and Königsbruck. On the 16th Mortier sent Beaumont after some 2000 hostile cavalry who were at Grossenhain. They fell back precipitately on Elsterwerda. Beaumont, on the 17th, was in communication with Lauriston's corps; on the 18th he returned to Moritzburg. Mortier was at Bischofswerda on the 17th. To Ney's army the orders sent were:—

THE PRELIMINARIES OF BAUTZEN 107

Lauriston received orders direct to march from Dobrilugk on Hoyerswerda, a copy being sent to Ney.[1]

Ney himself was ordered from Herzberg on Spremberg. These orders only reached their destinations on the evening of the 16th when, though Lauriston was at Dobrilugk, Ney was at Luckau, whither he had been ordered to march on the 15th and 16th. Napoleon, or Berthier, seems to have forgotten these previous orders. Moreover, the order, as sent to Ney, did not specify what troops were to go to Spremberg. Napoleon had intended Victor to take the offensive against Bülow, with the II. and VII. corps, and the 2nd cavalry corps. Ney had thus only the orders for Lauriston to move on Hoyerswerda, and for himself to move on Spremberg. Quite naturally, he assumed, as suggested by Jomini, his chief of staff, that all his force, except Lauriston, was to make for Spremberg, and he acted accordingly. In reality it was much better to do thus than to act as the Emperor had intended; for, by doing as he did, Ney was bringing all available forces to overwhelm the enemy's main army, whilst Bülow could easily be contained, in the event of his marching southwards, by a few thousands.

The route prescribed for Ney was not his shortest to Bautzen. Napoleon seems to have feared lest his appearance on the direct road should frighten the enemy into continuing his retreat on Silesia, the very last thing the Emperor desired. But by the morning of the 16th, Napoleon had received further reports which convinced him that the allies meant, under any circumstances, to defend themselves at Bautzen. He, therefore, in the afternoon, issued fresh orders to Ney, who was now to go to Hoyerswerda. The first order was sent at 1 P.M.,[2] as follows:—" The Emperor orders *you* to betake *yourself* with all diligence to Hoyerswerda." A later order (5 P.M.) says:[3] " The Emperor approves that you should arrive as soon as possible with your corps (in the singular) and that of Lauriston at Hoyerswerda." Then it goes on to explain that the Emperor

[1] *Foucart*, i. p. 204. [2] *Ibid.*, i. p. 217. [3] *Ibid.*, i. p. 218.

desired to send Victor, with Reynier and Sebastiani under him, to manœuvre towards Berlin, to retake that city; also, if possible, Spandau, and to pursue Bülow. This was the first Ney had heard of the Berlin project. He at once informed Victor of his mission, and ordered Reynier to stop at Luckau. This was on the evening of the 17th. That meant that Victor, with about 25,000 men, would be kept back from arriving for the coming battle.

By morning of the 17th, Napoleon seems to have come to the conclusion that Ney's original arrangement for bringing Victor and Reynier with himself was the better. At 10 A.M. Berthier writes to Ney: "Give orders to the Duke of Belluno (Victor), and to Generals Reynier and Sebastiani according to what you have ascertained regarding the enemy, and as you judge most suitable according to the circumstances. Everything leads to the belief that we are going to have a battle."

Ney at once acted on these orders by directing Victor and Reynier to leave Dahme and Luckau respectively on the 19th, and to march for Bautzen via Kahlau and Hoyerswerda. Unfortunately they had lost twenty-four hours, and could hardly reach Bautzen in time for the battle. For this the Emperor seems alone to blame. His hankering after the secondary objectives of Bülow and Berlin was a distinct falling away from his own principles. With the destruction of the main army of the allies, Bülow's ruin and the fall of Berlin must inevitably have followed, and the extra 25,000 men of Victor, Reynier, and Sebastiani would probably have made all the difference at the battle, as we shall see presently.

Ney's positions on the morning of 18th May were—

V. corps, less Puthod's division, Senftenberg.

III. corps and headquarters, Kahlau.

VII. corps, Luckau.

II. corps, Puthod's division (of V.), and 2nd cavalry corps, Dahme.

During the day Lauriston (V.) reached Hoyerswerda, his fourth division (Puthod) Finsterwalde, III. corps, Sorne.

Berthier's cypher despatch of 10 A.M. on the 18th from

THE PRELIMINARIES OF BAUTZEN 109

Dresden seems to show that the Emperor ignored the effects of his previous orders (of 5 P.M. on 16th) regarding the Berlin expedition. He now writes as if Ney had been ordered all along to march with all his forces on Bautzen. He says, "The Emperor informs you that we are within cannon range of the little town of Bautzen, which the enemy has occupied as head of his position, and where he has thrown up some entrenchments; that on the (enemy's) right are placed the Prussians, on the left the Russians; that he desires that, with General Lauriston *and all your forces united*, you should make for Drehsa[1] near Gottamelde; having passed the Spree you will find that you have turned the enemy's position; you will take up a good position there. The Emperor supposes that you are in a position to *reach Hoyerswerda completely* on the 19th. You will draw towards us on the 20th, and on the 21st you will be able to reach the position (described above), which will either have the effect of making the enemy retire farther, or of putting you in a position to attack him with advantage."[2]

The instruction to Ney to draw towards the main army on the 19th and 20th was apparently intended to lull any anticipations of the enemy of an attack on his right flank and rear by Ney. The movement of that marshal to his right would seem to point to a mere frontal attack. At the last moment, he would turn leftwards across the Spree to a position which would bring him down on and beyond their right.

On this 18th May, Napoleon, with the Guard, marched half-way to Bautzen, intending to be there early on the 19th. Orders were issued sending Mortier and Latour-Maubourg forward from Bischofswerda. As they came up, Oudinot was to come into line on the right of Macdonald, and, with the assistance of Latour-Maubourg, to thoroughly

---

[1] Brösa on the map.

[2] Foucart, i. 218, 219. The dates given are those in Berthier's despatch which differ somewhat from those in *Corr.* 20,024. Nor does the Emperor describe Drehsa as "near Gottamelde." Gottamelde is not shown on Petri's map. It is a small village in the neighbourhood of Guttau.

search the woods on the right, driving out any enemies found there. Bertrand was directed to get into communication with Lauriston and Ney at Hoyerswerda, where the Emperor expected them to be that day (19th). Beaumont was still to remain on the watch at Moritzburg.

In the instructions to Durosnel, Governor of Dresden, it is said, "the artillery will be parked on the left bank till the battle is decided, so that if the battle were lost we could pass to the left bank without losing anything"[1]—a characteristic mark of the Emperor's care in securing his own retreat, however certain he might feel of victory. Ney's orders of the 18th for the next day's march were designed to bring the V. corps on the right, and the III. on the left on to the line Zerna-Neudorf, facing south. He directed Lauriston to keep in communication with the main army towards *Kloster Marienstern*. From this it is clear that he was under the false impression that the allies were drawn up *west* of the Spree, and that Napoleon was facing them with his left at Kloster Marienstern. When Ney issued these orders he was acting on those of the Emperor of 10 P.M. on the 17th which, as conveyed by Berthier, were far from indicating clearly that the allies had crossed the Spree. They said, "Our army has nearly reached (touche à) Bautzen; the enemy's army and ours are in presence." That did not make it quite clear on which bank of the Spree the enemy was.

The orders of 10 A.M. on the 18th, saying the enemy occupied Bautzen (right bank of the Spree) "as the head of his position," made it quite clear that his main position was beyond the river, but they did not reach the marshal in writing till he arrived at Hoyerswerda towards noon on the 19th.

On the morning of the 19th the Emperor, with the main body, was posted thus in front of Bautzen :—

Headquarters and Old Guard, Klein Förstchen.

Young Guard and 1st cavalry corps, Gödau and behind it.

IV. corps (less Peyri's division sent to make connexion

[1] *Corr.* 20,025.

THE PRELIMINARIES OF BAUTZEN

with Lauriston at Königswartha), Gross-Welkau, with advanced Guard, Lubachau.

VI. corps, between IV. and the Dresden road, rather in front of the IV.

XI. corps level with VI., south of the Dresden road.

XII. corps on the right of XI., with an advanced guard in Guaschwitz. One of Lorencez's brigades of this corps was clearing the country on the right and right rear.

Of Ney's army, Lauriston (V. corps) was marching by Wittichenau for Zerna.

The III. corps was marching on Hoyerswerda.

The VII. and the II. corps and the 2nd cavalry corps also marching for Hoyerswerda, but still far behind.

Napoleon's orders to Ney of 10 A.M. on the 18th were carried by Major Grouchy, son of the future marshal. As he rode towards Hoyerswerda early on the morning of the 19th, he learnt that a hostile force was advancing from the direction of Bautzen. This news induced Lauriston to halt for fresh orders, after Ney should have heard it. Meanwhile, he ordered the V. corps to close up on Wittichenau and Maukendorf.

Ney, reaching Hoyerswerda about 11 A.M., received the clear orders of the 18th, and at once changed his own. The V. corps was now to march by Mortke[1] on Opitz and Lippitsch on the direct road to Klix and Brösa. The III. corps was to send Souham's division and Kellermann's cavalry brigade as advanced guard to Neudorf, the other four divisions to go half to Niesendorf and half to Königswartha.

The country between the Black Elster and the Spree was marshy, wooded, and covered with ponds to such an extent that it was not practicable to march through it at all in the autumn, and in the spring there were available only two narrow roads.[2]

Lauriston being still not clear of Hoyerswerda, the consequence was that the III. corps had to wait till even his

---
[1] This and a few other names do not appear on the maps. The general position is shown on Map III., inset (a).
[2] Jomini, *Vie de Nap.*, iv. p. 302.

baggage was gone before it could get forward on the road to Königswartha.[1]

It will be observed that Lauriston's corps, which was leading, was now to be passed across from Ney's right to his left. Evidently the marshal did this in order to have his left leading, and to be certain of reaching the Spree with it on the 20th.[2]

We now return to the allies and their movement on Königswartha, which had been correctly reported by Major Grouchy to Lauriston. They were, as Napoleon desired, entirely under the impression that they were about to be attacked, in their position behind the Spree, from the west only. On the 18th May a despatch was captured, which showed that Lauriston would be at Senftenberg on the 17th, and at Hoyerswerda on the 18th.[3] Though this enlightened the allies as to the fact that Lauriston was coming up, the direction of his march led them to believe that he would join Napoleon, and the attack would still be a frontal one from the west only. They also believed Ney to be a day's march behind Lauriston. This induced Wittgenstein to think that it might be possible to cut off Lauriston before he was supported. The plan was communicated to Barclay, who was to carry it out, in the evening of the 18th, and early in the morning of the 19th Wittgenstein wrote to him that, when he (Barclay) was heard to be in action, an attack would be made on the French left in front of Bautzen, in order to prevent its interfering with the expedition. This, von Caemmerer says, was nonsense; no preparations were ever made for such an attack.

---

[1] General von Cämmerer points out that Ney might have got over this difficulty by sending Lauriston's main body by Wittichenau to Königswartha, and detaining his baggage till the III. corps was clear of Hoyerswerda. Instead of that he sent Lauriston by the Maukendorf road, the III. corps had to wait till his baggage was gone, and only reached Königswartha with its advanced guard in the evening.

[2] In the above account of the orders to and by Ney, Col. Lanrezac's analysis and criticisms have been generally followed.

[3] Foucart i., p. 233 (Berthier to Bertrand), and p. 263 note.

THE PRELIMINARIES OF BAUTZEN 113

Barclay's force for this very risky adventure consisted of his own Russians and Yorck's Prussians, in all about 24,000 men. Tschaplitz, with the advanced guard, crossed the Spree, very early in the morning of the 19th, at Nieder Gurig, marching direct for Johnsdorf over the wooded heights beyond the French left.

Langeron and Rajewski, crossing at Klix, made for the same point by Milkel and Opitz. Yorck went farther north by Brösa, Guttau, Lomischau, and Lieske, through the woods towards Hermsdorf.

Tschaplitz's line took him within $1\frac{1}{4}$ miles of Bertrand's outposts at Lubachau, who observed and reported his march. But Bertrand took no action. He had already sent off Peyri's Italian division to Königswartha to get into touch with Lauriston. There it bivouacked about noon with total disregard of all measures of security. The outposts were badly placed, and no attempt was made to discover what there might be in the surrounding woods.

At 1 P.M. Barclay joined Tschaplitz, who was quite aware of the presence and unmilitary attitude of the Italians, since his scouts had been close up to their outposts. Of what ensued there is no very clear account forthcoming. All that is certain is that Peyri, whom the Russians believed to be Lauriston's advanced guard, was attacked and badly beaten, with a loss of 2860 men, including 750 prisoners. The pursuit only ceased at Wartha at 5 P.M., when Kellermann was met with Ney's advanced guard.

Yorck, meanwhile, had started at the same time as Langeron. Having to go by a road five miles longer, by Hermsdorf, Weissig, Neu Steinitz, and Wartha, against Lauriston's left flank, he should have started two hours earlier. At 3 P.M. he found the enemy in force at Hermsdorf. It was the head of Lauriston's corps. Yorck was fighting this when he received an order from Barclay to move to Johnsdorf as reserve.

Circumstances having changed since the order was dispatched, Yorck would have been justified in delaying compliance with this order. But his ideas of unhesitating

H

obedience induced him to attempt to break off his action and comply at once. As he was doing so, another order arrived from Barclay, who, having discovered that he was not engaged with Lauriston, but with Peyri's division of Bertrand's corps, now desired Yorck to hold on at Weissig. He did his best, and as he received reinforcements from Barclay, was able to put up a very good fight, though he could not recover the position he had evacuated. It was only late at night that, leaving his bivouac fires burning, he retreated on Klix, where he had been preceded by Barclay. Both rejoined the main army on the 20th, though it was not till after noon that Yorck was back. He had lost about 1100, Barclay about 900 men.

This expedition must be characterised as a very rash one, from which the allies escaped more by good luck than good guidance. They had sent about one-fourth of their whole army in the hope of striking a blow at Lauriston, whose corps, if complete, should have been 19,000 strong. The expeditionary force passed almost under Bertrand's nose, but he did nothing. Even Napoleon, when he heard the firing on his left rear at Königswartha, took no notice. He afterwards censured Bertrand for his slackness, but he must bear a considerable share of the blame himself.

Again, the allies had a great piece of luck in colliding only with Peyri's division and part of Lauriston's corps. Had Ney managed his march better, they might have had him also on their hands.

Napoleon, posted as he was in front of Bautzen, could have easily contained the allied main army with the VI., XI., XII., and Guard corps (86,000 in all against 72,000 allies), whilst he sent the rest of Bertrand's corps against the left and rear of Barclay and Yorck.

The attack on Peyri and Lauriston had a very remarkable effect on Ney. At 9 P.M. he wrote from Maukendorf to Berthier, saying that he had learnt from a prisoner that the enemy was marching on Hoyerswerda. "Two divisions," he added, "are here with me; it is at Buchwalde[1] that I

---
[1] Less than two miles south of Maukendorf.

THE PRELIMINARIES OF BAUTZEN 115

shall receive battle if the enemy attacks me to-morrow." He was clearly very much at sea still as to the real positions about Bautzen. For that he had no sufficient excuse after the receipt of the letter from Berthier saying the enemy held Bautzen as the "head of his position."

During the 19th there was no operation on the main front, except a reconnaissance by Eugen of Wurtemberg towards Quatitz, which only returned at 11 P.M.

CHAPTER IX

THE BATTLE OF BAUTZEN[1]

IT is now necessary to describe the field of the two days' battle of Bautzen.

The general line of division between the opponents on the 20th May was the river Spree, from about Doberschau, where it changes its course from north-west to a little east of north, to Leichnam beyond Klix. From Doberschau to Oehna, just below Bautzen, the stream flows in a steep-sided valley, some 150 feet in average depth. The command varies from bank to bank. Beyond Oehna, as far as the Gottlobsberg, about two miles lower down, the right bank generally commands the left. Beyond this point the river is bordered by meadows, in which, especially on the right bank, are numerous shallow, muddy ponds used for breeding carp, of which one sees a whole cart-load taken from a single pond. Through these ponds run a little branch of the Spree, which enables them to be filled or emptied when the fish have to be taken up. Across them, as in the case of the long line running north from Doberschütz, there are narrow causeways separating them into compartments. These ponds, and the marshy land around them, are a very serious military obstacle even for infantry. The Spree is here a small stream, comparable, perhaps, to the Mole about Dorking. It is fordable in most places in ordinary weather, though here and there are deep reaches, one of which is where the road from Nieder Gurig to Bautzen crosses above the former village between the Gottlobsberg and the Kiefernberg.

[1] In some accounts the first day's battle (20th May) is called the battle of Bautzen, whilst the second day's is called Wurschen. For plan of battle, see Map III.

THE BATTLE OF BAUTZEN

The extreme south of the battlefield was on the wooded heights of the Drohmberg and the Schmoritzberg, the last outliers of the Lusatian mountain in this direction.

The space enclosed between the Spree and the villages of Doberschau, Rieschen, Litten, and Kreckwitz is a rolling plateau of no very marked features. North-west of Kreckwitz is a mass of somewhat more marked elevation, known generally as the Kreckwitz heights.[1] North of this mass the field is generally flat, with a few knolls scattered about, the most notable being those between Malschwitz and Gleina, culminating in the windmill height south-west of the latter place. All this part of the field is dotted over with carp ponds, as shown on the map.

Roughly parallel to the Spree, on an average about two miles east of it, flows the Blösaer Wasser, from about Blôsa to Kreckwitz. Hence it flows past Purschwitz and Klein Bautzen to join the Löbauer Wasser. As a stream it is quite unimportant, but its valley, especially from about Auritz to Kreckwitz, was marshy, and an excellent protection for a position east of it. One feature outside the battlefield must be mentioned, the church spire of Hochkirch, where Frederick had been surprised by Daun. It is covered with copper, turned green with verdigris, and, standing out as it does on a commanding spur of the mountains, it forms a notable landmark, visible from almost every part of the battlefield, and from far beyond it.

The town of Bautzen had, in 1813, some 7000 or 8000 inhabitants. It was surrounded by an old wall, of which small portions are still to be seen on the river front. The deep narrow gorge of the Spree, west of the town, was hardly open to frontal attack, but could be turned by the stone bridge higher up, or from lower down.

The allies' first idea had been to defend the line of the Spree, but the objections to this were (1) the varying command of the bank; (2) the fact that the river was generally

---

[1] It was to a position on these heights, extending from about Kreckwitz to Burk, that Frederick the Great retired after his disastrous defeat at Hochkirch on the 14th October 1758.

fordable; and (3) the extent of the line as compared with their available forces.

They decided, therefore, on placing their main line behind the valley of the Blösaer Wasser, and only fighting an advanced guard action on the line of the Spree about Bautzen.

In addition to the natural protection of the valley of the Blösaer Wasser, they had carried out a very considerable amount of fortification on a line which generally offered an excellent field of fire. Their left rested on the hills, the Drohmberg and Schmoritzberg, which, with their woods and villages, made a strong support. The centre, from the hills to Kreckwitz, was covered with redoubts or batteries armed with a powerful artillery sweeping open slopes. The chief of these were :—

(1) One on the left, on the height north-east of Mehlteuer.

(2) One on a height behind Rabitz.

(3) Three between the Bautzen-Hochkirch road at Jenkwitz, and Baschütz.

(4) Three between Baschütz and the Bautzen-Weissenberg road.

(5) Three, in continuation of these, between the road and Litten.[1]

Besides these there were numerous smaller works along this line, and on the Kreckwitz heights villages were fortified and abattis set up in the woods. The French engineers, sent for the purpose later on, destroyed no less than 78 redoubts, batteries, and epaulements on the allies' position.[2]

The position, including the Kreckwitz heights projecting like a bastion on the right front, was generally a good one. Its left was within about 6 miles of the Austrian frontier, and, therefore, not likely to be turned by a large force.

---

[1] No traces of these redoubts are now apparent, except, perhaps, in a mound near the modern drill ground, which may represent one of the northernmost group.

[2] Foucart, i. p. 293, note.

THE BATTLE OF BAUTZEN

The weak points were its extent, and the danger of its being turned on its right from the north. It was excellent so long as it was only attacked from the west. With the advance of a strong force from Klix on Hochkirch, it was untenable for long, as the right was " in the air."

But all the allies' dispositions proceeded on the assumption that an attack was to be expected from the direction of Dresden only. On the 19th May, Gneisenau inferred, from the reports received, that there might also be an attack from the north, but his warnings were disregarded. There was a strong difference of opinion on several points between him and Wittgenstein. The hope of the allies was to be able to hold the French centre and right, whilst turning their left.

The strength of the allied army was as follows—[1]

I. Russians.

	Infantry	Cavalry	Cossacks	Artillery & Engineers.	Guns	Men
Miloradowich	8,800	3,400	1,750	650	54	14,600
Gortchakow	10,500	2,000	450	750	66	13,700
Grand Duke Constantine	11,300	5,350	—	3,250	252	19,900
Barclay de Tolly	9,150	1,800	1,220	1,420	84	13,590
[1] Kleist	1,400	420	550	180	16	2,550
	41,150	12,970	3,970	6,250	472	64,340

II. Prussians.

	Infantry	Cavalry	Cossacks	Artillery & Engineers.	Guns	Men
Blücher	17,040	4,710	—	1,550	90	23,300
Yorck	4,120	1,210	—	340	36	5,670
[2] Kleist	2,300	330	—	300	24	2,930
	23,460	6,250	—	2,190	150	31,900
Grand total	64,610	19,220	3,970	8,440	622	96,240

[1] Fruhjahrsfeldzug, ii. 181.
[2] Kleist's corps was partly Russian, partly Prussian, as shown.

A round 100,000 was made up by detachments on the French flanks and rear.

These troops were thus disposed—

(1) Miloradowich, holding the line of the Spree from Doberschau to Burk as advanced guard.

(2) Russian main body (Gortchakow) on the line Rieschen-Jenkwitz-Baschütz, supported by a powerful artillery from the reserve.

(3) Russian reserve infantry south of Canitz-Christina, cavalry and horse artillery on both sides of the Weissenberg road.

(4) Blücher, with a brigade on the Kreckwitz heights, in front of his main body.

(5) Barclay, with Yorck behind him at Guttau, stretching from Brösa to Klix, with Tschaplitz's advanced guard beyond.

The orders for the battle, issued on the 19th, attempted to provide for all contingencies, but missed the very one which occurred.

If Miloradowich found the enemy crossing with superior forces above and below Bautzen, he was to fall back on the heights between Auritz and Klein Jenkwitz.

In case the enemy attempted to advance against the main position, the following provisions were made:—

(*a*) If his attack was directed against the allied right, the army was to reinforce that flank by a "flank march," a very vague order, as von Caemmerer remarks.

(*b*) If the centre were attacked, Barclay and Kleist to attack the enemy's left flank.

(*c*) If the left were attacked, Barclay and the centre were to swing forward and drive the enemy against the mountains.

(*d*) So, too, if the attack were on both flanks, the right was to be strengthened so as to drive the French southwards.

No provision was made for what was to happen if Napoleon did not attempt the main position at once, or for the case of an attack from the north.

THE BATTLE OF BAUTZEN 121

Blücher was directed to move to his right, so as to have his left at Kreckwitz and right at Brösa, his line to the latter being completed by the Russian cuirassiers and Prussian reserve cavalry. Gortchakow was to move into Blücher's former position. Then the order for the move of the cavalry to Blücher's right was cancelled, and Yorck was ordered back to Litten. That decided Barclay to confine himself to the line Malschwitz-Gleina. Blücher, on the other hand, kept his main body east of the Kreckwitz heights, on which was Ziethen's brigade. Two battalions held Plieskowitz. Kleist was on the Kreckwitz heights and at Burk, Nieder Kaina, and Basankwitz.

Napoleon, anxious about his broken communications with Ney, had, about 7 A.M., ordered Soult, with Bertrand's corps and Latour-Maubourg's cavalry, to re-open them. Then, finding that they were again open, when he received Ney's letter of 9 P.M. on the 19th, he stopped his movement.[1] Napoleon, now assured of the retreat of Barclay and Yorck, decided to attack the line of the Spree, so as to give Ney more time to come up. About noon the VI. and XI. corps began the advance below and above Bautzen. Oudinot, with the XII., moved on Singwitz, linked to Macdonald's right by Reiset's cavalry brigade.

It was about 1 P.M. when Oudinot crossed by the bridge and a ford at Singwitz, driving the weak Russian line back on the Falkenberg till he was stopped by Russian cavalry. He had sent Lorencez's division[2] to the right. Finding the Drohmberg and Schmoritzberg weakly held, Lorencez got well forward towards Pielitz and Mehlteuer.

Whilst these events were occurring, Macdonald had got over the bridge above Bautzen, and had constructed two more bridges there. Marmont, from the heights near Oehna, had bombarded the opposite bank with sixty guns. Then, passing by a ford, he had got with Compans' division into the north-western suburb of Bautzen about 3 P.M.

---

[1] The fact that he ordered it on the 20th shows that he might well have done so on the 19th, to the probable undoing of Barclay and Yorck.

[2] Only one brigade. The other was clearing the woods on the right rear.

The Russians in Bautzen now evacuated it before the double threat of Marmont and Macdonald. Miloradowich, alarmed lest he should be cut off by Oudinot, ordered a general retirement, for which he was very unfairly blamed at headquarters.

Marmont's left had gone forward on Nadelwitz, and Macdonald to a position facing the heights of Rabitz. As the enemy retired, Marmont reinforced his left against Burk so as to support Bertrand's attack farther north. Behind Macdonald and Marmont, the Guard and two of Latour-Maubourg's cavalry divisions crossed and took post on the east of Bautzen. In the centre the fighting came to an end in this position.

We return to Oudinot before describing what happened in the north. The effect of Lorencez's advance on Pielitz and Mehlteuer had been very marked, for it confirmed in the mind of the Tsar his preconceived idea that Napoleon meant to cut the allies from Austria by turning their left and driving them northwards. Since the Tsar was really the supreme authority, his belief had a very serious effect on all the plans of the allies during both days of battle. Nothing would convince him that Napoleon's design was the exact reverse of what he had taken it into his head to assume. In reality, the Emperor's great design was to roll the allies up from their right against the Bohemian frontier. Nothing could be more natural in the circumstances; for he knew that Austria was not ready to declare against him, and would not be so for several weeks to come. Had she then found herself, still unready, with a defeated army driven over her northern frontier there was every probability that, like Prussia in 1805, she would give way and hasten to make her peace with Napoleon by refusing to allow the allies to utilise her territory. The allies themselves knew she was not ready, for Stadion had just brought a memorandum by Radetzky showing that it would not be till the middle of June, at the earliest, that Austria could have 120,000 men in Bohemia.

It was, therefore, Napoleon's wish to draw as many of the

THE BATTLE OF BAUTZEN 123

allied reserves as possible to their left wing, and prevent them reinforcing their right against the projected attack of Ney from the north. Alexander played into his hands by drawing on his already weak reserves to reinforce his left against Oudinot. Had Napoleon manœuvred as Alexander expected, he might, no doubt, have temporarily separated the allies from Austria, but there was nothing to interfere with their retreat on Görlitz, Liegnitz, and Breslau. Then the farther the French advanced the greater would have been the danger from Austria, busily arming on their right flank and rear.

The Tsar's erroneous view was not shared by Wittgenstein; but his opinion counted for little, and Alexander sent a substantial portion of his reserve against Oudinot.

The latter was now forced back by superior strength to Grubditz (Pacthod's division) and Denkwitz (Lorencez's), where he bivouacked for the night.

Meanwhile, Soult, on the French left, had advanced with Bertrand's corps. He succeeded, though with heavy loss, in reaching the Spree at the Gottlobsberg, and driving its defenders on to the Kiefernberg, but he only got a small force across the river there. At Nieder Gurig he also had a severe struggle to take the village and drive its garrison back on the main position at Doberschütz. Briesing was found unoccupied, and Soult's left pushed through it part of the way to Plieskowitz. Whilst Soult was attacking, Marmont's left division (Bonnet) had succeeded in driving Kleist from Burk, and eventually compelling his retreat on Litten. This operation had been facilitated by the movement of Friederichs' division down the valley of the Blösaer Wasser on Kleist's left against Basankwitz, which was taken. Soult's exit from the defile at the Gottlobsberg was barred by a single Prussian battalion on the Kiefernberg, which only retired in the night.

Ney, during the 20th, advanced to Brehmen. He was annoyed during the march by Lanskoi's and Tschaplitz's cavalry, but these were presently driven off by Kellermann and Ney's leading division. That night Ney's five divisions bivouacked at Sdier ; Lauriston was at and behind Särchen ; Puthod's division (of Lauriston's corps) was at Steinitz ; Reynier at Hoyerswerda ; Victor still far behind at Senftenberg.

The object of Napoleon's attack on the 20th had been to "fix" the enemy in his main position until he could bring up Ney on his right flank and rear. There was a certain amount of risk if the allies should make a determined counter attack on the IV., VI., XI., and XII. corps when they had crossed the Spree. On the whole, however, it seems probable that this would have failed, seeing that Napoleon still had the Guard and Latour-Maubourg's cavalry in reserve. With them he was very little inferior in strength to the whole allied army. Colonel Lanrezac points out that Napoleon did by design what the allies had done unintentionally at Lützen, namely, had attacked so late in the day that it was out of the question for the enemy to inflict a decisive defeat on him, even if they succeeded in compelling him to recross the Spree. If he had to do that he would still be in a position to carry out his design for the next day ; for the line of the Spree was not nearly so defensible for the allies as their main position behind the Blösaer Wasser.

Wittgenstein had, indeed, at one time contemplated such a counter attack, but it had been abandoned before the issue of his orders of the 19th ; for the order to Miloradowich not to hold on too long on the Spree was entirely inconsistent with any such idea.

During the night the allies held councils of war, both at the headquarters of the King of Prussia (Wurschen) and at those of the Tsar at Purschwitz. What was said at them has not been recorded, but von Caemmerer concludes that even then the allied commanders completely failed to recognise the danger of their position.

Napoleon had in reality only very imperfectly "fixed" the enemy. Had they not already unwisely decided to defend their main position under any circumstances, there was nothing in the events of the 20th to forbid their retreat

THE BATTLE OF BAUTZEN

during the ensuing night. That would have been their wisest course.

THE BATTLE OF THE 21ST MAY.

Napoleon's orders to Ney of the 18th only directed him on Drehsa (Brösa). On the 20th fresh orders were sent. They appear to have been issued about 4 P.M.,[1] to have been carried by Ney's own staff officer, and to have reached him only at 4 A.M. on the 21st.[2] They were signed by Berthier, and directed Ney to drive the enemy from Drehsa, and thence march on Weissenberg, so as to turn the enemy.

These orders, as von Caemmerer points out, were wanting in clearness, since they mixed up matters which should be kept distinct. The direction to march on Weissenberg could only come into force, he says, if it was desired to manœuvre the enemy from his position, or if he of his own accord withdrew from the battle. If the enemy were still in his position on the 21st, Ney ought to march, not south-east on Weissenberg, but due south on Hochkirch. Therefore, the Prussian writer thinks, there is nothing remarkable in Ney's replying that, as he heard firing in the direction of Hochkirch and Bautzen, he should await further orders before marching on Weissenberg. Here we must raise the question whether Napoleon ever meant "Drehsa near Gottamelde" to be sent to Ney as a direction. On Petri's map, which he is said to have used, there are two Drehsas, one (really Brösa) near Gottamelde (Guttau), the other south of Wurschen, in the direct line from Klix to Hochkirch.[3] Napoleon's order to Berthier speaks merely of Drehsa, without any description. Napoleon, who had studied

---

[1] Foucart, i. p. 289, note 2.   [2] *Ibid.*, i. p. 309, note 2.

[3] Petri was a Prussian officer of Frederick, and published his map in 1763. Why should he have made a mistake and written Drehsa for Brösa? (It seems probable Brösa was the right name as it is now.) The mistake may have arisen from the local pronunciation which sounds "ö" or "œ" as "e." The author himself was directed by a blacksmith at Nimmschütz to "Ena," which, on consulting the map, he found to be Œhna.

Frederick's campaigns, would know Drehsa south of Wurschen, as the strong position where Frederick made a stand to cover his retreat from Hochkirch to Kreckwitz. It was right in the centre of the space between the roads by which the enemy could retreat on Görlitz and Löbau, and the point on which, looking at his map at Dresden, he would naturally direct Ney; for the map did not tell him that Hochkirch spire was a much better landmark. Most writers assume that Berthier was right in adding the description " near Gottamelde." On the other hand, Jomini[1] says Napoleon indicated the Drehsa south of Wurschen, and that he (Jomini) got Ney to march on Hochkirch spire, which was the same direction.[2] Count Yorck von Wartenburg[3] also says Napoleon indicated " Drehsa in the rear of the allies," a description which does not apply to " Drehsa near Gottamelde." Again, Ney's main point of passage of the Spree would naturally be by the road at Klix. Why should Napoleon give him as a further line of direction one of scarcely a mile (the distance from Klix to Brösa)? The prolongation of this short line (Klix-Brösa) would carry Ney on parallel to the line of the main attack to a point north even of Weissenberg.

The bearer of Ney's reply to the order to march on Weissenberg reached Napoleon on the heights east of Bautzen after 7 A.M. The Emperor personally explained to him the enemy's position. Whether he told him where Ney was to make for is not clear. The staff officer was sent back with a pencil note as follows :—" The intention of the Emperor is that you should follow constantly the movement of the enemy. His Majesty has shown your staff officer the positions of the enemy, which are defined by the redoubts which he has constructed and occupies. The intention of the Emperor is that you should be this morning at 11 o'clock at the village of Preititz. You will be on the extreme right of the enemy. As soon as the Emperor sees you engaged at Preititz we shall attack

---

[1] *Vie de Nap.* iv., p. 311, note. [2] *Ibid.*, p. 305, note.
[3] *Napoleon as a General*, ii., p. 257.

THE BATTLE OF BAUTZEN 127

vigorously at all points. Cause General Lauriston to march on your left so as to be in a position to turn the enemy if your movement decides him to abandon his position."

It was perhaps proper in a "directive," which should leave a commander of a separate force a free hand, not to prescribe the direction to be taken after Preititz, but, on the other hand, the orders were much too definite in prescribing the hour at which Ney was to reach Preititz. Again, there is in the orders no clear statement of the Emperor's general plan, and of the part Ney was to play in it. The effects of this order will be seen later as the course of the battle is described, which may best be done in periods.

First period—up to 11 A.M.

Oudinot began the attack with the French right at daybreak. At first he was successful, Pacthod capturing Rieschen, and Lorencez storming Pielitz and Döhlen. This so alarmed the Tsar, who still believed in Napoleon's design to cut the allies from Bohemia, that he drew again on his weak reserves to reinforce Miloradowich. That general, with about 20,000 men against Oudinot's 15,000, now drove the latter back on to the Drohmberg and the heights east of Binnewitz. This was about 11 A.M. Oudinot, who had already asked for reinforcements, again appealed for them to the Emperor, who did not even reply.

On Oudinot's left, Macdonald got on to the heights of Rabitz, from which he maintained a heavy cannonade.

In the centre Marmont's three divisions stood inactive on the heights of Burk, with infantry occupying Nadelwitz, Nieder Kaina, and Basankwitz.

The Guard infantry stood in squares on the high ground north-east of Bautzen. Guard cavalry and Latour-Maubourg on the right of the infantry, behind Macdonald's left.

Soult, with Bertrand's corps, had announced that at daybreak he would be on the plateau east of the Spree. But Ziethen's battalion was only withdrawn from the Kiefernberg at dawn, and there were difficulties in constructing a bridge below the Gottlobsberg, where the water was deep. At 11 A.M. Bertrand was still not across, and it was not till 2 P.M. that he had 20,000 infantry, 1000 cavalry and 30 guns on the right bank. He was therefore very far from having done what Napoleon expected when he sent orders to Soult (at the same time as he sent those to Ney), to attack the enemy vigorously with three divisions advancing between Marmont and Ney.

Ney, on the French left, had started at between 4 and 5 A.M. to cross the Spree at Klix. As Lauriston's leading division reached Klix, it found Kellermann's advanced guard still in bivouac there. Crossing the Spree Lauriston met Tschaplitz's Russians, and turned leftwards towards Leichnam in order to outflank them. Lanskoi's Russian cavalry (2400) was still on Lauriston's left at Lomischau. Leaving four battalions, a squadron, and two guns to deal with Lanskoi, Lauriston marched on Brösa, Tschaplitz retiring from Salga before him through Brösa and Guttau, which latter he fired in order to delay Lauriston's passage of the Löbauer Wasser. Lauriston had only two divisions with him, as Ney had stopped Maison's, and sent it by Salga on Malschütz to protect his own right.

Ney now decided to attack Barclay, who stood on the heights of Gleina with about 5000 men, the rest of his 15,000 being 2400 with Lanskoi, 2 battalions in Guttau, 2 in the wood between Brösa and Gleina, and 3 in Malschütz. As Ney had some 18,000 men, Barclay fell back without serious resistance on Preititz with his main body, whilst he sent his reserve to reinforce Tschaplitz, who was now at Buchwalde east of Gleina. Barclay had already called on Blücher for reinforcements to be sent to Preititz. There, however, he was alarmed for his line of retreat by the advance of Lauriston, who had driven Tschaplitz back as far as the Schafberg east of Buchwalde, where the Russian was joined by Lanskoi and Barclay's reserve. Lauriston was now trying to turn his right.

Barclay, therefore, leaving only two battalions in Preititz, marched to Baruth to protect the line of retreat. It was

THE BATTLE OF BAUTZEN 129

10 A.M. when Ney found himself on the windmill heights of Gleina. On his right Maison was preparing to storm Malschütz; Lauriston had still not got beyond Guttau.

It was at this juncture that his staff officer, who had had to make a long round by Klix, returned with Napoleon's pencil orders and verbal explanations. Jomini urged Ney to advance at once on Preititz, but the marshal pointed to the order saying he was expected to be there at 11. Nothing would induce him to act otherwise than by the letter of the orders, and he remarked that an hour hence Maison would have taken Malschütz, and Lauriston would have got to Buchwalde. He decided to wait an hour. He had now got up the divisions of Souham, Delmas, Albert, Ricard, 23,000 infantry, so that he could have taken Preititz with the greatest ease.

Now, however, according to Jomini, Ney had got into his obstinate and not over clear head a new idea. "When Ney saw the fine heights of Klein Bautzen, he was carried away by the idea that they were the key of the position."[1] That made him hold that he ought to wait for the arrival of Reynier, and then attack the heights. Therefore, towards 11 o'clock, he adopted a half measure by sending Souham alone against Preititz. Delmas was echeloned, out of supporting distance, on Souham's right, whilst Albert and Ricard were kept right back in reserve. At the same time, orders were sent to Lauriston to close in on Ney's left. Lauriston, however, did not obey at once, for he saw that by a flank march he would merely lose time.

As we have said, Barclay had left only two battalions in Preititz, who could practically make no fight against Souham. Thus at 11 A.M. Ney had a division in Preititz, which was more or less of a literal compliance with Napoleon's orders. Had he had his whole corps there, and been on the move towards Hochkirch, as Jomini urged him, Blücher could hardly have held on to the Kreckwitz heights, and, the

---

[1] Letter from Jomini to Major Wagner, dated 15th April 1823, quoted by von Caemmerer in "*Fruhjarhrsfeldzug*, 1813." The "heights of Klein Bautzen" mean the Kreckwitz heights.

I

pressure in front of Soult being removed, that marshal also would have got forward.

Second period—11 A.M. to 3 P.M.

We left Oudinot, at 11 A.M., falling back before Miloradowich. At noon he again urgently demanded reinforcements. This time he got an answer: "Tell your marshal," said the Emperor to Oudinot's galloper, "that the battle will be won by 3 o'clock, from now till then he must hold on as best he may." As a matter of fact, Oudinot's position was not so bad as he imagined. He had not yet engaged his Bavarian division, and, when Macdonald on his left threatened an advance with his right from Grubditz on Binnewitz, the Russian advance came to a standstill, and Oudinot was able to hold on at Ebendörfel and on the heights in rear of Binnewitz.

Napoleon was quite satisfied; for Oudinot and Macdonald had drawn on themselves nearly the whole of the allies' left wing, and a great part of the reserve, which it was the Emperor's design to prevent being sent to the allied right. If Macdonald and Oudinot were forced back, so much the better, for that would facilitate the scheme for driving the enemy against the mountains.

The Tsar and the King of Prussia had taken post in the early morning on the heights near Klein Jenkwitz, on the Bautzen-Hochkirch road. Thence, they could, with a good glass, recognise the person of Napoleon about two miles off. At 9 A.M. the French Emperor, exhausted by a sleepless night, had lain down on the ground and gone calmly to sleep in the midst of his Guard. In this extraordinary position, with the enemy's shells bursting at times close to him, he slept till 11.

The Tsar, meanwhile, had become more and more convinced that the danger was to his left. In vain did Wittgenstein say to him, "I will wager my head that this is only a demonstration; Napoleon's idea is to outflank our right and drive us on Bohemia."[1]

When Napoleon awoke at 11 A.M. to hear the sound of

[1] *Danilewski*, p. 101.

THE BATTLE OF BAUTZEN 131

Souham's attack on Preititz, his view of which was shut out by the Kreckwitz heights, he ordered Marmont forward across the Blösaer Wasser between Nieder Kaina and the Bautzen-Hochkirch road. The infantry of the VI. corps, sheltered by the ground, now stood within twenty minutes' march of the enemy's redoubts, whilst the artillery kept up a tremendous fire.

Into the gap between Marmont's left at Nieder Kaina and Bertrand's right the Emperor sent Barrois' division of Young Guard who fired with artillery on Kreckwitz village on their left, and the redoubts south of Litten on their right.[1]

The rest of the Guard and Latour-Maubourg stood as reserve, with eighty guns, behind Basankwitz.

It was 1 P.M. before Bertrand, under Soult's orders, had his bridge ready close under the Kiefernberg, where it was defiladed from the enemy's artillery on the Kreckwitz heights. His artillery, which had hitherto kept silent, leaving the enemy to waste his ammunition, now opened fire from the Gottlobs and Kiefern Bergs to prepare the way for the advance, about 2.30 P.M., of Franquemont's Wurtembergers on Kreckwitz. This division, regardless of a murderous artillery fire, pushed gallantly on, forcing the allied batteries to retire from the Koppatschberg, which was stormed, and artillery brought up on to its flanks. One Wurtemberg battalion even got into Kreckwitz, but was driven out and almost all of it taken prisoner by reinforcements sent from Yorck's right at Litten.

Simultaneously with Franquemont's advance, Morand's division had one column moving against Plieskowitz from Briesing, another from Nieder Gurig on Doberschütz, and a third from the Galgenberg on the Weisser Stein.[2]

By 3 P.M. Blücher was forced back to the line Doberschütz-Weinberg-Kreckwitz (village).

[1] Two of Barrois' five regiments with half a battery had been sent there earlier.
[2] This appears to be the curious outcrop of white stone close to which one passes in walking by the cross road from Kreckwitz to Doberschütz.

We left Ney, at 11 A.M., with Souham's division in Preititz, or just arriving there. It will be remembered that Barclay, seeing Ney's advance on Gleina, had asked support from Blücher. In compliance with this demand, Blücher had, at 10 A.M., sent four battalions to the eastern slope of the Kreckwitz heights above Klein Bautzen. Then he ordered Röder to send three more battalions into Preititz. As the latter advanced along the left bank of the Blösaer Wasser, they met Souham debouching from Preititz and attacked so vigorously as to drive him back into it. The rest of Röder's brigade coming up, as well as a regiment sent by Kleist from east of Purschwitz, there ensued a desperate struggle in Preititz, the result of which was that Souham was driven from the village back on the divisions of Albert and Ricard. About 1 P.M. the three divisions fell back on Gleina heights.

Ney, who could now see the rear of the allied centre and knew that Napoleon had not yet attacked it, sent urgent calls to hurry up Reynier, who was just crossing the Spree at Klix, and to insist on Lauriston's closing in from the left.

The latter had manœuvred Tschaplitz off the Scharberg, and was following him towards Barclay, who now occupied the heights between Rackel and Briesnitz.

Lauriston, leaving Rochambeau's division and half his cavalry to contain Barclay, reluctantly marched with Lagrange's division and the rest of the cavalry by Buchwalde on Preititz. All told, he had only about 10,000 men, including Rochambeau; for Puthod's division was only just coming up to Gleina, and Maison's had been sent by Ney against Malschütz.

Maison, after storming Malschütz, had taken Plieskowitz, then being driven from it again, and only finally got possession of it when, towards 3 P.M., the Prussians retired on to the heights before the combined advance of Maison and that of Bertrand's left column from Briesing.

When Souham was driven from Preititz, Ney sent Delmas, supported by Albert and Ricard, to retake it. The village

THE BATTLE OF BAUTZEN 133

was now held by Kleist only; for Blücher had been obliged to recall Röder to form his own reserve. Kleist now (about 2 P.M.) saw Preititz threatened by Ney's three divisions in front, and by Lauriston on the right. The village was stormed by Delmas; then he was driven out again, once more re-took it, and finally held it as Kleist, alarmed for his retreat, fell back on the heights south-west of Belgern.

As Delmas advanced on Preititz, he had suffered from artillery fire from the northern slopes of the Kreckwitz heights. This seems to have confirmed Ney in his belief that he was bound to attack the heights. If the marshal was amenable in the council chamber, he took the bit between his teeth on the battlefield, and it was in vain that Jomini again told him that the decision lay in a march directed on the Hochkirch spire. He had now 32,000 men available, without counting the shattered division of Souham, Maison, Rochambeau, or Reynier. The "accursed heights of Kreckwitz," as Jomini styles them, continued to attract Ney.

As soon, therefore, as Delmas was in Preititz, he was ordered to face to his right for the attack on the heights, which would have to be made in face of a heavy artillery fire, and across a tract divided up by ponds with narrow causeways between them.

Third period. After 3 P.M.

During this period almost the whole interest of the battle centres round the Kreckwitz heights and the allied right. Blücher's position on these heights was becoming more and more perilous. Bertrand's advance had driven him back to the line Doberschütz-Weinberg-Kreckwitz, facing west. Maison was coming from the north; Delmas, Ricard, Albert, and Lauriston were advancing from the north-east; Barrois threatened Kreckwitz from the south.

Blücher had already called on Yorck for help; he could see Marmont's masses threatening the allies' centre, and the Imperial Guard apparently on the point of advancing from Basankwitz on Litten. Yorck was very weak in his position about Litten, but he at once sent off Steinmetz's brigade, which apparently was the force that destroyed the Wurtemberg battalion in Kreckwitz. As soon as Yermolow with part of the Russian Guard came up to relieve him south of Litten, Yorck, leaving behind only two battalions, started with the rest.

But it was too late, for Blücher, soon after 3 P.M., finding himself quite unable to resist the immensely superior forces advancing from three sides against the heights, decided to evacuate them. He had very little time to spare; indeed, Müffling says [1] that he warned Blücher that there was just a quarter of an hour left before the narrow gap in the circle of French would be closed. The old Prussian consented most reluctantly to retreat. Klüx was sent off first, followed by Ziethen. As they reached Kreckwitz, they met and passed through Steinmetz's and Horn's brigades of Yorck's corps. The Prussian troops retired in perfect order to a position north and south of Purschwitz, where Röder's brigade had already taken post. The cavalry covered the retreat, and succeeded in saving one of their batteries, which had very nearly fallen into the hands of the Wurtemberg cavalry.

Meanwhile, as the Prussians left the Kreckwitz heights, the tide of the French attack rose over them. Ney's men from the north and north-east, Bertrand's from the west and south, rushed on to the plateau to find no enemy left there, and to meet only their friends from the opposite side. The two corps were "clubbed" on the plateau, and it took an hour before they could get properly disentangled. Ney, as he reached the heights, saw to his disgust that the Prussians had slipped unharmed through the gap which he had left by his fatal right turn at Preititz, and were retreating in perfect order. He sent immediate orders to Lauriston to head them off, but it was too late.

It was not till Ney had taken Preititz for the second time that the Tsar at last realised that the danger was to the right of the allies, and that now there was nothing left but immediate retreat. Yermolow, with part of the Russian

[1] *Passages from my Life*, etc., p. 41.

THE BATTLE OF BAUTZEN

Guard, was sent off to support the right, and took Yorck's place south of Litten. His infantry was very weak, and, though with the cavalry and artillery they might have checked Barrois' Young Guard division alone, they could not withstand him as well as the Wurtembergers following the Prussians through Kreckwitz. Yermolow, therefore, fell back eastwards with the guns, covered by one of Yorck's battalions and by Corswant's cavalry.

In the centre, Napoleon still hoped, with Marmont's corps, Latour-Maubourg's cavalry, and the Guard, to drive the allied left on the mountains. But Eugen of Wurtemberg retired so slowly and threateningly along the Löbau road that all the troops of the allied left got safely away under his protection. Latour-Maubourg's inferior cavalry could do nothing against that of the Russians.

Orders for the allies' retreat were only issued at 4 P.M. It was to be in three columns; on the north Barclay, in a strong position at Briesnitz, and Rackel, was to hold on till the centre, the Prussians and Yermolow, got away to Wurschen. The southern column, Miloradowich, was to march on Löbau, covered by the left centre.

In this manner the retreat was carried out in perfect order. The French pursuit was hindered, not only by the action of the rearguards, but also by a violent storm of rain which broke over the field about 6 P.M. There was never the slightest foundation for the statement in Napoleon's bulletin that the retreat " soon became a flight."

Into the details of this retreat we need not enter. There were several sharp fights, by no means always ending in the victory of the French.

When darkness finally stopped the fighting, the allies stood thus :—

Barclay, north of Weissenberg, with rearguard (Tschaplitz and Dolffs' cavalry) at Gröditz.

Blücher and most of the Prussians east and south-east of Weissenberg.

Yermolow's division and Katzeler's cavalry brigade, Kotitz.

Russians (less Barclay and Yermolow), Löbau.

St Priest's rearguard, Hochkirch.

Immanuel, Kassarow, and Orlow were four or five miles south at Cunewalde.

The allies still had, after allowing for the losses of the day, some 45,000 men on the northern, and 40,000 on the southern road.

The French had reached the following points:—

XI. corps (Macdonald) at Meschwitz, south-west of Hochkirch.

XII. corps (Oudinot), behind XI., at Söritz and Blösa.

VI. corps (Marmont), Waditz, with cavalry at Canitz-Christina.

IV. corps (Bertrand), at and south of Drehsa.[1]

III. corps (Ney), and V. (Lauriston), Wurschen.

VII. corps (Reynier), Belgern.

Guard and Imperial headquarters, Neu Purschwitz.

The losses of the allies for the two days' battle are given by von Caemmerer as 10,850, of whom 2790 belonged to Blücher's corps. Very few prisoners were lost, and no trophies, except a few disabled guns, which had to be left behind.

The French lost at least double these numbers. The lowest estimate puts them at 20,000, the highest at 25,000. Perhaps it is safe to take von Caemmerer's of 22,500, inclusive of 3700 "missing," of whom 800 were prisoners, and the rest marauders and stragglers, many of whom rejoined later, or turned up at Dresden.

Napoleon had on the field on the 21st May—

        Ney's army   . 87,500
        Main army   . 115,000

        Total   . 202,500[2] with 543 guns.

[1] The Drehsa south of Wurschen.

[2] Statement given at beginning of Foucart, i. These numbers are exclusive of Victor and Sebastiani, who were not up. Lanrezac puts the total at 170,000 men, of whom, he says, only about 90,000 were seriously engaged, viz. the III., IV. and XII. corps, and parts of V. and XI.

THE BATTLE OF BAUTZEN 137

Yet he had only gained another Lützen, something very far short of the decisive victory which he hoped for, and had a fair right to expect.

Before going further, we may note here that Lanrezac freely admits that much of the failure of the French was due to the superior morale of the allied troops, especially of the Prussians, who were animated by a noble spirit of patriotism, and by the desperation of men fighting for the preservation of hearth and home. They had a long series of grievous wrongs to avenge. But this spirit alone could hardly have saved them against Napoleon's overwhelming superiority of numbers, had his scheme been executed as it was designed.

Von Caemmerer has remarked on the strong resemblance in general design between the battle of the 21st and that which the Prussians fought fifty-three years later at Sadowa. If we take the Blösaer Wasser as representing the Bistritz, the Kreckwitz heights as those north of Chlum, Napoleon's army as the Prussian I. and Elbe armies, and Ney's as that of the Prussian Crown Prince, the resemblance is obvious. There was, it is true, no river corresponding to the Elbe behind the allies, but the defile leading to Görlitz may be taken to represent that. Napoleon, for the first time in his military career, deliberately aimed at concentrating on and not short of the battlefield, and the event showed that the instruments at his disposal were not sufficiently good for his purpose. Not that he could blame for this anything but the system of centralised command which he had habitually employed, depriving his subordinate commanders of all initiative or self-reliance.

That the failure to make of Bautzen a complete and decisive victory was mainly Ney's fault is held by all critics. But the Emperor must bear his share of the blame, inasmuch as he chose Ney for a command for which he was very ill-suited. Perhaps most of the other marshals would have done no better, but with Davout, Soult, Marmont, or Gouvion St Cyr there was at least a better chance.

Von Caemmerer, whilst suggesting that possibly Napoleon

looked to Jomini to keep Ney straight, observes that the cases in which a Chief of Staff can make up for the deficiencies of his general are rare. With a man so impetuous as Ney, there was very little chance on the battlefield, where he allowed himself to be carried away by impulse, and became as obstinate as a mule.[1]

We have already, in detailing the various orders given to Ney, shown that they failed to explain to him with sufficient clearness the part he was expected to play, and the scheme of his master. We have also argued that the Drehsa which Napoleon originally meant was not the one "near Gottamelde," but the one rendered famous in Frederick's battle. Against this theory is the fact that the pencil note of the morning speaks of Ney's occupying Drehsa, and then marching on Weissenberg. But may not this order have been wrongly drafted by Berthier, who assumed that Drehsa "near Gottamelde" was meant? In favour of it is the fact that the earlier orders speak of Ney's taking "a good position" at Drehsa. There appears to be no position which could be called "good" at Brösa, whereas there is a good one at Drehsa south of Wurschen, one, too, the excellence of which had been practically demonstrated by Frederick.

Little has hitherto been said about Bertrand's delay in crossing the Spree. Yet it would seem he ought to have been across much earlier. He held the Gottlobsberg on the night of the 20th, and there was nothing to oppose him except Ziethen's single battalion on the eastern slope of the Kiefernberg. Surely he might have got on with his bridge building during the night? Had he been well forward with his attack when Ney took Preititz for the second time, it is possible the latter might have seen the advantage of getting across the Weissenberg road, so as to block Blücher's last avenue of escape eastwards. Bertrand, it is true, was weak; for practically he

---

[1] In the Waterloo campaign, when Soult objected to Grouchy as not sufficiently strong for the command of the right wing, Napoleon replied that he had given him two strong subordinates in Vandamme and Gérard.

THE BATTLE OF BAUTZEN 139

had only the two divisions of Franquemont and Morand, seeing that Peyri's had been rendered almost useless at Königswartha on the 19th. But he might very well have been reinforced from the centre. There were there the corps of Marmont and Macdonald, the Guard and Latour-Maubourg's cavalry. The allied position there was so strong as to be really unassailable, until the intended advance of Ney in its rear should render it no longer tenable. Marmont, the Guard, and a great part of Macdonald's corps did practically nothing beyond bombarding the enemy's main position. They could not have held him there, or prevented his retreating, had he not been determined to hold on. Therefore, the attack on the Kreckwitz heights might well have been begun by troops drawn from the centre, when Ney reached Preititz. That would have prevented Blücher's sending the troops which drove Souham from Preititz, and perhaps would have enlightened Ney as to the real state of affairs and his own task. His failure to appreciate the latter is shown by the way in which he weakened Lauriston by taking away from him Maison's division. With that additional force, and most of the cavalry, Lauriston would have been able to sweep away rapidly the weak forces of Barclay, instead of hesitating before them as he did. Moreover, Puthod's division should have been hurried up, as well as Reynier, and sent straight on to Lauriston, to whose corps it belonged. Instead of that, Puthod was kept at Gleina, and Lauriston was called in from the left. The latter measure was entirely opposed to the Emperor's order, " Cause Lauriston to march on your left, so as to be in a position to turn the enemy if our movement decides him to abandon his position." Ney entirely failed to appreciate his task, but for that Napoleon must bear a good deal of the blame. He might, as Colonel Lanrezac says, have easily arranged a meeting with Ney in the night of the 20th-21st, at which he could have explained the marshal's task beyond all possibility of doubt. We would venture to suggest that, possibly, the Emperor might have been better placed had he himself been with Ney's army, leaving Marmont or Soult in charge of the frontal attack. The great objection to that would probably have been that his presence in the north would have come to the knowledge of the allied commanders, and would have called their attention to the real point of danger. As it was, they (or rather the Tsar) persistently played into Napoleon's hands by strengthening their own left against Oudinot, and withdrawing their already weak reserves from the centre. Bautzen, comparative failure though it was, was perhaps the battle for which Napoleon prepared his plans, almost in detail, longer before its occurrence than any other. He was able to do so from the certainty which he had acquired some days before, that the allies were determined to fight a defensive battle on a carefully prepared and fortified position.

St Cyr's account of his interview with Napoleon, early in May at Dresden, is remarkable as an exposition of the Emperor's general views. After relating how Napoleon complained of the want of promise among his marshals, and then expounded his plan of attack at Bautzen, St Cyr continues: "The means on which Napoleon seemed to me to count most was the disposition he had made for turning the enemy's army by its right in its position at Bautzen. I observed to him that he seemed to me to be departing from his ordinary practice, inasmuch as I believed that he preferred attacks on the centre to those on the wings, whilst the latter seemed to have always been preferred by Frederick; that the first, whilst offering greater obstacles to be surmounted in the beginning, offered in the end, when they succeeded entirely, greater results, since it was almost impossible for an enemy, beaten and pierced in his centre, to avoid a complete rout and to effect a passable retreat. I added that this form of attack had always appeared to me most in accord with the nature of his genius, and the wish he had to be, on the day of battle, the sole spring of this great machine; that it lent itself better than any other to the union in his hands of all his resources. He replied, that he gave no preference to the attack on the centre over

THE BATTLE OF BAUTZEN 141

that on the wings; that his principle was to attack the enemy with the greatest force possible; that the nearest corps being once engaged, he left them to act, without troubling himself much about their good or bad chances; that he only took great care not to yield too easily to demands for succour from their chiefs. He cited as an example Lützen, where, he said, Ney had demanded immediate reinforcements, though he had still two divisions not engaged; he assured me that, in the same affair, another marshal [1] had also demanded them before having any enemy in front of him. He added that it was only towards the end of the day, when he perceived that the enemy was worn out, and had employed the greater part of his resources, that he united what he had been able to keep in reserve, in order to be able to launch on the field of battle a strong mass of infantry, cavalry, and artillery; that, the enemy not having foreseen this, he made what he called an "évènement," and by this means he had almost always obtained a victory." [2]

This very remarkable passage, if we may assume that it was not an unconscious afterthought of St Cyr, is a very clear profession of the Emperor's tactical faith.

At Lützen the "évènement" only partially came off, when Napoleon launched the Guard, supported by Drouot's great battery, on the quadrilateral of the four villages. At Bautzen, it never came off at all; for, owing to the failure of Ney's movement, the enemy was already in retreat, and the Guard did little or nothing. What he thought of the results of Bautzen is shown by Napoleon's remark, as he rode over the battlefield, "What! after such a slaughter, no trophies? These people will leave me no claws!" The words are curiously like those of Ney after Eylau.

[1] Marmont.   [2] *Hist. Mil.*, iv. pp. 40-41.

CHAPTER X

FROM BAUTZEN TO THE ARMISTICE [1]

IN the very early hours of the 22nd May the Russo-Prussian army resumed its retreat, both columns converging on Reichenbach. Thence to Görlitz there is a long defile, which they successfully negotiated, under the protection of their rearguards.

At 3 A.M. firing commenced at the outposts, which were in close contact all along the line. At 7 A.M. the French VII. corps (Reynier) set out for Reichenbach, with the 1st cavalry corps (Latour-Maubourg). On its left was the V. corps (Lauriston), in rear of it the Guard and the VI. corps (Marmont). The XI., followed by the IV., marched by Löbau; the III. took post at Weissenberg, and the XII. (Oudinot), which had suffered heavily in the battle, was left to rest at Bautzen, and to collect its detachments, including Lorencez's brigade from the right rear.

By 10 A.M. the Emperor, with the VII. corps, arrived before Reichenbach, and found Eugen of Würtemberg, with 6000 or 7000 men, standing on the heights to the east of the town to cover the retreat on Görlitz.

Reynier deployed for the frontal attack, whilst Lauriston manœuvred to outflank the enemy's right. The French were very cautious, and presently Napoleon, to expedite matters, ordered the Guard cavalry to cross the brook on which Reichenbach stands above the town, so as to threaten the enemy's line of retreat. As they got across and began to mount the heights, they were fired on by two batteries of horse artillery, and then charged by Russian cavalry. Latour-Maubourg joined in the fight, which was indecisive,

[1] Map I.

but, by 3 P.M., Eugen found his right seriously threatened by Lauriston. Having succeeded in his task of gaining time for the main body, he fell back on his reserves at Markersdorf on the way to Görlitz. It took the French an hour to rearrange their advance, and then, when they arrived before Markersdorf, Eugen retired again on a position short of Görlitz.

Reynier's men being very fatigued by the long marches they had made in the last few days, their commander requested permission to halt. Napoleon's reply was a peremptory order to move on Görlitz

Whilst the VII. corps was coming to the attack, a round shot passed close to the Emperor. It killed on the spot Kirgener, the general of engineers, who had conducted the siege operations at Danzig in 1807, and then mortally wounded the Grand Marshal Duroc, who died twelve hours later. There was, perhaps, none of his subordinates, except Lannes, who lost his life four years before at Essling, whom Napoleon regarded with such personal affection as Duroc. As in the case of Lannes, he was genuinely affected by this loss, though one cannot but feel that he would have shown better taste had he not inserted in his bulletin of the 22nd May a full, and perhaps doubtful, account of his last interview with the dying man. It was a good opportunity for a "coup de théâtre," and that Napoleon could never resist. Yet he must have been feeling that death was now beginning to take heavy toll amongst his old friends and servants, who, so far, had escaped with wonderfully little loss. Three weeks earlier he had lost Bessières, and on this fatal day of Reichenbach he lost Bruyère, Kirgener, and Duroc. Mortier, who was talking to the last two when they were struck, had a very narrow escape. Perhaps the most remarkable evidence of Napoleon's feeling in the matter is the fact that he ordered the combat then proceeding to be broken off.

That night the V., VI., and VII. corps and the Guard were about Markersdorf,[1] whilst the IV. and the XI. were a little south of Reichenbach; III. corps at Weissenberg;

[1] Four miles east of Reichenbach.

Victor, with the II. and Sebastiani's cavalry, behind at Baruth. Thanks to the Emperor's personal presence with his leading corps, he had got from them fourteen hours of marching and fighting, over a distance of $17\frac{1}{2}$ miles. The cavalry fighting had mainly devolved on the Guard, who lost 300 men, whilst Latour-Maubourg, nearly double their strength, lost only about 100. The VII. corps lost about 400.

At Görlitz the allies had again divided into two columns, one marching on Bunzlau, whilst the other took the southern road towards Lauban and Löwenberg. During the 23rd May there was again some fighting between Lauriston's advanced guard and the rearguard of the allies on the road to Bunzlau. In the night of the 23rd-24th the positions were as follows:—

French—
V. corps, Hochkirch, on the road to Waldau.
VII. corps, Troitschendorf.
VI. corps, Hermsdorf.
Headquarters and Guard, Görlitz.
XI. corps on the road to Schönberg, with an advanced guard in that place.
IV. corps, south of Troitschendorf.
III. corps, Weissenberg.
II. corps, Krobnitz.

The columns of the allies were respectively at Waldau and Lauban.

On the 24th and 25th of May there were frequent rearguard actions, serving to delay the French pursuit, which was further kept back by bad roads and difficulties in crossing rivers, especially the Neisse and the Quiess. Consequently, Napoleon's programme for each day was not worked up to, and on the evening of the 25th the positions reached were as follows:—

V. corps and 1st cavalry corps, between Wolfshain, Thomaswalde, and Martinswalde.
VII. corps, Neu-Jaschwitz.
VI., Alt-Jaschwitz and Ottendorf.

FROM BAUTZEN TO THE ARMISTICE

The XI. and IV. corps, the former at Stekicht, the latter towards Wenig Rächnitz.

Guard and III. corps approaching Bunzlau.

The II. corps, at last coming up, was on the left at Thommendorf, after a march of 20 miles.

The corps which had the greatest difficulty on this day was the XI., which came upon the Russian rearguard, and was engaged with it from 10 A.M. till 10 P.M. So vigorous was the resistance of the 10,000 Russians that Macdonald was induced to believe he had been engaged with forces triple his own. The IV. corps, following the XI., had turned to the left at Seifersdorf to make a link with the left column. When the sound of Macdonald's action reached Bertrand, he again turned towards the right to give assistance, but arrived too late according to Macdonald, though Bertrand says that it was the appearance of his advanced guard on their right which at last induced the Russians to give way.

In the allies' camp there was again a serious divergence of views. Wittgenstein's position had become impossible, with Alexander passing orders and taking counsel over his head, and he tendered his resignation, which was accepted, and Barclay appointed in his place, he being a commander acceptable at Prussian headquarters. But Barclay's views were practically identical with Wittgenstein's. He saw that the allied army was melting away, being now reduced to 80,000 men, very much demoralised by defeat and retreat. He, therefore, wished to fall back on Poland to completely reorganise the Russian army. This did not at all suit the views of the Prussian leaders, such as Blücher and Gneisenau, who were all for fighting again, and who viewed with dismay the prospect of a complete evacuation of their own territory, and the consequent stoppage, in great part, of their recruitment of fresh levies. At this juncture, Alexander again intervened with a compromise, which, to some extent, satisfied the Prussians, who had many complaints against their allies, for having, as they alleged, failed in assisting them in the matter of supplies. It was arranged that the retreat, instead of continuing due eastwards, should be diverted towards the south-east on Schweidnitz. This would mean still holding on to Silesia, and, at the same time, keeping in touch with Austria, whose intervention was urgently desired. Yet Schweidnitz was a dangerous point on which to retreat, since it gave Napoleon an opportunity of again outflanking the allies on the right, of cutting their line of retreat on Warsaw, and of forcing them against the Austrian frontier. Austria was not ready yet, and it was very problematical what she would have done at that time had the Russians and Prussians been forced over her boundary. A lateral retreat like this necessarily implied the resumption, sooner or later, of the offensive by the allies, and they were hardly in a state for that at present.

On the 26th May there was friction between Ney and Marmont, an evil symptom, seeing that, however much they might squabble amongst' themselves when the master was not present, the French marshals generally kept their personal disagreements in the background when Napoleon was at hand. Marmont resented being placed under Ney's orders, and was anxious to get away from him. Accordingly, he persuaded himself that the enemy had only a rearguard on the Bunzlau-Liegnitz road, and that the bulk of his forces was retreating on Löwenberg and Goldberg. He had been ordered by Ney to march on Ottendorf, and he now, under the circumstances represented by him, demanded permission to move instead on Löwenberg. This Ney refused, and Marmont continued on Ottendorf on the 25th. But Napoleon had been much struck by Marmont's reiterated asseverations that the greater part of the enemy was towards Löwenberg, and that nothing but Prussians had passed through Bunzlau. At 6 A.M. on the 26th he issued orders to the following effect—

(1) Ney, with the V. and VII. corps, to move on Hainau, with one advanced guard on Liegnitz and another towards Glogau.

(2) Marmont, with his own corps and Latour-Maubourg, to manœuvre in communication with Macdonald and

FROM BAUTZEN TO THE ARMISTICE 147

Bertrand, to turn the right flank of the enemy on the southern road.

(3) III. corps to take post 2½ miles in front of Bunzlau under orders of Ney.

(4) As there was a report that part of the enemy had disappeared northwards, Victor, with the II. corps, was to reconnoitre towards Sprottau, and to follow anything that might be making for Berlin. Victor during the day discovered that this report was false.

It was 3 P.M. when Maison's division, at the head of the V. corps, passed through Hainau. It was now only 4000 strong. Maison marched to the heights east of Michelsdorf, a couple of miles out of Hainau, on the road to Liegnitz. He was in a gently rolling country, quite open, and well suited for cavalry action. An enemy standing behind any of the ridges was invisible except from the ridge itself, and might lie hidden within a very short distance of his opponent, if that opponent did not send cavalry on to the heights to reconnoitre. Maison was marching about as carelessly as Peyri had done on the 19th, though his skirmishers had been all day bickering with those of the enemy. For the protection of his flanks he had nothing but some 50 troopers, and they performed their duty so perfunctorily that they did not even take the trouble of riding on to the nearest heights to see what was in the next valley. Chastel's cavalry division, which should have been with Maison, had stopped short of Hainau, under the impression that their day's march was over. Just as Maison halted beyond Michelsdorf, a mill on his right flank burst into flames. The fire was a signal arranged by the Prussian general Ziethen. Immediately afterwards a Prussian horse artillery battery appeared on the heights, only 400 yards from Maison's position, and opened fire on his division. At the same moment, a mass of 3000 cavalry surging up from the valley beyond, galloped down the hill against the right flank of the French infantry, who had already began to prepare to bivouac.

Before they could assume a formation for defence, the Prussian horsemen were in their midst, sabring and riding over the almost defenceless infantry, who fled in the wildest disorder to the village of Michelsdorf. There they fortunately found two battalions of another division, who were able to check the pursuit and drive off the Prussian cavalry. The arrival, at the double, of Puthod's division, finally put an end to the danger. The attack had lasted only a few minutes, but in that short time Maison lost over 1000 men in killed, wounded, and prisoners, and five guns. It was fortunate for him that the Prussian charge fell upon him when he was still close to the village. Had he got farther from shelter, probably his division would have been cut up. Ziethen had intended to let him do so, but had given the signal for attack sooner than arranged, because, being informed of the approach of Reynier, he thought, if he waited, he might be too late. In this charge Dolffs, the leader of Blücher's reserve cavalry, was killed.

Farther to the French right, Marmont, Bertrand, and Macdonald had all been delayed by various causes, and, when at last they came upon the Russian rearguard a little east of Pilgramsdorf, night was already falling, and an attack was no longer feasible. On this day the allies' main body had crossed the Katzbach and stood with its right at Liegnitz, left at Goldberg.

On the 27th May Lauriston got to Gross Rechern, east of Liegnitz, with Reynier on his right, watching towards Jauer. Headquarters and the Guard were in Liegnitz, the III. corps at Hainau, with Marchand's division at Bunzlau.

On the French right, Marmont marched on Kröitzsch to cut the road between Goldberg and Liegnitz, whilst the IV. and XI. corps continued towards Goldberg. Between Pilgramsdorf and Goldberg Macdonald found a strong Russian rearguard. He sent against the enemy's cavalry the division of Latour-Maubourg's cavalry which he had with him, but the French cavalry behaved badly, and had the worst of the fight.[1] When the French infantry attacked

---

[1] Macdonald reported that "the cuirassiers did their duty, but the other regiments did not support them." (Foucart, ii. p. 148.) Macdonald himself headed the last charge, and was abandoned by his men.

FROM BAUTZEN TO THE ARMISTICE 149

the enemy retired, and Macdonald, passing through Goldberg, took post between the Liegnitz and Jauer roads, on Marmont's right. Bertrand, following Macdonald, had found Marmont crossing his front and stopped at Giersdorf.

Victor had occupied Sprottau and cut off a Russian artillery convoy.

On the 27th the allies began their movement on Schweidnitz. Their right reached Mertschütz, with a rearguard at Kloster-Wahlstadt; the left marched from Goldberg to Jauer, rearguard at Hermannsdorf. On the 28th the French left stood fast. On the right, Marmont, crossing the Katzbach, drove back a detachment of the enemy, the strength of which Marmont probably overstates at "several thousands."

Macdonald reached Jauer, Bertrand Hermannsdorf.

Victor, far on the left at Sprottau, marched to Primkenau, where he was in communication with Glogau, the blockade of which had been raised by the enemy.

The allies on this day reached Striegau.

On the 29th May, the III. corps moved up to Liegnitz, leaving Marchand at Hainau; the V. and VII. corps, followed by the Guard, moved towards Neumarkt. But the Emperor stopped the VII. at Kloster-Wahlstadt, at which Ney took offence, as he had ordered Reynier to keep in line with Lauriston, and the counter order was, perhaps owing to Berthier's carelessness, not at once communicated to him. He asked to be replaced in the command of the advanced guard, pleading his wounds as an excuse. Like the rest of the marshals, he was showing signs of weariness of the war. There was a good deal of trouble in pacifying him.

On this day the allies reached Schweidnitz, which they found not a fit place to stop at, as the fortifications, demolished in 1807, had not been restored.

On the 30th May, Reynier came abreast of Lauriston, who remained stationary. Guard and headquarters Neumarkt. The VI. corps and Latour-Maubourg moved to Eisendorf and Ober Moys. The IV. and XI., though ordered to Striegau, only moved a short way out of Jauer, as Macdonald heard that the main body of the allies was retiring on Schweidnitz.

Victor advanced to Randten.

On the 31st May, Lauriston got to within three miles of Breslau, driving before him Schuler's detachment, of 5000 or 6000 men, which, falling back from before Glogau, endeavoured to cover Breslau.

The VII. corps took post at Arnoldsmühl, the III. closed on Neumarkt, where headquarters and the Guard remained. The VI. did not move from Eisendorf. The IV. and IX. were ordered to occupy Striegau, but both commanders, exaggerating their difficulties and the strength of the rear-guard opposed to them, ended by not getting forward at all.

Marmont, too, raised a very unnecessary cry about the danger of his position, for which he was severely snubbed by the Emperor. Evidently most of the corps commanders were suffering from severe attacks of nerves.

On the 1st June, Napoleon, now aware that the enemy was retreating on Schweidnitz, arranged his army thus.[1] Headquarters and Guard, Neumarkt.

V. corps, main body Kryptau and Mochbern, facing south; a detachment in Breslau, and a division at Purschwitz. Chastel's cavalry at Hartlieb.

VII. corps, Purschwitz.

III. corps, south of Neumarkt, with Marchand at Liegnitz.

VI. corps and two divisions of cavalry at Eisendorf and Moys.

IV. and XI. corps about Jauer.

Victor was ordered to prepare to march back on Sagan, en route to support Oudinot at Hoyerswerda in a movement on Berlin, of which more anon.

From the 2nd to the 4th June, when the armistice was finally arranged, the French made no movement of importance. But it was otherwise with the allies, for Barclay, on the 2nd June, when a suspension of hostilities began, pointed out that, should Napoleon close to his left on

Positions marked on Map I.

FROM BAUTZEN TO THE ARMISTICE

Breslau, the allies would be in great danger of being cut from the Oder. In consequence, it was decided to move more to the east, so as to be within reach of the Oder between Ohlau and Brieg. The river was to be bridged.

On the two succeeding days the Russo-Prussian army moved to the line Strehlen-Nimptsch. On its right was Schuler's detachment and the head of Sacken's corps, now arriving from Poland.

To Blücher and Yorck this seemed symptomatic of a return to the former Russian idea of a retreat on Poland, and they wrote to the King of Prussia proposing that, if the Russians crossed the Oder, the Prussians should leave them, and retire along the Bohemian mountains, whilst the Silesian landwehr assembled about Neisse and Glatz.

Before describing and discussing the armistice, it is necessary briefly to mention what had been taking place in Napoleon's rear since Bautzen.

Oudinot had been left behind after the battle, with instructions to gather in Beaumont from Moritzburg, and his own detachments, including Lorencez's 2nd brigade. He was then to march on Berlin. He was only able to reach Hoyerswerda on the 27th May.

Bülow, meanwhile, had collected some 30,000 men, of whom a large proportion were landwehr, at present of very little fighting value, and had marched towards Luckau as soon as he felt the relaxation of pressure due to Napoleon's concentration on Bautzen.

On the 28th May, he attacked Hoyerswerda, where he expected to find only a weak detachment, instead of the whole XII. corps and Beaumont's detachment. He was badly repulsed. Then, hearing that Victor was moving on Sagan, he proceeded to disperse his troops along a front of over sixty miles, in an attempt to cover Krossen and Berlin at the same time. Had Oudinot marched promptly on Luckau, the Prussian rallying point, he might have destroyed Bülow's separated forces in detail. But he delayed until Bülow, realising his danger, had concentrated by forced marches. When Oudinot appeared at Luckau on the 6th

June, Bülow had practically his whole force there in a strong position. Now, when it was too late, Oudinot rashly attacked. In the action which followed he was badly beaten, and, after losing 2000 men, had to retreat with the rest on Uebigau. Bülow's men were too tired to pursue at once, and, when the Prussians began to move on the 9th, his operations were stopped by news of the armistice. On the lower Elbe, Davout had been joined by Vandamme, and also had 8000 Danes placed at his disposal, owing to the decision of their king to throw in his lot with Napoleon. Walmoden, commanding on behalf of the allies at Hamburg, finding himself unsupported by Bernadotte's Swedes from Mecklenburg, evacuated the place, which was occupied by Davout on the 30th May. Lübeck fell into the hands of the French on the 1st June, so that they occupied the whole of the 32nd military division before operations were stopped by news of the armistice.

On the French lines of communications farther south, there were constant raids of Cossacks and other bodies of "free" troops, which did a great deal of damage, and kept up a constant feeling of alarm and confusion. Czernitchew's Cossacks, on the 25th May, destroyed a cavalry "regiment de marche"; on the 30th, they captured a convoy of artillery escorted by 1600 Westphalian troops, and forced four battalions, marching up to the rescue from Brunswick, back on that place. But the most serious affair was an attack upon Leipzig itself, which was full of sick and wounded, besides parks, and a "division de marche" of cavalry, under Arrighi. The latter were absolutely untrained as yet, and useless for fighting. Woronzow, the Russian general observing Magdeburg, resolved on an attempt to surprise Leipzig. Leaving before Magdeburg only 1000 cavalry and 7000 Prussian landwehr, he crossed the Elbe near Dessau with some 5000 infantry and cavalry, in the night of the 5th-6th June, to meet Czernitchew from the Bernburg direction with another 1200 cavalry before Leipzig. He marched hard, following Napoleon's example in carrying his infantry in wagons or

FROM BAUTZEN TO THE ARMISTICE 153

other conveyances. At dawn on the 7th June, he reached Leipzig and made short work of the helpless French cavalry recruits. He was actually entering the town, when he was stopped by notification of the armistice.

Any full account of the political negotiations after the return of Napoleon from Russia is beyond the scope of this military history of the campaign, but a general outline of them, as affecting its course, is necessary.

Napoleon, as soon as he was back in Paris, endeavoured to get into direct communication with the Tsar, with a view to the conclusion of an arrangement with him in which Prussia and Austria should play no part independent of himself. Though Napoleon did not succeed in this, negotiations were constantly more or less on the "tapis." When the French army reached Dresden, Austria had sent two emissaries to the contending parties, Count Stadion to the allies, Count Bubna to Napoleon.

Stadion's instructions from Metternich represented as the aim of Austria's armed neutrality the attainment of a durable peace, with a curtailment of French influence and possessions east of the Rhine. The curtailment proposed was very considerable. Poland was to be restored to its position before the last peace of Vienna, Prussia was to receive back all her old possessions, France to renounce all claims in Germany east of the Rhine, Holland to be independent, the states of the Church to be restored, and all French garrisons to be withdrawn from Italy. Austria was to be reinstated in all that she possessed in Italy previous to the Peace of Lunéville. Tyrol, the Illyrian and Dalmatian provinces also to be returned to her. France was to renounce all claim to suzerainty in Germany, or to special influence in the kingdom of Italy.

That was the maximum, to which it was hopeless to expect Napoleon to agree. As a minimum, Austria proposed to exact the following concessions: surrender of Dalmatia and Illyria, dissolution of the Grand Duchy of Warsaw, a new boundary between Austria and Bavaria, return of South Prussia to Prussia, abandonment by Napoleon of his possessions on the right bank of the Rhine, and dissolution of the Rhenish Confederation. There was not much probability of the Emperor's accepting even these terms, except under compulsion.

Stadion also brought a memorandum showing when Austria would be in a position to join the allies in the field, in the event of Napoleon's refusing these terms.

The upshot of the negotiations was the "Programme of Wurschen," in which the allies laid down as their aim—

(1) Restoration of Austria to her position previous to 1805.

(2) Restoration to Prussia of her possessions previous to 1806.

(3) Dissolution of the Rhenish Confederation.

(4) Independence of Germany.

(5) Dissolution of the Grand Duchy of Warsaw.

(6) Independence of Holland.

(7) Restoration of the ancient dynasty in Spain.

(8) Entire freedom of Italy from French influence.

This was even more than the Austrian maximum, and Stadion said plainly his country would certainly not fight for all this.

Meanwhile Bubna, who had only left Vienna after receipt of the news of Lützen and the retreat of the allies, was singing a considerably softer tune at Dresden. Nothing was said of the Austrian maximum. The points pressed were the dissolution of the Grand Duchy of Warsaw, the return to Austria of Illyria and Dalmatia, and the surrender of the French possessions beyond the Rhine. The readjustment of the Austro-Bavarian frontier, the abandonment of the Protectorate of the Rhenish Confederation, were only lightly touched upon as desirable, and the independence of French influence of Central Europe was only suggested as conducive to permanent peace. Napoleon, however, knew a good deal more about Austria's real aims from his ambassador at Vienna, and from the King of Saxony.

The interviews between Bubna and the Emperor were somewhat stormy, and the latter eventually discovered that, if he was to negotiate for peace, or even for an armistice, he was expected to retire behind the Elbe, and to comply with other conditions which, under the circumstances of the moment, he was certainly not willing to accept.

The next step taken was on the 17th May, when the battle of Bautzen was clearly imminent. Napoleon despatched Caulaincourt to endeavour again to negotiate separately with Alexander. His instructions of that date [1] directed him to endeavour to get into personal communication with Alexander, who had known and liked the Duke of Vicenza when he was ambassador at Petersburg. He was to represent to the Tsar that it would be to his advantage to negotiate directly with Napoleon, rather than to allow Austria the credit of acting as mediator. The French Emperor was to be represented as desirous of avoiding the impending bloodshed, whilst Austria was to be held up as having treated Russia scurvily, and as acting from selfish motives. Every effort was to be used to flatter Alexander, and induce him to look upon himself as the destined arbiter of Europe.

These are secret instructions. The open instructions, of course, do not allude to all this, but state that Napoleon is prepared to agree to the assembly of a Congress at Prague, or some other neutral place, for the settlement of terms of peace. Napoleon said that he was willing to conclude an armistice with the allied armies, in order to allow time for peace negotiations, and to avoid bloodshed.

Another letter, probably ante-dated, was sent to the Emperor of Austria, expressing Napoleon's readiness to agree to a Congress. Nothing came of this before the battle of Bautzen, for Caulaincourt was politely refused permission to pass the allied outposts.

The day after the battle found the allies ready to open negotiations, though they did so through Stadion and not direct. From this time the negotiations proceeded regularly though slowly. The most remarkable point in the correspondence is Napoleon's eagerness to conclude an armistice,

[1] Foucart, ii. p. 135.

156 NAPOLEON'S LAST CAMPAIGN IN GERMANY

which has been characterised by Jomini, and by the majority of later writers, as the greatest mistake he ever committed in his whole career as a general-in-chief.

In the end, he accepted terms differing materially from those he wanted. He wished the armistice to extend over the whole period of peace negotiations. If that could not be obtained, he must have it for at least three months, plus fifteen days' notice before hostilities recommenced. He told Caulaincourt that anything less than two and a half months would be too short to enable him to reorganise his cavalry. He wanted Breslau to be included within the French line of demarcation, and there were other points on which he laid stress. In the end, he accepted an armistice of about seven weeks [1] with only six days' notice, and with Breslau placed in the neutral strip, in which neither side was to keep troops. The French line in Silesia was, roughly, that of the Katzbach to its infall into the Oder; the allies' line was that of the Striegau Wasser. The French were limited, on the north, by the northern frontier of Saxony, from the Oder to Wittenberg on the Elbe. From Wittenberg downwards they were confined to the left bank of the Elbe, except that they were to hold the islands in the river, and so much of the 32nd military division as might be actually in their possession at midnight on the 8th June. Danzig, Mödlin, Zamosc, Stettin, and Küstrin were to be regularly supplied with provisions every five days by the besiegers, and, if Hamburg was still only besieged by the French, the same provision was to hold good.[2]

We must now consider Jomini's dictum as to the inexpediency, from his own point of view, of Napoleon's conclusion of the armistice of Poischwitz.[3]

In the first place, it must be noted that the idea of an armistice was no sudden conclusion on the Emperor's part,

---

[1] Afterwards extended to 10th August.

[2] As a matter of fact Davout had possession of Hamburg, Lübeck, and the whole 32nd military division well before the 8th June.

[3] This armistice is dated "Pleiswitz" (Foucart, ii. p. 355). Lanrezac, and many others, call it the "armistice of Poischwitz," and Lanrezac adds the alternative name of "Neumarkt."

FROM BAUTZEN TO THE ARMISTICE 157

arrived at in consequence of his failure at Bautzen, and in his subsequent endeavours to bring the allies to a general action. He had already expressed his desire for it in his instructions to Caulaincourt of the 18th May, two days before the battle.

His reasons for wishing it he subsequently stated as (1) the necessity for time to organise his cavalry, and (2) the danger impending from a declaration of war by Austria, situated as she was on the flank of any further forward movement.

Many critics have treated with disdain the story of the influence of the cavalry idea. But, in the instructions to Caulaincourt, issued through the Minister for Foreign Affairs on the 29th May,[1] it is quite clearly stated that Napoleon wishes time to re-establish his cavalry. That letter was secret, containing an outline of instructions and addressed to the Foreign Minister; it clearly expresses the Emperor's real thoughts, and it indicates that the story of the influence of this consideration was not an invention of St Helena days. With this before us, it is impossible to argue that Napoleon was not influenced by the question of cavalry. Whether the Napoleon of earlier days would have allowed himself to be dominated by such a consideration, or by fear of Austria, is quite a different matter, which we will consider presently.

What was his position before the suspension of arms on the 2nd June? Up to that time he could perfectly well have broken off the negotiations on several grounds.

On the 1st June he stood[2] on the line Jauer-Breslau, facing south, with the V., VII., VI., III. corps. The Guard and 1st cavalry corps were on the shorter line, Ober Mois-Breslau, whilst the allies were concentrated near Schweidnitz, with only a rearguard at Striegau. Napoleon could, as Lanrezac points out, have easily placed the whole of his army, including Victor's corps and Marchand's division, in thirty-six hours, between the Weistritz and the Neisse, barring the allies from the Oder between Ohlau and Brieg,

[1] Foucart, ii. p. 174.   [2] See positions marked on general Map I.

by which section they afterwards proposed to establish their communications. He would have been there before they began to move on the 3rd. Schuler's detachment was too weak to interfere seriously with this movement. The allies must, then, either have fought with their backs to the mountains, or have hurried south-eastwards to take up a position the communications of which with Poland would still have been seriously threatened. If they fought, they would do so with an army which had already suffered two defeats and had been necessarily demoralised by a long retreat. They could hardly have hoped for victory against the French, who, if they too were demoralised, were not so much so as the allies. Defeat entailed their being driven on to the mountains and the Austrian frontier, and, it must be repeated, the Austrian army was not ready in Bohemia, and would not be so for another month. The chances were all in favour of Austria not daring to espouse the cause of the allies after a third defeat, even if it had only been another Bautzen. On the other hand, a retreat behind the Neisse would have accentuated the differences of opinion between the Prussian and the Russian leaders, and, in all probability, would have induced the former to separate from their allies, leaving them to fall back towards Poland alone. That must almost certainly have led to the destruction of the Prussians, for once the Russians had started for Poland they could have been easily contained, and prevented from returning westwards, by part of the French army, whilst the rest of it dealt with the Prussians with at least double their numbers. Besides, the Russians would probably have been disgusted at what they would have deemed the desertion of the Prussians, and would have abandoned the idea of a return to help them. There probably still survived amongst the Russians some of the ideas of Kutusow, which were opposed to fighting other people's battles in Central Europe, now that the invader had been expelled from Russia.

On the 4th June, when the allies had moved to the line Strehlen-Nimptsch, Napoleon's chance was gone, and the armistice was concluded.

Of course there was always the difficulty about want of cavalry against Napoleon's moving to his left, but he had advanced so far notwithstanding it, and it would seem that it was worth his while to try one more throw for decisive victory.

In a recent English work it is argued that where Napoleon felt the pinch of his inferior cavalry was, not so much in reconnoitring, as on the battlefield itself; that, owing to it, his men were compelled to advance on the battlefield in formations constantly ready to repel cavalry, and that they were therefore hampered and delayed in their movements. But that argument would have applied equally at Bautzen. On the other hand, the French superiority in infantry was so great that Napoleon could hope for decisive victory even with the weak cavalry he had.

The acceptance of the weak cavalry theory has been attributed mainly to German criticisms, based on the want of cavalry for reconnoitring and screening purposes. Yet the French critic, Colonel Lanrezac, does not see it in this light, and concurs in the verdict of Jomini as to the mistake of the armistice. He, like Yorck von Wartenburg, sees in it a falling off on the part of Napoleon from his former standards. He will not have it that either the want of cavalry, or the threat of Austrian intervention, justified the armistice from Napoleon's point of view. He had advanced in 1805 with Prussia threatening him in flank, and in 1806-1807, with Austria in a similar position.

CHAPTER XI

DURING THE ARMISTICE. PREPARATIONS AND PLANS OF CAMPAIGN

THERE is not the slightest reason for supposing that either Napoleon or his opponents had any expectation that the Congress of Prague would lead to peace between parties whose views of its terms differed so very widely. Each side, as well as Austria, utilised the period of the armistice to the fullest extent for recruiting and increasing its forces for the new campaign, which all saw to be inevitable.

Napoleon, after arranging for the cantonments to be occupied by his troops during the suspension of hostilities, left Neumarkt on the 4th June. After stopping to inspect his troops and attend to affairs generally at Liegnitz, Hainau, Bunzlau, Görlitz, and Bautzen, he arrived at Dresden on the 10th June. His headquarters, when he was in the Saxon capital, were in the Marcolini Palace,[1] but he spent by no means the whole of the armistice in Dresden. From the 10th June to the 9th July he stayed there, working hard at arrangements for the coming campaign, and attending to the innumerable other affairs which could be dealt with by no one less phenomenally gifted with the power of hard work. Even in the midst of all this cabinet work, he was constantly riding or driving all over the neighbourhood of Dresden, till there was scarcely a yard of it which he did not know "comme sa poche."[2] Between the 9th July and the 15th August he was absent from Dresden on seventeen

---

[1] Now the Friederichstadt Municipal Hospital.

[2] Space will not allow of a description of Napoleon's daily life in Dresden. It is very fully and admirably described in Odeleben's account of the campaign, which has been translated into both French and English.

PREPARATIONS AND PLANS OF CAMPAIGN

days, including a week given to a visit to Mainz to meet Marie Louise, through whom he hoped to influence Austria. He also visited Wittenberg, Dessau, Magdeburg, Leipzig, Luckau, Lübben, Würtzburg, and Bamberg.

Napoleon began the settlement of his plans for the new campaign at once.

On one point the Emperor was decided from the very first. He had no intention whatever of retiring behind the Rhine, there to await the attack of united Europe. Nor would he even retire behind the Saale. He would utilise as his forward base, not the comparatively small stream of the Saale, but the line of the great river Elbe, one of which he held all the permanent passages from Bohemia to its mouth, and on which all these passages were covered by fortified bridge heads of more or less strength.

That he was right, from his point of view, not to retire behind the Rhine is now universally admitted. There was certainly no necessity for his doing so after the events of the spring campaign, in which he had inflicted two severe, though not decisive, defeats on the allies, and had pushed forward again right up to the Oder.

Supposing he decided on a defence of the Rhine, what would have been the consequences? He would at once have lost, for good and all, his control over the states of the Rhenish Confederation, which he well knew were seething with the spirit of revolt, only waiting their opportunity to throw off his yoke. In addition, he would lose Italy, Naples, and Holland. Peace on the basis of the Rhine frontier was not at all what he was prepared to accept, even if that would be granted, and even of this there was no certainty. If he had to fight behind the Rhine, he would find a large proportion of his forces absorbed by garrisons of the too numerous fortresses, and he would lose all the garrisons he had left behind in the fortresses of the Vistula and the Oder. The numbers required for garrisoning the French fortresses are estimated as high as 150,000, and he would be far better off in Central Germany with these 150,000 available in the field, than in France with them locked up. The Rhine may, therefore, be set aside at once.

As for the Saale, that was a comparatively small stream, easily passable in many places, and with no fortress-protected permanent passages.

Undoubtedly, therefore, he rightly decided for the Elbe.

His first cares, having decided on the Elbe as a base, were for the protection of its fortified passages, and for the collection of supplies of all sorts on it.

The great fortress of Magdeburg, in those days one of the strongest in Europe, required little or nothing in the way of strengthening of its means of defence. Torgau, and still more Wittenberg, required a good deal, and their strengthening as fortified places was taken in hand at once. Of Dresden we will speak presently. Above Dresden, the fort of Königstein, and the Lilienstein rock, stand opposite one another, like two grim sentinels commanding the Elbe, which flows, hundreds of feet below, between them. Königstein, as the guide who shows one round it is careful to explain, has "no military value" in the present day. It is a mere shell trap now, but in 1813 it was different; the army which held it and the Lilienstein could have just as many bridges between them as it could possibly want in perfect safety. Napoleon had two built, and one at Pirna, all with bridge heads. Between Königstein and Pirna lies the famous camp in which Frederick the Great blockaded, and eventually compelled the surrender of the Saxon army in 1756. The "camp" is a perfectly open, almost level plateau, extending like a great shelf from Königstein to Pirna. The palace of the Sonnenstein at Pirna, though hardly to be called a fortress even in Napoleon's day, was still useful as a support, and was, in September 1813, cleared of the lunatic asylum which occupied it, and used as a temporary fort. On this great shelf, protected towards the west by the valley of the Gottleuba brook, there was room for a large army, which would be right on the left flank of any advance from Bohemia by the left bank of the Elbe on Dresden. To connect Königstein with Bautzen

PREPARATIONS AND PLANS OF CAMPAIGN 163

via Stolpen the Emperor had a road constructed or improved. Dresden itself had been a fortress up to 1811, though never a really strong one, lying as it does in a hollow commanded by considerable heights on both banks of the river, and with the Dresden Forest, on the right bank, coming close down to the Neustadt.[1] By 1813 a great part of the fortifications, especially those of the Altstadt, had been demolished. Napoleon had already, in May, started work on the reconstruction of the Neustadt as a bridgehead on the right bank. As it became more and more evident that Austria might join the allies, he started fortifying the Altstadt as a bridgehead on the left bank to meet any attack on that side from Bohemia. The Neustadt, surrounded by new works and the patched-up remains of the old, was by the end of the armistice a formidable place, quite proof against a "coup de main." With the Altstadt it was different, for the defensive works were of much less strength, owing mainly to want of time. The old enceinte, of which the outline can still be traced by the alignment of the Ringstrasse and by a mound and pond near the Opera House, was as far as possible reconstructed and armed. Its field of fire was greatly hampered by the circle of suburbs ("schlags," as they were locally termed), which had grown round it to a distance of 600 or 700 yards. Still, guns on some of the old bastions could sweep the ground beyond these "schlags." The outer edge of the suburbs was put in a state of defence by the loopholing of houses and garden walls, the barricading of doors and windows, the deepening of ditches, and other temporary devices. In front of the main entrances "tambours" were constructed, whilst the smaller entrances to the town were blocked up. Streets were cleared so as to afford free passage for artillery within the suburbs, and the squares and open places were kept free for the posting of reserves.

About 200 or 300 yards beyond the outer line of the suburbs Napoleon had built five redoubts or lunettes, with

[1] The part of Dresden on the right bank of the Elbe. The more important part on the left bank is called the Altstadt.

a small "flêche" in addition close to the Elbe above Dresden. These works covered the space between the river above the town and the tributary Weisseritz below it.

To facilitate communication across the Elbe, the Emperor had made two boat or raft bridges, one above and one below the stone bridge, within the limits of the city.

The works were by no means complete in the end of August, as may be seen from a letter of the 25th August from Napoleon to Rogniat.[1] At that date the Altstadt was in a condition to resist a "coup de main" by forces approximately equal to the garrison, but perhaps not one by forces greatly superior. It certainly could not hold out for eight days against very superior strength, as Napoleon believed on the 13th August.[2] In addition to these greater fortifications, others were carried out at Meissen, and, in the form of blockhouses, redoubts, and batteries, at various points between Dresden and Magdeburg. It was found impossible, owing to the lie of the ground on the left bank and Napoleon's confinement to that bank by the terms of the armistice, to fortify a position opposite the mouth of Plauen canal, below Magdeburg, as was desired.

Hamburg, the only strong place on the lower Elbe, was in a different position from Dresden. Its possession was of great importance to Napoleon, for it cut off the allies from direct communication with England, and also served to keep Denmark to the alliance with him which she had made. But it was far removed from the main theatre of operations, and, unlike Dresden, could not look to the presence close at hand of a great army for its protection. All that Napoleon could spare to hold it were the 40,000 or 50,000 French and Danes whom he had placed under the command of Davout. Hamburg must depend for its defence on this unsupported force, and Davout himself must look to Hamburg as his place of refuge against the advance of superior forces in Northern Germany.

The Emperor would have wished it to be strong enough

[1] *Corr.* 20,465.   [2] *Corr.* 20,373.

PREPARATIONS AND PLANS OF CAMPAIGN 165

to hold out for at least two months against a regular siege, but there was neither time nor money available for its fortification on this scale. Yet Davout's energy and skill were such that he held firm till long after the fall of his master, and only surrendered under the orders of the new government of 1814. He has been much abused for his conduct at Hamburg, but Germans themselves, notably Count Yorck von Wartenburg and Sporschil, have not hesitated to say that what he did was necessary for the execution of his task, and that "There is certainly no military power in Europe but will wish for men like Davout to command besieged fortresses."[1] Davout may have been severe, unjust in particular instances, yet, looking to his position as a commander under Napoleon, he certainly did his duty splendidly, and merited the highest praise.

Having decided to use the line of the Elbe as his base, Napoleon set to work to provision and supply it in such manner that it should be really a base, not a mere line of defence. He wished to make himself, and he did make himself, independent temporarily of his communications with France. "What is important to me," he wrote, "is not to be cut from Dresden and the Elbe; I care little for being cut from France."[2]

The Emperor's most important arrangements for provisioning his army and his base are contained in his letter to Daru of the 17th June:[3]—

(1) From Erfurt 20,000 hundredweights of flour were to be forwarded to Dresden, 500 a day for 40 days.

(2) From Magdeburg to Dresden, by land and water, 40,000 hundredweights.

(3) In the markets of Saxony and Bohemia 20,000 hundredweights to be bought, and 10,000 in Bamberg and Baireuth.

These measures would collect 80,000 hundredweights of flour in Dresden by the 20th July.

(4) The neighbourhood of Dresden was to supply daily

---

[1] *Napoleon as a General*, ii. p. 267. [2] *Corr.* 20,398
[3] *Corr.* 20,142.

30,000 rations of bread, of which 18,000 would be for immediate consumption, and 12,000 would go into store.

(5) All military train battalions coming from Mayence or Wesel were to fill up their wagons with flour or rice.

(6) Ten days before hostilities recommenced, all caissons were to be sent from the army to Dresden to fill up with flour for the troops.

(7) By the end of the armistice, each corps was to have ready baked ten days' supply of biscuit, six days' "pain biscuité," and four days' bread.

(8) In Glogau was flour representing 1,000,000 rations, for the use of the garrison. Enough for 2,000,000 more rations for the army was to be bought.

(9) The flour sent from Magdeburg to Dresden was to be replaced by 50,000 hundredweights of corn from Hamburg, and 50,000 more collected in the 32nd Military Division. There were numerous mills for grinding it worked by the Elbe at Magdeburg.

(10) Brandy, wine, and rum to be sent from Hamburg to Magdeburg.

(11) In Erfurt 500,000 rations of biscuit, and 10,000 hundredweight of flour to be kept always in stock, to replace what was sent to the front.

(12) 6000 cattle to be requisitioned in the 32nd Military Division.

36,000 meat rations to be delivered daily by Saxony at Dresden.

4000 or 5000 cattle to be kept in reserve at Dresden.

Magdeburg and Erfurt to send their beef supplies to Dresden, replacing them by local purchases.

(13) The Emperor, considering rice to be a valuable preventive of dysentery, ordered an ounce to be supplied daily to every man. As he required 20,000 hundredweight to last till the 20th September, he had to procure 14,500, for which he relied chiefly on attachments of ships at Hamburg and Bremen. In addition to all this, the army was to live at first as much as possible on the country, husbanding the four days' rations which each man carried. It was hoped,

PREPARATIONS AND PLANS OF CAMPAIGN 167

by increasing the rice and decreasing the bread ration, to make it possible for the men to carry twelve days' food. On paper there appeared to be no possibility of a shortage of food ; but orders were certainly not executed to the full, and the French soldier in the autumn campaign often found himself marching and fighting on a very empty stomach. St Cyr relates how his conscripts, arriving at Freiberg, found the question of their food had been entirely forgotten.

Orders were issued for the organisation of an ambulance battalion with 600 wagons, and for hospitals at Dresden, Leipzig, Torgau, Wittenberg, and Magdeburg, capable of providing for 24,000 sick and wounded, and 11,000 convalescents. But the hospitals, in the end, were not half what was required, and their condition was often indescribably horrible.[1]

In addition to fortifying and provisioning his base, Napoleon carried out a most elaborate system of reconnaissance. The whole probable theatre of operations, within his own lines, was flooded with surveyors and map makers, for the existing published maps were wretched.[2] St Cyr was employed for a month, from the 5th July, in inspecting the fortifications at Königstein and the Lilienstein, and in making himself thoroughly acquainted with all the roads, passes, and military positions between Bohemia and Stolpen on the right bank of the Elbe, and from Dresden as far as

---

[1] The following ghastly description of a Dresden military hospital is taken from *Die französische Armee* in 1813, p. 160 :—

"The pestilential hospital smell became more suffocating as we advanced, making breathing difficult as we found ourselves in this great incurable ward. At broken windows, stopped up with rags or dirty straw, sat disfigured, wretched soldiers, buried alive in that horrible place. Still more terrible were the sights as we entered the hospital itself. On bundles of mouldering straw, mixed with filth and ordure, lay dead and dying side by side. From the confused mass attendants sought to separate the corpses, as one picks the rotten apples from a heap. The sick and wounded lay helpless all around in the pestilential atmosphere of that room, abandoned to their fate, without care or attention. Here and there a solitary surgeon was met, where a hundred would not have sufficed."

[2] Petri's was the one hitherto used. It was made in 1763, and was so unreliable that no modern tourist would condescend to use it for planning a walking tour.

Hof on the left. We have already mentioned Napoleon's daily drives and rides over part of this country.

The armistice, which had originally been for seven weeks, was subsequently extended to the 10th August, with six more days after denunciation before hostilities commenced. That would be on the 17th; but Blücher had already on the 15th began to move into the neutral zone near Breslau. Into the controversy regarding his conduct in this matter it is not necessary to enter. The armistice was duly denounced by the allies on the 10th August, and two days later Austria, in a lengthy document,[1] declared war against Napoleon.

Both sides had been busy during the armistice recruiting their forces. Napoleon by the time of its conclusion had collected in Germany very nearly the whole of his forces likely to be available for the present. The allies, on the other hand, though already considerably superior to him in numbers, were still awaiting the arrival of Bennigsen with 60,000 of the Russian reserve army, and Prussia was daily adding to her forces by the recruitment of fresh levies. We have already shown the strength of the opposing forces at the conclusion of the armistice.[2]

Napoleon had probably from the very beginning of the armistice begun elaborating his plans for the next campaign. He did not communicate them to any of his subordinates till the very eve of the opening of hostilities. He kept them back, no doubt, for two reasons; first, because he relied on himself alone for the elaboration of a great scheme; secondly, because up to the last he hoped to keep Austria, at the worst, neutral, though he felt that in settling his plans he must keep on the safe side by considering her as an enemy.

In describing, and later in criticising, his plan, it is necessary to keep before our eyes the facts as they appeared to him in the light of the somewhat meagre information which alone he could obtain, owing to the general hostility of

---

[1] Printed, with Napoleon's marginal comments in *Corr.* 20,376.
[2] *Cf. supra*, chaps. ii. and iii.

PREPARATIONS AND PLANS OF CAMPAIGN 169

Germany to him. It would be unreasonable to judge of them in the light of facts which Napoleon did not, and could not, know when he formulated his scheme. He believed that Austria could bring against him in Bohemia not more than 100,000 men, after allowing for the forces which she must keep to watch Wrede with the Bavarians, and Augereau on the Inn, and the army of Italy on the Isonzo.

The main army of the allies he assumed to be that in Silesia, which had retired before him in May and June. The Tsar and the King of Prussia he believed to be with it, as they actually were up to the first week in August. The strength of this army he estimated at less than 200,000 men, considerably less as it seems to us; for, on the 12th August, he wrote: "I am far from believing that the Prussians and Russians together can have 200,000, *counting those whom they have at Berlin aud in that direction*.[1]

At what strength he estimated the army of Bernadotte in the north, protecting Berlin and threatening Hamburg with Walmoden's detachment, it is difficult to say. It is not stated in his instructions either to Davout or Oudinot.[2] In any case, he clearly underestimated both its numbers and quality; for, with 120,000 men advancing concentrically on Berlin, he expected to occupy that capital within a week of the opening of the campaign, and to be able to push on to the relief of Stettin and Küstrin, driving the Swedes to return to their own country, and the Russians and Prussians across the Oder.

He estimated his own forces at about 420,000, exclusive of the garrisons of the Elbe fortresses, and of course of those of the Oder and the Vistula.

The actual strengths are thus stated by von Caemmerer[3]:—

[1] *Corr.* 20,360. On the other hand, he says (*Corr.* 20,365) that he is *equal* in force to the armies of Silesia and Bohemia, and (in *Corr.* 20,360) he computes his own "equal" force at 300,000, which would seem to show he allowed 200,000 for the army of Silesia alone.
[2] *Corr.* 20,353 and 20,365.
[3] *Die Befreiungskriege*, 1813-1815, p. 38.

	Allies.	Napoleon.
Field army,	512,000	450,000
Reserve army and besieging forces,	143,000	nil
Garrisons of fortresses,	112,000[1]	77,000[2]
	767,000	527,000

The Emperor's scheme is promulgated provisionally in two letters of the 12th August, addressed to Ney and Marmont,[3] and to Oudinot.[4] In the former he says the plan of operation will only be definitely fixed by the ensuing midnight.

The scheme is this: The main army was to be concentrated on the defensive between Görlitz and Bautzen, and in the entrenched camps at Dresden and Königstein. It would consist of the I., II., III., V., VI., XI., and XIV. corps, with the 1st, 2nd, 4th, and 5th cavalry corps, and the Guard; in all nearly 300,000 men. With these he would be in a position where he could not be cut from his supplies at Dresden or from the Elbe, and where he could wait to see what the Russians and Austrians were going to do, and profit by the turn of events. He would prefer to be at Liegnitz or Bunzlau, for there he would be in a position to prevent a flank march by the army of Silesia towards Berlin and the rear of Oudinot. But, as Liegnitz was eight, and Bunzlau six marches from Dresden, a position at either of them would risk his being cut from Dresden, whereas between Görlitz and Bautzen (four and two marches respectively from Dresden) he would be safe; if defeated he would be nearer the Elbe than the enemy, and able to take advantage of their mistakes. The Austrian headquarters were at Hirschberg, and Napoleon expected their advance through the mountains by Zittau.

The instructions to Oudinot will be dealt with in more detail when we come to his operations. Briefly they, and those to Davout,[5] required Oudinot, with the IV., VII., and

---

[1] Fortresses in Prussia and Bohemia.   [2] On the Elbe, Oder, and Vistula.
[3] *Corr.* 20,360.   [4] *Corr.* 20,365.   [5] *Corr.* 20,357.

PREPARATIONS AND PLANS OF CAMPAIGN 171

XII. corps, and the 3rd cavalry corps, to advance on Berlin, and thence on Stettin. He would have 70,000 to 75,000 men. Davout, with 40,000 (including 15,000 Danes), would simultaneously advance from Hamburg on Berlin, drawing on himself as many as possible of the enemy. Between Davout and Oudinot would be Dombrowski with 3000 or 4000 Poles, and Girard with 8000 or 9000 men. Altogether there would be about 120,000 men moving concentrically on Berlin.

Whilst his left was gaining Berlin, the Emperor would overwhelm the Silesian and Bohemian armies, or, if he were defeated, retire on Dresden.

Then, in marked contrast to anything he had done before, he invites criticism of his schemes by Ney and Marmont, and goes on to defend it. "I suppose all should finish with a great battle, and I think it is better to deliver it near Bautzen, two or three marches from Dresden, than at six or seven marches; my communications will be less exposed; I shall be able to subsist more easily, all the more so that during this time my left will occupy Berlin and sweep the lower Elbe, an operation which is not hazardous, since my troops, in any case, have Magdeburg and Wittenberg to retreat upon." He again hankers after Liegnitz, but rejects the idea as involving a division of his army, and a possible long retreat with flank exposed to attack from Bohemia.

Then he goes on: "It seems to me that the present campaign can only lead us to a good result if, to begin upon, there is a great battle. . . . However, it appears to me that, in order to have a decisive and brilliant affair, there are more favourable chances in holding ourselves in a more concentrated position and awaiting the arrival of the enemy."

Briefly summarised the scheme was—

(1) Offensive in the north, with 120,000 men converging on Berlin.

(2) Defensive with 300,000 men between Görlitz and Dresden, waiting for the enemy to move, and always ready to profit by his mistakes.

This scheme, as modified next day,¹ leaves the Berlin project unchanged. But there is a considerable change in the defensive scheme ; for the III. and V. corps are to be placed on the Katzbach between Hainau and Goldberg, with VI. and XI. in second line on the Bober, between Bunzlau and Löwenberg.

Why had the Emperor gone back to the idea of holding Liegnitz and Bunzlau, which he had condemned as dangerous only the day before? No reasons are stated, and it can only be inferred that his dread of the Silesian army slipping away unperceived north-westwards, between him and the Oder, overcame his fear of being cut from Dresden.

Here it will be convenient to set out the disposition of his forces under these final orders.²

(1) Facing east, in first line on the Katzbach were Ney (III. corps), Lauriston (V.), and Sebastiani (2nd cavalry corps). Altogether 78,000 men (of whom about 13,000 cavalry) and 226 guns.

Behind them, in second line on the Bober, Marmont (VI.), and Macdonald (XI.) 52,000 men, 182 guns.

(2) Facing south about Zittau. Poniatowski³ (VIII.), 8000 men.

(3) In reserve, about Görlitz. The Guard, Victor (II.), and Latour-Maubourg (1st cavalry corps). In all about 100,000 men (of whom about 25,000 cavalry), and 330 guns.

(4) At Bautzen. Vaudamme⁴ (I.) and Kellermann (4th cavalry corps), about 37,000 men (about 5000 of them cavalry), and 88 guns.

(5) About Dresden, Pirna, and Königstein. St Cyr (XIV.), L'Heritier (5th cavalry corps), garrisons of Dresden, Königstein, and Lilienstein. In all 35,000 men (about 5500 cavalry), and 198 guns.

[1] *Corr.* 20,371 and 20,373.   [2] See diagram. Map III., inset (*b*).
[3] Poniatowski, it will be remembered, had been carried off to Gallicia in February by Schwartzenberg. During the armistice he had been allowed to rejoin the French through Austria.
[4] Vandamme was on the march from the lower Elbe, and only reached Bautzen on the 17th August.

PREPARATIONS AND PLANS OF CAMPAIGN 173

(6) The army operating against Berlin was thus distributed :—

(a) Bertrand (IV.), Reynier (VII.), Oudinot (XII.), Arrighi (3rd cavalry corps) concentrating on Luckau, 67,000 men (8000 or 10,000 cavalry), and 216 guns.

(b) Girard and Dombrowski, between Luckau and Wittenberg, 13,800 men (1500 of them cavalry), and 23 guns.

(c) Davout (XIII.) in front of Hamburg, 37,500 men (of whom about 2000 cavalry), and 94 guns.

The position of the army under the immediate command of Napoleon was really this. There were three strategic advanced guards. The first on the Katzbach in an open country, was very strong, two infantry and one cavalry corps. The second at Zittau, was weak, but, on the other hand, it was guarding very easily defensible passes, and moreover, it could be supported in a single march by 100,000 men of the Görlitz group, and very shortly by 37,000 more from Bautzen. The third was not very strong on the left bank of the Elbe, but it had the entrenched camp at Dresden to fall back upon, and could be supported in a day, and a half by the 37,000 men at Bautzen.

Napoleon puts the matter thus :

The Austrians, if they take the offensive, must do so on one of three lines. First, if they debouched by the Peterswalde road on the left bank of the Elbe, they would, even with 100,000 men, be delayed in the strong positions which St Cyr could find between the mountains and Dresden.[1] He would retire on Dresden which could be reached by Vandamme in a day and a half. The two together, with over 70,000 men, could easily hold out till the arrival of Napoleon from Görlitz (four marches) with the Guard and II. corps raised the force to over 150,000 men.

Secondly, if they attacked by Zittau, as Napoleon expected they would, they must meet Poniatowski, the

---

[1] St Cyr knew all this country thoroughly, thanks to his deputation for the purpose of studying it during the armistice.

Guard, and II. corps. Before they could advance any distance they would find themselves faced by 150,000 men. If the Silesian army moved westwards simultaneously with the Austrian advance by Zittau, it would encounter the two corps on the Katzbach which, as they fell back towards the Bober, would be raised to 130,000 by the two on that river. This army would unite at Bunzlau.[1] In a day and a half Napoleon could add to them such of the Görlitz group as he deemed superfluous for dealing with the Austrians. He would probably have dealt with the Austrians first, driving them back through the mountains, and then turning on the Silesian army.

The third possible movement of the Austrians was to join the Silesian army by Josephstadt. In that case the whole French army, except Oudinot and Davout, would assemble on Bunzlau.

It will be observed that nothing is said of the converse of the last case, namely, the march of the Silesian army to join that of Bohemia, and advance by the left bank of the Elbe. That was what actually happened, except that only the larger half of the Silesian army went to Bohemia, leaving Blücher with about 90,000 men to face the French on the Katzbach. That, of course, shifted the centre of gravity of the allied armies from Silesia to Bohemia, and made the army of Bohemia their principal army. That Napoleon could not know to be in progress when he prepared his scheme. We shall see presently how he dealt with the altered circumstances, when they came to his knowledge.

As regards this scheme for the defensive army, all critics seem to be agreed that it was as nearly perfect as was possible in the circumstances, and a most admirable design for the use of interior lines. Later on we shall see it failing in the execution.

Three questions have been raised: (1) whether the Emperor was right in deciding for the defensive as

---

[1] "Bautzen" is in the text (*Corr.* 20,373). But is not Bunzlau meant? The subsequent reference to sending troops from Görlitz seems to indicate this.

PREPARATIONS AND PLANS OF CAMPAIGN 175

opposed to the offensive; (2) whether he was wise, whilst acting defensively with his main army, to act offensively with another part; (3) if the last question is answered affirmatively, was Berlin the best direction for the offensive?

The idea of acting on the defensive was repugnant to Napoleon's genius, and he had never yet adopted this course. His previous successes had been gained by a vigorous offensive. We may be certain he would only adopt the defensive if circumstances absolutely required it. If he decided for the offensive he would have to operate in one of three directions: against the Silesian army eastwards; against the Bohemian southwards; or against Bernadotte and Berlin in the north, and of course he must operate with the bulk of his forces, or so large a force as to be much superior to the enemy attacked.

Assuming, as he did, that the Silesian was the main army he would certainly wish if possible to attack it. But, if he advanced in great force against it, the probabilities were it would retire before him without fighting. He would be drawn away eastwards, without gaining the great victory which alone would be of real value to him. In the meanwhile, the Bohemian and Northern armies, closing in behind him, would seize his base on the Elbe, and his store house, Dresden, which was too weak to resist long.

The idea of an attack on the Bohemian army was more tempting; for a decisive victory over the Austrians might yet tear them from the arms of their allies, and even bring them back to the French alliance. If he could bring them to a general action towards Prague he might well hope to make an end of them, before the Silesian army could come to their assistance.

But what certainty was there that the weak Austrian army would not retire hurriedly before him, and that he would not strike a blow in the air? If he penetrated far into Bohemia, in pursuit of the retreating enemy, he risked being surrounded, as he afterwards was at Leipzig, or being forced to the very difficult, perhaps impossible, operation of changing his line of operations to one through south

Germany. Besides, when he was making his plans, it was still not certain that Austria would declare war. If he was to hope for a success against her, it was absolutely necessary to make a dash for Bohemia the moment the armistice came to an end.

There remains the case of an offensive against Bernadotte. Here, again, Napoleon had many temptations to the offensive, and he showed, by his decision in favour of an attack on Berlin and north Germany with part of his army, that he could not entirely resist them. In the first place he was very bitter against both Prussia and Bernadotte. Marmont goes so far as to say: "Passion prompted him to act quickly against Prussia. He desired the first cannon shots to be fired against Berlin, and that a startling and terrible vengeance should follow immediately on the renewal of hostilities."[1] But, undoubtedly, there were substantial advantages offered by a successful attack on Bernadotte. Berlin itself had no political or strategical value, since the government was no longer there, and the magazines and treasury were empty. But a decisive defeat of the northern army of the allies would give the Emperor possession of the greater part of Prussia, and of its great resources. It would probably drive Bernadotte to desert his allies, and compel the rest of their troops to seek safety beyond the Oder. The capture of Berlin would certainly produce a great moral effect in Germany, and the establishment of the French in and north of the Mark of Brandenburg would cripple the Prussian recruiting arrangements. Moreover, an advance towards the Oder would result in the relief of Küstrin and Stettin, with the addition of their garrisons to the field army. But there were grave objections to a general offensive in this direction. It would draw Napoleon far away from south Germany, where he required to keep a firm hand on the wavering states of the Rhenish Confederation. It would leave his base exposed to the united attack of the Silesian and Bohemian armies against the inferior forces which alone he could afford to leave behind for its protection. He

[1] *Mém.*, v. 139

would probably lose Dresden with all the vast military stores he had collected there. His communications with Mayence would probably be permanently cut, and he would be reduced to a line via Hamburg and the lower Elbe, which had not been prepared. On the whole, then, it seems that Napoleon was undoubtedly right in deciding for the general defensive. He need have had less care for his base on the Elbe had he been, as he had been in earlier wars, at the head of superior forces. But, on this occasion, he was certainly numerically inferior, perhaps inferior even in the fighting qualities of his troops. It must be remembered that the idea of a purely passive defensive never could have entered his head. Indeed, he specially warns his marshals against such conceptions when he writes to Ney and Marmont, " I need not say that, whilst disposing yourself in echelons, it is indispensable to threaten to take the offensive."[1] On the other hand, acting generally on the defensive, he felt himself safe. "What is clear," he writes to St Cyr on the 17th August,[2] " is that no one can turn an army of 400,000 men, planted on a system of fortresses, on a stream like the Elbe, and able to debouch at pleasure by Dresden, Torgau, Wittenberg, and Magdeburg." No doubt the Austrians might turn this base by a wide movement through south Germany by Baireuth, but in that case, says the Emperor in the same letter, "I wish him 'bon voyage' and let him proceed, being quite certain that he will return faster than he went."

So much for the case of the general offensive, as opposed to the general defensive. Now the question remains whether, having decided for the latter, Napoleon was justified in taking the offensive with part of his army. On this point critics are more divided in opinion.

Count Yorck von Wartenburg[3] seems to approve the whole plan for the campaign, though his discussion of the partial offensive on Berlin gives reason to doubt if he really thinks there was "a just proportion between the advantages

[1] *Corr.* 20,360. [2] *Corr.* 20,398.
[3] *Napoleon as a General*, ii. 280-82.

178 NAPOLEON'S LAST CAMPAIGN IN GERMANY

to be gained and the stake involved." Von Caemmerer [1] does not distinguish clearly between the general and the partial offensive on Berlin, though, on the whole, he seems to condemn the former.

Of Napoleon's contemporaries, Marmont and St Cyr, in the replies which he invited from them, both unhesitatingly condemn the idea. The former deprecated the separation of the Emperor's forces into three armies, one for Berlin, one to cover it against the army of Silesia, and a third to cover it against an advance by the Bohemian army by the left bank of the Elbe. He added his famous prophecy, so soon to be realised: "I fear greatly lest on the day on which your Majesty has gained a victory, and believe you have won a decisive battle, you may learn that you have lost two."[2] By the course proposed, Napoleon, he thought, was depriving himself of forces which he would require on the Elbe and upper Spree to ensure a decisive victory over the allies' main army, a victory which, once gained, would carry with it as a consequence the fall of the north. Bernadottes' army could be contained by a single corps in front of Torgau and a few threats from Magdeburg and Hamburg. He advocated the offensive southwards, which, he said, would take the army from exhausted Saxony into a richer country.

St Cyr was equally opposed to the partial offensive on Berlin. According to his own account,[3] the marshal warned his master that he had underestimated both the numbers and the fighting value of Bernadotte's army. What St Cyr wished to do was to leave 150,000 men well posted between Magdeburg and Dresden, whilst, with the other 250,000 Napoleon undertook a great offensive movement against the Austrians in Bohemia towards Prague. The Emperor replied that he had not the time to make these movements, or to take up a plan entirely different from his own, already thought out. St Cyr maintained that the Austrians would move by the left bank of the Elbe, which was opposed

[1] *Die Befrieungskriege*, 1813-1815, p. 43.
[2] *Mém.*, v. pp. 140 and 207.
[3] *Hist. Mil.*, iv. p. 59, etc.

PREPARATIONS AND PLANS OF CAMPAIGN 179

to Napoleon's belief that they would come by Zittau. Grouard [1] agrees with the two marshals in condemning the offensive on Berlin.

Friederich [2] goes into this question more fully and clearly than most critics. He first asks the question whether the offensive with part of the army was justifiable in any direction. He holds that Napoleon, being in this case numerically inferior to the forces opposed to him, was bound by his own principles to seek decisive battle with the most powerful force available. Clearly a victory decisive of the result of the war was only to be sought against either the Silesian or the Bohemian army, one of which certainly was the enemy's main army. Napoleon clearly meant to seek a decisive battle with one of these, though waiting for them to move before deciding on his actual first objective. To act on the defensive with his main army, and at the same time to act offensively with a considerable force, was to leave himself less strong than he might have been at the decisive point. No success against a secondary army could be of decisive importance, however great it might be in itself. He holds, therefore, that Napoleon was guilty of a serious error in deciding for the offensive with any part of his army before it was clear where the final decision was to be sought. If, however, it were to be held that a partial offensive was justifiable, he thinks that the direction of Berlin promised the quickest and best results.

Considering all these opinions, it seems safe to hold :—

(1) That Napoleon was absolutely right in his decision for the general defensive.

(2) That his offensive against Berlin was a mistake, based, as it would seem, largely on his underestimate of the value of the Prussian levies.

(3) That where he failed was in the chain of assumptions, not in accordance with facts, to which he was led by the information available.

He certainly made a fatal mistake in selecting Oudinot

---

[1] *Stratégie Napoleonienne*, p. 49, etc.
[2] *Die strategische Lage Napoleon's*, p. 29.

for the command of a more or less independent army. That marshal, though no doubt a capable commander of a division, perhaps even of a single corps, was not of the calibre to command an army of 70,000 or 80,000 men. Whether any of Napoleon's lieutenants was fit for it is perhaps doubtful. Of those then in Germany, Davout, Marmont, and St Cyr were alone possible.[1] The last-named marshal himself says, speaking of an earlier part of the campaign: "In my opinion there was not then in the whole of the belligerent armies a single man capable of commanding a greater number (than 50,000 men)."[2]

Napoleon's orders display absolute unity of command, and a self-confidence which it is impossible to blame, considering what the Emperor was, as compared with all other leaders of his time. On the side of the allies a very different state of affairs is disclosed, one which Napoleon reckoned as an important advantage to himself. There could be no unity of command where so many divergent interests were involved. Every plan had to be evolved in consultation between the several sovereigns concerned, and the final result was necessarily a compromise. Napoleon's scheme was evolved from his own brain, in his cabinet, without anything of the nature of a council of war. It was divulged to his own commanders only at the last moment. The allies spent days and weeks in consultation and debate. Among the many advisers of the allies, since the death of Scharnhorst, the only men who had a true conception of the necessity for vigorous concentric action, and the bringing of the enemy's main army to a decisive battle, were Toll the Russian, and Gneisenau the Prussian, now Chief of Staff to Blücher.

It is not possible for us to describe in detail the many schemes which came under discussion. They began with one drawn up by Toll on the 9th June. Simultaneously with this Radetzky had proposed another. Toll's plan was modified by Barclay. Bernadotte sent in three plans, all of which, as might be expected, aimed more at his own

[1] Soult had gone to Spain.   [2] *Hist. Mil.*, iv. 16.

PREPARATIONS AND PLANS OF CAMPAIGN 181

advantage than at that of the allied cause generally. He wanted to be appointed Commander-in-Chief of the whole allied army, an arrangement which would have suited no one but himself, and, perhaps we may add, Napoleon.

Then came a scheme drawn up by Knesebeck, and two more prepared by Borstell and von Boyen. Knesebeck wanted to have two-thirds of the armies in Bohemia, and one-third in the north. The result would have been to divide the command between Bernadotte and an Austrian, leaving Prussia and Russia out altogether. As a mean between Toll's and Knesebeck's plans, it was proposed to give Bernadotte a large command in the north, to make the Bohemian army the main one, by moving all but about 55,000 of the Silesian army to its aid, and to leave these 55,000 under a Prussian. This plan was apparently accepted by the Russians, though it left them with no command. But Austria preferred Knesebeck's plan, which contemplated transferring the whole Silesian army to Bohemia. It had apparently been generally assumed by the allies that Napoleon would act on the offensive against Bohemia.

On the 9th July, the Tsar, the King of Prussia, and Bernadotte met by arrangement at Trachenberg, north of Breslau, and spent the next three days in consultation. Bernadotte, it may be remarked, could not be persuaded to believe that Austria would join the allies. He thought she would wait till both parties were exhausted, and then step in.

In the end, a protocol was drawn up, the responsibility for which is claimed by Toll, and also by von Boyen. It terms were briefly these :—

(1) As a general principle for guidance, it was laid down that all forces of the allies should aim at the direction of the enemy's main force, and that forces operating on his flanks or rear should aim, by the shortest road, at his communications.

(2) The main body to take up a position from which it could advance against the enemy in whichever direction he

might move. The bastion-like projection of Bohemia would facilitate this.

(3) From 90,000 to 100,000 men to move, a few days before the end of the armistice, from the army of Silesia, by Landshut, Glatz, Jung Bunzlau, and Budin, to join the Austrians, raising their numbers to over 200,000 men.

(4) Bernadotte to leave 15,000 or 20,000 men to watch Hamburg, and with 70,000 to take post about Treuenbrietzen, so as to be able to advance on Leipzig, crossing the Elbe between Torgau and Wittenberg.

(5) The army of Silesia to follow the enemy as he retired on the Elbe, but not to engage in any important action, unless under circumstances of peculiar advantage. On reaching the Elbe it would endeavour to cross between Dresden and Torgau, to unite with Bernadotte. Should that be found impossible, it would march at once to join the Bohemian army.

(6) The Bohemian army would move, according to circumstances, on Eger, Hof, or Silesia, or would retire towards the Danube. Should Napoleon attack it, Bernadotte would endeavour, by forced marches, to fall on his rear.

(7) Similarly, if Bernadotte were the object of attack, the Bohemian and Silesian armies would fall on Napoleon's communications, and compel him to a general battle.

(8) All allied forces to act on the offensive, with the enemy's camp as their objective.

(9) Bennigsen, with the Russian reserve army, to march by Kalisch towards Glogau, ready either to attack the enemy or to prevent his advance on Poland.

The whole scheme is, according to Friederich, a compromise between the ideas of Toll, Knesebeck, and Bernadotte, with traces of those of Borstell and von Boyen. It is based on the assumption that Napoleon's first attack would be on Austria and the Bohemian army. To Toll is to be attributed the idea of the offensive, and the fixing of the objective, not in a geographical point, but in the enemy's army. That was not in accordance with the

PREPARATIONS AND PLANS OF CAMPAIGN 183

ideas of Austria, who, if she had learnt something in tactics from Napoleon, had completely failed to grasp his strategical ideas. Even her best general, the Archduke Charles, now in retirement, had shown by his writings that he was still largely dominated by 18th century ideas of manœuvring, rather than seeking a tactical decision.

It will be observed that the Trachenberg protocol only prescribed the avoidance of a great battle in the case of the Silesian army. That was necessary, both because the army was weak, and because its commander, Blücher, was notoriously hot-headed, and required definite instructions to prevent him from hurling himself on Napoleon, of whom he alone was not afraid.

Whilst the Trachenberg scheme was being evolved, Radetzky, Schwartzenberg's chief of staff, had worked out another scheme, under which any of the armies which might be attacked by Napoleon was to go on the defensive, whilst the other two advanced.

When, therefore, the Trachenberg plan was sent for the approval of Austria, she insisted on making the instructions to avoid a general action with Napoleon, unless under very advantageous circumstances, applicable to all three armies. In order to secure her adhesion, the others agreed to this at Reichenbach on the 19th July.

No written record of the final arrangements, which may be called those of Trachenberg-Reichenbach, has been traced, but it is supposed that they are summarised in a memorandum drawn up by Schwarzenberg, in November 1813, of which the main points are these:—

(1) Fortresses encountered by the allies to be masked, not besieged.

(2) The main force to operate on the enemy's flank and communications.

(3) By attacking his communications he was to be forced either to detach, or to hurry with his main army to the threatened point.

(4) He was only to be attacked when divided, and when the allies were largely superior.

(5) If the enemy advanced in mass against one of the allied armies it would retire, whilst the other two advanced.

(6) The point of union for all the armies to be the enemy's headquarters.

These rules show that the allied leaders were still under the influence of 18th century ideas. They were afraid of bringing on a great battle by a general concentric advance, and hoped by small measures to carry out a dilatory scheme. This, notwithstanding the fact that they over-estimated their numbers as compared with Napoleon's. It is clear, as Friederich remarks, that Napoleon's teaching was lost on them, and the early part of the war could only lead to partial decisions. It was only later that the allied leaders found themselves, almost against the wishes of many of them, forced to a final decision at Leipzig.

CHAPTER XII

FROM THE END OF THE ARMISTICE TO THE BATTLE OF DRESDEN

NAPOLEON left Dresden in the afternoon of the 15th August, quite satisfied with his plans. Two days earlier he had said : " I have allowed for everything ; the rest depends on Fortune." After inspecting the fortifications round the Lilienstein, he proceeded along his new military road to Stolpen, and on to Bautzen, which he reached at 2 A.M. on the 16th. He remained there till the evening of the 17th, busy with his orders for the operations now commencing.

On the 16th[1] he received information from a reliable spy that on the 12th, the Russian[2] army had left Reichenbach and started for Bohemia, except the corps of Sacken, which had, on the same day, debouched with Blücher and Kleist from Breslau, where they had no business to be during the armistice. On the 15th they had captured French vedettes. Under these circumstances, the Emperor expressed his intention of placing 100,000 men on the position of Eckartsberg behind Zittau, and occupying on the 17th Rumburg, Schluckenau, and Georgenthal. Here he would menace Prague by the shortest road, and would be in communication by Neustadt with Königstein. Macdonald was asked if, with his own (XI.) corps, the V., and 5000 or 6000 cavalry (about 60,000 in all) he could hold a position which the Emperor understood to exist at Löwenberg, whilst Ney, with 70,000 or 80,000, took position between Bunzlau and Hainau. Mortier would be at Lauban

[1] *Corr.* 20,390, to Macdonald.
[2] The march had really begun on the 7th. This Reichenbach is south-east of Schweidnitz.

with three divisions of the Guard to-day (16th). "When I am certain that Blücher with Yorck, Kleist, and Sacken (who cannot be more than 50,000 men) is advancing on Bunzlau, and that Wittgenstein and Barclay de Tolly are in Bohemia, en route for Zwickau or Dresden, I shall march in force to carry away Blücher." Napoleon's estimate of Blücher's army is entirely wrong, for it consisted of the Prussians of Yorck, and the Russians of Sacken, St Priest, and Langeron, altogether at least 90,000 men.

In the evening of the 17th Napoleon was at Reichenbach, on the 18th at Görlitz. Here he learnt that Wittgenstein, with 40,000 Russians, had reached Bohemia, and that the Austrians had passed the Elbe for an unknown destination.

Vandamme, whose first division was only just arriving at Stolpen, was ordered to Rumburg, where he would find the 42nd division of St Cyr's corps and would keep it, if St Cyr were not hard pressed. Also he would have 3000 Guard cavalry under Lefebvre-Desnoettes. The Emperor was going to Zittau, possibly to Rumburg. "It is possible I might enter Bohemia at once to fall upon the Russians and catch them 'en flagrant délit.'"[1] Accordingly, Napoleon moved to Zittau on the 19th, still waiting to get a clearer idea of the enemy's intentions. During the day he went forward in person with a strong reconnaissance as far as Gabel. By this means he ascertained that the Austrians were marching westwards, followed by a large Russian force. Clearly there was not likely to be a serious attack on Zittau for the present. "When the enemy learns that I have been at Gabel, he will march on this point with all his forces."[2] But before he could arrive Vandamme would have had four or five days in which to fortify himself in the passes about Rumburg, and so would Victor at Gabel. Vandamme's whole corps, Lefebvre-Desnoettes' Guard cavalry, Victor's and Poniatowski's corps would be available for the defence of the passes, about 65,000 men. The Emperor was off to destroy Blücher, as he hoped, and he calculated that these 65,000 men, fighting to the last

[1] *Corr.* 20,408, to Vandamme.   [2] *Corr.* 20,421.

FROM ARMISTICE TO BATTLE OF DRESDEN 187

extremity in very strong positions, could easily hold the enemy's main army till his own return. He still apparently either did not believe in an advance of the allies on Dresden by the left bank of the Elbe, or, if he thought they contemplated it, he believed that his own appearance at Gabel would bring them back.

He was back at Görlitz by 2 P.M. on the 20th, ready to move against Blücher, who that evening stood east of the Bober opposite Löwenberg. Facing him, on the left bank, on the line Löwenberg-Bunzlau, were Ney (III.), Lauriston (V.) and Macdonald (XI.); Marmont (VI.) and the Guard were coming up. By evening on the 20th Napoleon had reached Lauban, whence he issued orders for the attack. "My intention is to attack to-morrow. The Prince of the Moskowa will attack what is in front of him, and, after passing the Bober, will move on Alt-Giersdorf to form my left. The Duke of Ragusa will be, at 10 A.M., two leagues (5 miles) from Löwenberg on my left. You will debouch at Löwenberg with General Lauriston, the XI. corps on the right of Löwenberg. My Guard, horse and foot, will be at Löwenberg by noon."[1] The Emperor now estimated Blücher at 100,000, or rather less, which was fairly correct.

The attempt to destroy Blücher failed completely. Napoleon saw Löwenberg captured without difficulty. The bridge over the Bober, which had been partially destroyed, was repaired, and the French advanced against the heights beyond, only to find Blücher retreating. Napoleon put this down to want of confidence in their generals on the part of the allies. He was, of course, ignorant that the retirement was in accordance with the Trachenberg arrangement. Next day he wrote to Maret:[3] "It appears that their army of Silesia had not advanced with as much rapidity as was contemplated by the general plan of the allies, and their belief that we should repass the Elbe. They thought they had only to pursue, and consequently, as soon as they saw our columns debouch to reassume the offensive, they

[1] *Corr.* 20,428, to Macdonald, midnight, 20th August.
[2] *Corr.* 20,437, of 22nd August.

were filled with fear, and one was convinced that the chiefs wished to avoid a serious engagement. The whole plan of the allies has been founded on the assurance, given them by Metternich, that we should repass the Elbe, and they are much disconcerted to find it is otherwise." But he also shows that he realises the incompetence of his own subordinates; for he continues: "In general, what is most regrettable in the position of affairs is the little confidence which the generals have in themselves; wherever I am not personally present, the enemy's forces appear to them considerable."

In the same letter he shows that he is beginning to believe the Austrians are making for Dresden. That he welcomes as entailing a battle. "Since we can arrive at no result without a battle, the most fortunate thing that could happen is that the enemy should march on Dresden, since then there would be a battle."

During this day (22nd) the French continued to advance eastwards. There was a fight between Lauterseifen and Pilgramsdorf, and by evening the enemy was driven beyond the Katzbach. The Emperor himself went to about half-way between Löwenberg and Goldberg, and then returned to the former in the evening. There he received an important letter, dated Pirna, 21st August (noon), from St Cyr[1] in which that marshal very frankly stated his view of the position. The Austrians, he said, now reinforced by a large part of the Silesian army, were posted in two lines behind the Erzgebirge, on the left bank of the Elbe, and he believed they meant to swing round their left towards Wittenberg, shutting in Dresden and Torgau. However much he hoped for it, St Cyr could not believe Napoleon's movement on Zittau would draw them back in that direction. They would hope to contain him with their right on the upper Elbe, whilst they blockaded Dresden and Torgau so closely that it

---

[1] *Hist. Mil.*, p. 372. Napoleon's reply (*Corr.* 20,445) is dated "Görlitz, 23rd August 1813," and refers to "your letter of 22nd August at 11 P.M." There is palpably some mistake about the dates, as the letter quoted above is undoubtedly that to which the Emperor was replying.

would be impossible to issue from them, even if they did not fall.

In his reply,[1] Napoleon, without distinctly admitting his acceptance of St Cyr's theory, shows plainly that he realises the danger threatening Dresden, and that he must hurry to its assistance. He assumes that St Cyr has left no boats on the left bank of the Elbe, and that he has made safe the communications between Dresden and Königstein by the right bank. He promises that he will soon have 200,000 men at Dresden. St Cyr had reported that the Russians and Prussians were already in contact with his outposts, and that he did not believe the Königstein passage was safe, once he had to withdraw his army.

As Napoleon was about to leave the eastern army, he entrusted its command to Macdonald, christening it the "Army of the Bober."[2] He stated its total strength at 100,000 men. Macdonald's principal task was to hold in check the enemy's army of Silesia, to prevent it from operating either against Napoleon's communications towards Zittau, or against Oudinot towards Berlin. Therefore, Macdonald was to push Blücher back beyond Jauer, and then to take post on the Bober. Three divisions of the III. corps were to hold a fortified position near Bunzlau. Another similar position at Löwenberg was to be held by three divisions of the XI. corps, with the 4th division in reserve on the Queiss. The V. corps was to hold a position near Hirschberg. Communications were to be behind the Bober, along the left bank of which fortified posts were to be constructed at every $1\frac{1}{4}$ miles, so as to prevent Cossacks crossing. Each flank of the whole position was to be strengthened by a strong body of cavalry and infantry, reconnoitring and preventing the enemy from turning it. A great deal of field fortification was prescribed, both in the front line and in Marchand's second line on the Queiss. When this position was thus occupied and fortified, Napoleon believed that it would be impossible for the enemy either to

---

[1] *Corr.* 20,445, Görlitz, 23rd August.
[2] *Corr.* 20,442, of 23rd August, to Berthier.

turn it by an advance between its right and the Riesengebirge, or to move between its left and the Oder towards Berlin. The army was to be kept in a state of mobility, and, if the enemy took the offensive, and advanced, Macdonald would be strong enough, unless Blücher were greatly reinforced, to issue from Löwenberg, or some other point, and attack him.

It certainly looked as if the Emperor's rear was thoroughly protected during his march on Dresden. But the choice of Macdonald for this important semi-independent command was not a wise one. In order that there might not be difficulties, owing to the presence of more than one marshal out of the Emperor's sight, Ney was summoned to headquarters. It would, of course, have been out of the question to leave him with the Bober army under Macdonald, his junior in rank as marshal. Unfortunately, Ney did not get the order[1] which summoned him to headquarters, and directed transfer of the command of the III. corps to Souham, yet he marched for Bunzlau with the III. corps. It is not clear what induced him to do this.

On the 24th August, the Emperor wrote to Maret, in cypher, directing him to pass on the orders to St Cyr, whose opinion was again invited on them. He said: "My intention is to move to Stolpen. My army will be assembled there to-morrow. I shall spend the 26th there in preparations, and rallying my columns. On the 26th, in the night, I will send my columns by Königstein, and at daybreak on the 27th, I shall be in the camp of Pirna with 100,000 men. I shall operate so that the atttack on Hellendorf begins at 7 A.M., and I shall be master of that place at noon. Then I shall place myself astride of that communication, and seize Pirna. I shall have two bridges ready to throw at Pirna, if necessary. Either the enemy has taken as his line of operation the road from Peterswalde to Dresden, in which case I shall be in his rear with all my army opposed to him, whilst he cannot assemble his in less than four or five days; or he has taken his line of operation

[1] *Corr.* 20,440, to Berthier.

FROM ARMISTICE TO BATTLE OF DRESDEN

by the road from Kommotau to Leipzig. In that case he will not retire, and will move on Kommotau; Dresden will be relieved, and I shall find myself in Bohemia, nearer than the enemy to Prague, on which I shall march. Marshal St Cyr will follow the enemy as soon as he appears to be disconcerted. I shall mask this movement by lining the bank of the Elbe with 30,000 cavalry and light artillery, so that the enemy, seeing all the river lined, will believe my army to be at Dresden. . . . I assume that, when I undertake my attack, Dresden will not be attacked so as to be able to be taken in twenty-four hours."[1]

The scheme was beautifully simple, but it all depended on St Cyr's being able to hold Dresden unsupported against the allies. This Napoleon evidently felt to be the weak point, for he said his scheme might have to be modified in consequence of the enemy's movements.

Meanwhile, the allied army of Bohemia had been slowly pressing on towards Dresden. Schwarzenberg's first idea had been to march on Leipzig, according to Napoleon's second supposition, but, as he crossed the Erzgebirge, he changed his plan to a direct advance on Dresden. St Cyr's troops were everywhere forced back by superior numbers, only the 42nd division remaining behind at Königstein, and between that fortress and Dresden on the Pirna plateau.

On the 22nd, Wittgenstein had appeared at Hellendorf, driving in the French outposts on Berggiesshübel. The French XIV. corps was watching the whole line, some seventy-five miles, from the Elbe to Hof. At Berggiesshübel there were only available the 43rd division and L'Heritier's cavalry, which had replaced Pajol's, detached to the right towards Freiberg.[2]

A sturdy resistance was made, but when, in the afternoon, Wittgenstein began to turn the position, the French retired to Zehista, where they again held out till nightfall.

On the same afternoon, the 44th division had been brought up from the old road to Teplitz to support the 43rd at Zehista. The XIV. corps was ordered to take up

[1] *Corr.* 20,449, dated Görlitz, 24th August.   [2] See Map IV. (*b*).

a position next morning near enough to Dresden to be certain of not being cut from it. The 45th division, which had been fighting on the 22nd near Dippoldiswalde, took post on the 23rd on the heights of Räcknitz a couple of miles outside Dresden; the 44th was on its left. The 45th then retired to the Pirna suburb of Dresden.

Pajol had also been attacked towards Freiberg on the 22nd, and his cavalry driven back on two battalions of the 45th division supporting him. On the 23rd he stood, with his right on the Mulde and his left at Rabenau, watching the enemy's movements in this direction and towards Leipzig.

L'Heritier's cavalry was on St Cyr's left.

On the 23rd a Russian light division approached Dresden by Zehista, drove in the French outposts, but made no serious attack. Desultory skirmishing continued on the 24th. On the 25th these Russians were driven back from the heights of Strehlen, enabling the French to see that heavy columns were moving towards Dresden. L'Heritier's cavalry lost three guns in this affair, thanks to Murat's [1] rashness, if we may credit St Cyr. The latter refused now to follow the suggestions of the King of Naples, who advocated withdrawing the whole army within the fortifications of Dresden, and kept his infantry as far out as the heights beyond Strehlen. Fortunately for him, the allies could not make up their minds to a general attack that day, which might very well have resulted, looking to their immense superiority of numbers, in the capture by storm of the Altstadt. This failure to attack is universally condemned; for St Cyr had not more than about 20,000 men, and it is scarcely possible to suppose he could have held the weak defences of Dresden very long against the enormous forces which the allied commander might have hurled upon him on the afternoon of the 25th. But Schwarzenberg had clearly no inkling of the neighbourhood of Napoleon, and chose to wait till next day for his attack, when he hoped to have the Austrian army up.

[1] Murat had been fetched back from Naples to command the cavalry, and also to remove him from the temptation of Austrian intrigues.

FROM ARMISTICE TO BATTLE OF DRESDEN

The allied sovereigns were on the heights of Räcknitz between 9 and 10 A.M. on the 25th. The Tsar and Moreau,[1] who accompanied him, saw clearly the weakness of St Cyr, and wanted to make an immediate attack, but Schwarzenberg insisted on waiting for the Austrians. Late that evening Wittgenstein came personally to Barclay at Räcknitz with a request to be allowed to storm the city during the night. Barclay refused on the ground of superior orders prohibiting an attack that day. The golden opportunity was lost.

We now return to Napoleon. Leaving Görlitz on the 24th, he was at Bautzen by 3 P.M., the Guard being expected there the same evening. By 7 A.M. on the 25th, he was at Stolpen, still intent on his plan of crossing with 100,000 men at Königstein, to seize the enemy's line of operations by the Peterswalde-Dresden road; Vandamme was at Neustadt and Stolpen on this day. The Guard, and Latour-Maubourg's cavalry, on the road from Bautzen to Stolpen, Victor and Marmont still a day's march short of Bautzen.

The Emperor was anxious about Dresden, on the holding of which it depended whether he could leave it alone whilst he debouched from Königstein. His doubts on the subject are evidenced by letters to St Cyr and to Rogniat, his engineer-general. He had also sent Gourgaud to Dresden to bring information on the subject. Gourgaud arrived at Stolpen at 11 P.M. on the 25th with such a poor account of the Dresden fortifications, and their chance of being able to hold out, that Napoleon, no longer daring to carry out his great scheme, decided to march direct to the Saxon capital with the bulk of his forces. At 1 A.M. on the 26th the new orders issued. The Guard and Latour-Maubourg were to start at once for Dresden, Victor and Marmont to follow. Between 9 and 10 A.M. the

[1] Moreau had, at the instance of the Tsar, returned from America and joined the allies. He was thought much of by Alexander, who constantly consulted him. Whatever sympathy might be felt for him on account of the past he largely forfeited by consenting to serve against his own countrymen.

Emperor himself was in Dresden, busy examining the fortifications and reconnoitring. The troops, which he was hurrying up, began to arrive soon after himself. He had not entirely given up the Königstein and Pirna expedition, but he left it to Vandamme alone, with his own corps, to be joined by Mouton-Duvernet with the division (42nd) which St Cyr had left behind about Königstein.

Here we must pause to describe the neighbourhood of Dresden, especially the left bank of the Elbe, which, during this and the succeeding day, was to be the scene of very notable events.[1] The student of military history at the present day has to exercise a good deal of imagination in studying the battlefield of Dresden; for the city, which had only some 30,000 inhabitants in 1813, now has about half a million, and has spread far and wide over what was, in 1813, open country with villages scattered about, the names of which now stand for quarters well within the city area. The old fortifications had by 1813 been only partially dismantled, now they have entirely disappeared. The city lies in a broad, open valley, astride of the Elbe, which in 1813 was spanned within the walls by only one stone bridge, that which led from opposite the royal palace to the Neustadt.

The Altstadt was enclosed by the remains of the old enceinte, but suburbs ("schlags," as they were locally called) had already extended on an average 600 or 700 yards beyond it, covering its field of fire. The western suburb, the Friedrichstadt, beyond the river Weisseritz, extended much further. The Neustadt, on the other hand, was in a much better condition for defence. The enceinte had been reconstructed by Napoleon since his re-occupation of Dresden in May, and several fresh forts had been built. It was only during the armistice, as Austria seemed to be likely to join the allies, that much attention had been given to the defences on the left bank. What had been done in the way of temporary fortification during

[1] Map IV. (a).

FROM ARMISTICE TO BATTLE OF DRESDEN 195

the armistice has already been described. But the works were still incomplete and defective, as is shown by Napoleon's letter of the 25th to Rogniat (his engineer-officer), saying he would feel reassured about Dresden if he knew that "the three entrenchments already marked out were ready, if the barricades in the town were finished, and if the Pirna ditch were properly excavated."[1]

The Altstadt had three weak lines of defence—

(1) The ring of lunettes.

(2) The barricades, palisades, and garden walls of the suburbs.

(3) The old enceinte.

With a strong garrison, and an enemy of not very great superiority, it was safe; but it certainly was not so when the allies could attack with 100,000 men a garrison of little more than 20,000.

We have said there were defects in the works. Some of them were these. The lunettes I., II., III. were out of sight of one another, and therefore incapable of mutual support. In front of No. IV. there was a good deal of dead ground, and there was a large building, the Feldschlösschen, in which an enemy could effect a lodgment within 300 yards of it. There were no redoubts beyond the Weisseritz, and the Friedrichstadt suburb on that side was very poorly fortified.

Outside the eastern suburbs stretched for some 2000 yards, with a breadth of 1000, on perfectly level ground, the Grosser Garten, which was very much the same in 1813 as it now is, with its palace in the centre forming a sort of réduit. Its importance to the defender is obvious; for, so long as he held it, he was on the flank of any advance against the city along either its northern or its southern side, and the part between it and the Elbe was also open to artillery fire from the opposite bank against the right flank of an attack, provided, as was the case in 1813, the defender was in undisputed possession

[1] *Corr.* 20,465.

of the right bank. At some distance outside its eastern and northern sides was the Landgraben, a drainage cut running, according to the undulations of the country, either in a low embankment or in a sunken ditch. It was not much of an obstruction to infantry, or even to cavalry, but it was so to artillery; for the foot-bridges across it were not wide enough for the passage of guns. Artillery could only cross by the main roads.

The country between the Grosser Garten and the Elbe was only slightly undulating, and was open, except for a large wood, about Blasewitz and south-west of it, which was of no great importance.

The next section of the semicircle is different; for within 1000 yards of the southern suburbs the ground begins to rise to the line of heights which, from Tschertnitz to Briesnitz, surrounds the southern and western sides of Dresden. From Tschertnitz these heights curve back southwards, whilst beyond the Weisseritz they trend forwards towards the Elbe at Briesnitz.

At Räcknitz the level is about 250 feet above Dresden; beyond the Weisseritz it is greater, but the crest is further from the city.

The ridge is cut through above Plauen by the little river Weisseritz, flowing through a precipitous gorge 200 feet or more in depth, which was only passable with great difficulty by one or two bad roads for a mile or so above Plauen. The Weisseritz is now carried away from below Plauen to the Elbe at Briesnitz; in 1813 it flowed straight down to the Elbe between the city and the Friedrichstadt suburb. In ordinary weather it was generally fordable, but in torrential rain, such as fell on the 27th August 1813, it became a serious obstacle, only passable at the bridges, of which there were four of stone and two of wood between Coschütz and the Elbe.

Beyond the Weisseritz, the heights were in places rather more intersected by ravines than those between the stream and Tschertnitz. These ravines specially favoured attacks on some of the villages on the slopes; but most of this country was open, and excellently suited for cavalry.

The troops immediately available for the defence of the city on the 26th August were:—

(*a*) Three divisions of St Cyr's corps, about 15,000 men, the 42nd division being at Königstein.

(*b*) About 4500 Westphalians.

(*c*) 1 French and 1 Italian cavalry regiment, and 2 Polish squadrons.

(*d*) A few Dutch, Polish, Saxon, and Baden allies.

Of these, the Westphalians were set apart as the regular garrison. The XIV. corps occupied the 1st and 2nd lines of defence. Of the three divisions, the 43rd on the left held the space between the Elbe and redoubt III., the 44th held the Grosser Garten, and the 45th had to hold the whole space thence round to the Friedrichstadt. The line, except in the Grosser Garten, was necessarily very thinly occupied.

On the other side, during the night of the 25th-26th, the Russians on the allied right held Blasewitz and the great wood, Striesen, Grüna, and the Grüne Wiese, with outposts in front.

The Prussians were in Prohlis, Torna, Leubnitz, and Ostra.

More Russians held Gostritz and behind it.

Colloredo's and Lichtenstein's divisions (Austrians) were on the heights behind Räcknitz.

Chasteler's two divisions arrived at 8 P.M. on the right bank of the Weisseritz, about Plauen, with the French outposts close in front of them.

The 2nd Russian Guard division, the 1st Grenadier division, the 3rd Cuirassier division, and the Prussian Guard cavalry, all under Miloradowich, were still at Dippoldiswalde. Klenau had only just reached Freiberg. Schwarzenberg had at last made up his mind to attack Dresden on the 26th August. Had he done so with vigour in the early morning of that day, he would probably have been still in time to storm it before the arrival of Napoleon's reinforcements, of which the nearest was half Teste's division of the I. corps, which was half way between Dresden and Stolpen. But, in order to take the city, there must be no hesitation in the attack, and it was necessary to have fascines and scaling-ladders ready for storming the old enceinte. Schwarzenberg had prepared none of these things, and his orders were anything but decided. He seems to have meant to divide his attack into two portions, a sort of preparatory reconnaissance in force during the morning, to be followed at 4 P.M. by the general attack, which should have commenced ten or twelve hours sooner, and should have been carried straight through. The attack was to be made in five columns.

1st column. Wittgenstein, with 10,000 Russians on the right, to make a demonstration, drawing on himself as much as possible of the enemy's attention.

2nd column. 35,000 Prussians to attack, as a demonstration, the Grosser Garten.

3rd column. Colloredo, with 15,000 Austrians, to demonstrate towards redoubt No. III., covering the heavy batteries in that direction.

4th column. Chasteler (less his grenadier division) to occupy Plauen and cover the leftward march of the 5th column.

5th column. 35,000 Austrians under Bianchi to attack Lobtau and work down, beyond the Weisseritz, to Friedrichstadt and the Elbe.

Chasteler's grenadier division (10,000) to act as reserve towards Coschütz, and, if necessary, to support the rest of the corps at Plauen.

Cavalry divisions, Nostitz and Lederer, to act as a further reserve between Coschütz and Kaitz.

The advance of the left wing and the bombardment of the place were to be held back till 4 P.M., when the forces of the enemy had been drawn away by the attacks of the right and centre.

Thus Schwarzenberg was bringing to the attack of St

Cyr's 20,000 men well over 100,000, and, had he pushed them boldly in in the morning, there can be little doubt that they would have carried everything before them, before even the arrival of Teste's division, which started only at 4 A.M.

CHAPTER XIII

THE BATTLE OF DRESDEN[1]

(a) THE 26TH AUGUST

FIRST *Period, up to noon.*—The first of the allies to attack were the Prussians advancing from the south against the nearest part of the Grosser Garten. The French had evacuated Strehlen at 4 A.M., an hour before Ziethen, supported by Pirch, moved from it against the Grosser Garten. The Prussians made but slow progress, and it was only as Roth, with the Russian advanced guard, came to their assistance, by attacking the north-eastern corner of the garden, that they were able to push slowly forward.

Roth appears to have attacked between 7 and 8 A.M., and, by the latter hour, when they had been already fighting for three hours, the Prussians had only mastered the outer half of the garden as far as the palace in its centre. By 9 A.M. they had got about half-way from the palace to the city end of the garden. Here they were ordered to break off the fight for the time. On the right of the Prussians the Russians began their advance between the Grosser Garten and the Elbe between 7 and 8 A.M. As they advanced from the Blasewitz wood they suffered severely from the artillery fire of the Marcolini fort on the right bank of the Elbe. They could make little progress till the Prussians, aided by Roth, got forward in the garden, and the Russians coming from Striesen planted a strong battery on a slight elevation, the Windmill height. Covered by this, they succeeded in capturing the building known as Engelhardt's, near the Elbe.

[1] Map IV. (*a*).

THE BATTLE OF DRESDEN

An attempt to advance on the Hopfgarten was repulsed. No further progress was made before the general lull in the battle, which began about noon. On the Prussian left between Zschertnitz and Räcknitz operations up to noon were confined to an artillery duel with the opposite French lunettes.

The Austrian attack towards Plauen began about 6 A.M. By 9 they had driven the French back past the Feldschlösschen, which was stormed, and on to redoubts Nos. IV. and V. From the Feldschlösschen the French artillery fire from redoubt IV. failed to drive the Austrians, as, the walls of the building being of lath and plaster, the French shells passed straight through them without setting fire to the building. A serious mistake had been made by the French engineers in not destroying this building before the battle. On the other hand, Austrian advances against redoubts IV. and V. were driven off by the fire of those forts, supported by the guns of one of the bastions of the old enceinte.

Thus when the fighting died away about noon the allies had attained the following positions. The Russians on the right stretched from Engelhardt's to the Grosser Garten, of which about three-fourths of the length was in possession of their own left and the Prussians. In the centre no progress had been made. On the left, up to the Weisseritz, the Austrians were close in front of the French redoubts IV. and V. Beyond the Weisseritz the Austrians had driven the French out of Lobtau. On the extreme left, Meszko's division had met with little opposition, and had succeeded in getting as far forward as Schusterhaüser on the Elbe.

In Dresden, meanwhile, the early attacks spread the greatest alarm among the inhabitants, who were aware that the allied troops were especially bitter against them, on account of alleged ill-treatment of Russian and Prussian prisoners. Confidence was to a great extent restored by the appearance of Napoleon between 9 and 10 A.M. Men began to say, " There is Napoleon. Things will soon be very different."[1] There was no longer any talk of abandoning homes and escaping across the river. The Emperor was still reputed invincible in Germany.

Leaving Stolpen in his carriage at 5 A.M. he had mounted his horse as soon as he came in sight of Dresden from the hills above. At the Marcolini (Meissenberg) fort he stopped to watch the Russian advance, and to direct more artillery on them. Then he galloped into Dresden, paid a visit of a few moments to the king, and hurried off to inspect the defences. St Cyr found him, between 11 and 12, on the French left, on foot in the midst of the horse artillery, which at the moment was not firing, as the pause in the battle had commenced. Then the Emperor rode along the defences towards the right. The garrison was terribly weak. Behind the garden walls in many places there was only one man to every ten paces. At the Dippoldiswalde road he went farther forward to observe the enemy. Arrived at redoubt IV., he was annoyed to find the Feldschlösschen in the enemy's possession and ordered St Cyr to retake it. The battalion sent for the purpose succeeded for a moment, but was driven out again. Having passed along the whole of his line, Napoleon returned to the Schloss Platz, where he took his position at the head of the stone bridge, watching the arrival of his troops and directing them to their posts in the line. Teste, with eight battalions, arrived first, and was sent to Friederichstadt, where Murat was put in command of this infantry, of the 1st cavalry corps, when it arrived at 2 P.M., and of Pajol's cavalry of St Cyr's corps.

Next came Decouz's and Roguet's Young Guard divisions under Mortier. These were sent to the suburbs on the

---

[1] Aster, *Schilderungen der Kriegsereignisse in und vor Dresden*. This author was a Saxon officer of artillery in Dresden in 1813. After his retirement from the service he wrote most careful accounts of the battles of Dresden, Kulm, and Leipzig, and other events in the war. He supplemented his personal knowledge of facts by the most careful local inquiries, and his facts appear to be accepted generally by modern German writers.

As regards these stories against the citizens of Dresden which were current in the Russo-Prussian army, he denies that there was any foundation in fact for them.

THE BATTLE OF DRESDEN 203

left. Two more divisions of Young Guard, under Ney, went to the Dippoldiswalde and Falken " schlags," left and right of redoubt IV. The Old Guard remained in the city in reserve, sending only one regiment to each of the suburbs of Pirna (on the left), Falken (centre), and Freiberg (on the right). The Guard had marched 90 miles in the last seventy-two hours, and that not on good roads but alongside of them, for Napoleon kept the roads for his guns and wagons, whilst the infantry and cavalry marched on a broad front across country. Latour-Maubourg's 78 squadrons went to behind Friederichstadt, where the public slaughter-house now stands, and there also were Pajol's 46 squadrons—23,000 cavalry in all. The rest of Teste's division, when it arrived, followed the first 8 battalions to Friederichstadt. It was between 3 and 5 P.M. when Roguet's 14 battalions and Barrois' 10 of the Young Guard arrived. These went to the suburbs on the right bank of the Weisseritz. The general reserve of Old Guard, under Friant and Curial, counted 10 battalions and 30 guns in the Altstadt, besides the 3 regiments sent as special reserves to the right, centre, and left. These were all the troops Napoleon could expect for this day's battle. We have somewhat anticipated in noting their arrival.

On the side of the allies, the Tsar and the King of Prussia stood, about 11 A.M., on the heights of Räcknitz in company with Jomini,[1] Moreau, and their other advisers and staff. They could clearly see the stream of Napoleon's soldiers hurrying to Dresden by the Bautzen road beyond the Elbe. Yet, the glow of bivouac fires towards Stolpen in the previous night should have warned the allied leaders that a great army was approaching. Jomini, clearly realising that the capture of Dresden was now hopeless, counselled retreat to Dippoldiswalde, and the Tsar agreed with him.

[1] Jomini had been Ney's chief of staff at Bautzen. He went over to the allies just before the end of the armistice. His defence of his conduct attributes it largely to Napoleon's refusal to let him leave his service in 1810, and to his disapproval of Napoleon's ambition. But it is difficult to avoid the suspicion that, had Ney's recommendation of him for appointment to a division after Bautzen been accepted, he would not have gone over. His case is different from Moreau's, inasmuch as he was a Swiss, not a Frenchman.

But the King of Prussia thought otherwise. Hours of discussion followed, ending in the decision to countermand the general attack fixed for 4 P.M. Whether Schwarzenberg deliberately neglected to give the counter-order, or whether there was a misunderstanding, it is certain that the three guns, the prearranged signal for attack, were fired and the battle recommenced.

Second Period, from 4 to 6 P.M.—It was towards 4 P.M. when Napoleon was informed that the allies appeared to be preparing for a general attack. Galloper after galloper was dispatched to hurry the march of the approaching French reinforcements.

The Russians on the allied right were still much annoyed by the French artillery beyond the Elbe, and, farther to their left, hampered in their movements by the Landgraben. French troops, too, had been pushed out along the Elbe, sheltered by an embankment constructed to restrain floods, and by several villas and farms. Nevertheless, the Russian right advanced for some distance victoriously from Engelhardt's, capturing Anton's and Lämmchen. In the centre they got little beyond the windmill height. On the left, between the Landgraben and the Grosser Garten, they pushed close up to redoubt II., but all their efforts to storm it were repulsed.

The Prussians in the Grosser Garten also arrived in front of redoubt II., which they attempted to storm along with the Russians on their right. They, too, were driven off here, as well as from the adjoining Prince Anton's garden, which was protected by a wall with a ditch in front of it.

Kleist, with his Prussians, advanced from the Rothe Haus against the Bürgerwiese and the Hospital garden.[1] In the attack on the latter they were joined by the right of the Austrians. Kleist had arrived within ten yards of the Dohna suburb when the Austrians on his left gave way before the terrible fire. At this juncture, too, Serurrier, with

---

[1] On the outer edge of the Dohna Schlag to the east of redoubt III. The Bürgerwiese is the open space cutting into the Schlag. Prince Anton's garden is directly behind the Grosser Garten.

THE BATTLE OF DRESDEN

St Cyr's 44th division, broke out from the Bürgerwiese, compelling Kleist to retire.

The signal guns for the general attack were followed immediately by the advance of numerous Austrian columns in the space between Kleist's left and the right bank of the Weisseritz. As the Austrian right advanced against the Hospital garden and redoubt III., they found their movement facilitated by the ditches and channels which then scored the slopes below Tschertnitz and Räcknitz.

The fate of the extreme right in this period has been noticed above in connexion with Kleist's attack. Two columns farther to the left were directed on redoubt III. Notwithstanding the support of their own and of Russian guns pushed forward with them, the Austrians were almost stopped by the terrible fire of the redoubt and the French batteries on either side of it. The two leading Austrian lines had already given way, when suddenly the work was silent. The supply of ammunition had given out. Seizing their opportunity, the Austrians dashed forward once more, mounting the parapet of the redoubt and engaging in a desperate hand-to-hand conflict with its defenders, who were nearly all killed or wounded before the remains at last retreated and sought shelter in the gardens behind.

The next Austrians on the left nearly got possession of the gardens; a few, indeed, penetrated into them, but the latter were turned by French reserves. In one of these attacks on the gardens several hundred Austrians, hemmed in against the walls by the French reserves, were compelled to surrender. So desperate was the fighting in this part that it is said that in redoubt III. alone 180 French and 344 Austrian dead were found in the evening, after its recapture.

The attack on redoubts IV. and V. was less successful. In redoubt IV. the allies' artillery fire wrought such havoc that 96 of its small garrison were *hors de combat*, and the fort was deserted for the moment. As the Austrian infantry rushed forward from the Feldschlösschen to seize it, French reserves issued from the "schlags" in rear and drove the enemy back to their starting-point. Two attacks, from

Kohler's Garden and the "Meisterei," on redoubt V. likewise failed before the steady fire of the French. A third attack from the Tharandt road met with the same fate. Beyond the Weisseritz, on the signal for the general advance, Bianchi pushed on towards Friedrichstadt from the positions gained before noon. He was met by a heavy artillery fire in front from the Freiberg road, and by a flanking fire from redoubt V.

On the extreme left, Meszko's men were in front of Cotta and Schusterhaüser, and a small party even got along below the Elbe bank to nearly opposite Uebigau. Thence, however, they had to fall back hurriedly, to avoid being cut off by French reserves and cavalry.

Napoleon, in Dresden, had been anxiously marking the course of the battle during this period, waiting for all the troops he could collect before making his counter-attack. By 5 P.M. he had some 70,000 men in the Altstadt and in the line of defence. The allies had about 150,000 on the field, but they had acted throughout with want of decision, and had kept nearly two-thirds of this great army in reserve.

Alarm had once more taken hold of the unfortunate citizens as they saw great masses of the allies pouring down from the heights, and the shells began to burst in all directions in the suburbs. Many houses were in flames. There was a general rush for safety in the cellars.

The streets were full of French troops, especially the open spaces in the suburbs where reserves were massed, ready to move at a moment's notice to any gravely threatened point. Amongst these troops the bursting shells produced only a feeling of exhilaration and eagerness. They were to fight under the immediate command of a leader whom they still believed to be invincible.

Aster tells a curious story of a battery which received orders to be ready to move into the fighting line. The men were dust-stained and untidy after their long march. The moment they heard of the order, each man began to get out of his haversack his parade uniform, which it was thought suitable to don on such an occasion. Comical scenes ensued, as men, in the act of changing their trousers, had to skip off as they might to avoid a shell about to burst. All were laughing and cheery, as if about to go to some fête. Such was the spirit of Napoleon's soldiers.

Third Period, from 6 P.M till dark.—The tide of the allied advance had reached its height towards 6 P.M. Their front line is shown on the plan, and it was one which made matters look very black to the uninitiated. Not so to Napoleon, who, between 5 and 6 P.M., had issued orders for the counter-attack which commenced at the latter hour. Ney, who had been ordered to take command in the Falken and Blinde "schlags" behind redoubt IV., had no fresh charger up. The Emperor, seeing his difficulty, turned to Caulaincourt saying he could lend Ney his horse. The Duke of Vicenza hesitated for a moment. "Descendez," was Napoleon's brief, stern order, and Caulaincourt instantly dismounted and changed chargers with Ney.

As soon as the orders for the general advance were issued, the Emperor left the Schloss Platz to watch their execution. First he went to the bridge of boats above the stone bridge, thence he was guided by Count Nostitz to the Rammischer "schlag," near the Elbe on the French left. Hence he passed through the Pirna and See "schlags," so close to the foremost line of the enemy that one of his orderly officers and several of his suite were wounded. It was 8 P.M. before, being finally satisfied that everything was going as he wished, he returned to the king's palace.

Meanwhile, on Napoleon's extreme left, the 3rd and 4th divisions of the Young Guard under Mortier began to issue, about 6 P.M., from the Ziegel "schlag" close to the Elbe. At that moment an ammunition wagon blew up, and the terrified horses dashed wildly amongst the troops. For a moment they were delayed, then Roguet advanced close to the Elbe, whilst Decouz attacked the Russians at Engelhardt's, driving them back on the Windmill height, which, after a desperate hand-to-hand struggle, was taken at 7 P.M.

By 8 P.M. the French on this wing had driven the Russians back into the Blasewitz wood and Striesen.

Wittgenstein was now so hard pressed that he personally rode over to Barclay to ask for reinforcements. Klüx's Prussian brigade was sent up to behind Striesen, which village the Russians evacuated only at midnight.

Simultaneously with this advance, three more columns of Mortier's troops issued from behind redoubt II., and from Prince Anton's garden, driving back Wittgenstein's left and the Prussians, whose attack had just failed. By 7 P.M. the French had driven the allies through half the length of the Grosser Garten to the palace. Here the fight swayed backwards and forwards till, at 8 P.M., the Prussians, still holding the palace, were separated from their antagonists only by the width of the central cross avenue. At that hour the turmoil of the struggle gave place to a still more ghastly silence, broken only by the groans of the wounded.

About redoubt III. the counter-attack began very soon after the Austrians were in possession of it. It was facilitated by the threat to the Austrian flank, due to Ney's advance by redoubt IV., to be described presently. The attack on the captured redoubt was commenced by a column of the Young Guard from the west of the Hospital garden. The first attempt failed, though about 50 men got in through a gate in the gorge of the work which, being closed behind them, left the little party isolated in the midst of about 500 Austrians. Refusing the enemy's calls to surrender, the gallant band held firm against tenfold numbers. As no officer was with them the drum-major took command, brandishing his baton, with which he promptly felled the Austrian leader. Help was at hand, and this little band of heroes held their ground till what remained of them was rescued by a fresh irruption, through the palisading, of their comrades, now reinforced by two regiments led by Berthezène. The redoubt was now recaptured, and some 400 Austrian prisoners were taken in it.

Ney, from the Falken and Blinde "schlags," had begun

to advance about the time the Austrians took redoubt III. He passed on both sides of redoubt IV., threatening by his movement the flanks of the Austrians in front of redoubts III. and V. His right column marched from the paper-mill on Kohler's garden, from which it drove the Austrians. The left column, charging along the upper Plauen road, failed in its first attempt to retake the Feldschlösschen. The second succeeded in taking it at the point of the bayonet. After this the Austrians in this quarter fell back fighting towards Plauen till darkness stopped the combat. In the low ground on the right bank of the Weisseritz the enemy, now reinforced by Chasteler's grenadiers, still held on, though suffering heavily.

During Ney's attack, Dumoustier issued from the Freiberg "schlag," drove the enemy in front of him across the Weisseritz, and recaptured the Chaussée Haus near the crossing of the Freiberg road. The Austrians retired to Riesentzien's garden,[1] which they still held, destroying the wooden bridge near it.

Beyond the Weisseritz, Teste's infantry, with part of Dumoustier's, issued from the Lobtau "schlag" against Altona and the neighbouring buildings. The Austrians made a desperate resistance in the buildings, but were eventually driven from all but a small inn at Klein Hamburg, which they evacuated at midnight. In this combat even Pajol's cavalry took part. As darkness fell, the Austrians on the Tharandt road withdrew behind Lobtau and bivouacked south-west of it. The village was occupied by neither party during the night, but the Austrians still held Cotta, Dölzschen, Nauslitz, Rossthal, Wolfnitz, and Nieder- and Ober-Gorbitz.

As a result of the day's fighting, the line of French outposts, marked on the plan, shows that they had regained practically all that they had lost earlier in the day.

Between 9 and 10 P.M. there were brought to Napoleon at the Royal Palace 700 Austrian prisoners, most of whom had been captured in or near redoubt III. After inspecting

[1] Marked "garden" on plan; just north of Plauen.

them by torchlight, the Emperor distributed crosses to the battalion of Young Guard escorting them.

The day had been fine, but towards midnight rain began to descend in torrents, which continued for the rest of the night, and during the whole of the next day.

If terror still reigned amongst the citizens, the French troops were jubilant over the great success which they had undoubtedly gained against vastly superior numbers. Moreover, their spirits were further raised by the knowledge of the approach of strong reinforcements, and by the fact that they were amply supplied with food and drink in the midst of the magazines and resources of Dresden.

During the night there was a constant stream of reinforcements pouring into the Altstadt over the three bridges across the Elbe.

In the evening of the 26th August Napoleon was inclined to believe that the allies would retreat in the night, but he issued orders for his troops for the next day, in the event of a fresh battle, should the enemy decide to maintain his position. During the night there arrived

II. corps (Victor), 36 battalions, 2 squadrons, 68 guns.

VI. corps (Marmont), 40 battalions, 8 squadrons, 78 guns.

Guard cavalry (Lefebvre - Desnoettes), 10 squadrons, 6 guns.

These raised the total available on the 27th to 180 battalions, 137 squadrons, 486 guns. At most, after allowing for losses on the 26th, these could not amount to more than from 120,000 to 125,000 men. The allies, on the other hand, had 158,000 men (less the losses of the 26th) actually on the field, and expected the arrival of 21,000 more with Klenau early next morning.

Nevertheless, the feeling in their camp was one of general despondency. They had gained little or no ground as the result of the day's fighting. This was attributable mainly to Schwarzenberg's indecision, and the confusion of his orders. It was almost impossible to say whether he aimed at a general attack, or merely at a reconnaissance in force. He had missed the great opportunity for storming Dresden

THE BATTLE OF DRESDEN

before Napoleon's arrival with reinforcements. There had been no unity of command, no co-operation of the various columns. Amongst the troops all confidence had disappeared; they were filled with the dread of Napoleon's presence. Moreover, they were very short of food and drink, owing to the wild confusion prevailing amongst the supply columns on the miserable roads between Dresden and the Erzgebirge. The best road, that by Peterswalde, was already threatened by Vandamme. That general, crossing by the Königstein bridges, had, by 5 P.M., got across 34 battalions and Corbineau's cavalry, but no artillery. With these he had attacked the inferior observing force under Prince Eugen of Wurtemberg. Though Eugen's men held out bravely till dark, they were obliged by their weakness to evacuate during the night the whole Pirna plateau, and the town itself. Eugen's appeals to headquarters for reinforcements had resulted in nothing but his supersession in the command by Osterman Tolstoi, who was ill and unfit for the task.

Eugen, seeking above all things to protect the rear of the army at Dresden, had abandoned the Peterswalde road and fallen back to a position north and south of Zehista, facing the Elbe. This was known both to the allies and to Napoleon.

At the council of war at allied headquarters there were again many differences of opinion and lengthy discussions, which ended in a decision to hold on next day to the heights before Dresden.

When the allied troops had, during the night, taken up the positions ordered by Schwarzenberg, whose orders Friederich considers by no means clear, they stood as follows:—

1. RUSSIANS AND PRUSSIANS

(*a*) Russian advanced guard, still holding Blasewitz weakly, stretched in a feeble line from the Elbe at Blasewitz to Grüna, where its left was supported by the Prussian reserve cavalry.

(*b*) The Russian 5th infantry division was spread from Torna to Leubnitz, with Ziethen's and Klüx's Prussians behind and on its right.

(*c*) The rest of the Prussians stood, two brigades between Leubnitz and Gostritz, one behind Gostritz; landwehr cavalry in 3rd line; reserve artillery in front of Nothnitz.

(*d*) Miloradowich's Russians held Tschertnitz, Klein Pestitz, and Mockritz.

2. AUSTRIANS

(*a*) Between Tschertnitz, Klein Pestitz, Coschütz, and Plauen were the corps of Colloredo and Chasteler, and Lederer's cavalry in 1st line. Civillart's division and Moritz Lichtenstein's cavalry in 2nd. In 3rd line Nostitz's cavalry.

Ignaz Gyulai, with the reserve, consisting of Weissenwolf's and Bianchi's divisions and Schuler's cavalry, was at Gittersee. These troops had been brought back from beyond the Weisseritz, on Klenau's promise to be on the field early in the morning of the 27th.

(*b*) Beyond the Weisseritz, Weissenwolf was in command. On his right in Dölzschen, Rossthal, and Neu Nimptsch, with detachments in front, were Czöllich's brigade, two infantry regiments sent ahead by Klenau, and two squadrons of cuirassiers. As reserve to these, Messery's brigade stood between Pesterwitz and Alt Franken.

On the left was Meszko's division, at and to the left of Nieder Gorbitz and Leutewitz, supported by Mumb's brigade.

The Austrian and Russian artillery trains, when they came up in the night, were sent to Nothnitz and Mockritz.

Napoleon's arrangements, which were completed before midnight, were these:—

(*a*) On his right, beyond the Wiesseritz, Murat commanded Victor's corps and 6 battalions of Teste's division, besides 68 squadrons of Pajol's and Latour-Maubourg's cavalry.

(*b*) From the right bank of the Weisseritz to beyond

THE BATTLE OF DRESDEN 213

redoubt III., Marmont commanded his own corps (VI.) and Normann's cavalry brigade.

(c) On Marmont's left, St Cyr, with the XIV. corps and Jacquet's cavalry brigade, stood behind Strehlen with his left in front of the south-east corner of the Grosser Garten.

(d) Ney, with Barrois' and Dumoustier's Young Guard divisions, was to advance through and on the north side of the Grosser Garten.

(e) On Ney's left was Mortier, with Decouz's and Roguet's Young Guard divisions. On his extreme left was Nansouty with two divisions of Guard cavalry.

Comparing the positions of the opponents, we find that Napoleon had beyond the Weisseritz about 35,000 men (12,000 of them cavalry) and 106 guns, opposed, until Klenau's arrival, to 24,000 allies with only 34 guns, and including less than 2000 cavalry. Once the French were in possession of Plauen, the allies would be cut off, by the gorge of the Weisseritz, from all hope of rapid support from their reserves in the centre. Klenau was supposed to be coming up from between Freiberg and Tharandt, but he did not arrive in time to support the isolated allied left wing. The 24,000 men beyond the Weisseritz were too strong for a mere corps of observation, not strong enough to fight a serious battle. Moreover, on a day of torrential rain, as the 27th August was, infantry was comparatively useless; for their muskets could often not be fired owing to their primings being damped.

In the centre, from Plauen to Strehlen, the allies had about 100,000 men opposed to 41,000 of Marmont and St Cyr. There were 83 squadrons of allies in this section, where they could be of comparatively little use. Napoleon only had a couple of cavalry brigades here. He had no intention of a serious attack in the centre; for his plan, notwithstanding his inferior numbers, was to attack on both wings, driving the allies off their two best roads to Bohemia on to the wretched tracks through the mountains between the roads via Peterswalde and Freiberg.

The allied right wing consisted of about 24,000 men,

including 83 squadrons. Napoleon's left, taking Ney as its right, had about 40,000 infantry and 10,000 cavalry.

It was all-important to the allies not to be cut from the Pirna-Peterswalde road, which was by far the best they had. Though the centre of their position was naturally the strongest, they massed two-thirds of their army on it. What they should have done, apparently, was to confine their defensive to the country on the right of the Weisseritz, and to strengthen their right especially. As for the left, beyond the Weisseritz, they would have been wise to attempt no defence of it.

(*b*) THE BATTLE OF THE 27TH AUGUST

When day broke on the 27th, the rain was still descending in torrents, and it was almost dark; a depressing outlook for all, especially for the allies, conscious as they were of failure on the previous day. Moreover, their commanders felt themselves handicapped by being able to see through the mist but a small area of a country which they knew indifferently, whilst Napoleon knew it thoroughly.

At 6 A.M. Mortier, on the French left, began his advance with Roguet on the left and Decouz on the right. The Guard cavalry followed the former.

By 7 A.M. Roguet had taken Blasewitz without serious fighting, and was proceeding to clear the Blasewitz wood. South of the wood Decouz was supported by Ney's two divisions, advancing on his right along the north edge of the Grosser Garten, from which the Prussians had retired at daybreak. The Russians, driven from Grüna, retired on Seidnitz, and, as Roguet with the French left swung round from Blasewitz, the whole of the Russian advanced guard (Roth) fell back to a position extending north-eastwards from Seidnitz to the Elbe.

The French were now pivoting on their right at Seidnitz, their left moving on Tolkewitz, threatening to surround Roth's right. Wittgenstein now ordered Roth, who was making a stubborn resistance, to retire on Reick and Prohlis, so as to join the right of the allied main position at Torna.

THE BATTLE OF DRESDEN 215

He still held firmly to Seidnitz, where his left repulsed several French attacks.

As soon as the Russians had evacuated Tolkewitz, the French cavalry passed through it towards Laubegast, and drew up south of it in two lines, facing the Pirna road.

Meanwhile the French had at last taken Seidnitz, whence Roguet set out to attack Gross- and Klein-Dobritz. The cavalry, at the same time, advanced towards Leuben. Nansouty, by passing Leuben and wheeling to his right, threatened the retreat of the Russians in Dobritz, and determined them, after repulsing several of Roguet's attacks, to retreat to Reick and south-east of it. This movement Nansouty made no attempt to harass with his cavalry, as apparently he might have done, seeing that the infantry were unable to fire their muskets in the wet. On the other hand, the allies had 62 squadrons on their right, which might have annihilated Nansouty's 28. Possibly the difficulty of seeing any distance in the blinding rain may account partially for the inactivity of the cavalry on both sides.

Whilst Mortier was thus getting forward on the left, Ney had reached Grüna. St Cyr, on his right, had taken Strehlen, between 8 and 9 A.M., without much difficulty, since it was only defended by one Prussian battalion, which presently retired to Leubnitz, where the Prussians still held the right bank of the Kaitzbach. St Cyr had not yet moved the main body of his corps beyond a position between the Grosser Garten and Strehlen, but he had posted a powerful battery on the rising ground just east of the latter place, with which he was firing heavily on Tschertnitz and Leubnitz.

Such was the position at 11 A.M., when Napoleon reached Leubnitz. The Emperor had betaken himself, at 6 A.M., to a post just behind redoubt IV., where a great bonfire was lighted for him, and a tent pitched. Here he remained till 10, waiting for news of Murat's attack with his right beyond the Weisseritz. At that hour he received a report which satisfied him that all was going well in that direction, and that he might now go to look after his left. Riding through the Pirna suburb and the Grosser Garten, he reached Seidnitz about 11 A.M., and at once ordered an attack on Reick. The village was strongly protected on the north and east by the Landgraben, here about 8 feet deep, flowing in a channel 6 to 8 feet wide at the top. The channel ran along an embankment 10 to 12 feet high, and 18 to 20 feet thick. The French attack was made on both sides of the angle where the watercourse turns from north-east to north-west. Meeting the Russians in front on the embankment, and charged in left flank by Russian and Prussian cavalry, the French were driven off with heavy loss. The attack was renewed with reinforcements, but the defenders would not yield till a French shell fired the north part of the village and reduced them to the southern part. In the smoke the Russians failed to see that the French had almost surrounded them, and when they attempted to retreat on Prohlis, they found themselves cut off. Then they sold their lives as dearly as they could in a fierce hand-to-hand struggle in the houses. It was not till noon that the French were finally in possession of Reick, where the horror of the scene was enhanced by the burning of many in the raging fire.

The remains of Roth's force fell back on Torna. Beyond Reick the French advanced but a short way after noon, though they continued to bombard and set on fire the villages in front of it. After witnessing the storming of Reick, Napoleon betook himself to St Cyr's corps. This he now found with its right in Strehlen, and left in contact with Ney's right at Grüna.

Presently the relief of the Prussians in Leubnitz by the Russians induced a belief that they were retreating, and an attack was at once made on the village from Strehlen. The French got into the nearer part of it, but, swept with grape by two guns at the church, and then charged with the bayonet by two Prussian battalions, they were driven out again. A second attack failed before it reached Leubnitz.

It was at this juncture that Napoleon arrived on the scene. He was furious at the failure of the attacks, and

THE BATTLE OF DRESDEN 217

ordered a third, to support which he had added horse artillery guns to the battery east of Strehlen. This attack was nipped in the bud by a storm of artillery fire directed on the French as they issued from Strehlen. Skirmishing continued along the Kaitzbach till evening, when the French surprised, and got into the north-east corner of Leubnitz, whence they were promptly ejected again.

It was 1 o'clock when Napoleon, disgusted with his failure at Leubnitz, started on his return journey to redoubt IV. On the way he ordered a horse artillery battery forward to fire on the enemy's battery near Räcknitz. After a few rounds it stopped firing, and, on his inquiring the reason, he was informed that the object battery had withdrawn. He then ordered his own battery to fire on a group of horsemen a little to the left of Räcknitz. The first shot fired had momentous results; for the ball hit Moreau as he was riding just in front of the Tsar. It tore through his right leg above the knee, passed through his horse, and shattered the left leg also.[1]

Before this, the Tsar, seeing things going badly on the right, had, on the advice of Jomini and Moreau, directed Barclay and Wittgenstein to attack Mortier's front with all available reserves, whilst Kleist and Miloradowich attacked his right towards Strehlen and Grüna. The plan was good; but Barclay objected that, if it failed, he would lose all his artillery, as, in the muddy state of the country, he could not get his guns up the hill again. This remonstrance arrived just as Moreau was wounded, and in the confusion no reply was sent. Barclay, therefore, did nothing; and the counter attack never came off, though Danilewski[2] and Jomini say Kleist and Miloradowich had actually changed front to the

---

[1] Moreau behaved heroically, calmly smoking a cigar, whilst both his legs were amputated by the Tsar's surgeon, Wylie, at a farm a short way in rear. "I am done for," he said, as Alexander spoke to him, "but how good it is to die for the good cause, under the eyes of so great a monarch." He was carried, suffering great agony, to Laun, in Bohemia, where he died a week later. His body was embalmed and taken to St Petersburg, where it was buried with great pomp.—*Danilewski*, p. 173.

[2] *Danilewski*, pp. 143-145.

right ready for it. Perhaps, too, the ardour of headquarters for this move had cooled in consequence of the news just received, that Vandamme, at Pirna, had driven Eugen of Wurtemberg off the Peterswalde road. The news, perhaps, did not reach Napoleon till later, as the Saxon general, Gersdorf, who had received it, had been sent to inform the King of Saxony of the impending victory of the French.

Marmont's troops, all along the line from redoubt III. to the Weisseritz, had been heavily fired on since early morning by a long line of Austrian guns, extending almost continuously along the heights from Räcknitz to above Plauen. On his right the French had driven the Austrians from all the gardens and houses right up to Plauen. Beyond this, nothing happened on Marmont's front.

We must now describe the course of events beyond the Weisseritz. The Austrian main position on this side rested its right on the gorge of the Weisseritz at Dölzschen. Thence it passed through Nauslitz, Rossthal, Neu Nimptsch, and Nieder Gorbitz, almost up to Leutewitz.

Murat started his advance against this line between 6 and 7 A.M. Victor's corps (II.) assembled opposite the Weisseritz woodyard, near the bridge on the Freiberg road. Thence they were to spread out fanwise in four columns moving towards Nauslitz, Rossthal, Wolfnitz, and Nieder Gorbitz. The artillery was in advance covered by skirmishers, the corps cavalry followed the main body of the infantry.

Teste's division assembled behind the rising ground at Lobtau. Pajol's cavalry took post between Victor and Teste, whilst Latour-Maubourg's squadrons came up on Teste's right, having the Saxon Guard cuirassier regiment on his extreme outer flank moving towards Leutewitz.

Victor's artillery, pushing forward, opened a heavy fire on Nauslitz and the Austrian guns there, whilst the infantry advanced in four columns. The 1st, on the left, followed the small ravine (perhaps better described as a hollow road) which leads up the slope to between Rossthal and Dölzschen. The 2nd column attacked the gardens about Nauslitz, the 3rd went by the right of Nauslitz, the 4th moved by the

THE BATTLE OF DRESDEN 219

Freiberg road against Wolfnitz and Nieder Gorbitz. The cavalry followed in rear of the infantry.

The 1st column, covered by the ravine and the orchards on either side of it, had little difficulty in reaching its head, where it found itself close to the Austrian position between Rossthal and Dölzschen.

The 2nd column was not so fortunate, and had to make several attacks before it was in possession of Nauslitz. Thence it followed the two ravines which lead, one into Rossthal, the other rather to the left of it. The ravines were admirably suited to the French infantry, adepts in the use of cover, and as the 1st and 2nd columns issued from them, the Austrians between Dölzschen and Rossthal gave way, retiring partly on each of these villages. The 1st column now turned to its left, hemming the now separated right of the enemy against the great ravine of the Weisseritz. At the same time, the 2nd column turned to the right against Rossthal, which they stormed, taking 300 prisoners.

From Rossthal the 2nd column attacked the right flank of the Austrians opposing the 3rd column, and drove them partly towards Neu Nimptsch and partly on Pesterwitz. Neu Nimptsch was also stormed by the 3rd column. The 4th column, advancing on Nieder Gorbitz, had stormed Wolfnitz. The defenders of Nieder Gorbitz were surrounded and captured in a ravine between Neu Nimptsch and Alt Franken with the aid of Victor's cavalry, which was now up on the height between Neu Nimptsch and the Austrian reserves of Messery towards Pesterwitz.

During the attacks on the other villages, Meszko's troops had fallen back from Nieder to Ober Gorbitz and to the west of it, where Mumb's brigade had joined them.

About noon the Austrians from Wolfnitz, and those now driven out of Ober Gorbitz, were in considerable disorder in the open space between the latter village and Neu Nimptsch. Victor's cavalry was preparing to charge them, so they formed themselves into four squares as far as possible. Their muskets, however, would not go off in the rain, and they were ridden down by the French cavalry. Many were cut down, a great many more taken prisoners, and only a few got away to Pesterwitz.

The capture of Ober Gorbitz had cut Meszko completely from Alois Lichtenstein's division at Neu Nimptsch, so that the Austrian line was now pierced in two places, between Dölzschen and Rossthal, and between Neu Nimptsch and Ober Gorbitz.

As soon as Victor's cavalry had destroyed the four squares as above described, Pajol's cavalry had moved along the Freiberg road.

Whilst all this was happening in the Austrian centre and right, between the Freiberg road and the Plauen gorge, Murat, with the main body of the French cavalry and Teste's infantry, had advanced against Meszko's left and Mumb's brigade west of Ober Gorbitz. The Austrians fell back, as they were bound to do, after the ruin of the troops in the centre. Indeed, by this time, when it was too late to save a disaster, Weissenwolf had ordered a general retreat. His left was to make its way by Pesterwitz to the Weisseritz in rear below. Czöllich, with the right, was to reach the same point by Potzschappel.

The French cavalry followed Meszko. Teste's right moved round Gompitz to Pennrich, which they easily took, as Meszko's attention was fixed in front of him. He and Mumb retreating in squares, now found themselves with their retreat by Pennrich cut off by Teste's infantry there, and attacked by the cavalry of Murat and Pajol on the other three sides. The Austrian infantry, unable to fire their muskets, and threatened by cavalry and artillery, laid down their arms and surrendered.[1] Four entire regiments

---

[1] Marbot, no doubt, refers to this part of the battle in his famous story of Bordesoulle riding up to an Austrian square, and calling on it to surrender as it could not fire. When they replied that his cavalry equally could not charge in the heavy mud, he clinched the argument by opening out and showing a battery of artillery ready to fire. The Austrians at once gave in. The story may or may not be true.

The neighbourhood was an unpropitious one for the Austrians, for it is within two miles of Kesselsdorf, where they and their Saxon allies were so badly beaten by the "Old Dessauer" in 1745, though, it is true, very few Austrians actually fought that day.

THE BATTLE OF DRESDEN

were captured here, with Meszko and Mumb. The Saxon cuirassiers who, during the fights at Wolfnitz and Nieder-Gorbitz, had marched from Leutewitz to Ober Gorbitz, had already taken two Austrian squares of 2000 men.

We must return for a moment to the Austrian right, which had been hemmed against the gorge at Dölzschen by Victor's left column. Protected in front by a garden wall facing towards Rossthal, they had behind them as means of retreat nothing but a very difficult and steep footpath from Dölzschen down to the Weisseritz at the point where the Felsenkeller brewery now stands, and a bad steep road from their left along the face of the cliff.

For some time they managed to keep the French off, but about 2 P.M., a shell fired Dölzschen, and the village was rushed in the consequent confusion. Some of the defenders, pursued by the French fire, got away by the path or the road, and attempted to scale the opposite heights, which are in many places sheer precipices. Those who got so far narrowly escaped drowning in the swollen Weisseritz. One battery succeeded in getting down the bad road, but could not cross the stream short of Potzschappel, as the bridge had been destroyed. Numerous prisoners were taken in Dölzschen. Here the French infantry broke into the wine cellars and indulged in what Aster calls a "Bacchus-feast," which might have cost them dear had there been any Austrians to make a counter attack. There were plenty in sight, just across the gorge, where the reserves stood; but they were compelled to look idly on at the destruction of their comrades, to whom they could bring no help in time.

By 2 P.M. the whole Austrian left beyond the Weisseritz had been practically destroyed. The number of prisoners taken was enormous, Aster thinks 15,000 is not too high a figure to take.[1]

---

[1] With regard to prisoners, the author found the following returns in the Paris records—(1) One showing 1407 prisoners received at headquarters up to midnight on the 26th, and 4209 more up to 7 P.M. on the 27th. (2) Prisoners in Dresden on the 29th August, 12,535.

These two returns give rise to a suspicion that the numbers taken at Dresden may

What remained of this unfortunate left wing got into the Weisseritz Valley about Potzschappel, whence they reached the Dippoldiswalde road by Rabenau, far in rear of the allies' main position. Some who tried to escape to Freiberg were followed by French cavalry and lost many prisoners. They probably hoped to meet Klenau, but that general had marched by Tharandt. When he heard of the disaster to the Austrian left, he at once moved to his right to the Dippoldiswalde road.

Victor's cavalry had found Alt Franken still occupied by Austrians. They were shelled by horse artillery, and the village was stormed by French infantry from Ober Gorbitz, just as its garrison was retiring on Pesterwitz.

All fighting on this side of the Weisseritz was over by 3 P.M., though the French cavalry continued the pursuit as far as Herzogswalde, taking many prisoners and some guns.

In the rear of the allies, Vandamme had not done very much on the 27th August.[1] Even on that morning he had not got his corps completely across the Elbe at Königstein, but Mouton-Duvernet[2] was able to occupy Pirna, and the plateau above it, whilst Phillippon's division took post to the left of Krietschwitz, and Corbineau's cavalry advanced to between Langen Hennersdorf and Berggieshübel. A battalion was placed on the Kohlberg, the hill at the junction of the Gottleuba and Seidnitz Valleys.

Vandamme, deceived partly by the thickness of the weather, partly by the reports of a doctor who had been captured from the enemy, believed he was not strong enough to attack till the whole of his corps was up. At 4 P.M.,

have been exaggerated. But there is a later return showing the total number received up to the 8th October at 23,518 (over 15,000 Austrians). The greater part of these must have been taken at Dresden, for there were few other large captures of prisoners by the French. Of the 590 others who deserted from the allies only sixteen soldiers were Prussians, and not a single officer! 478 are classed as "miscellaneous," *i.e.* neither Russians, Austrians, nor Prussians.

[1] Map IV. (*b*), and Map I.

[2] 42nd Division belonging to St Cyr's corps, but temporarily under Vandamme.

THE BATTLE OF DRESDEN

hearing of the progress of the battle at Dresden, he prepared to march next day on Berggieshübel and Hellendorf.

At 3 P.M. the battle at Dresden was nearly over, the artillery fire had ceased. At 4 P.M., Napoleon, wet to the skin, with the famous cocked hat reduced to pulp by the rain and hanging limply about his ears and down his neck, rode through the Dippoldiswalde suburb to the palace. Behind him marched 1000 Austrian prisoners. Later on 12,000 more[1] came in from beyond the Weisseritz, including Meszko, two other generals, sixty-four officers of high, and many of lower rank. Fifteen Austrian standards were borne by the grenadiers of the Old Guard; twenty-six guns, and thirty ammunition wagons followed. Save the one battery which escaped from Dölzschen, practically the whole of the Austrian artillery of the left wing was there.

"When an army of 120,000 men, in the presence of 180,000 enemies, deploys from a bridge-head, then surrounds the enemy on both wings, and seriously damages both; when it compels a whole division to lay down its arms in the open field, when it brings in immediately from the battlefield 13,000 prisoners fifteen standards, and twenty-six guns, that is a quite undeniable victory." So says von Caemmerer,[2] thinking apparently of less honest historians, who would attempt to deny that at Dresden Napoleon gained one of his most remarkable, though almost his last, great victories.

Could he have carried out his original plan of holding the allies before Dresden, whilst he, with 100,000 men, instead of Vandamme with 40,000, issued by Königstein on their rear, the result would perhaps have been decisive of the whole campaign. But the weakness of Dresden diverted him from his purpose, and as it was, he owed much to the irresolution of the allies, to their postponement of the attack on the city till the 26th, and to its general feebleness during the hours in which he was bringing up his reinforcements. Yet it is tempting to speculate what might have happened had he kept to his original plan, and sent 40,000 of

---

[1] See previous note on this subject.
[2] *Die Befreiungskrieg* 1813-1815. p. 56.

his nearest troops to support St Cyr, whilst with 100,000 he himself crossed at Königstein. Would not St Cyr, with another 40,000 men, have been able to hold on at least to the Altstadt behind the old enceinte, for the scaling of which the allies had made no preparations? Would the allies have dared to continue their attack on Dresden after the 26th, perhaps even after noon on that date? By that time they might well have learnt, from Eugen of Wurtemberg, that Napoleon himself was crossing at Königstein. Would not that have sent them hurrying back to Bohemia, harassed and delayed by St Cyr with 60,000 men? Napoleon at Stolpen, be it remembered, was nearer to Königstein than he was to Dresden, and he had at least as good a road. Latour-Maubourg and the Guard were also nearer to Königstein than to Dresden; Victor and Marmont no farther from one than from the other.

However, this is mere speculation, and we must return to actual facts. These were, that the allies had been badly defeated at Dresden, that they had lost probably at least 25,000 men, that the Peterswalde road was already intercepted by Vandamme, and the next best road, by Freiberg, was in Murat's hands. They were practically confined to the bad tracks between the two, on which their movements, hampered by the congestion of trains, must be slow. By the Peterswalde road Napoleon could be across the Erzgebirge and in Bohemia, ready to meet them there as they debouched from the difficult passes of the mountains. We shall see presently how he lost his chance. On the 26th and 27th August his genius flashed forth, he was the Napoleon of Austerlitz, Jena, and Friedland; on the following days he relapsed into the declining energy of 1813.

His unerring appreciation of the advantages to himself of the separation of the allied left by the Plauen gorge recalls his similar estimate of the position of the Russian left at Friedland, separated by the smaller obstacle of the mill stream from the centre and right. His bold resolve to attack on both wings, notwithstanding his inferiority of

THE BATTLE OF DRESDEN 225

numbers, was a novelty with him. The only question is whether he might not have still further weakened his centre in order to strengthen his left, and break in the allied right; that is, whether he might not have added at least half of St Cyr's corps to his left.

He owed much, no doubt, to the faults of his enemy, to the massing of the allied army on its centre, to the neglect of the right, and especially to the collection in the centre of the great mass of their cavalry, where it was useless. If the support of Dresden rendered Napoleon's centre safe, the allies equally were safe in their centre. Possibly their action may have been due to their belief that he would always make his great effort to break the centre. That was an idea held by St Cyr, as we have already seen when that marshal discussed the plan for Bautzen.[1] Still, Bautzen itself should have warned them that he allowed himself to be tied down by no such hard and fast rule.

Again, they committed a grave error in leaving their exposed left wing miserably weak both in guns and cavalry, the two arms which could do most in the pouring rain of the 27th August, in an age when neither breech-loaders nor even percussion caps had been invented to do away with the necessity for primings, which could not be kept dry.

One thing must be said in favour of the allies' treatment of their left wing, namely, that they had good reason to believe Klenau would have joined it early in the morning, nearly doubling its strength. They had not reckoned on that commander's slowness, due doubtless to the terrible meteorological conditions, and had been content to accept his assurance that he would be up in time. It is not, however, clear why Klenau should have gone by Tharandt instead of by Kesselsdorf. He started that move before he knew of the ruin of the allied left. Surely the allies should have known that Klenau was delayed in time to repair their error to some extent by sending reinforcements, from their reserve at Gittersee, across the Weisseritz to the left wing.

When their right wing was hard pressed, the proposal for

[1] *Supra*, p. 140.

a strong counter attack with Kleist and Miloradowich came to nothing, partly on account of Barclay's rather weak objection, partly on account of the depressing effects of Moreau's mortal wound, and the news of Vandamme's progress at Pirna. The former, however it may have affected Alexander, was after all only an incident, the latter was an additional reason for attempting to clear the Pirna road, as well as for the despatch of reinforcements from the centre to Osterman at Zehista.

For the counter attack on Napoleon's left, cavalry might also have been sent to the right from the centre, where it was standing idle. It may also be remarked that the Russo-Prussian cavalry, already available on the right, might well have displayed more activity than it did against Nansouty's.

CHAPTER XIV

FROM DRESDEN TO KULM[1]

AT 7 P.M. on the 27th August Napoleon ordered Ney to be informed, "that the enemy is not in retreat, that he only regarded the affair of yesterday as an attack that had failed, that it is doubtful if he will commence his retreat to-night."[2] In the same orders Ney was to be informed that, "everything leads to the belief there will be a great battle tomorrow, and that the enemy is numerous." An hour later the Emperor was still making preparations for a renewal of the battle, even to prescribing the garrisons of the redoubts.[3] Precisely when he came to the conclusion that the allies would not renew the battle, and had begun their retreat, is not quite clear. Apparently he was not quite sure at daybreak on the 28th, when he returned to his old position near redoubt IV. The orders, if there were any in writing, which he then issued to Marmont and St Cyr have not yet been found, but it is certain that by 9 A.M. those marshals were in the allies' position of the 27th on the heights, which was now empty. The rain had ceased, but for some time a thick mist obscured the view.

On the afternoon of the 27th, after Moreau's fall, a council of war was held by the allied commanders round a badly burning camp fire. The King of Prussia advocated renewing the battle next day. Jomini still counselled retreat to Dippoldiswalde. The majority were for retreat right back to Bohemia, and their opinion was supported by the statement of Schwarzenberg that bread, shoes, and ammunition were all wanting, and not to be procured.

[1] Map IV. (b).   [2] *Corr.* 20,479.   [3] *Corr.* 20,481.

Thousands of men were barefooted, their shoes having been sucked off their feet by the mud. There was, he maintained, no hope of taking Dresden, no advantage to be gained by fighting another battle. Retreat in the night was decided on. About 4 P.M. Toll and Radetzky produced a draft order to the following effect :—

(1) Barclay, with Wittgenstein, Kleist, and the Russo-Prussian reserves, to march by Dohna, Berggieshübel, and Peterswalde to Teplitz.

(2) All the Austrians on the right bank of the Weisseritz to go by Dippoldiswalde, Altenberg, and Eichwald to Dux and Brüx in Bohemia.

(3) Klenau, and the remains of the left wing beyond the Weisseritz, to march by Tharandt, Freiberg, and Marienberg towards Kommotau. This direction was upset by the fact that the remains of Czöllich's and Alois Lichtenstein's divisions had joined Klenau at Potzschappel and marched with him to Gittersee.

Radetzky's orders assigned one road to each column, but they were not all available. That on the left by Kesselsdorf and Herzogswalde to Freiberg was already in the hands of Murat's cavalry. If Klenau marched by Tharandt on Freiberg, he could not reach Naundorf, the junction of that road with the one from Kesselsdorf, before night on the 28th. The road, already bad when the allies advanced, had been rendered almost impassable by twenty-four hours of rain. The column might well be attacked by the French at the passage of the Mulde near Freiberg. Klenau, therefore, alarmed at the risk, decided to march by Rabenau to Pretzschendorf, whence he would endeavour to reach the Chemnitz-Kommotau road at Marienberg. In the end he reached Pretzschendorf on the 28th, Gross Waltersdorf on the 29th, Marienberg on the 30th.

The head of the centre column reached Altenberg on the 28th, Dux on the 29th. Its rearguard (Moritz Lichtenstein) was at Wendisch-Carsdorf on the 28th, Falkenhain on the 29th, Altenberg early on the 30th.

Barclay, with the right column, also thought Radetzky's

FROM DRESDEN TO KULM

orders impracticable, for he believed Vandamme was with 35,000 or 40,000 men on the Peterswalde road between himself and Teplitz, whilst Napoleon with 50,000 men from Dresden was following him. Believing that to follow the new road would endanger the very existence of his command, he ordered :—

(1) The reserves to march by the Dippoldiswalde road.

(2) Kleist by Maxen and Glashütte.

(3) Wittgenstein to cover the retreat on the heights of Leubnitz and Prohlis.

(4) Osterman, if he found the main road blocked by Vandamme, to join the rest by Maxen.

Had these orders been carried out, the result would have been the meeting of 120,000 men on the single bad road from Dippoldiswalde to Bohemia. The resulting confusion would have been almost unimaginable, and by the time the great crowd of disordered troops reached the passes leading down to Bohemia, Vandamme would have arrived at their mouths, via Peterswalde, quite unopposed. As it was, the Russians and Prussians of Barclay's column marched at nightfall on the 27th for Dippoldiswalde. The main body going by Lockwitz, Maxen, and Hausdorf, only reached Furstenwalde on the 29th. Their night march to Dippoldiswalde, though they were not pursued, was one of dreadful suffering for the weary, hungry men on a wretched road in pouring rain. Had there been any immediate pursuit, nothing could have saved them from destruction. Klüx, standing as rearguard at Leubnitz, followed the rest on the morning of the 28th, via Possendorf.

It was not till 9 A.M. on the 28th, when the allies had disappeared from the heights, that Napoleon's orders[1] for the pursuit were issued, St Cyr and Marmont being already on the enemy's position of the previous day.

St Cyr was directed to march on Dohna, following the enemy and keeping in the plain between Dohna and the Elbe, so as to be always in sight of Mortier, who was ordered to Pirna, where Napoleon would join him. Van-

[1] *Corr.* 20,483.

damme was to be informed of the orders, and, as soon as he and St Cyr were in touch, he was to take his whole corps on to the heights of Berggiesshübel and Hellendorf. No orders appear to have been issued to Marmont on the 28th beyond one of 9 P.M.[1] directing him to follow and do as much harm as possible to the enemy.

Osterman and Eugen of Würtemberg had waited in vain for reinforcements on the 27th. On the morning of the 28th they heard of the results of the battle at Dresden, and that Barclay was to retreat by the Peterswalde road to Teplitz. Wolzogen, who brought the orders from the Tsar, was also to say that they could easily hold Zehista till Barclay's arrival. At the same time, however, Barclay's orders arrived saying he was going by the Dippoldiswalde road, and that Osterman would march by Maxen if the Peterswalde road was already blocked by Vandamme. As the latter contingency was already known to have occurred, it appeared to be the duty of Osterman and Eugen to march by Maxen. Eugen vigorously urged the fatal consequences of thus leaving the new road open to Vandamme; but Osterman demurred to running any risks with the precious Russian Guard. Even Wolzogen supported Eugen, and in the end, when Eugen had threatened to go off with his own corps alone to Peterswalde, Osterman gave in, on condition Eugen would take the entire responsibility on himself. This he did in a letter to the Tsar. Nevertheless, Eugen continued to be hampered by the anxiety of Osterman and Yermolow to keep the Guard out of danger.

Vandamme at this time had Quiot's brigade on the plateau above Pirna, with a battalion of light infantry on the Kohlberg. On Quiot's left was Mouton-Duvernet, beyond him Dumonçeau; Philippon's division and Corbineau's cavalry at Hennersdorf. The allies now drew in all the troops they had north of Zehista for a demonstration against the Kohlberg and Krietschwitz, under cover of which the Guard and artillery marched for Hellendorf.

Vandamme soon saw through this, and at 3 P.M. sent

---

[1] *Marmont. Mém.*, v. 222.

FROM DRESDEN TO KULM

Quiot hurrying along the Gottleuba valley, whilst the demonstration was dealt with by other troops.

When the head of the Russian Guard reached Berggiesshübel it found the enemy in the woods, and had to force a passage with the bayonet. The Guard reached Peterswalde without serious loss. The 2nd corps, following them, was driven off the road by Quiot and part of it had to escape by by-paths to Hellendorf during the night. When Eugen, about 5 P.M., assembled the remains of his corps at Hellendorf, he had but 2000 men left.

In front of Hellendorf Vandamme stopped his pursuit for the night. There he had the brigade of Prince Reuss and the cavalry of Corbineau and Gobrecht. The rest of his troops were on the road between Berggiesshübel and Hellendorf, and on either side of it.

We now return to Napoleon after he had issued his 9 A.M. orders for the pursuit. Shortly afterwards he rode off towards Pirna. On the way, at 9.45 A.M., he received a dispatch from Vandamme, who stated that the enemy was retreating across his front with 25,000 men, and that he was being attacked. As we know, he had been deceived as to the enemy's strength. Napoleon, however, felt certain that he could have no great force before him. He was convinced that the right of the allies was making for Maxen, their centre for Dippoldiswalde, their left for Marienberg and Annaberg. He thought it desirable to draw St Cyr closer to Marmont, who was following the main body of the enemy. If Murat bore south-west from Freiberg he would come on their flank and rear. He had begun to think he could do more with Murat, and that Vandamme's 40,000 men were ample to drive on Eugen of Wurtemberg and to make connexion by Tetschen with Poniatowski at Gabel. Satisfied with the progress of affairs, he decided to send the Old Guard back to Dresden and to stop the Young Guard at Pirna.

Getting into his carriage at Pirna, he started back to Dresden. With the story that Napoleon was compelled by illness to return to Dresden we will deal later. At 4 P.M., "one league from Pirna," Napoleon stopped to dictate an order to Vandamme which was sent by Berthier. Vandamme was to move on Peterswalde with the I. corps, 42nd division, Corbineau's cavalry, and Prince Reuss' brigade of the II.[1] Pirna would be held by Mortier. "The Emperor desires you to unite all the forces which he places at your disposal, and with them to penetrate into Bohemia, overthrowing the Prince of Wurtemberg, if he opposes you. The enemy, whom we have defeated, appears to be retiring on *Annaberg*. His Majesty thinks that you could arrive before him on his communications of Tetschen, Aussig, and Teplitz, and there take all his carriage, ambulances, baggage, in fine, everything which marches behind an army. The Emperor orders the boat-bridge at Pirna to be removed, in order to be able to throw one at Tetschen." [2]

At Dresden Napoleon heard of Macdonald's defeat on the Katzbach; he had already heard of Oudinot's at Gross Beeren.

Late that night (28th) he received Vandamme's report of 8.30 P.M. saying that the enemy had been beaten and was in flight. His orders to Vandamme thereon are not yet forthcoming, but as that general next day occupied Aussig instead of Tetschen, and threw a bridge at the former, it may be presumed they directed him to do so.

During the whole of the 28th the French were pursuing in four columns directed respectively on Freiberg (Murat), Dippoldiswalde (Marmont), Maxen (St Cyr), and Berggiesshübel (Vandamme), capturing many prisoners and guns, with much material of all sorts. The interest of the 29th and 30th August centres mainly about the operations of Vandamme.

---

[1] Teste's division, except Quiot's brigade, was with Victor. Vandamme had Prince Reuss' brigade in exchange.

[2] Du Casse (*Le général Vandamme*, ii. 504) quotes this despatch with the name "Altenberg," instead of "Annaberg," which, as will be seen later, makes a considerable difference in the question as to the responsibility for Vandamme's subsequent defeat. The name in the "Registre du Major Général" at Paris is "*Annaberg*" which seems to show beyond doubt that Du Casse's version is wrong.

During the night of the 28th-29th Osterman sent a report to Teplitz, where he believed the Tsar to be, saying he was compelled to retire before Vandamme, and must cross the Eger.

In the early morning of the 29th Osterman started first with the Russian Guard. At 6 A.M. there was a rearguard action about Hellendorf, in which the allies were driven back. In this fight Prince Reuss, on the French side, lost his life. There was another rearguard action about Peterswalde, in which a flank attack by French cavalry from Raitza, east of Peterswalde, had considerable influence. Schachowski, the allied commander, lost 1000 men. He made another stand at Nollendorf, and again at Vorder Tellnitz. Thence he was followed to Kulm, where yet another fight took place about 10 A.M., the confusion of which was added to by the intrusion of some unfortunate villagers returning from church.

Osterman's envoy to the Tsar had not found him at Teplitz, but he found there the King of Prussia and the Austrian Emperor. The latter rode off to Laun, but the King, realising the situation, at once sent off to Osterman, pointing out the danger to the army of his retreat beyond the Eger. He added that it would endanger the personal safety of the Tsar, who was still in the mountains. This latter consideration convinced Osterman that the time had come for making use of his Guard. Frederick William also despatched his adjutants in all directions in search of troops to support Osterman at Priesten.

Alexander left Altenberg, where he had slept, early on the 29th. At 2 P.M. he was on the crest of the mountains on the road to Dux. Thence he saw what was happening at Priesten. He at once ordered Colloredo, who was nearest him, to Priesten. The Austrian refused on the ground of Schwarzenberg's orders.[1] The latter could not be found, but the Tsar found Jomini and Metternich. The latter assumed the responsibility of sending Colloredo to Priesten, saying that circumstances had changed since Schwarzenberg's

[1] *Danilewski*, p. 150-152.

order. Meanwhile, Osterman had taken up a position at Priesten facing east, with his left on the wooded heights above Straden, his centre in and west of Priesten, and his right between Priesten and Karbitz. He had, at the beginning of the action, about 14,700 men; by the end of the day he had received reinforcements raising his numbers to, at most, 20,000 men.

The scene of the battle of the 29th and 30th August is the slope below the last really steep part of the Erzgebirge. Kulm is a short mile from the real foot of the mountains, though there is a fairly steep slope all the way down from the railway station of to-day to the village, which is of a fair size. At Tellnitz, $2\frac{1}{2}$ miles north-east of Kulm, the road by which Vandamme arrived comes winding round the angle of the hill from Nollendorf. In Kulm itself there is a knoll rising 100 or 120 feet above the village, and affording an excellent view of the surrounding country. The road from Kulm to Priesten is of the "switchback" class, Priesten being at the top of the second rise, not counting the slight rise about 300 yards out of Kulm.

South of Kulm there is a wood in which is the "Schloss," and beyond that more hills, between Karbitz and Deutsch-Neudörfel. Vandamme had got possession of Kulm by 10 A.M., but his troops were still spread out in a long column in the pass over the mountains. Believing apparently that he was only going to have another small rear-guard action, like those he had already had earlier in the morning, he sent Reuss' brigade to try and cut the Russians from the mountains by their left. Tactically this was perhaps the better course, as the protection of the marshy ground on the other flank was stronger. Strategically, however, he would have done much better to have turned their right, driving them into the mountains, and on to the heads of their own columns as they debouched by the Geiers Berg pass and those farther west.

First, Straden was taken by the French, and retaken by the Russians. Then, as nine battalions of the 42nd division arrived, it was again taken. About noon, more troops

FROM DRESDEN TO KULM

having now come up, Vandamme began his advance on Priesten, whilst his right wing attacked the Eggmühl, the support of the Russian left on the spur of the hill. They even succeeded in getting a gun on to the spur above it. On the other hand, two battalions of French here fell into a Russian ambuscade, and were mostly taken prisoners. Up to 2 P.M. a furious combat raged all along the line from the Eggmühl to Priesten. The latter village was taken by greatly superior French forces, who, when they attempted to push beyond it, were driven back by artillery fire, and then ejected from the village by infantry.

At 2 P.M. Philippon arrived with fourteen fresh battalions. The Russians now began to yield on the left and in the centre, and it was only when Eugen insisted on sending in part of the Russian Guard, much against Yermolow's[1] wish, that they were able to hold their own for a time. Then Priesten was again taken, and again lost by Vandamme. It was by this time filled with dead and wounded. The Russian general, Krapowitzki, was killed in the hand-to-hand combat, and Osterman had his left arm carried away by a round shot.

The Russian position was very critical, with French reinforcements constantly arriving. Only one Guard battalion and the cavalry remained in reserve. Fortunately, some of the troops collected by the Tsar and Frederick William were now coming up. At 5 P.M. Vandamme made his decisive attack. It was momentarily checked, north of Priesten, by the Russian infantry. But at that instant two cuirassier regiments led by Diebitsch charged the left of the French, and an Uhlan regiment fell on the other flank. Before these charges the French fell back on Corbineau's cavalry, which was south of the road between Kulm and Priesten. Then more cavalry came to the aid of the Russians.

This decided Vandamme to abandon his attack till he could get up the rest of his troops. They kept arriving throughout the night. During the night Vandamme sent

[1] Commanding the Guard.

300 sappers to throw a bridge over the Elbe at Aussig, where he already had a battalion. He was under the impression that he was certain to receive support during the next day from Mortier or St Cyr.

The Russians had put up an excellent fight in the last position in which it was possible to cover the issue of the main army from the mountains. For this the credit was mainly due to Eugen of Wurtemberg, who, with 15,000 troops, had done what Barclay with 100,000 had not dared to attempt, namely, to force his way by the Peterswalde road. Perhaps it would have been better to fight at Kulm, but Priesten was a good position. Vandamme's chief fault had been in attacking piecemeal, instead of waiting for the arrival of a considerable force.

The losses had been heavy; the Russians lost 6000 men, the French probably nearly as many.

Elsewhere the pursuit by the French had been rather feeble, though they had taken great numbers of wagons and much material, which had to be abandoned on account of the badness of the hill roads. In two places the pursuers found regular lines of piled arms, and great quantities of boots sticking in the mud, where they had been left behind by the exhausted battalions of the enemy. The sufferings of the allies from hunger, cold, wet, and mud up to their knees had been almost indescribable. Their positions in the night of the 29th-30th were:—

> Klenau and the divisions Weissenwolf and Alois Lichtenstein at Gross-Waltersdorf.
> Civillart and Crenneville at Sayda, south-east of Waltersdorf.
> Colloredo and Bianchi between Dux and Teplitz.
> Chasteler on the road to Dux.
> Wittgenstein on the heights of Altenberg.
> Kleist at Furstenau and Liebenau.

As for the French, Murat only reached Lichtenberg, instead of Frauenstein, where Napoleon expected him to be. He probably got the Emperor's orders of the morning

FROM DRESDEN TO KULM 237

of the 29th[1] too late to enable him to comply. This was lucky for the allies, as had he been there he would have come upon Klenau's flank and probably done great harm.

Marmont, following Wittgenstein, got as far as Falkenhain. St Cyr, following Kleist, had a sharp fight with him at Glashütte. A good cavalry charge, led by Colonel Blücher, delayed him considerably. St Cyr and Pajol, in the mistaken belief that this was a flank guard and not a rear guard, marched by Rheinhardsgrimma, expecting to find Kleist retiring by that valley. This direction led St Cyr into Marmont's area near Falkenhain. He consequently stopped at Rheinhardsgrimma, and sent to Pirna for orders, but found both Napoleon and Berthier gone. Kleist thus had an opportunity of which, as we shall see presently, he availed himself.

Meanwhile, the allied headquarters had reached Priesten in the evening of the 29th. The King of Prussia had been in the neighbourhood most of the day, Barclay arrived at 5 P.M., Schwarzenberg at 6, and the Tsar later. The Austrian Emperor, as we know, had gone off to Laun.

As no Austrian troops were at present engaged, Schwarzenberg left matters to be arranged by the two sovereigns concerned. Vandamme had been held all day, and it was clearly necessary to go on holding him on the 30th, if the allies were to debouch in safety from the Erzgebirge. With the 50,000 men on whom they could count for the 30th the task was easy, always provided Napoleon did not support Vandamme with other troops. So far, there were no signs of the Emperor's approach. Unless he arrived in the small hours of the 30th, the allies might well hope to defeat Vandamme before Napoleon was up. They decided, therefore, on the offensive, a course recommended, it is said, by Toll and Jomini.

There was no news of Kleist, and his absence caused much alarm. Still, there was a chance that he might appear in Vandamme's rear. Colonel Schuler was despatched to find him, and urge this course on him if possible. So great

[1] *Corr.* 20, 485.

was the apprehension regarding Kleist that Schuler was told to try and bring away the young Prince Frederick of the Netherlands, who was with the Prussian general.

The two monarchs then rejoined Schwarzenberg at Dux. One anxiety which they felt was lest Augereau and the Bavarians on the Inn should, on hearing of the victory of Dresden, march to meet Napoleon as he entered Bohemia. So great was the alarm that, though Blücher's victory on the Katzbach had been reported, Schwarzenberg sent to him, requiring him to march with 50,000 men into Bohemia at once.

Meanwhile, this is what had happened to Kleist. His orders were to reach the southern side of the mountains and support Osterman in the Teplitz valley. The bearer of the order, however, reported, from personal observation, that the road to the valley by Graupen was hopelessly blocked. That over the Geiersberg by Ebersdorf was also blocked, and could not be cleared in less than twenty-four hours. That left Kleist no hope save in a return to the Peterswalde road, along which Vandamme was known to have passed. However, cavalry patrols reported it to be now clear of the enemy. That was not true, for Vandamme's troops were passing along it all night. The risk was great, and Kleist was hampered by only having a wretched map of 1721, on which several actually existing roads found no place. The cavalry now reported a practicable track along the crest of the mountains, through Streckenwald to Nollendorf.[1] The other forest roads, running through deep valleys, were impracticable for large forces. Kleist's acceptance of this route was received with satisfaction by his subordinates, and was communicated to headquarters. Kleist announced his intention of attempting to cut his way, sword in hand, through Vandamme's corps. His orders were for assembly at 3 A.M., and announced that he was moving on Vandamme's rear.

Leaving Kleist to his difficult and dangerous march, we return to the opposing forces at Kulm.

[1] Marked BB on Map IV. (*b*).

Into the details of Vandamme's battle of the 30th, we do not propose to enter at great length, for its importance was far greater from a strategical and general, than from a merely tactical, point of view.

Vandamme took up a position with his right well up into the hills above the Eggmühl, his centre across the Teplitz road in front of Kulm, and his left south of the road, stretching as far as the Striesowitz Berg. His cavalry were on this wing. Allowing for his losses on one hand, and his reinforcements on the other, he had about 32,000 men left.

The allies faced him across the Teplitz road, with about 44,000 men. Their left was opposite Vandamme's right on the hills, centre at Priesten, right stretching as far as opposite Böhmisch Neudörfel—reserve at Sobochleben.

They proposed to fight a defensive action with their left, whilst the right turned Vandamme's left and drove him in on to the mountains. It was hoped that Kleist would close his line of retreat by the Nollendorf road.

The battle began at 7 A.M. Vandamme's right, meeting at first with some success, was presently checked by Russian reinforcements. The advance of the allies' right began at 8 A.M. The Striesowitz Berg was taken after a severe struggle, and the allies began to press forward towards Arbesau, compelling Vandamme to set up a defensive flank with Quiot's and Dunesne's brigades against them. Their cavalry soon began to get round the left even of this. It was beginning to be doubtful if Vandamme, with his left thus threatened, could hold on at Kulm much longer.

We now return to Kleist who, in the darkness and cramped space, had only succeeded in starting his march at 5 A.M., two hours later than he intended. At 8 A.M. he had reached Nollendorf, having sent Ziethen to his left on Peterswalde as rearguard. At Nollendorf there was more confusion, and it was not till somewhere about 11 A.M. that the head of his column began to appear round the hill above Tellnitz.

The battle about Kulm was in the condition above described when the sound of Kleist's first cannon shots reached the ears of the combatants. Vandamme felt sure that they came from Mortier's or St Cyr's men hurrying to his assistance; the allies knew better. Vandamme was soon undeceived. His decision was taken with the greatest promptitude. His artillery, or the greater part of it, must be abandoned to its fate, after checking the main attack as long as possible, whilst the cavalry and infantry did their best to cut their way back to Peterswalde through Kleist's corps.

The fight which ensued in the space between Schande, Arbesau, and Tellnitz was a glorious one for the young French troops. It was so confused that it is almost impossible to understand it, except by standing at the Austrian and Prussian monuments, where the road from Aussig joins that from Tellnitz to Kulm, and following the details book in hand. French guns were lost, and for the moment replaced by others captured from the Prussians. There was desperate fighting at Schande, Arbesau, and on the road. Great numbers of French were captured, after fighting to the last cartridge, in the villages; many were driven into the hills above. Part actually cut their way through to Jungferndorf, where, utterly exhausted, they encountered the comparatively fresh rearguard of Ziethen, and many of them were killed or taken.

The woods were full, not only of French, but also of Prussians, who, in various episodes of the confused fighting, had been driven there. Kleist himself only escaped capture by getting into the woods and passing by by-paths, through Schönwald, to a point on the road between Peterswalde and Nollendorf, where he learnt from Ziethen that the victory was complete. Parties of French and Prussians wandered at times peacefully together in the woods, on the mutual understanding that one party should be prisoners to the others, according to the eventual result of the battle.

Vandamme remained with the defenders of Kulm till all hope had vanished. Then, as he sought to escape alone to the hills, he was captured and taken to the Tsar. There he dismounted, and theatrically kissed his charger. He was kindly received by the Tsar, and, two days later, was sent off to Russia, where he remained a prisoner till the fall of Napoleon. Somewhat to the scandal of Danilewski, who considered that he should have been looked upon only as the unfortunate general, he met with many insults on his way through Germany.[1] Perhaps that was hardly to be wondered at, considering his notorious brutality in former times. Haxo, whom Napoleon had sent to him as adviser in engineering matters, was taken about the same time as Vandamme. Dunesne fell at the head of his men when they met Ziethen. The I. corps had been half destroyed. The prisoners alone numbered 8000 to 10,000; the killed and wounded probably raised the loss to 15,000. The prisoners included many generals and officers of high rank. There fell into the hands of the allies 82 guns, 200 wagons, 2 eagles, and 3 standards. The allies stated their loss at 3319 killed and wounded, but Friederich considers this probably under the mark, as Kleist's artillery alone is known to have lost nearly 600 officers and men. The French detachment at Aussig escaped by Königswald and reached the Lilienstein late the same night, without their guns or wagons, which they had to abandon in the woods, where they were led astray by some peasants (formerly Austrian soldiers) whom they compelled to act as guides.

On this day it was only at 11.30 that St Cyr began to move. He had, as we know, waited for orders when he found himself on the 29th in rear of Marmont. The orders[2] which reached him at the hour above named, said that, in his actual position, he had better support Marmont, though the Emperor would prefer to see him between Marmont and Vandamme.

Marmont, pursuing the enemy before him, drove a rearguard from Altenberg, and again from the Zinnwald plateau, and followed almost up to Eichwald, where in the evening he heard through St Cyr of Vandamme's disaster.

Napoleon's conduct of the pursuit after Dresden, and his responsibility for Vandamme's disaster, have been much

---

[1] *Danilewski*, p. 161. [2] Berthier to St Cyr, *Hist. Mil.*, p. 388.

discussed, often with considerable prejudice on one side or the other.

The first question that arises is, why did not the Emperor start his pursuit much earlier than 9 A.M. on the 28th? The answer to that question has already been given in quotations from his correspondence of the evening of the 27th August, which show that, at that time, he was strongly of opinion that the battle would be renewed next day. He hardly appreciated the difficulties of the allies, or the very severe shaking they had received. Next day he went to the opposite extreme, by estimating his victory too highly.

Exactly when he became convinced that the allies had retreated is not quite clear, but it seems very doubtful if it was before his return to redoubt IV. at 5 A.M. on the 28th. It may be said the mere fact of his return there proves that he still expected a renewal of the battle; but it is not alone conclusive proof; for, in his letters of the night before, he had given that as his post early on the 28th. Ought he to have been aware of the retreat at an earlier hour? It is easy to say he should have been informed of it; but when it is remembered that the night was pitch dark, that it still rained hard during the earlier portion of it, and that the rain was followed by a thick morning mist, the difficulties of reconnoitring are apparent. Moreover, the heights on which the allies stood were a very effective screen, even in daylight, for movements going on behind them. Even on the morning of the 28th, it was only when Napoleon, riding with Marmont, reached the heights above Räcknitz, that he could plainly see the streams of troops passing over the hills in rear which, though higher, are defiladed from the low ground near Dresden by the heights near the town.

When he reached Dresden on the 26th, almost his first inquiry was for news of Oudinot. He had already heard rumours of the defeat at Gross Beeren. With the possibility of having to defend Dresden, the weakness of which he had seen, and his rear against an advance of the allied

Northern army, he must have felt that his hopes of being able to pursue the main army far into Bohemia were vanishing. He had probably, by the morning of the 28th, heard rumours of Macdonald's disaster on the Katzbach. By the evening he heard the news definitely. That rendered the idea of an advance on Prague even less feasible. Still, calculating that the main body of the allies was going by Dohna and Dippoldiswalde, with their left by Freiberg, he might still hope to reach Teplitz by the shorter and better road (by Peterswalde) with the three nearest corps of Vandamme, Mortier, and St Cyr. At Teplitz he would still have time to inflict great damage on their columns as they debouched in disorder from the passes, pursued by the rest of his army, Marmont, Victor, and Murat. That was why he rode off to Pirna.

When, however, on the way to Pirna, he saw Barclay's movement westwards, he was convinced that the allies were going by roads farther to the west than he had at first expected. If, as Napoleon now fancied, they were going by Annaberg, he would meet nothing at Teplitz and would merely strike a blow in the air. He began to think that he could do more harm to the allies by the movement of Murat and Victor on his right, than by sending forward his left.

Though it would be useless to send three corps to Teplitz, he could yet send Vandamme alone, without much risk of his falling in with the main body of the enemy, but with the probability of his being able to do them immense harm, by destroying all their resources towards Aussig and Tetschen, whilst they themselves were far away west. Hence his orders to Vandamme of 4 P.M. on the 28th. Those orders spoke only of the overthrow of the weak corps of Eugen of Wurtemberg, and of the capture of "everything which marches behind an army." There was no mention of fighting a great battle. Mortier was stopped at Pirna, St Cyr was sent farther west, and Vandamme was informed of this. Clearly, when those orders were sent, the Emperor had abandoned the idea of any great incursion into Bohemia, for he believed the allies to be moving so far to the southwest that he had no longer any chance of reaching the southern issues of the passes before them.

Yorck von Wartenburg argues that Napoleon sent Vandamme unsupported on a dangerous mission, and that he cannot be supposed to have held an erroneous view of the situation as regards the direction of the allies' retreat. The order to Vandamme, however, shows, as Friederich points out, that Vandamme's operation was meant to be, not a great one, but merely one of "la petite guerre" on a somewhat large scale. Nothing is said of what Vandamme was to do if he met the main body of the allies; for Napoleon thought he had no chance of doing so. He wrote that "the enemy whom we have beaten appears to have taken the direction of Annaberg." Vandamme was only ordered to attack Eugen of Wurtemberg if he made any opposition, and Eugen's strength was not half Vandamme's.

At 7.30 A.M. on the 29th, Napoleon writes to Murat that "to-day, 29th, at 6 A.M., General Vandamme has attacked the Prince of Wurtemberg near Hellendorf," etc.; also that Vandamme was marching on Teplitz with his whole force.[1]

It is quite clear, then, that Napoleon knew Vandamme was marching on Teplitz, that he approved his doing so, and that he had no intention of supporting him either by Mortier, who was ordered to stay at Pirna, or by St Cyr, who had been ordered "to follow the enemy on Maxen and in all directions he may have taken."[2] The same direction had been given to Marmont, substituting Dohna for Maxen. As has been said, the Emperor believed the enemy to be going mainly for Annaberg. If he should go, as he did, by Altenberg, it might be expected that he would issue from the mountains so closely pursued by Marmont and St Cyr

---

[1] *Corr.* 20,486. How Napoleon, at Dresden, could have heard in an hour and a half of the result of Vandamme's action at Hellendorf is incomprehensible. The hours given make it doubtful if the letter was written so early as 7.30.

[2] *Corr.* 20,485. Dresden, 29th August, 6.30 A.M.

that he would be in disorder, and scarcely a serious danger to Vandamme. Moreover, if he did issue there, Napoleon had perhaps a right to expect that a general of Vandamme's experience would, if he found himself hard pressed, make good his retreat on Nollendorf. But clearly the Emperor did not expect the enemy's main body to go in that direction. Had he done so, he would probably have ordered Mortier to support Vandamme, as he actually did on the 30th, when it was too late.[1]

He had also a right to expect Vandamme to confine himself to the task prescribed for him, namely, the capture of all that was on the enemy's communications at Teplitz, Tetschen, and Aussig, and not to engage in an enterprise which was too great for his strength. Where Napoleon seems really to have been to blame was in assuming, on insufficient grounds, that the enemy was going by Annaberg, and in putting himself, by returning to Dresden, in a position where he was not able to correct that false assumption. It was not till 4.30 P.M. on the 29th August that he was disillusioned about the line of retreat of the enemy, "whose whole army is retiring by Altenberg on Teplitz."[2] It was not till at least eight hours later, perhaps a good deal more, that he wrote to Mortier to find out what was happening with Vandamme, and to support him with two divisions if necessary.[3] Clearly the order to Mortier should have been despatched by 5 P.M. on the 29th, and should have ordered him to march at once. Mortier would have received that order, at latest, by 7.30 or 8 P.M. He could have reached Peterswalde early on the morning of the 30th, and would, in all probability, have met and destroyed Kleist there, or at any rate have come upon his rear between Peterswalde and Nollendorf. That order it seems should have been issued with reference to Vandamme's probable situation at Teplitz, and without any reference to Kleist's march in the early morning of the 30th, a march of which Napoleon could know nothing, and which he had no reason to expect; for he could know nothing of

[1] *Corr.* 20,494. [2] *Corr.* 20,491 to Murat. [3] *Corr.* 20,494.

the complete blockage of the Prussian general's direct route to the plains by Graupen, or by the Geiersberg.

Nevertheless, Friederich thinks that, as the Emperor could not know Vandamme's exact position, and as he had a right to expect so experienced a general to adapt himself to the altered circumstances and retire on Nollendorf, he was not so much to blame as appears at first sight. Grouard, on the other hand, as well as Yorck, thinks that Napoleon was alone to blame.

Now for the case for and against Vandamme. Napoleon wrote on the 1st September to St Cyr: "That unhappy Vandamme, who appears to have killed himself, had not left a sentinel on the mountains, or a reserve anywhere; he threw himself into a gulf without reconnoitring in any way. If he had only had four battalions and four guns in reserve on the heights, all this disaster would not have occurred. I gave him positive orders to entrench himself on the heights, and only to send parties to disturb the enemy and obtain news."[1] Of any such order to Vandamme there is no trace at present.

On the other hand, Du Casse[2] says, on the authority of Vandamme, that he had orders from Napoleon to go "tête baissée" for Teplitz, and that he need have no care for his flanks and rear, which would be safeguarded by St Cyr, supported by Victor (*sic*). He also says that, in his report of the 28th (8.30 P.M.), Vandamme said, "I attack them to-morrow, and march on Teplitz with the whole I. corps, if I receive no orders to the contrary." This would be very important evidence in favour of Vandamme, and against Napoleon, were it supported by documents. But Du Casse says Napoleon, believing Vandamme was dead, seized his papers in Dresden, and, presumably, destroyed anything telling against himself. As for the original orders, Vandamme destroyed them just before he was taken prisoner. Anyhow, at present, they are not forthcoming, except the report of 8.30 P.M. on the 28th, which the author found in

---

[1] *Hist. Mil.* iv., p. 391.
[2] *Le général Vandamme*, ii. pp. 505, 511, 512, 532, 533, 540.

the Section Historique de l'Etat Major-Général at Paris. There also he found an account of Kulm written by Gobrecht some years later.[1] Its handwriting, misspelling, and bad grammar are a curious example of the bad education of a man in the position of the commander of a cavalry brigade. The remarkable part of it is that in which Gobrecht says that Vandamme told him, during the battle, that Mortier had orders to support him from Pirna with the Young Guard. This seems to confirm Du Casse's assertion that Vandamme was aware, on the morning of the 30th, of Napoleon's orders of that date to Mortier. If so, Napoleon must have issued them very soon after midnight.

To go fully into this controversy as to the respective shares of blame to be borne by Napoleon and Vandamme would require much more space than we can afford. On the whole, the evidence so far available seems to point to Napoleon as the culprit, as Yorck and Grouard hold him to be. His great fault would appear to be in having returned to Dresden, though Friederich thinks it was not unnatural that he should do so, looking to the news of Gross Beeren and the Katzbach, and to the possibility that the heavy losses which fell on the Austrian army at Dresden might cool the ardour of the Emperor Francis Joseph in the cause of his new allies.

As for Napoleon's censure of Vandamme for not leaving a rearguard in the hills, Friederich thinks it could have done no real service in stopping Kleist, and that Vandamme was right to bring every man he could on to the battlefield. We would venture to suggest that even a few squadrons left on the road would have given Vandamme notice of Kleist's approach by 8 A.M., when the Prussians got to Nollendorf. It took them more than two hours to reach the battlefield at Tellnitz, and during that time Vandamme might quite possibly have escaped, at anyrate without total ruin. The finger-post at Vorder Tellnitz marks " Aussig 8 kilometres," only 5 miles. The French had a detach-

[1] It is printed, but apparently revised in spelling, etc., in Bertin's *Campagne de* 1813, pp. 117-122.

ment at Aussig busy building a bridge. Might not Vandamme have escaped in that direction, seeing the allies' right was largely composed of cavalry? At Aussig he could have crossed the Elbe, and got away to join Poniatowski at Gabel.

If that is not considered feasible, there is the route now followed by the railway by Königswald. At the present time, at any rate, it is not a difficult country, at least not till the descent on Tetschen begins. Had Vandamme taken that road, as soon as he heard from his rearguard (if he had had one) of the approach of Kleist, it is extremely improbable that either Kleist or the main army would have followed him by it, and from Tetschen he could probably have got back to Saxony by either bank of the Elbe. At Tetschen, as well as at Aussig, he would no doubt have picked up the enemy's supplies in sufficient quantity to support himself.

Of the other French generals, Mortier, looking to the Emperor's orders up to the 29th, can hardly be blamed. St Cyr is blamed by Thiers, and it certainly seems that he acted rather feebly in the night of the 29th in waiting for orders, instead of keeping close on the heels of Kleist. Here again Napoleon must share the blame; for it is apparent, from St Cyr's account,[1] that the marshal had not been informed of the departure of headquarters for Dresden on the previous afternoon.

There is one more question, viz., whether the story told by Pelet, Thiers, and others of Napoleon's being obliged to return to Dresden by an attack of illness, the result of exposure, is true. Friederich thinks he had sufficient reasons for leaving Pirna without this. Irrespective of this, it may be noted that the illness is mentioned neither by Odeleben nor Marmont. Indeed, Odeleben says that the Emperor started for Dresden " with the greatest tranquillity, and very cheerfully." Moreover, it does not seem by any means clear why a man suffering, as Napoleon is said to have done, from fever and severe pains

[1] *Hist. Mil.*, iv. p. 123.

in the stomach should have wanted to start off on a long drive to Dresden, instead of resting at Pirna, where there is no reason to suppose he could not have found fairly comfortable quarters.

On the side of the allies much credit is due to the Tsar and the King of Prussia for their action in collecting troops to support Osterman at Kulm, a difficult matter, as was shown by Colloredo's refusal to obey till Metternich interfered.

To Kleist is due almost the whole credit for the fact that Vandamme was almost annihilated instead of getting away, in part at least, as he might have done, had not the Prussians appeared in his rear. Yet Kleist had very little idea of the great success awaiting him when he started on his march. He only hoped to be able to cut his way through to safety. Had it not been for the blocked roads leading by the shortest way to the plains, and the fear that St Cyr would be on him before he could clear them, Kleist would almost certainly have attempted to descend to the plains by Graupen, or by the Geiersberg. In that case there would have been nothing on Vandamme's rear. To march back to the Peterswalde road was, for Kleist, a counsel of despair. He deserves all credit for following it. He received his reward in finding himself in a position to complete a victory which almost counterbalanced all that Napoleon had gained at Dresden, and infused a fresh spirit of hope into the half-desponding allies.

CHAPTER XV

THE KATZBACH[1] AND GROSS BEEREN

MARMONT'S prophecy of the 16th August had already been fulfilled before the end of the month; for the results of Napoleon's victory at Dresden had been more than counterbalanced by the defeats of Vandamme at Kulm, of Macdonald on the Katzbach, and of Oudinot at Gross Beeren. We must turn back a little in time to describe the two latter defeats.

When Napoleon left the army of the Bober on the 23rd August, he decided to take Ney with him, so as to leave Macdonald as the only marshal with that army. The orders of the 23rd,[2] which were clear enough, that Ney was to join the Emperor in person, leaving the III. corps under Souham, miscarried, and it was only on the 25th that Napoleon learnt from Macdonald that Ney had gone off *with his corps* towards Bunzlau.[3]

Napoleon's instructions to Macdonald have already been described.[4]

On the 24th August Macdonald's command stood thus—

III. corps[5] at Rothkirch, west of the Katzbach, two battalions in Liegnitz.

V. corps at Wolfsberg and Röchlitz, on the right bank beyond Goldberg.

XI. corps behind Goldberg, on the left bank.

On that day Blücher, already beginning to suspect

---

[1] Map ii. (*b*) and Map i.   [2] *Corr.* 20,440.
[3] *Corr.* 20,463. It is not quite clear what orders induced Ney to march the III. corps westwards.   [4] *Supra*, p. 189.
[5] Now only four divisions, as Marchand's had been provisionally transferred to the XI.

THE KATZBACH AND GROSS BEEREN 251

Napoleon's departure, had issued orders for a general reconnaissance by Sacken on Liegnitz, by Yorck between Liegnitz and Goldberg, and by Langeron between Goldberg and Schönau.

By the 25th he had come to the conclusion that Macdonald was taking up a position on the left bank of the Katzbach. He ordered, for the 26th, Sacken to advance on Malitsch; Langeron on Hermannsdorf; Yorck, supported by Sacken, against the left flank of the enemy opposed to Langeron.

The Katzbach, a stream of small importance in dry weather, but liable to sudden floods in heavy rain, flows north-east from Goldberg to Liegnitz. Three or four miles before it reaches the latter it is joined on its right bank by the Wuthende[1] Neisse, the name of which suggests its character as a stream liable to sudden spates of great violence. The space been the Katzbach and the Neisse is not very elevated or hilly, whilst the right bank of the latter stream rises in formidable heights to the plateau east of it, which is open and fairly level.

On the 26th Macdonald also had decided on the offensive, believing apparently that Blücher was still on the defensive towards Jauer, and that he would retire towards Breslau as soon as he saw the French advancing on Jauer.

Blücher, equally intent on the offensive, also expected to find the enemy on the defensive behind the Katzbach. He now believed that the III. corps was at Liegnitz, the V. and XI. at Goldberg. At 11 A.M. he, consequently, changed his orders. Sacken was to hold the III. corps at Liegnitz in front, whilst Yorck fell on Souham's right flank. At the same time Langeron was to protect Yorck's rear by containing the two corps supposed to be at Goldberg.

Meanwhile, Macdonald, proposing to reach the plateau in front of Jauer on the 26th, and to attack Blücher on the 27th, if he still held fast there, issued the following orders:—

[1] "Raging" or "roaring."

III. corps to cross the Katzbach below Kroitzsch, and seek to reach the Liegnitz-Jauer road.

XI. corps (less Ledru's division) and Sebastiani to cross the Katzbach at Kroitzsch, then to cross the Neisse, and march towards Jauer on the right of the III.

V. corps (only two divisions) to advance from Goldberg by Seichau on Jauer, always on the left bank of the Neisse.

The marshal, alarmed by the appearance of St Priest on his right flank, sent Puthod's division of the V. corps with orders to reach Schönau on the 27th, and to detach one brigade still farther to the right to Hirschberg, whither also Ledru's division of the XI. corps was to go.

Thus Macdonald proposed to advance with widely separated forces :—

(1) 12,000 men detached to protect his right against St Priest, who was no serious danger.

(2) 22,000 men were to go with himself from Goldberg towards Jauer, partly direct, partly by Schönau.

(3) 67,000 to go to the left, across the Katzbach and Neisse, and descend on the enemy's right in his supposed position at Jauer.

Before Blücher's orders of 11 A.M. on the 26th issued, the two advancing armies had met and begun the battle.

At the commencement the opposing forces were thus grouped :—

On the left bank of the Neisse, Langeron with 31,000 men faced Lauriston with 23,000.

On the plateau of the right bank were the allied forces of Yorck and Sacken, 55,000 strong; against these were advancing, though much separated, the XI. and III. corps, and Sebastiani's cavalry, about 67,000 in all.

Blücher was quite as surprised to find the French on the offensive as Macdonald was to find Blücher advancing.

About 11 A.M. the allied advanced guard, after beating off one attack on Kroitzsch, evacuated it and fell back across the Neisse. The infantry on both sides were generally unable to fire their muskets, as the rain was very much what it was on the 27th at Dresden.

THE KATZBACH AND GROSS BEEREN 253

Then confusion began to be introduced into the French advance by the crossing of Sebastiani's cavalry from Kroitzsch, and the XI. corps (now commanded by Gérard) from Goldberg. However, the Prussians had left the passage of the Neisse open, and the French now began to mount to the plateau in two columns, the stronger, on the left, by the paths leading to Janowitz, the weaker, on the right, by Nieder Weinberg and the Kuhberg. In both columns the infantry and cavalry were mingled, and the latter caused much confusion by their efforts to get through the former to the front. The first of the infantry only began to reach the plateau, a battalion at a time, towards 1.30 P.M.

Meanwhile, Lauriston with his two divisions of the V. corps had found Langeron in a strong position, with his right on the Neisse and his line extending about 5000 paces to the Mönchsbach, on which his left rested. His front was protected by the Silberfliesz brook and the Plinsengrund, and he had light troops pushed forward. Lauriston began his advance with a small detachment on his right, moving along the valley towards Buschhäuser, and then sent his main body across the Plinsengrund in five columns. Langeron's advanced guard was driven back on to his main position on the line Schlaupe-Buschhäuser. Langeron was now alarmed. He reported, incorrectly, that he was attacked by superior forces, and began falling back. He was anxious to retire on Jauer.

At 2 P.M., Lauriston was preparing for a decisive attack. At the same time, the centre group of the French on the plateau, the XI. corps and Sebastiani, was partly on the line Klein Tinz-Gross Janowitz-Ober Weinberg. All told, they did not exceed 27,000 men, including a considerable proportion of the force which was still trying to climb the heights leading from the Neisse to the plateau.

Opposite them were 55,000 Prussians and Russians of Yorck's and Sacken's corps. They could not hope for the arrival of Souham with the III. corps for hours to come. He was still not up to the Katzbach.

Yorck had his advanced guard between Bellwitzhof and Christianenhöhe, his main body just in front of the line Bellwitzhof-Triebelwitz, in two columns.

Sacken was moving on Yorck's right, on Eichholz.

Neither Macdonald nor Blücher was altogether responsible for the condition of affairs. The former had no reason to expect that Souham's advance would be so slow as it was; the latter could see very little in the blinding rain, and it was only when Gneisenau and Müffling rode forward that they were able to report the advance of about 3000 French cavalry, and a strong force of infantry, on Janowitz. They concluded that, if Yorck advanced at once, he would be at the hollow road from Nieder Krain before the French could possibly have 20,000 men up to oppose him.

As Yorck started, he was forced to detach two battalions to hold Schlaupe, which was threatened by Lauriston, and the loss of which would separate him from Langeron.

Sacken, at the same time, had got his artillery on the Taubenberg, and was firing heavily on the French, whose left he threatened.

Blücher advanced with Yorck's men, encouraging them, and telling them to use the bayonet, as their muskets would not go off.

"Now, my children," said the old man, "I have enough French over here; now at them." There was some delay, owing to Yorck's obstinately wanting to advance in line, till Blücher insisted on his re-forming column.

Space will not allow us to go into the details of the fierce hand-to-hand struggle, with bayonets and clubbed muskets, which ensued. Sacken's troops joined in, his cavalry overthrew that of Sebastiani, which they attacked in front and rear. Yorck's cavalry too, pushing through the infantry, added to the discomfiture of the enemy, who, despite the bravery with which the French fought, was gradually driven back to the edge of the plateau, and in many places over it. In one place the pile of overturned guns and ammunition wagons completely blocked the Nieder Krain road. Some of Souham's men had now arrived through Kroitzsch and

Nieder Krain. For a moment they had some success against the Russian cavalry, now disordered by their own success. Then Yorck's infantry once more turned the tables, and the whole of the French who had ascended the plateau from the Neisse were sent streaming down again in wild confusion. The river, which had been small in the morning, was now a raging torrent, in which many of the fugitives were drowned in attempting to cross it elsewhere than by the overcrowded bridge at Nieder Krain. That village was captured by the pursuing Prussians before darkness finally stopped the combat in this direction.

Whilst these events were occurring, Sacken had turned in pursuit of some still formed bodies which were trying to escape across the Katzbach towards Dohnau. Here he met the divisions Albert and Ricard of the III. corps, who had crossed the Katzbach at Schmogwitz, too late to retrieve the fortunes of the day. The bridge had been carried away by the raging stream, which had to be forded with the water up to the men's hips. Only twelve guns could be got across. As the two divisions advanced on the heights of Klein Schweinitz, they found them held by Sacken's artillery. At 7.30 P.M. they returned to Schmogwitz, where they were constantly annoyed by Cossacks, till 2 A.M., when they marched for Hainau.

On the French right, Lauriston had at first met with some success. Hennersdorf and the Weinberg[1] were stormed, and both Langeron's wings driven back. It was not till 4 P.M. that Langeron realised that his own somewhat feeble conduct was endangering the rest of the army. Blücher now sent Yorck's reserve brigade to assist him by an attack on Lauriston's left from across the Neisse. Langeron, too, began to act with some energy, and before darkness fell he and Yorck's brigade had retaken nearly all that had been lost earlier on this side. Lauriston still held on to Hennersdorf.

[1] That is the Weinberg between Hennersdorf and Hermannsdorf. Langeron had also troops, withdrawn from his right, on the other Weinberg just west of Peterwitz.

The night after the battle was almost more terrible for the allies than for the French. Yorck's landwehr were soaked to the skin, their linen trousers clung to their legs, and most of them were without shoes. So fearful were their trials that only the strongest amongst them held out. Next morning one battalion had only 202 men fit for work out of 510 who had gone into action. In another the proportion was 271 to 577. On the other hand, another battalion, which took the precaution to fit themselves out with the cloaks and shoes of the French dead, only lost 93 men. According to the allies' reports, they took 36 guns, 110 wagons, and 12,000 to 14,000 prisoners, but Friederich thinks these figures are under the mark. There is no return of Blücher's losses, though they were certainly heavy.

The battle on the Katzbach was an encounter unexpected by either general. Each thought the other on the defensive. Macdonald did not expect to meet Blücher short of Jauer; the old Prussian, on the other hand, believed the French to be standing at Goldberg and Liegnitz, and hoped to contain the former body with Langeron, whilst he fell with two corps on Souham alone.

Macdonald meant to march all his corps on Jauer. Lauriston was to go direct from Goldberg; Gérard and Sebastiani were to go in a single column by Kroitzsch and Nieder Krain to the plateau on the right bank of the Neisse, and thence on Jauer. Souham was to cross the Katzbach at Schmogwitz, below the infall of the Neisse, reaching the plateau at the same time as Gérard. But the unfortunate mistake under which the III. corps had started for Dresden delayed its arrival, though that was not the only cause.

But what was Macdonald doing on the offensive at all? The Emperor's instructions, whilst professing to leave him a good deal of latitude in detail, distinctly prescribed a defensive rôle, until the enemy himself took the offensive; then, "the enemy in taking the offensive will march on several points, whilst the Duke of Tarentum, on the contrary, should unite all his troops on one point, in order to debouch in force against him (the enemy) and at once to reassume the

THE KATZBACH AND GROSS BEEREN 257

initiative."[1] Blücher was, as a matter of fact, resuming the offensive, but Macdonald did not know it, and believed he was advancing against an enemy still on the defensive, and that at or beyond Jauer, the point to which the previous instructions [2] had required him to be driven.

"The principal object of this army (Macdonald)," said this order, " is to hold in check the army of Silesia, and to prevent it moving on Zittau to interrupt my communication, or on Berlin against the Duke of Reggio. I desire him (Macdonald) to push the enemy to beyond Jauer, and then at once to take post on the Bober."

It may be said that Macdonald's first task was to drive back Blücher to Jauer. There had been a fight at Goldberg on the 22nd, and it was on the 23rd that Blücher fell back on Jauer, where he was on the 24th, expecting to be attacked. This part of the task was, therefore, practically completed when Napoleon was dictating his instructions on the 23rd. It cannot be supposed that he contemplated its being done over again at once, and it appears that Macdonald should first have fixed himself in the prescribed position on the Bober, and waited there till he had definite information of Blücher's fresh offensive. Then would have been the time for him to make a united attack on the divided forces of Blücher, not on the Katzbach, but within easy reach of his own fortified line, Löwenberg-Bunzlau.

But Macdonald, in the operation he undertook, made another very serious blunder in detaching the divisions of Puthod (V. corps) and Ledru (XI. corps) far to his right, where they could be of no use to him, and were guarding against a danger which was largely imaginary. When Puthod heard of the disaster to the main army, he saw that it was impossible for him to rejoin it at Goldberg without falling in with Langeron. Hoping to rejoin it behind the Bober, he made for Hirschberg, where he found the bridge over the Bober gone, and the stream too swollen for its restoration to be possible. Marching down the right bank of the Bober, he was at Löwenberg on the 29th. There

[1] *Corr.* 20,443.   [2] *Corr.* 20,442.

again the bridge was gone, and he failed to restore it. Bunzlau alone remained with a bridge, and that place had already been reached by the allied cavalry. Puthod, pursued by Langeron, now found himself hemmed in against the Bober. On the heights of Plagwitz, a little east of Löwenberg, he resolved to sell his liberty as dearly as possible. But, attacked by enormously superior numbers, he had no option but surrender, with what remained of his division, after an obstinate fight.

As for Macdonald, his whole force repassed the Katzbach during the night of the 26th-27th. On the 27th Langeron attacked Lauriston at Goldberg and drove him to a farther retreat on Löwenberg, where he arrived that evening, after losing 18 guns. More fortunate than Puthod, he was able to reach Bunzlau, where he, as well as the other corps, crossed the Bober.

Macdonald evidently feels that he has no case, for his memoirs set up little in the way of defence beyond complaints of the failure of his subordinates to carry out orders properly. Souham certainly was unaccountably slow in his movements, but it seems unjust to blame Puthod. The marshal blames Sebastiani for ascending the plateau with all his cavalry, and the artillery for taking guns up on to it, when they could hardly be moved in the deep mud, and had only a narrow road, which was soon completely blocked, by which to retreat.

The blame for this grievous failure must be borne by Macdonald; it is impossible to lay any of it at Napoleon's door, except as regards his choice for the command of a marshal who, if he stands above many of his fellow-marshals as an honest, well-meaning man, was certainly one of the least competent of them as a commander.

Napoleon's instructions, if intelligently carried out, should have ensured the army of the Bober against misfortune, and it must be remembered that the Emperor had not stinted Macdonald in the number of his troops, which was at least equal to that of Blücher's army.

We have now to describe Oudinot's movements, after the

THE KATZBACH AND GROSS BEEREN

close of the armistice, against Berlin. Napoleon's orders to him have already been stated.[1]

On the 18th August[2] Oudinot had his three corps (IV., VII., and XII.) concentrated at Baruth, only three marches from Berlin. From Baruth he marched to his left to Luckenwalde, which he reached on the 20th. Why he went by Luckenwalde, instead of direct on Berlin, is not very clear, unless it was to pick up Arrighi. He turned northwards towards Berlin on the 21st; the XII. corps, with Oudinot himself, marched by the Trebbin road on the left; Reynier in the centre by Munsdorf;[3] Bertrand on the right by the Blankenfelde road. The allied outposts fell back on Trebbin, Munsdorf, and towards Zossen. Trebbin was taken by a frontal attack by Pacthod, combined with a flank attack by Reynier from Munsdorf. Beyond that nothing particular happened on the 21st or 22nd, by the evening of which latter day Bertrand held Juhnsdorf. Reynier was north of Wittstock, and Oudinot north of Trebbin.

Oudinot's orders for the 23rd apparently anticipated no serious opposition on that day. The XII. corps, with Fournier's cavalry division, was to March on Ahrensdorf; the VII. to march on Gross Beeren; the IV. and the cavalry divisions of De France and Beaumont to advance to Blankenfelde.

The divisions of Raglowich, Lorge (cavalry), and the Wurtembergers were left behind to guard the rear.

The advance was through a thickly-wooded country, much cut up by watercourses and marshes, offering no facilities for lateral communication between the somewhat widely separated columns.

The dispositions led up to two separate actions.

Opposed to the French right column was Tauenzien, who, after failing to retake Juhnsdorf from Bertrand on the previous evening, had bivouacked at Blankenfelde. He had about 13,000 men and 32 guns.

---

[1] *Supra*, p. 170.   [2] Maps I. and II. (*c*).
[3] Not shown on Map I. It is east by north from Trebbin, and west by south from Wilmersdorf.

It was 9 A.M. on the 23rd when Bertrand began to advance against Tauenzien, who had his troops south of Blankenfelde and on either side of it. He did not occupy the village itself, as his landwehr were not properly trained in village fighting.

The position was protected on both flanks, but not in front, and it was too close to the wood east of Blankenfelde, which offered good cover for a French approach.

At 10 A.M. Bertrand sent Fontanelli against Tauenzien's front, and six battalions into the wood on his left. From this they could not issue, owing to heavy Prussian artillery fire. A desultory fight continued till 2 P.M., without any decisive result. Then Bertrand withdrew, apparently thinking that Reynier's advance on Gross Beeren must presently compel the Prussians to evacuate Blankenfelde.

It was not till 3 P.M. that Reynier appeared before Gross Beeren, which was weakly occupied. The Prussians were soon driven from it, and Reynier, thinking the fighting was over for the day, proceeded to bivouac with Sehr's Saxon division just west of Gross Beeren, Durutte on Sehr's left, and Lecoq left of Durutte. The windmill height was occupied, and the cavalry was behind Durutte.

Bülow had marched in the morning from Heimersdorf to Ruhlsdorf, by order of Bernadotte. Hearing the firing at Blankenfelde, he returned to Heimersdorf, which he reached at 1 P.M. His troops were tried with this march in torrential rain.

At 2 P.M. Borstell came up and took post east of the road from Gross Beeren to Berlin, whence, at 3 P.M., he heard the sounds of the fight at Gross Beeren. Von Boyen, sent out to reconnoitre, met the Prussians retreating from that place. He reported that Reynier might easily be attacked as he debouched from the forest. Bülow, therefore, decided to advance.

Reynier had his right supported by Gross Beeren, on the east side of which a marshy ditch, 5 or 6 feet deep in places and running north and south, prevented the village being turned on that side. The windmill height, rising

THE KATZBACH AND GROSS BEEREN 261

20 or 30 feet above the plain just west of Gross Beeren, would have afforded a good view, but for the heavy rain. As it was, the French were unable note Bülow's advance till he was close up.

Reynier's weak point was his left, on which he quickly recognised that he could not hope for help from the distant XII. corps. If it were turned, he would be in danger of being driven off his line of retreat. Therefore, he drew up the whole of Lecoq's division in a great square with a few guns to protect it. Between 5 and 6 P.M. Bülow was firing from a distance of 1300 yards with 62 guns against 44 French. The artillery duel lasted for one and a half hours, when the arrival of Borstell raised the Prussian numbers to 80 guns against, at most, 69 French. The Prussian infantry, 300 yards behind the guns, had already suffered considerably before the advance began.

Borstell was intended to act as reserve to Bülow's attack, but, instead of that, he moved to his left to Klein Beeren, whence he proceeded to attack the wood east of Gross Beeren. The wood was only held by one Saxon battalion which, unable to fire its muskets in the rain, had to retreat into the village. Gross Beeren was now attacked from the north by Krafft's division, and from the east by Borstell, whilst the Hessen-Homburg division advanced on the windmill height. The village was stormed, and an attack was then commenced from it against the east side of the windmill heights. Before this combined attack the French on the heights soon began to fall back in disorder. A brave attempt by two Saxon battalions to stop the Prussians as they descended from the heights failed.

Whilst Reynier's right had thus suffered defeat, Durutte and Lecoq, farther to the left, had scarcely been damaged.

Durutte was now sent to attempt the recapture of the windmill heights, but his division gave way completely when they met the fugitive Saxons of Sehr. All broke and fled together to the wood.

Lecoq, too, failed in an attempt to retake the heights, where the Prussians were now established with superior forces.

Reynier, now despairing of retaking the heights, employed Lecoq's division to cover his retreat, as he fell back by the Neu Beeren road. Thus covered, he was able to retreat in good order. There was some cavalry fighting, as Borstell attempted to pursue, but Reynier was not seriously molested, and by 10 P.M. was back at his bivouac of the preceding night, at Löwenbruch, with Sehr's, Durutte's, and Lecoq's divisions.

Bülow's divisions, unable to continue the pursuit in the darkness, had bivouacked about Gross Beeren, when suddenly a fresh fight broke out. Oudinot's XII. corps had reached Ahrensdorf at 6 P.M. Hearing the sounds of the battle at Gross Beeren, the cavalry division of Fournier and Guilleminot's infantry went in the direction of Ruhlsdorf. It was 8 P.M. when Fournier came upon the battlefield; Guilleminot was half an hour later. Then ensued a confused fight between Prussian hussars and the French cavalry, and the struggling crowd bore down on Bülow's infantry, who were powerless to assist where friend and foe were so mixed up. The French cavalry had arrived by Neu Beeren on Bülow's right. It was only at Heimersdorf that the combatants got separated from one another, and the French returned by roundabout ways to Neu Beeren.

This fight was of no real importance to either side, except in so far as it influenced Bülow who, warned by this attack of the proximity of the XII. corps, withdrew all his troops to Heimersdorf, except Thümen and Borstell, who remained on either side of Gross Beeren.

During the night Oudinot met Reynier, who assured him that his corps was not fit to renew the battle. Accordingly, Oudinot withdrew his whole army to its starting-point, abandoning for the present all hope of gaining Berlin.

The losses were not very heavy. The Saxons lost 2000 men, 7 guns, and 60 loaded wagons.

Durutte and Lecoq lost 1000 men and 6 guns.

Bülow's loss was only about 1000 men and 200 horses.

THE KATZBACH AND GROSS BEEREN 263

It is apparent, from a letter from Napoleon to Macdonald,[1] that Oudinot had been very nervous about the country through which he was to advance. The Emperor writes: "He (Oudinot) was no longer afraid of the inundations; that monster had disappeared as he advanced." Nevertheless the country was much cut up by woods, marshes, and drainage cuts, and it was not possible to move straight across country in the Napoleonic manner. Friederich remarks that Oudinot must either have advanced, as he did, in three columns, or he might have left a weak retaining force at the Juhnsdorf defile, whilst he strengthened Reynier by sending the greater part of Bertrand's corps with him. He did not expect to meet a strong force as he debouched from the north side of the forest, and he started the XII. corps so late that it never got out of the forest at all on the 23rd. Bertrand might have forced his way out, but did not, as he relied on the advance of the VII. corps to open a way for him. The result was that only the centre one of the three columns debouched, and that opposite the strongest part of the enemy's line.

Oudinot should have arranged to unite his three columns behind the northern edge of the forest, and to have issued from it with all three together. Instead, Reynier alone issued, and that in isolation. He was probably unwise to fight when he did. He could easily have retired to the forest again, whither Bülow would not have dared to follow. When he did fight, he left Sehr's division to fight superior forces at first, instead of supporting him at once with all his troops

As for the allies, Bernadotte might have supported Bülow against Reynier's left with one of his corps, whilst with the other he contained Oudinot. He refused assistance, on the ground that he believed Oudinot had Victor's corps as well as the XII. and Arrighi. He would have had to use his Swedes, and, as we have said before, his great object was not to engage them. He thought Bülow, with 38,000 men, was strong enough to deal with Reynier's 27,000, and

[1] *Corr.* 20,454.

he knew that Tauenzien had stopped Bertrand, so there was no danger in that direction.

Bülow would have done better to attack Reynier's left, but, as a matter of fact, Gross Beeren was so weakly held that the attack on it succeeded easily. Borstell played a great part in the battle, but, on the other hand, his division being Bülow's only reserve, his move into first line was very risky. Had Bülow been in greater difficulties when attacked by Durutte and Lecoq, he would have had no reserve whatever available. As a result of Oudinot's repulse at Gross Beeren, Girard, from Magdeburg, found himself isolated in the midst of the allied army of the North. He was attacked at Hagelberg, near Belzig, by Hirschfeld and Czernitchew's Cossacks, and driven to seek safety again at Magdeburg, considering himself fortunate in losing only 1200 prisoners.

Napoleon's opinion of Oudinot's conduct is given in his orders for his successor, Ney.[1] "The Duke of Reggio never attacked the enemy, and he has been so clever as to let one of his corps attack separately. If he had attacked vigorously, he would have overthrown him everywhere."

Davout's advance from Hamburg had not had much effect, and Oudinot's retreat necessarily compelled him also to fall back.

For Oudinot's failure it seems impossible not to agree with Grouard in considering that the blame must fall entirely on the marshal. Setting aside the mistake that Napoleon probably made in taking the offensive towards Berlin at all, there was no reason why Oudinot should have suffered defeat, even if he did not find it possible to reach Berlin. In this case, as in that of Macdonald, Napoleon can hardly avoid blame for having selected, for a semi-independent mission, a commander who was at most qualified for the subordinate command of an army corps.

[1] *Corr.* 20,502, dated 2nd September, to Berthier.

CHAPTER XVI

THE SECOND ADVANCE AGAINST BLÜCHER, AND NEY'S DEFEAT AT DENNEWITZ[1]

ON the 30th August Napoleon drew up a long note on the general situation of his affairs, which is of the greatest importance.

He begins by assuming that Macdonald would rally on the Bober; he did not mind if it was as far back as the Queiss.

Were he to withdraw Poniatowski and send him to the Berlin army, the passes at Zittau, leading to Macdonald's rear, would be unguarded, and it would be necessary for Macdonald to fall back on Görlitz, or even on Bautzen. A single corps at Hoyerswerda would suffice to guard the rear of the Berlin army. It would take Poniatowski four days to get to Kalau. Supposing the Emperor were to decide to give up all idea of an expedition to Bohemia and join the Berlin army, he would leave Murat in front of Dresden with St Cyr, Marmont, Victor, Vandamme (whose destruction was not yet known), and Latour-Maubourg, with his left on the Elbe, facing south. If Murat were forced to retire on Dresden, Napoleon could be back there from Luckau as soon as Murat. At the same time, Macdonald, with his left at Weissenberg, and holding Bautzen and Hoyerswerda, would protect Dresden on the right bank of the Elbe. Thus Napoleon would have two armies covering Dresden on the defensive, whilst he himself was marching to take Berlin, and transferring the theatre of war to the lower Oder. If he had 60,000 men at Stettin, he would be menacing the blockade at Danzig, and threatening the

[1] Maps I. and II. (d).

Russian frontier, which would probably induce the Russians to leave Bohemia, in order to defend their own territory.

He had two possible plans of operation. The first, to march on Prague. The objections to this were, that he could not now reach that place before the allied army of Bohemia, and against that he might not be able to take it. Moreover, he would be in person at the extreme end of his line, which he recognised was not a suitable position for him, considering the demonstrated incapacity of his lieutenants. His position would be specially critical if Blücher attacked Macdonald. Again, Oudinot's army, as well as Davout's, would be reduced to the strict defensive, and about the middle of October he must lose 9000 men by the capitulation of Stettin. He goes on to remark that he would be holding an enormously long line on the Elbe, from Prague to Hamburg. Any breach effected by the allies in that line must mean his own immediate retreat on the Rhine. He sums up the Prague idea thus: "Thus the project of going to Prague has objections—(1) I am not certain of getting Prague; (2) I should there find myself with my chief forces in quite another system, and, finding myself in person at the extremity of my line, I should not be able to go to threatened points, and mistakes would occur. That would carry the war to between the Elbe and the Rhine, as the enemy wishes. As a third objection, I should lose my fortresses on the Oder, and should not be on the way to Danzig."

Then he deals with the project of an advance on Berlin, towards which he is evidently drawn. He would be in the centre, protecting the Elbe from Dresden to Hamburg; he would obtain an immediate result in drawing the Russians away from the Austrians, who, with only 120,000 men, would be reduced to the defensive between Dresden and Hof. He would be threatening Prague without going there. Even the Prussians would not stay in Bohemia when their capital was lost, and the Russians would be alarmed for Poland.

The Russians and Prussians in Bohemia might insist on

THE SECOND ADVANCE AGAINST BLÜCHER

a fresh advance on Dresden, but that could not be before fifteen days. By that time, the Emperor would have taken Berlin, re-victualled Stettin, and have got back to Dresden with his army united. "Finally, in my present position, no plan is admissible under which I am not present in person in the centre."

Then, in order to get a general picture of the two projects for comparison, he sketches out the movements of each.

1st—Prague project. He would have to go there with the I., II., VI. and XIV. corps, leaving Davout in front of Hamburg, Oudinot at Wittenberg and Magdeburg, Macdonald at Bautzen. "In that situation I should be on the defensive, leaving the offensive to the enemy. I should threaten nothing. It would be absurd to say I was threatening Vienna. The enemy could mask my army of Silesia and send his corps by Zittau to attack me at Prague; or else, masking the Silesian army, he could detach to the lower Elbe and march on the Weser, whilst I was at Prague; I should have nothing left but to gain the Rhine as quickly as possible. . . .

"2nd hypothesis. Now the I., II., VI. and XIV. corps and Latour-Maubourg can rest peacefully round Dresden without fear of the Cossacks; Augereau's corps will move up on Bamberg and Hof, the army of Silesia on the Queiss, or the Bober, and Bautzen; no anxiety for my communications; my two armies of Hamburg (Davout) and Reggio (Oudinot), will be towards Berlin and Stettin."

In a postscript he calculates that next day (31st) he will have 30,000 men at Hoyerswerda, and 54,000 of Oudinot's three corps, over 80,000 in all, for the Berlin expedition, not to speak of Davout. If he took his headquarters to Luckau, he would be two marches from Torgau, three from Dresden, four from Görlitz, ready to go where he wished, and either to send all he wanted to Berlin, or to go there himself. Communications between Dresden, Torgau, and Berlin could be maintained by 10,000 cavalry, of whom 3000 could be taken from Murat. All this is very unlike the old Napoleon, in that there is little or nothing about a great battle for the overthrow of Schwarzenberg, Blücher, or Bernadotte. On the contrary, it is full of considerations of mere geographical points, and of something very like the old 18th century war of manœuvres.

He definitely abandons all idea of a decisive blow at the main army of the allies; he had practically done so already on the 28th, when he left the pursuit to his lieutenants, without even appointing one of them to the general command.

The whole note shows that he was prejudiced in favour of the march on Berlin and Stettin; for he argues against the advance on Bohemia on the ground that two of his armies would be reduced to the defensive, but takes no objection to the same fact in the case of the Berlin project. Surely, too, as Grouard points out,[1] it was essential to the proper utilisation of interior lines to take the offensive in one direction only, whilst remaining on the defensive in the others. So far, since the armistice, Napoleon had been attacking in every direction at once. In two directions he had failed, through the incapacity of his lieutenants. In the third he had missed a great opportunity, after Dresden, of inflicting perhaps mortal injury on his true objective, the army of Bohemia.

He was now planning a vigorous offensive northwards and north-eastwards, leaving the army of Bohemia to recover itself, which it was still in a position to do without much difficulty.

But his vigorous offensive, led by himself, was destined not to take place, and it ended in his deputing Ney to carry it out with inferior forces—scarcely a better choice of a commander than Oudinot. Though Napoleon had accepted as the better the project of going himself towards Berlin, circumstances prevented his execution of it. In the first place, the news of Vandamme's disaster at Kulm deprived him of one of the corps which he proposed to leave under Murat at and before Dresden. It is true he set to work to reconstruct the I. corps; but nothing could replace the men

[1] *Stratégie Napoléonienne. La campagne d'automne de* 1813, p. 156.

THE SECOND ADVANCE AGAINST BLÜCHER

who had been lost at Kulm. Teste's division had to be again withdrawn from Victor for the reconstruction of the corps, which was put under Lobau. News of the most unsatisfactory character regarding the state of demoralisation of Macdonald's army made it more and more doubtful how far it could be depended on to hold on at Görlitz, or even at Bautzen.

As for the army of Berlin, the Emperor was furious at Oudinot's incompetence, and superseded him in the command by Ney. Oudinot had much better have been withdrawn altogether from that army, where he was still allowed to command the XII. corps. He resented his supersession as an injustice, and was not in the least inclined to work willingly, to the best of his ability, with Ney, who, after all, and as the event further showed, was not much more competent than himself for semi-independent command.

The orders to Ney were dictated in full on the 2nd September.[1] They recite that Oudinot has deemed it necessary to retire to a position two marches above Wittenberg, thus enabling Tauenzien to send detachments towards Luckau and Bautzen, to harrass Macdonald's communications. "It is really difficult to have less head than the Duke of Reggio." The Emperor was himself about to move his headquarters to Luckau. Ney was to march with his new command to Baruth, reaching it on the 6th, when the Emperor would be at Luckau with a corps ready to support him, and Ney would be only three marches from Berlin, which he could reach and attack on the 9th or 10th. Napoleon still speaks with contempt of the allied army of the North as, "all this cloud of Cossacks and pack of bad landwehr," which would fall back on Berlin as soon as Ney advanced. After the orders to Ney, comes one of severe censure of Oudinot.

But the Emperor had to abandon even the idea of supporting Ney with one corps from Luckau, for a bitter cry for help reached him from Macdonald who, with his army utterly demoralised and reduced by 20,000 men by

[1] *Corr.* 20,502 to Berthier.

the events on the Katzbach, had fallen back on Bautzen and the Bober. He must be succoured at once.

On the 3rd September Napoleon left Dresden, after sending on to Bautzen the Guard, Marmont (VI. corps) and Latour-Maubourg. He reached Harthau that night. Next morning he rode forward to Hochkirch, encountering everywhere bands of stragglers and fugitives from Macdonald's army, offering the strongest proof of the terrible demoralisation of that force. The Emperor was so furious that he gave a childish exhibition of temper, by drawing his pistol to shoot a village cur which ran out and barked at him. When the pistol missed fire, he hurled it at the dog. Then he burst out furiously at Sebastiani who, he said, had mishandled his cavalry. He was so angry that Caulaincourt had to be careful to keep away from him any one who had been concerned. At Hochkirch he met Blücher's advanced guard who, in the evening, were forced back by the superior numbers of the French. Napoleon had at once taken the offensive, sending Murat with the III. corps and Latour-Maubourg by Wurschen; Macdonald, with the V. and XI. corps and Sebastiani on Murat's right; and Poniatowski on Lobau. All these had opposed to them only Blücher's advanced guard of 10,000 men. Napoleon himself was with the centre.

Blücher very soon found out that he was now opposed by Napoleon in person, and, in accordance with the Trachenberg-Reichenbach arrangements, proceeded to retreat. Napoleon followed him as far as Görlitz. He now realised Blücher's design to retire as soon as the Emperor himself was in the field against him. Avoiding the attempt to draw him away from Dresden into Silesia, Napoleon returned from Reichenbach, with the Guard and Marmont, to Bautzen in the evening of the 5th, arriving there at 2 A.M. on the 6th. Now he again proposed a dash northwards. On the 6th he ordered Marmont and Latour-Maubourg to Hoyerswerda, an order which was at once countermanded in consequence of news that the Bohemian army was again advancing on Dresden. Thither the

NEY'S DEFEAT AT DENNEWITZ 271

Emperor must go in person, and he also ordered Latour-Maubourg thither, whilst Marmont was ordered to Kamenz, to be ready to move on Dresden at a moment's notice.

Macdonald was left to pursue Blücher who, on the 6th, re-crossed the Queiss without serious molestation. That evening Napoleon was again in Dresden, after less than four days' absence.

This same 6th September witnessed the undoing of Ney, though Napoleon was not aware of it till the night of the 8th.

When Ney took over command of the army of Berlin on the 3rd September, the three corps stood on the arc of a circle north of Wittenberg—Bertrand (IV.) on the right, Oudinot (XII.) in the centre, Reynier (VII.) on the left. The allies were very widely scattered, but when, on the 4th September, Oudinot made a demonstration towards Zahna, Bernadotte drew his corps closer together, though they were still not closely concentrated. On his left was Tauenzien's corps at Zahna, in the centre Bülow, on the right, about Lobbese, Stedingk, Winzingerode, and the division of Hirschfeld, which had recently defeated Girard.

Ney's orders for the 5th directed the 58,000 men whom he commanded to move thus:—

XII. corps to start first, followed by the IV., both marching towards Zahna and Juterbogk. The VII. was to march northwards at first, and then turn to the right towards Baruth, thus forming a flank guard to the other two, and threatening the right of the enemy at Zahna. Bernadotte's plan was for Tauenzien to oppose the French advance at Zahna with an advance guard, whence he would retire on his main body at Dennewitz and Juterbogk. The rest of the North Army, moving leftwards, would fall on the left flank and rear of the French.

When Oudinot's attack fell upon Tauenzien's advance guard at Zahna, Reynier was marching south of him, as was evidenced to the Prussians by the clouds of dust. Zahna was taken after a severe fight, and the defenders retired, partly direct by the Juterbogk road, partly by Gadegast and Oehna.

Ney's positions at night were—

XII. corps—Pacthod's and Guilleminot's divisions in front of Sayda; Fournier's cavalry and Raglowitch's Bavarians behind Gadegast.

VII. corps about Zahna.

IV. corps and Lorge's cavalry at Seehausen and Naundorf.

For the 6th, Ney's orders directed Reynier to advance on Rohrbeck by Gadegast and Oehna. Oudinot was to wait at Sayda till the VII. had passed Oehna, and then to march in the direction of Dahme and Luckau, where the Emperor was supposed to be.

Bertrand to march south of Juterbogk, guarding the left flank of the march on Dahme.

The IV. corps started a little before 8 A.M.

The VII., though it had farther to go, started later, and then, instead of going by Gadegast and Oehna, went direct to Dennewitz.

Oudinot, meanwhile, waited at Sayda for the VII. to pass on its way to Gadegast. Owing to Reynier's deviation from the route by Gadegast he never did pass, as Oudinot was told to expect. Oudinot appears not to have started till he got orders, between 1 and 2 P.M., though he had been ready to do so from 10 A.M. A strong north-west wind was raising clouds of sand, which obscured his view. The consequence of all this was that the three corps reached the battlefield at considerable intervals, between 10 A.M. and 4 P.M.

The battlefield of Dennewitz is generally, speaking, a sandy plain with woods and low knolls scattered about it. It is crossed by several brooks flowing in deep channels, of which the most important is the Agerbach, flowing from Nieder Görsdorf to Dennewitz and Rohrbeck. The country offers advantages to all arms. There are good artillery positions on the knolls, which form a screen for reserves behind them, and the plain is open for cavalry. Infantry can find good supports in the villages of Gölsdorf, Dennewitz, and Rohrbeck, in the various woods, and in the passages of the Agerbach.

When Bertrand with the IV. corps reached Dennewitz,

NEY'S DEFEAT AT DENNEWITZ

he saw Tauenzien in front of him. He at once deployed Fontanelli's division beyond the brook, with Lorge and Morand on his left. The latter division, in support, had at first to remain in Dennewitz, for want of room to deploy beyond the brook.

Tauenzien had his artillery (19 guns) on the knoll north of Dennewitz, his infantry behind them.

Fontanelli's attack began about 11 A.M., and was at first completely successful. Both Tauenzien's wings were driven in, and the situation was only saved for the time by a charge of Prussian cavalry. The landwehr had got somewhat out of hand, and had fired wildly over the heads of their own skirmishers.

The French, however, hearing of Bülow's approach on their left, had not dared to push home their attack on Tauenzien's right. Nevertheless, that general, though practically defeated, had held out long enough to give Bülow time to arrive. The latter had started from Eckmannsdorf at 10.30; by 12.30 the heads of his columns were arriving at Nieder Görsdorf. His first attack, with Thümen's brigade, which joined Tauenzien's right, was badly repulsed by Morand. Then the Hessen-Homburg division arrived, and compelled Morand to retire eastwards from the heights north of Nieder Görsdorf, though he did so in good order. A pause in the fighting now occurred, during which the French took up, about 2.30 P.M., a new position north of the brook, with their left resting on the Dennewitz windmill height and fronting westwards. Thümen and Tauenzien now made a combined attack on the wood north-east of Nieder Görsdorf, on which the French right rested. Though a vigorous defence was made by the Wurtembergers, the wood was eventually captured and many prisoners taken. In consequence of this, the French were compelled to fall back on Rohrbeck. Bertrand's effort to restore the battle with his last reserve of two Wurtemberg battalions failed completely. He had been badly defeated, and Thümen was now in possession of everything north of the Agerbach.

It was 2 P.M. when Reynier, with the VII. corps, began

to reach the field. There were still no signs of Oudinot's approach. Ney, who had arrived, sent a brigade of Durutte's division (VII. corps) across the brook. This, in conjunction with Bertrand's corps, succeeded with difficulty in retaking the windmill height, which the Prussians had occupied. The French were, however, again driven from it, and by 4 P.M. Thümen had got through Dennewitz and stood with his troops in a semi-circle facing south, between Dennewitz and Rohrbeck. Bülow, meanwhile, had brought up Krafft's division south of the brook.

Reynier, owing to the heavy wind, knew nothing of the battle till, about 1 P.M., he met Lorge's defeated cavalry between Oehna and Rohrbeck. Sending Durutte on to Dennewitz, he turned leftwards with his two Saxon divisions, which, with De France's cuirassiers, went against Bülow's right, south of the Agerbach. The Saxons took part of Gölsdorf about 2.30 P.M., but were driven out again. The space between them and Durutte was filled by De France's cuirassiers.

Reynier, finding himself too weak to do much, sent to hurry up Oudinot, who had began to arrive about 3 P.M.

Bülow, seeing that the French were now gathering strength, had thrown in Borstell with his last reserve, and sent an urgent demand for reinforcements to Bernadotte. Bülow was now advancing on Gölsdorf. Before he got there, however, Oudinot had brought up Guilleminot's and Pacthod's divisions behind the Saxons, and had posted a strong battery on Reynier's left. Thus supported, Reynier had recaptured Gölsdorf without difficulty.

Bülow's position was now very critical, for Bernadotte's Swedes and Russians were still two or three miles off. He might very well have been rolled up from his right, or driven away from the troops beyond the brook, had not Ney seized this moment to ruin his own chance of success.

As usual, the Prince of the Moskowa had been carried away by impulse on the battlefield. Standing where he did on the heights south-east of Dennewitz, he could see little of what was going on on the left, for the air was thick

NEY'S DEFEAT AT DENNEWITZ 275

with the whirling dust. He judged only by what was nearest to him, and he believed that the decision lay in that direction, whereas it clearly lay on his left. He proposed to make an attempt to restore the battle on the right by a vigorous attack with Oudinot's corps and what remained of Bertrand's. Orders were sent to Oudinot to march to his right. When they reached him, that marshal was with Reynier, who begged him to leave at least one division to complete the success at Gölsdorf. But Oudinot, still smarting under his supersession by Ney, maintained that he was bound to obey the order literally. He had already started towards Rohrbeck when Borstell attacked the Saxons in Gölsdorf. The 156th regiment, which was just following the rest of Oudinot's troops, stopped to assist in the defence. But the Prussians attacked with such fury that the Saxons, after losing nearly 1500 men, were driven from the village, and only saved from total destruction by a timely charge of De France's cuirassiers.

It was 5 P.M. when Bertrand had been driven from Rohrbeck, long before Oudinot could arrive. The Prussians again held the whole field north of the Agerbach.

Bülow, too, was now beginning to receive Russian and Swedish reinforcements, especially artillery. Before these, Reynier's Saxons, shattered and disordered, were falling back eastwards, carrying away Oudinot's troops as they marched on Rohrbeck.

In vain did Ney and Reynier endeavour to turn the flight into an orderly retreat. Panic and confusion reigned supreme. Ney, at 6 P.M., had ordered a retreat on Dahme, but his orders only reached part of the troops, which fled in different directions, pursued by the enemy's cavalry and artillery. Reynier and Oudinot made direct for Torgau; Ney, with Bertrand, went towards Dahme, where they were joined by Raglowich's Bavarians, who had scarcely been engaged. Dahme was evacuated by a Prussian detachment which had held it.

Of Reynier's corps, one column went by Langen-Lipsdorf, Körbitz, and Wendisch Linde, reaching Annaburg at daybreak, and Torgau at mid-day on the 7th. Another column started on the Dahme road, then turned towards Schönwald, and reached Wendisch Ahlsdorf at 11 P.M. They were at Torgau by 2 A.M. Oudinot's three divisions, though they had borne less of the stress of battle, fled as wildly as the rest by Schweinitz and Annaburg to Torgau.

Ney, finding himself at Dahme with only a small part of his army, decided also to make for Torgau. As he left Dahme, he was attacked by Wobeser from Luckau, who took the village and over 2800 prisoners. He picked up another 400 as he pursued Bertrand who, having left Dahme at 3 A.M., only reached Herzberg by 9 p.m. on the 7th.

In the fight at Zahna, the battle at Dennewitz, and the subsequent actions in the pursuit, the Prussians had lost about 10,500 men killed and wounded. The losses of the Russians and Swedes were probably not serious.

Ney, on the other hand, had lost about 22,000 men, of whom 13,500 were prisoners, 53 guns, 412 wagons, and 4 standards. His army was utterly disorganised, more so even than Macdonald's on the Katzbach.

Ney, like Oudinot at Gross Beeren and Macdonald on the Katzbach, had not expected a battle. Had he done so, perhaps he would have held his corps more together, in which case he might well have defeated Tauenzien and Bülow before Bernadotte could come up. Possibly he might have split the allied army in two.

His information regarding the enemy was very poor. He had not utilised his cavalry properly. His object being to reach Dahme, there was no need to go so far north as he did. He might have marched two of his corps straight there, using the third as a flank guard on his left, as he had done on the previous day. He was so furious when he found Bertrand engaged at Dennewitz that he remarked to a Wurtemberg general, "Mais nom dieu, mon général, quelle cochonnerie fait ce Bertrand," which shows clearly that he did not expect a battle, or desire one, that day.

NEY'S DEFEAT AT DENNEWITZ 277

Once engaged, he, as usual, let himself be carried away by his fiery temperament, and became a corps commander rather than a general-in-chief. Consequently, his outlook became localised, and he completely failed to see that it was his left which should have been reinforced, or that victory against Bülow's right would be decisive, whilst victory in the opposite direction would only drive the Prussians back on the support of Bernadotte.

Had he taken up a defensive position behind the brook with his right, and reinforced his left with Oudinot, he would, at the worst, have had a safe retreat open, either on Dahme or Torgau. Oudinot was in a position to judge the position better, but he obeyed Ney's order to move to the right without remonstrance, and without any attempt to explain the true situation to the commander-in-chief. He must share the blame for the defeat with Ney.

Friederich considers that the allied leaders worked well together. Tauenzien, not hesitating to engage superior numbers, trusted to the support promised by Bülow. When Tauenzien, and the whole of Bülow's corps were arrayed against Bertrand and Reynier, the Prussians were the stronger, but Oudinot's arrival turned the scale against them.

Bernadotte has been charged with delay, but Friederich shows that he was not really to blame on this occasion; for, up to 10 a.m., it was uncertain whether Ney meant to march direct for Berlin, or was moving to his right. Nor was there any information as to whether he was likely to be supported by Napoleon. In view of the possibility of Ney's moving direct on Berlin, Bernadotte could not safely march towards Juterbogk earlier than he did. Though his troops took no great part in the battle, the 36 guns which he was able to get up prevented the French from rallying towards Oehna and covering their retreat.

Bernadotte's troops marched over 9 miles between 11 A.M. and 2 P.M., when they reached Eckmannsdorf. The remaining $6\frac{1}{4}$ miles to Dennewitz were covered by 5.30 P.M.

and, considering the heat of the day, they cannot be accused of want of activity in covering over 15 miles in 6½ hours. Bülow might possibly have obtained greater results by bringing up all his troops south of the brook, but that would have risked Tauenzien's destruction in the meanwhile.

CHAPTER XVII

FROM THE 6TH SEPTEMBER TO THE END OF THE MONTH

THE movement of the allies from Bohemia, which had brought Napoleon back in a hurry to Dresden on the 6th September, differed considerably from that which led to the battle of Dresden. Instead of an advance of the whole of the army of Bohemia on the left bank of the Elbe, Schwarzenberg was now moving with 60,000 Austrians on the right bank towards Rumburg and Zittau, and threatening the right flank of the French operating against Blücher. Barclay was left in Bohemia with the Russians and Prussians, and the two Austrian divisions of Lichtenstein and Klenau. He was to advance through the mountains towards Dresden, spreading reports that he was only waiting for siege guns to take the place. This, Schwarzenberg hoped, would compel Napoleon to concentrate, and afford an opportunity for the destruction of Macdonald by Blücher in his front, acting with Schwarzenberg against the French right.

If Napoleon moved south in force from Dresden, Barclay was to avoid a battle, to retire on Teplitz, and, if he still found himself threatened by superior forces, even to cross the Eger.

Schwarzenberg's plan of taking a large force to the right bank was apparently due to the belief that Napoleon contemplated a movement to his right into northern Bohemia, by Zittau and Rumburg, as soon as Blücher had been forced back.[1] That might end in his getting to Prague in rear of the allies, if the main army all remained on the other side of the Elbe.

[1] *Danilewski*, p 19c.

Such a division of the allied main army into two groups, separated by a great river like the Elbe, across which Napoleon could pass at pleasure at Dresden, Pirna, or Königstein, was very risky in the face of such an opponent.

On the 4th September[1] St Cyr, with the XIV. corps, had his right at Borna, centre at Berggiesshübel, left at Königstein and the Lilienstein. Advanced guard and cavalry (Pajol) at Hellendorf, Oelsen, and Breitenau. The left division (42nd) astride of the river, watched the left flank of an allied advance on Rumberg, the right of one on Dresden. For the latter purpose it had six battalions distributed between the redoubts at Cunnersdorf and Hennersdorf, and Krietschwitz on the Pirna plateau, with one more at Pirna. In the evening of the 5th September Pajol, with the advanced guard, was pressed back by the Russians and Prussians to Berggiesshübel and Borna, where he took post behind the 44th and 45th divisions.

On the 6th St Cyr had again to retire till he stood, on the morning of the 7th, with his advanced guard stretching from Pirna to the heights of Zehista and Zuschendorf. He still had most of the 42nd division about Königstein. His main body was at Dohna, Mügeln, and Heidenau. Here he stood fast all day. During the day Napoleon arrived. St Cyr gives an account of his interview with the Emperor, which is unfortunately too long for quotation. According to him, Napoleon admitted having lost an opportunity, on the 28th August, by not supporting Vandamme. St Cyr replied that he had now another opportunity of a battle with the Bohemian army, but the Emperor's thoughts seemed to be far away in the direction of Bernadotte and Blücher.[2] On the morning of the 8th St Cyr's position was on the left bank of the Müglitz. His advanced guard was driven in across the stream, but parts of it still held on in Dohna and Heidenau. About 2 P.M. Napoleon returned from Dresden, where he had slept the night before. St Cyr says he hesitated to attack till all his troops were up from Dresden, which meant doing nothing till next

---

[1] Map IV. (*b*).   [2] *Hist. Mil.*, iv. p. 137.

morning. At last, however, the XIV. corps was sent forward, its repassage of the Müglitz being facilitated by its retention of Dohna and Heidenau.

The enemy, after a sharp fight, fell back beyond Zehista. Barclay's force was much scattered, since Lichtenstein's Austrians had been sent towards Freiberg, and Klenau's by the Chemnitz road. They were linked to the Russians and Prussians on the right by Kasarow at Maxen, where he was supposed to be in a position to turn St Cyr's right.

That night the XIV. corps stood with its right at Köttwitz, left in front of Sedlitz.

During his supper, at which St Cyr was a guest, Napoleon received a full account of Ney's defeat at Dennewitz. His reception of it was remarkable. The man who, a few days before, had burst out in furious abuse of Sebastiani for his real or supposed mishandling of his cavalry, now received this crushing news with the utmost calmness. No word of ill-humour, or of abuse of Ney or the other generals, passed his lips. Everything was put down to the difficulties of the art of war, which were so little understood. A curious remark which he made was that no great soldier, except Turenne, had ever learnt much of war by experience, and he admitted, in his own case, that he had never done anything better in the fullness of his experience than his first campaign in Italy. As for the Dennewitz disaster, he discussed it, says St Cyr, "with all the coolness he could have brought to a discussion of events in China or in the preceding century."[1]

Daybreak on the 9th saw Napoleon at the front, where he eventually accepted St Cyr's proposal to march by the old road, by Dohna and Furstenwalde to Teplitz, in order to arrive on the enemy's rear as he retreated by the Peterswalde road. As soon as Wittgenstein discovered what was happening, he set out towards Peterswalde, the French marching parallel to him by the old road, and for some time actually in sight. That night there were at Furstenwalde, Lefebvre-Desnoettes' Guard division, two divisions

[1] *Hist. Mil.*, iv. p. 148, etc.

of the XIV. corps, and Pajol's cavalry; the third division of the XIV. was at Breitenau, and a reconnaissance of the Guard had driven the enemy's flankers out of Oelsen. The Emperor's headquarters were at Liebstadt.

Napoleon's presence had been recognized and reported to Schwarzenberg, who now hurriedly ordered back his troops from the right bank of the Elbe towards Dux, and recalled Klenau and Lichtenstein from the directions of Chemnitz and Freiberg. By 10 A.M. on the 10th the XIV. corps was on the Geiersberg, just above the field of Vandamme's action of the 29th August. Napoleon arrived in person an hour later.

From the Geiersberg he looked down on the plains below, where he saw the Russians and Prussians hurrying in all directions to prepare for the attack which they expected to fall upon them, constantly changing their positions as their columns emerged from the Nollendorf road. The weather being fine, he could count every file in the enemy's ranks, and could see exactly what he had before him. The 43rd division of St Cyr's corps was already half-way down the steep slope, and sappers were rapidly clearing the road for the artillery. Not an Austrian was to be seen, either of those beyond the Elbe or of those to the west.

But already some of the French artillery had got into difficulties in a premature descent of the road, and the dangers foreshadowed by this may have had a good deal to do with Napoleon's decision not to follow St Cyr's suggestion of a descent into the plain, with the object of defeating the Russians and Prussians whilst still far from their Austrian allies. He would retire, he said, leaving St Cyr for the present to keep up the alarm which appeared to exist in the Russo-Prussian camp.[1]

St Cyr expresses his astonishment that the man who had not hesitated at the passage of the Alps with a mere hand-

---

[1] Odeleben (i. p. 277) says Napoleon only abandoned the scheme of a descent from the Geiersberg with great regret, on an unfavourable report on the possibilities of the road for artillery. A single breakdown might ruin everything.

ful of troops, should have refused to take this smaller risk which held out such strong hopes of a brilliant success. He was convinced that the Emperor could no longer hope to assemble an army sufficient to beat his enemies united, but he might very well defeat the Russians and Prussians alone. It must be remembered, though, that however calmly he appeared to take the disaster of Dennewitz, Napoleon doubtless felt the risk of engaging in a descent into Bohemia when Bernadotte might even now be crossing the Elbe and marching on Leipzig.

On the 11th the allies, below still, at first seemed to be expecting an attack from the mountains. Presently, when nothing happened, they began making small attacks on the foot of the Geiersberg. In the Nollendorf-Peterswalde direction, whither Napoleon had himself gone by Breitenau, there was some artillery firing, directed by him. It was only that evening that Austrians from beyond the Elbe began to reach Teplitz—two divisions of them—and take post as reserve behind the Russian right.

When Napoleon left St Cyr on the 10th, he would have slept at Ebersdorf or Furstenwalde, but there was absolutely no accommodation. Even at Breitenau there was only the parish priest's house, and that had to be cleaned before the Emperor, who was not squeamish, could use it for himself and Berthier. All Saxony was ruined by the constant advance and retreat of the tide of war; the part adjoining the Bohemian frontier was perhaps the worst; for within the last few weeks the allies had advanced and retreated through it twice, and the French the same. There was not much to choose, from the wretched inhabitants' point of view, between the starving French soldiers and "Russia's savage warriors," as the Cossacks are described on a stone just outside Dresden, which still records the horrors of their occupation of Räcknitz. Odeleben's description of the frontier is worth quoting. "The troops were short of food; they were obliged to sleep, in the cold autumn nights, on the damp ground of the mountains. There was no forage for the horses, the frontier villages were entirely destroyed, every house which was not built of stone had been pulled down to feed the bivouac fires; the whole neighbourhood bore the stamp of the horrors of war. . . . The soil, already ten times turned over, was again ransacked in the search for a few potatoes."

It was on the morning of the 11th, as Napoleon went by a difficult path through Oelsen towards Peterswalde, that his escort met Prussian cavalry. The latter, unable to avoid the superior French force, were attacked and beaten. In this combat there was wounded and taken prisoner, near Peterswalde, Colonel Blücher, son of the victor of the Katzbach. It was late when the Emperor at last reached Nollendorf, where Lobau took post with the I. corps, of the withdrawal of which from behind him St Cyr only learnt on the 12th; a curious example of the inefficiency of Napoleon's staff work.

At Peterswalde the Emperor lodged at the house of the parish priest; all the other inhabitants had fled. Next day he returned to Pirna, where he ordered the construction of a fortified bridge-head.

St Cyr retired with the 43rd division to in front of Breitenau, the 45th between Liebstadt and Borna, the 44th and Pajol still watching the enemy from Furstenwalde, linked, by a post at Streckenwald, to the I. corps at Nollendorf, and by another at Lauenstein to Victor (II. corps) at Altenberg. The 42nd division, after following the retreating Russians from Königstein towards Peterswalde, was back again at Langen-Hennersdorf.

On the 14th Lobau was attacked and driven back behind Berggiesshübel. For this affair the allies had made preparations as if they were attacking a whole army, instead of a single corps, with only Dumonçeau's weak division as advanced guard.

On the 15th St Cyr, whose advanced guard was now forward again as far as Breitenau, expected an attack, but nothing happened, except a small affair on its right rear, which was exposed, owing to the withdrawal of Victor, which again only came to St Cyr's ears accidentally at a very late period. The attack on Lobau brought Napoleon once more southwards with reinforcements. Lobau had now been placed under St Cyr, but the Emperor, being present in person, of course took command.

On the 16th Napoleon advanced on Peterswalde by the road from in front, whilst St Cyr co-operated on the enemy's left by Oelsen and Schönwald. The enemy was driven from Peterswalde and Nollendorf, where the Emperor himself arrived in weather so misty that it was impossible to discern from the heights what was happening in the valley below.

On the 17th, in the early morning, Napoleon went to the chapel of Nollendorf. Though the weather was still nearly as thick as the day before, he sent troops down the road, whilst others filled the woods on its sides. These, after some fighting, were cleared, and the French reached the plain. Napoleon himself went to Tellnitz. The sky had cleared somewhat, but the view was still obscured, and it was impossible to judge of the enemy's forces. Then there broke a sudden storm of artillery fire, the source of which was uncertain in the mist. It appeared that there was a strong allied column about Kninitz, on the road to Königswald, which seemed to be endeavouring to cut off the French retreat by the Nollendorf road. Napoleon had to take measures for occupying this village and guarding his retreat with his reserve. Some of his troops had now advanced almost to Kulm, when torrents of rain put a stop to the fighting. Napoleon himself went back for the night to Peterswalde. His troops still held Tellnitz on the 18th, and on that day he again went forward to Nollendorf and Kninitz. As he issued from the neighbouring wood, he had to turn back before an attack of some of the enemy's cavalry. Ascending again to the heights, he was now able to see the enemy, and remarked to Berthier : "All I see are two corps of about 60,000 men each, which will need an entire day to unite for attack."

Making over the command to Lobau, he then returned to Pirna, convinced that his army was not strong enough to remain where it was, and that the time had passed for an invasion of Bohemia.

On the 16th he had written to Lobau[1] that the enemy's "principal forces in this direction are on the Peterswalde 'chaussée,' which it is important to him to hold, in order to be sure that I do not take the offensive whilst he is engaged in his operations." The operations referred to—that is, those on the right bank of the Elbe towards Rumburg—had already been abandoned. The Emperor's move into Bohemia on the 17th does not appear to have been intended to be more than a reconnaissance for the purpose of gaining information.

Napoleon's rearward communications had throughout the campaign been much harassed by the operations of partisans who had displayed the greatest activity and enterprise. So serious had the losses become that, on the 11th September,[2] the Emperor directed Lefebvre-Desnoettes to take up the special duty of clearing off the Cossacks and others. He was reinforced up to 4000 cavalry at Freiberg, where he was on the 14th,[3] besides another 2000 under Lorge, withdrawn from Ney. A division of Victor's corps was ordered to Freiberg. The cavalry was to sweep the whole country west of the Elbe in rear of the army; Margaron, the governor of Leipzig, was to help; and, finally, Augereau was ordered, on the 17th,[4] to march with his whole corps from Würzburg by Coburg to Jena, whence he was to keep open the passages of the Saale and protect the rear of the army with the 11,000 men he would have left, after sending one of his divisions to join the I. corps.

Considerations of space forbid our entering into the details of this partizan warfare, but this seems a convenient place for a brief statement, anticipating somewhat, of the principal operations of the allied flying columns in the French rear.[5]

Prince Kudaschew was sent during the battle of Dresden with a party of cavalry to carry despatches to Bernadotte.

---

[1] *Corr.* 205,72, dated Pirna, 16th September, 8 A.M.
[2] *Corr.* 20,543.   [3] *Corr.* 20,562.   [4] *Corr.* 20,576.
[5] For fuller accounts, see Danilewski.

After a most adventurous ride to the North, across the Elbe and back again to Bohemia, he was able to give information as to the unprotected state of the French communications. In consequence of his news, Thielmann[1] and the Austrian Count Mensdorf were sent off to operate on the Saale, and between Leipzig and Erfurt, against the French convoys and reinforcements. Their force consisted chiefly of Cossacks. On the 12th September Thielmann was at Weissenfels, where he took 1000 prisoners and 26 guns, and seized the defile of Kösen. On the 18th he took Merseburg and 2000 prisoners. Mensdorf acted with equal vigour, cutting off convoys, despatch riders, etc. It was against these two that Lefebvre-Desnoettes was sent. At the same time, the allied free corps had been strengthened by seven Cossack regiments under Platow. These, with Thielmann, attacked Lefebvre-Desnoettes at Altenburg on the 28th September, drove him out, and captured 1000 prisoners from him.

About this same period a still more important raid was carried out from the north. Czernitchew, with 2300 Cossacks and cavalry and 6 guns, crossed the Elbe, and marched rapidly on Cassel, the capital of Jerome Bonaparte's kingdom of Westphalia. Spreading false reports regarding the direction of his march, he unexpectedly appeared before Cassel on the morning of the 28th September, and defeated some French infantry, taking 6 guns from them. Then he attacked 2000 French troops approaching the place and dispersed them. Returning to Cassel, he induced the garrison to surrender it, and captured a number of guns. Jerome had fled in haste on Czernitchew's first appearance. After proclaiming the end of the Westphalian kingdom, Czernitchew returned unharmed to Bernadotte.

On the 16th September a raid of Walmoden's troops crossing the Elbe destroyed a detachment of Davout's corps at Görda. This detachment was on its way to Magdeburg.

Later, on the 17th October, Tettenborn surprised and took Bremen, far in Davout's rear.

[1] Formerly Saxon commandant of Torgau. He went over to the allies in May.

These are only a few of the exploits of the allied partizans. A full record of their doings would fill a volume. Some more of them are chronicled in an order of Napoleon of the 19th September,[1] prescribing precautions against surprise to be taken by officers commanding detachments.

These extensive expeditions of considerable bodies of cavalry far in the French rear are a peculiarity of this campaign, which is the only instance of their employment on a large scale in a European war. Similar raids played a considerable part in the American Civil War of fifty years ago. In this case, as in 1813, the raids were generally carried out in a country the inhabitants of which were often sympathisers with the raiders, to whom they supplied food, forage, and information. Moreover, there were few or none of the modern facilities for sending information to the other side. It seems more than doubtful what success such raids could hope for in these days of telegraphs in Europe. There has recently been another example of such a raid in the Russian expedition under General Mistshenko against Yinkon in the Japanese rear, in January 1905.[2] The raid can hardly be deemed a great success, and it was only possible to carry it out at all owing to the route taken being through an area devoid of telegraphs, in which the inhabitants were not likely to go out of their way to give information to either side. Looking to the intensity of the anti-French feeling in Germany in 1813, it would have been impossible for Napoleon to have made such raids, and, in 1814, for a similar reason, the invading allies could not continue their practice of 1813 in France.

The Emperor was now waiting at Pirna for the enemy to offer him an opportunity. The inactivity which is a marked characteristic, surely a strangely novel one, of Napoleon's conduct during the greater part of September, was very dangerous; for the surrounding armies were

---

[1] *Corr.* 20,595.
[2] See Vol. V., German Official Account of the Russo-Japanese War (English translation). The question of such raids is discussed at some length at pp. 37 *et seqq.*

gradually closing in on him, threatening to convert the strategical advantages of holding the interior lines into the dangerous position of being tactically surrounded. Moreever, Bennigsen with 50,000 or 60,000 men was now coming up to reinforce the allies, whilst Napoleon could look for very few fresh troops beyond the 16,000 of Augereau's (IX.) corps ordered up from Würzburg. Saxony was almost completely exhausted, and the provisioning of the army was day by day increasing in difficulty. "The army is not nourished. It would be an illusion to regard matters otherwise."[1] So wrote Napoleon on the 23rd September, and at an earlier date he had sent Marmont and Murat, with the VI. corps and two cavalry corps, to Grossenhain to cover a convoy of food coming up the Elbe to Dresden. The magnitude of the covering force shows the immense importance which the Emperor attached to this supply.

On the 19th Napoleon received a report from Macdonald to the effect that his flankers on the left had been driven from Pulsnitz on Radeberg. Thereupon, the Emperor ordered two divisions of Young Guard, under Mortier, to cross the Elbe at Pirna, and advance to Lohmen on the way to Stolpen. This movement was to be concealed from the enemy by Poniatowski at Stolpen, and Napoleon indicated his intention, if the weather improved, of moving to drive Blücher back beyond Bautzen, on which he had advanced as soon as he found Napoleon was no longer with Macdonald. Next morning, Napoleon writes to Marmont that the weather has been too bad to move, but, as he also says Macdonald's report of the enemy's force towards Radeberg was an exaggeration, that is perhaps the chief reason for delay.

On the 19th September the XII. corps was dissolved and distributed thus :—The two French divisions, amalgamated into one under Guilleminot, were made over to the VII. corps (Reynier). The Bavarian division was relegated to escort duty with the parks. Oudinot was recalled on the 25th to headquarters, and put in command of two divisions of Young Guard.

[1] *Corr.* 20,619.

On the 21st September a new set of orders[1] was issued from Pirna, where the Emperor still stayed, complaining that the weather was too bad for any movements.

The Old Guard was sent to Dresden, Mortier, with a division of the Young Guard to hold Pirna. To St Cyr was given the command of his own (XIV.) corps, the I. and the V., the last-named being called in from Macdonald's army. St Cyr's duty was to guard the Elbe from Pilnitz to Königstein, and to watch the roads from Bohemia between the latter place and Freiberg. The Emperor reckoned he would have 40,000 to 50,000 men—Victor to hold Chemnitz, with his left towards Freiberg, right towards the Saale; Marmont to Freiberg; Macdonald, with the XI. corps, to the command of which alone he was now reduced, to fall back to the exits of the forest in front of Dresden. All this would enable the army to rest.

Ney was charged with the defence of the Elbe from Magdeburg to Torgau, with the IV., VII. and III. corps. There was news that the enemy was throwing a bridge at Dessau, which required Ney to move the IV. and VII. towards Wittenberg. Murat and Marmont, who had, at Grossenhain, protected the convoy from Torgau, would now pass the Elbe at Meissen. If the news of the bridge at Dessau were confirmed, they would proceed at once to Torgau. This was a conditional modification of the orders sending Marmont to Freiberg.

A later order[2] directed Macdonald to support Poniatowski, and prevent his being driven from Stolpen, which was alleged to be threatened by the enemy.

On the 22nd the Emperor writes,[3] at 2 A.M. from Dresden, to Macdonald that, as it seemed uncertain what were the movements of Blücher's army, he should carry out a reconnaissance in force, with the object of ascertaining where his main forces were. The Emperor would probably be behind in support. Then he decided to go in person to Macdonald's front.[4] He reached Harthau the same day,

---

[1] *Corr.* 20,603 and 20,604.   [2] *Corr.* 20,607.
[3] *Corr.* 20,609.   [4] *Corr.* 20,612.

FROM 6TH SEPTEMBER TO END OF MONTH

after driving Blücher's advanced troops back with the III. and XI. corps and capturing Bischofswerda. On the 23rd the advance continued, Blücher, as usual, falling back to Förstgen, short of Bautzen. According to Odeleben, the Emperor showed signs of irresolution at Harthau. After watching the retirement of Blücher, he returned to Harthau.

He had heard from Ney that the enemy had completed a bridge over the Elbe at the mouth of the Black Elster, and could cross when he chose.

Napoleon had now decided that the time had come for abandonment of all territory east of the Elbe, excepting that immediately in front of the fortresses and bridges. He would have one bridge at Königstein, one at Pilnitz, three at Dresden, one at Meissen, and, of course, those at Torgau, Wittenberg and Magdeburg. All would be defended by powerful bridge-heads, and Macdonald, recalled to Dresden would hold strongly the issues from the Dresden forest. He would watch the enemy, and, if the latter undertook any offensive operations, the Emperor would fall upon him and compel him to battle.

As Count Yorck points out,[1] Napoleon came to this decision at the dictation of the enemy, not, as when he decided to retire behind the Passarge in 1807, of his own free will.

We must here return for a few moments to the doings of Ney and his opponents after the disastrous battle of Dennewitz, and to those of Blücher. Ney, having assembled the remains of his army at Torgau on the 8th September, crossed to the left bank of the Elbe and went to Düben, where he had his hands full with the task of reorganizing his army.

Bernadotte, on the other hand, sent Bülow to besiege Wittenberg, though, as that general was very ill-provided with siege artillery, there was not much prospect of his gaining any material success at an early date. In order to shut in the fortress on the left bank, and to be ready for a passage of the Elbe, Bernadotte, about the 15th September,

[1] *Napoleon as a General*, ii. p. 324.

began building three bridges—one below the mouth of the Black Elster, one at Rosslau, and one at Acken, both the latter below Wittenberg. On the 21st September, Ney, alarmed by a false report that the whole of Bernadotte's army was about to pass the Elbe, set his troops in motion towards Wittenberg.

On the 24th, when the enemy appeared in some force opposite Wartenburg, Ney drew up his army there. Bernadotte at once removed his bridge and withdrew.

Blücher was now about to make a momentous move. After the defeat of Dresden, Schwarzenberg, fully expecting an invasion of Bohemia by Napoleon, sent urgent orders to Blücher to march to his assistance with 50,000 men. Blücher could hardly be expected to divide his army, taking 50,000 men to Bohemia and leaving the rest to face Macdonald. The victory of Kulm changed the aspect of affairs, and this scheme dropped for the moment. On the 7th September it was revived. Blücher was ordered to march by Rumburg, sending his baggage by Zittau, to Böhmisch Leipa. Bennigsen, when he came up, was to march direct to the Elbe. If the French evacuated the right bank, he was to blockade Königstein, Dresden, and Torgau. If they continued on the right bank, he was to keep in touch with them, avoiding a general action. Regarding these arrangements, however, Blücher was consulted at the instance of the King of Prussia, and in consequence of what he said, orders of the 12th, recognising that Blücher was already near the Elbe, transposed his rôle and that of Bennigsen. Blücher proposed that he should march, not to Bohemia, but to his right, in order to join the North army, whilst Bennigsen, now nearly up, went to reinforce the Bohemian army. Blücher would remain in Eastern Saxony long enough to cover the flank march of Bennigsen to Bohemia. The latter was expected to reach Zittau about the 20th September. He actually reached Leitmeritz on the Elbe on the 27th.

As Bennigsen approached, Radetzky (Schwarzenberg's Chief-of-Staff) proposed, on the 22nd September, that the whole army of Bohemia should start on a fifteen days' march by Hof to Baireuth, in order to threaten Napoleon's communications with France. It will be remembered that such a movement was one of the contingencies contemplated by Napoleon at an earlier date. He then remarked that, if the allies went off in that direction, he would be content to wish them "bon voyage," in the certainty that they would come back quicker than they had gone. Had they done so, he would have been left time to fall upon Bernadotte and destroy him. Fortunately for the allies, Radetzky's wild scheme met with no encouragement. On the other hand, it was decided now to operate through the Erzgebirge, not on Dresden as heretofore, but by Chemnitz direct towards Leipzig.

Thus, just when Napoleon decided to bring his whole army over to the left bank of the Elbe, the allies were preparing, first, for Blücher's flank march to his right to join Bernadotte, secondly, for the advance of the Bohemian army on Leipzig.

The withdrawal of the French army to the left bank began on the 24th September. Mortier went to Dresden. Souham and Lauriston were called in to the same place, to reach it on the 26th. Poniatowski was to march by Fischbach and across the Elbe at Dresden, covered by Macdonald and Sebastiani at Weissig. Marmont and Latour-Maubourg were ordered to cross at Meissen, leaving L'Heritier, with the 5th cavalry corps, to watch at Grossenhain.

On the 25th the positions of the French were these—

Macdonald (XI. corps), Weissig.

Lauriston (V. corps) and Guard, Dresden.

III. corps (Souham), VI. corps (Marmont), and 1st cavalry (Latour-Maubourg), Meissen

VIII. corps (Poniatowski), marching on Waldheim to support Lefebvre-Desnoettes in his operations against Thielmann's and the other allied "Free-corps."

South of Dresden, under the general command of St Cyr, were his own (XIV.) corps at Pirna and Borna.

I. corps (Lobau) at Berggiesshübel.

II. corps (Victor) at Freiberg.

Ney, with the IV. (Bertrand) and VII. corps (Reynier), was in front of Wartenburg.

Napoleon was now beginning seriously to look forward to the time when he must retreat over the Rhine, as is evidenced by his order [1] to Clarke to prepare the French fortresses on the Rhine for defence.

As September closed the positions on both sides were these—

French.—XI. corps (Macdonald), Weissig.

I. and XIV. corps (Lobau and St Cyr), south of Dresden, the latter linked to the XI. corps by the Pirna bridge.

II. corps (Victor), Freiberg.

Guard, Dresden.

V. corps (Lauriston), near Dresden, on the Leipzig road.

VIII. corps (Poniatowski), on the Waldheim-Leipzig road, acting with Lefebvre-Desnoettes' column.

IV. corps (Bertrand) and VII. corps (Reynier), under Ney, between Torgau and Wittenberg, on the left bank of the Elbe.

III. corps (Souham), VI. corps (Marmont), and 1st cavalry corps (Latour-Maubourg), towards Meissen, ready to support Ney if the enemy passed the Elbe.

IX. corps (Augereau), marching on Jena.

Bavarians (30,000 under Wrede) opposed to 30,000 Austrians on the Inn.

Davout (XIII. corps), in Hamburg.

Allies.—Army of Bohemia, between Aussig and Brüx, with Klenau towards the passes leading to Chemnitz.

Blücher, at and about Bautzen.

Bernadotte, Herzberg to Zerbst.

On the 25th September the time had come when Blücher could, without exposing Bennigsen, begin his march to the right to join the northern army. He left, to face Macdonald and Dresden, Tscherbatow with 8000 Russians, and Bubna with 10,000 Austrians.

[1] *Corr.* 20,646, dated 27th September.

On his left his flank march was covered by the Russian cavalry under Wassilsikow, before whom Latour-Maubourg fell back from Grossenhain across the Elbe at Meissen.

Of the allied army of the North, Bülow had advanced to Wartenburg, where he threw two new bridges.

Tauenzien had reached Jessen.

The rest were at Barby and Rosslau.

Means of passage were provided also at Rosslau, Acken, and Barby.

The chapter in von Caemmerer's "strategical survey" of this campaign which deals with this period is headed "Indecision on both sides," and that is certainly the most marked characteristic of the three weeks succeeding the 6th September. With the allies generally this frame of mind was the rule. We see Bernadotte, after Bülow's victory at Dennewitz, hanging about without making any serious attempt to reap the fruits of his success by crossing the Elbe; building bridges, and then removing them as soon as an enemy appeared. Blücher, no doubt, knew his own mind, but he was restrained by superior orders, and compelled to wait in order to cover the march of Bennigsen. Schwarzenberg was perhaps the most irresolute of all, moving forward first by both banks of the Elbe, then hurrying back again as Napoleon moved south from Dresden, then making feeble advances towards Dresden, only to withdraw the moment Napoleon showed any disposition to move south again.

But indecision, such as he showed at this time, was certainly not characteristic of Napoleon in his better days. It looks almost as if, like a tiger surrounded by hunters, he was half bewildered, and unable to make up his mind to do more than make short dashes, first on one part, then on another, of the circle which was steadily closing in on him. The time had really come for him to abandon much more than the right bank of the Elbe. The rescue of the garrisons of the Oder and Vistula fortresses was no longer to be hoped for after Dennewitz, but the Emperor could still have carried with him in his retreat those of Hamburg, Magdeburg, Wittenberg, Torgau, and Dresden. Including the troops in Dresden, he had still 270,000 men in the open field, though his losses since the armistice are estimated by von Caemmerer at 140,000 to 150,000. Adding the garrisons of the Elbe fortresses, and deducting the German allies, who would no doubt desert him, he could still have returned to the Rhine with at least 250,000 men. The Elbe had played its part, and the Emperor seemed to be succumbing to the temptation, so dangerous to weaker leaders, to allow himself to be tied to fortresses. The real fact was that he could not make up his mind to part with his dominion in Germany, which he knew must collapse with his own withdrawal. Nor could he be certain what his reception in France would be.

The despot in him was suppressing the general, whose purely military view of the situation would probably have insisted on sacrifices which the Emperor could not endure. Thus we see him satisfied to frighten back first Blücher, then Schwarzenberg, then Blücher again, without dealing a really serious blow at either. His decision to advance northwards had withered under the shock of Ney's defeat at Dennewitz, coupled with the Emperor's discovery of the fearful demoralisation of Macdonald's army.

CHAPTER XVIII

NAPOLEON'S QUEST OF BERNADOTTE AND BLÜCHER

ON the 1st October, Ney, fearing that Bülow might pass at Wartenburg and cut him from Dresden, ordered Bertrand to the former. It was, however, Blücher who was now at Wartenburg. He had marched to Jessen, setting free Bülow and Tauenzein to return to Bernadotte. Sacken, having performed his function as flank guard, had now rejoined Blücher.

Bertrand was in Wartenburg on the 2nd October, in front of the Prussian bridge head, which was at the salient of the bend of the Elbe in the neck of which Wartenburg lies.[1] The Prussians had selected this place as quite theoretically suitable for forcing a passage, but they had omitted to reconnoitre the area within the bend, and were ignorant of the fact that it was exceedingly unfavourable for deployment after they had crossed under the protection of their artillery sweeping the peninsula. It was marshy and cut up by backwaters which, when the Elbe was in flood, were quite impassable, and were so in great part at all times. The village of Wartenburg stood behind one of these, and also had in front of it an embankment to protect it from floods. It was right in the centre of the neck, and was practically safe against a mere frontal attack. It could only be reached by troops passing along a narrow strip of land between it and the Elbe, in the part above the bridges.

Whilst the Prussians underestimated the defensibility of the Wartenburg position, Bertrand erred in the opposite direction; for he had only recently seen it at a time

[1] Map IV. (c).

when the Elbe was in very high flood. He believed it to be almost impregnable.

At 7 A.M. on the 3rd October, Prince Charles of Mecklenburg passed the Prussian bridges with three battalions of Yorck's corps. It was only when he got to the left bank that he was compelled to acknowledge that his guides had told him correctly that Wartenburg could only be reached by the narrow strip of land along the Elbe on his left leading to Bleddin. This strip was enclosed between the Elbe and a backwater or overflow pond.

Yorck himself, following over the bridges, sent Prince Charles against Franquemont's Wurtembergers who held Bleddin.

Steinmetz's brigade went against the front of Wartenburg. They got as far as the embankment running across the peninsula in front of Wartenburg, but could get no farther, and with difficulty held on there against the fire of the French beyond the old watercourse parallel to the dam, between it and the village.

Between Steinmetz and Prince Charles, Horn's brigade was brought up, with Hunerbein's in reserve.

It was 1 P.M. before Prince Charles could make his advance against Bleddin. Then he gradually drove Franquemont back towards Wartenburg, in which was Morand's division, with Fontanelli's in reserve. Presently, however, the progress of Horn's advance, on Prince Charles' right, interposed between Franquemont and Morand, compelling the former to fall back to his right with 900 infantry and 200 cavalry. His artillery was practically annihilated. It was about 2 P.M. when Bleddin fell into the hands of the Prussians.

Steinmetz was still holding on at the embankment with the utmost difficulty, and Horn's men had equal difficulty in getting forward over walls and ditches against the southeast side of Wartenburg.

Blücher had now come upon the field. He was very anxious, and sent orders to Prince Charles that he must take Wartenburg at any cost. That commander had now available only some 600 or 700 men, and 9 guns, but he boldly advanced against the south-west of the village whilst Horn continued against the south-east. By 3.30 P.M. Morand was driven in disorder from it. Bertrand had been very slow to perceive the danger which threatened his right.

He now began his retirement in two columns, under cover of his artillery on the heights behind Wartenburg. Morand led the left column, Fontanelli (who had been in reserve west of Wartenburg) the right. Both columns were near the river below Wartenburg.

As Fontanelli marched his right flank was attacked by Mecklenburg's cavalry, who took some guns and prisoners. Morand suffered from the fire of artillery beyond the Elbe, which followed him as he retired.

The Prussian weakness in cavalry prevented any effective pursuit.

Friederich gives Yorck's losses at 67 officers and 1548 men. If the French lost perhaps somewhat less in killed and wounded, they lost, on the other hand, 1000 prisoners, 11 guns, and 70 wagons. Bertrand's strength at the commencement was about 13,000 or 14,000 men, with 32 guns. He appears to have thought that the passage at Wartenburg was only a diversion to withdraw attention from the real crossing, which he believed to be at Rosslau.

Yorck brought into action a force slightly inferior to Bertrand's, but he had behind him, what Bertrand did not realise, the whole strength of Blücher's army.

On the 4th October Blücher's Silesian army completed its crossing at Wartenburg, leaving only Thümen to blockade Wittenberg, and Wobeser in front of Torgau. On the same day Bernadotte, crossing at Rosslau and Barby, marched up the Mulde.

The appearance of Bernadotte on his left and of Blücher on his right compelled Ney to fall back towards Delitzsch. Holding the passages of the Mulde, he might have engaged either Bernadotte or Blücher separately, but was debarred from thinking of this by the fact that he had little more than half the strength of either of them.

Meanwhile, on the 2nd October, Napoleon sent Murat to Freiberg to take command of an army comprising the II., V., and VIII. corps, and the 5th cavalry corps, to oppose the Bohemian army, which had once more passed the Erzgebirge, aiming now no longer at Dresden, but direct at Leipzig. On the 3rd October it had 70,000 men holding the heads of the passes on the line, Ebenstock, Annaberg, Marienberg; 80,000 still south of the mountains, on the line Kommotau-Karlsbad; Bennigsin with 50,000 at Teplitz and Aussig.

The army of Silesia, of 64,000 men, was fighting at Wartenburg; that of the North, 76,000 strong, held the passages of the Elbe at Rosslau, Acken, and Barby.

On the 4th October Klenau's advanced guard entered Chemnitz, but was driven out by Lauriston who, in turn, was compelled by Platow to retire on Mittweida.

The news of Blücher's passage at Wartenburg reached Napoleon on the 5th, though only through Marmont, and without details. He at once ordered the III. corps, from about Meissen and Riesa, to join Marmont. The latter, taking command of the two corps (III. and VI.) was to march on Torgau, picking up there all available men in the the depôt. He was then to re-establish the bridge on the Mulde at Düben and to join Ney and Dombrowski. Augereau was to go to Leipzig, and form its garrison in union with the 6000 men already there under Arrighi. It was a matter of urgency, the Emperor said, to throw the enemy back over the Elbe before he was reinforced.[1]

Ney was to have command of Marmont's force as soon as it reached him. This was explained to Marmont as necessary, looking to Ney's seniority.[2]

The division of the Guard still on the right bank of the Elbe was ordered over to the left, by which it was to march to Meissen, where Oudinot (now commanding two divisions of Young Guard) would fix his headquarters.

To Murat[3] orders to the following effect were sent. It

[1] *Corr.* 20,695.   [2] *Corr.* 20,696.   [3] *Corr.* 20,698.

BERNADOTTE AND BLÜCHER

was important to be at Chemnitz, at which place and at Zschoppau, Victor should take up a good position—Poniatowski to move to Penig. The Emperor believed there was only Klenau with 14,000 men in this direction.

St Cyr received orders (1) to withdraw the Pilnitz bridge to Dresden; (2) to post Lobau with headquarters and one division at Pirna; (3) to bring his own headquarters to Dresden with two divisions; (4) to guard the left bank from Dresden to Pirna with cavalry.

The Emperor's general plan was decided on, though there were still some details on which he had not made up his mind. At 9 A.M. on the 6th[1] he wrote to Marmont that he would be the same evening at Meissen with 80,000 men, having his advanced guard at the junction of the roads from Leipzig and Torgau. He expected the III. corps to be at Torgau, but was not certain in which direction Marmont might have sent it. His present idea was to march on Torgau, to cross there to the right bank of the Elbe, in order to cut off the enemy and destroy his bridges, without being compelled to storm his bridge heads on the left bank, and also to prevent any possibility of his avoiding a battle by slipping back to the right bank.

The Emperor's main force was to be brought to bear, under his own command, on Blücher and Bernadotte, whilst Murat contained Schwarzenberg's movement on Leipzig, and St Cyr with Lobau defended Dresden. Murat had only about 45,000 men.

In the afternoon of the same 6th October St Cyr arrived at Dresden, and had a long interview with Napoleon, who explained his plan of holding back, with Murat, the Austrian advance sufficiently long to enable himself to finish with Blücher and Bernadotte before Schwarzenberg reached Leipzig.

Then he hoped to fight another battle disposing of Schwarzenberg. He spoke to St Cyr of various positions south of Dresden, but impressed specially on him the paramount importance of defending the city itself. Thither

[1] *Corr.* 20,705.

he hoped to return, continuing to make it the pivot of his operations, after defeating the enemy in a great battle or battles. On this occasion he was so vehement that St Cyr thought it best to attempt no argument.

At midnight the Emperor sent for him again. He said that having received news of Ney, he had now decided to take St Cyr and Lobau with him against Bernadotte and Blücher, abandoning Dresden.

St Cyr's report of his remarks[1] runs thus: "I am certainly going to have a battle; if I win it, I shall regret not having had all my troops under my hand; if, on the contrary, I suffer a reverse, in leaving you here you will be of no service to me in the battle, and you are hopelessly lost. Moreover, what is Dresden worth to-day? It can no longer be the pivot of the operations of the army, which, owing to the exhaustion of the surrounding country, cannot subsist there. This city cannot even be considered as a great depôt; for you would find in it subsistence for a few days only. There are in Dresden 12,000 sick who will die, since they are the residue of the 60,000 who have entered the hospitals since the commencement of the campaign. Add to this that the season is advancing, and that the Elbe, once frozen over, no longer offers a position. I wish to take up another for the winter, refusing my right on Erfurt, and stretching my centre along the Saale, which is a good position in all seasons, because the heights of the left bank are always excellent for defence. I shall rest my left on Magdeburg, and that city will become for me of greater importance than Dresden." . . . Here he describes the greater strength of Magdeburg as compared with Dresden, and then continues: "Besides, I repeat, I want to change my position; Dresden is too near Bohemia; as soon as I make the smallest movements from the neighbourhood of the city to approach Bohemia, the enemy's armies, having a very short distance to cover, will return to it, and I have no means of cutting them off by moving on their rear. Finally, by the more distant position I am going to

[1] *Hist. Mil.*, iv. 185.

occupy, I wish to 'leur donner un cul'[1] (you understand me?), in order to be able to strike great blows, to force the allied sovereigns to a solid peace, putting an end to the calamities of Europe."

St Cyr duly received orders on the 7th[2] for retreat to Dresden, for sending the sick down the Elbe to Torgau, and to be ready to evacuate the city on the 8th and 9th.

It was 1 A.M. on the 7th October when Napoleon dictated the following note[3] on "the movements of the different corps d'armée":—

" 1st. To make a forced march on the 7th to Wurzen. I can have my headquarters there with the cavalry of Sebastiani, that of the Guard, and the corps[4] of Oudinot, 10 miles from Wurzen, so as to be at Leipzig to-morrow (8th) if absolutely necessary.

" 2. The III. infantry corps will probably be at Wurzen, since the Duke of Ragusa has directed it on the Mulde.

" 3. General Lauriston can take position at Rochlitz; he has only three leagues ($7\frac{1}{2}$ miles) to march; the Duke of Belluno can go to Mittweida, commencing his movement rather late; they will be in communication with Prince Poniatowski, who is at Frohburg. To-morrow they can be at Frohburg, thus containing the head of the enemy's army.

" Marshal St Cyr can turn to-day (7th) the I. and XIV. corps on Dresden, occupy Meissen to-morrow (8th) and commence his movement, evacuate Dresden the 9th,[5] and make forced marches on Wurzen.

" As a result of this movement, I shall be able to do what I choose. From Wurzen I can go to Torgau against the enemy, debouching from Wittenberg (myself), or turn my whole army on Leipzig for a general battle, or repass the Saale.

" *Details.*—The King of Naples would move on Mittweida, masking his movement; he would only evacuate Flöha in

---

[1] In the English translation of *Napoleon as a general*, this phrase is translated, "to form a blind alley." The author feels some doubt as to whether this was the Emperor's precise meaning.
[2] Berthier to St Cyr. *Hist. Mil.*, iv., p. 431. [3] *Corr.*, 20,711.
[4] Four divisions Young Guard. [5] Printed 7th. The 9th is clearly meant.

the night of the 7th; the enemy would not know till the morning of the 8th that there is no longer any one on the road from Chemnitz to Dresden.

"General Lauriston would reach Rochlitz, and would only leave Mittweida when the head of the II. corps had arrived.

"On the 8th the II. corps would move on Rochlitz, and would be in observation from Rochlitz to Frohburg, holding Colditz, so as to link itself with the army. It would remain there till further orders, unless pressed by the enemy; in that case it would approach Leipzig, without allowing itself to be separated from the Mulde.

"On the 8th the army commanded by me in person would be at Wurzen.

"On the 10th the corps of Marshal St Cyr would be at Wurzen."[1]

Thus at 1 A.M. the Emperor had decided to abandon

[1] It will be observed that we have not quoted the long note of the 5th October, accepted by Yorck as probably genuine. It is given in M. de Norvins' *Portefeuille de* 1813, vol. ii. p. 366. Yorck admits that it is not usual for Napoleon, in such notes, to speak of corps by their numbers, as he does throughout this alleged note. But this is not very convincing evidence; for he does so speak of them occasionally in the undoubtedly genuine note of 1 A.M., on the 7th; though he only does so when it is necessary to distinguish part of the command of a general having more than one corps under him. What seems to us to throw much more doubt on the authenticity of the document is the way in which the writer speaks of himself as "the Emperor," or "His Majesty," expressions which find no place in his other notes of this period. They, as well as the indication of corps by their numbers instead of by their commanders, would probably be used by a person trying to imitate the Emperor, and yet forgetting himself for the moment. M. de Norvins, in his preface, does not indicate precisely whence he obtained this note, or the evidence of its authenticity. If it were genuine, there seems no special reason why it should have been omitted by the publishers of the correspondence; for it is, as Yorck remarks, "a true picture of the state of affairs at the time, and of the Emperor's views."

On the other hand, why should any one concoct such a note? Once more, there is against its authenticity the fact that there are several palpable mistakes in the numbers of the corps. One of these, the writing of "quinzième corps" for "quatorzième corps," was not in the least likely to be made by the Emperor, for there was no such corps as the "15th." Even his secretary would probably not have allowed such a slip, if made, to pass.

On the whole, while admitting that the document may possibly be genuine, its authenticity seems so open to doubt that we prefer not to rely on it. Possibly French writers, now working at the records in Paris, may hereafter be able to clear up the point.

BERNADOTTE AND BLÜCHER

Dresden, and to leave Murat no longer in connection with it.

Twelve hours later all is changed. Napoleon, writing at 1 P.M. on the 7th from Meissen,[1] tells St Cyr he has decided to hold on to Dresden. The convoys are to proceed thither, the marshal is to hold the positions in front of Pirna all the 8th, and to send a detachment to Nossen.[2] The fortifications of Dresden to be improved, supplies got in, wounded sent out, etc. The Emperor, hoping for a battle immediately, moving by Torgau, would have his communications open by both banks with Dresden.

Here was an inexplicable change in the whole plan, a change which was absolutely inconsistent with the Emperor's guiding principle of uniting the greatest possible forces for battle, and neglecting secondary matters, in the certainty that all would be rectified regarding them by decisive tactical success at the main point. He was now leaving two whole army corps to hold a place which certainly was now of quite secondary importance. Yet, unless we are to believe that St Cyr's account of the midnight interview on the 6th October is a pure invention, Napoleon had explained precisely and correctly why it was useless for him to hold Dresden, nay worse than useless, for to do so would deprive him of two corps on the battlefield. It is impossible to see in this decision to hold on to Dresden anything but a vast deterioration in Napoleonic strategy. Count Yorck considers it, "not so much the mistake of a general, as the obstinacy of a ruler, who will not admit that he can be compelled to relinquish anything, and who, not without reason, is alarmed for the continuance of his rule, based only upon force, so soon as he gives any indication that this force has diminished."[3]

On the evening of the 7th the opposing forces in the north stood thus :[4]—

French.—III. corps (Souham) at Torgau.

[1] *Corr.* 20,719 and St Cyr, *Hist. Mil.*, iv. 433 (for hour of dispatch).
[2] Apparently to maintain touch with Murat as well as with Meissen.
[3] *Napoleon as a General*, ii. p. 338.   [4] Map I., inset (*c*).

Guard, Macdonald (XI. corps) and Sebastiani at and near Meissen.

Marmont (VI. corps) at Taucha.

Ney (IV. and VII. corps) at Bennewitz (adjoining Wurzen).

Latour-Maubourg watching the Elbe to Torgau.

Allies.—*Bernadotte* with about 30,000 men at Dessau and 40,000 at Zorbig and Jessnitz on the west of the Mulde.

Blücher.—Yorck's and Langeron's corps, and head-quarters at Düben.

Sacken at Mockrehna, midway between Eilenburg and Torgau.

Blücher held the passages of the Mulde at Mühlbeck, Düben, and Eilenburg.

A day's march separated the Northern and Silesian armies, and Blücher was filled with a very reasonable though very violent distrust of his Gascon colleague.

Napoleon had from 140,000 to 150,000 men concentrated about Wurzen on the 8th, and he believed that Blücher was with 60,000 at Düben. That was generally correct, and, moreover, Blücher's position, facing Leipzig, offered his left flank to Napoleon at Wurzen.

The Emperor, in a letter dated Wurzen, 9th October, at 9 A.M., to Murat,[1] sums up his views of the situation and his intentions. He says that he is starting for Wittenberg, which is besieged. He counts on attacking Blücher at Düben, where his information points to the presence of that general with 60,000 men, whilst Bernadotte is at Dessau with 40,000. He hopes to be at Wittenberg on the 9th, to raise the siege, and, passing to the right bank, to seize the enemy's two bridges at Wartenburg and Dessau. He had issued orders for the advance.

(1) The three divisions of Guard cavalry (Lefebvre-Desnoette's at Leipzig, Ornano's and Walther's) were summoned to Eilenburg.

(2) Arrighi, at Leipzig, was told that that city was

[1] *Corr.* 20,735.

BERNADOTTE AND BLÜCHER

covered in every direction but those of Halle and Dessau, and it was explained to him with what forces he could defend it in those directions.

(3) Ney was ordered to march with the III. corps at 6 A.M. by the right bank of the Mulde on Eilenburg. He was to send Reynier with the VII. by the left bank, to which he would cross at Eilenburg. Bertrand, who was on the right at Schildau, to move on Mockrehna. Sebastiani was also placed under Ney, who thus commanded the III., IV., and VII. corps, the division of Dombrowski, and the 2nd cavalry corps. The Emperor would himself support Ney with the whole of the Guard.

(4) Marmont to march at 6 A.M. by the left bank towards Düben. Latour-Maubourg, and all the cavalry of the Guard to go with him.

(5) Macdonald to start at the same hour from Dahlen for Mockrehna, in support, if necessary, of Bertrand.

The Emperor was anxious to have possession of Düben the same day, and, if the enemy were not more than 30,000 strong there, he would be attacked in the evening. Napoleon would be in person at Eilenburg at 8 A.M., marching with 120,000 men on Düben.

It is time to see what was happening on the allies' side between Blücher and Bernadotte. On the 6th October Blücher wanted his colleague to take a strong position in front of Merseburg, whilst he himself stood between the Saale and the Mulde. Thus placed, each would threaten the flank of an advance by Napoleon against the other.

On the 8th October the Crown Prince wrote to Blücher to the effect that, since their mission was to hold Napoleon till the Bohemian army could come up on his flank and rear, there were only two alternatives open to them. The first, which was clearly the one he favoured, was immediate retirement to the right bank of the Elbe. The second was retirement to the left bank of the Saale. In the event of Blücher's accepting the second alternative, he was requested to take up his bridge at Wartenburg and send it (by land of course, as it could not pass through

Wittenberg and Magdeburg by water) to Ferchland, 25 miles below Magdeburg. Bernadotte would either remove or destroy his bridge at Rosslau, and would leave six battalions to defend that at Acken. Bernadotte was dying to get back across the Elbe, to avoid Napoleon, of whom he was in mortal dread, and to get away by Ferchland if he could not get Blücher over the Elbe direct. He did not give any real consideration to the Bohemian army. The first alternative would have spelt ruin for Blücher, who would in all probability have been caught by Napoleon when he was in the very act of crossing the Elbe. He unhesitatingly chose the second, and promised to march at once. The great risk in going behind the Saale was lest the allies should lose their communications with Berlin. Blücher said that Yorck, with his right column, would reach Jessnitz in the evening of the 9th, his headquarters would be near Mühlbeck. He would only leave a few companies at Wartenburg, which could rejoin Wobeser before Torgau. He also said he would make a demonstration against Eilenburg, as he thought it necessary to cover the westward march.

Blücher's orders required Yorck to pass the Mulde at Jessnitz; Langeron near Bitterfeld; Sacken, who was the farthest to the left and from Düben, was to pass at that place, but he would probably be in contact there with the French.

Napoleon's march on the 9th progressed without opposition worthy of mention. Ney was at Düben by 3 P.M. At Probsthain Sebastiani dispersed some of Sacken's troops, and he, as well as Bertrand, followed Sacken towards Kemberg. The French advance had come sooner than Blücher expected, so nothing came of his proposed demonstration, and Sacken, finding it impossible to cross the Mulde at Düben before the French came up, turned northwards, and, by dint of hard marching through the night, got across at Raguhn, which he only reached at 10 A.M. on the 10th. Yorck and Langeron reached Jessnitz and Mühlbeck respectively. Blücher and Bernadotte were united on the 10th towards Zorbig. The French positions in the evening of the 9th were—

II., Ney's advanced guard, beyond Düben.
VII., Düben.
III., Lausig.
Dombrowski at Priestäblich.
Napoleon and Guard—Eilenburg.
IV. corps south-east of Mockrehna.
XI. corps, Mockrehna.

On the 10th Napoleon remained at Eilenburg, sending letters and orders, till after 10 A.M. Then, after a parade of his cuirassiers, he set off in his carriage to Düben, where the letter-writing begins again at 3 P.M., when he had taken up his residence in the little water-surrounded château. The correspondence of this day is fairly voluminous, but it is strangely uncertain in its tone. It is wanting entirely in that decision which generally characterises the correspondence of the Emperor when he is in hot pursuit of some great object. He was suffering under the grievous disappointment of having missed the blow which he had aimed at Blücher, and, moreover, it is clear that he is unable to guess with any certainty how the old Prussian has evaded it, or where he has gone. There are a great many "ifs" used. There are no less than five letters to Maret, Duke of Bassano, much of their contents repetition or speculation, a great deal about the movements of the King of Saxony, who was under Maret's charge at Wurzen, and so on.

Napoleon is at times despondent on the subject of Murat's capability of holding the Bohemian army back from Leipzig, and tells Maret[1] what he proposes to do if Murat has to abandon it. "My intention is, if the King of Naples were obliged to evacuate Leipzig, to repass the Elbe with all my army, throwing the army of Silesia and Berlin on to the right bank, and taking all the time to destroy it; or, if it prefers to abandon its bridges, to leave it on the left bank and take my line of operation on the right bank from Dresden to Magdeburg." According to Friederich, it is not

[1] *Corr.* 20,746.

credible that Napoleon ever entertained the idea, attributed to him by some modern French writers, of abandoning everything west of the Elbe, and operating, based on it from Magdeburg to Dresden, towards the Oder. Surely this passage indicates clearly that he did intend, at one time at least, to go to the right bank. He again refers to the idea of passing to the right bank in a letter to Reynier,[1] in one to Berthier,[2] and in one to Arrighi.[3] The correspondence of this day shows how uncertain the Emperor felt as to Blücher's own and Sacken's movements. He says, in the letter to Reynier just mentioned, (1) that Sacken was making for the Wartenburg bridge, (2) that all reports show that the enemy is retiring from all directions on Dessau. He orders Reynier to Wartenburg and also Bertrand,[4] both letters being dated 4 P.M. But, in a postscript to that to Bertrand, he says Sacken had left Leipnitz at 6 A.M. and got to Raguhn. Of his prospects he writes to Murat at 5.30 P.M.:[5] "To-morrow, the 11th, either I shall have swept away the enemy or I shall have destroyed his bridges and thrown him on to the other side of the river (Elbe). Having thus driven off the army of Silesia, I can, on the 13th, be at Leipzig with my whole army." Then he proceeds to estimate Murat's strength thus:—

	Infantry.	Cavalry.
VIII. corps (Poniatowski)	5,000	3,000
V. corps (Lauriston)	12,000	500
II. corps (Victor)	16,000	1,200
IX. corps (Augereau)	8,000	3,000
Arrighi from Leipzig	8,000	3,000
5th cavalry corps (L'Heritier)	...	2,000
	49,000	12,700

and says that, on the 12th, he could send another 20,000, raising Murat to 80,000. If Murat had only Kleist and Wittgenstein against him, they could not have more than

---

[1] *Corr.* 20,750.   [2] *Corr.* 20,752.   [3] *Corr.* 20,749.
[4] *Corr.* 20 757.   *Corr.* 20,754.

BERNADOTTE AND BLÜCHER

50,000 men. If Klenau was with them, they might have 80,000. On the 11th the Emperor's uncertainty and irresolution continued. In the early hours he is convinced that the whole army of the enemy is concentrated at Dessau, with a great quantity of baggage. He proposes to march by the right bank of the Elbe on the Rosslau bridge. Reynier, Sebastiani, Dombrowski are to pass at Wittenberg as soon as possible, so as to make way for Bertrand, Macdonald, and the rest of the army to pass. Bertrand to see that the Wartenburg bridge is gone. Ney, meanwhile, to remain at Gräfenhainchen, watching the roads to Dessau, Raguhn, Jessnitz, and Mühlbeck, and supported by the Emperor with the Guard about Kemberg. Marmont to come back to the right bank of the Mulde, leaving only Lorge's and Nordmann's cavalry on the left to scout towards Bitterfeld and Delitzsch,[1] and enough infantry to force the enemy out of Bitterfeld.

At 3 P.M. he has heard that there is no enemy at Raguhn, and very few at Dessau.[2]

By 3 A.M. on the 12th he learns that, on the 10th, Blücher was marching on Halle. Ney is ordered[3] to Dessau. As soon as Reynier had mastered Rosslau on the right bank, Ney was to destroy the enemy's bridge-head and throw two bridges there. Ney to call up Bertrand from Wartenburg, Oudinot to remain at Gräfenhainchen. Marmont to go towards Delitzsch to watch towards Halle and Leipzig. Macdonald was only to pass at Wittenberg if Reynier required assistance beyond that of Sebastiani.[4]

At 10 A.M. he draws up a note "on the union of the different corps d'armée at Taucha," in the following terms:[5]—

"I am ordering Ney to Düben. He will not receive this order till 2 P.M., his troops can start at 3; he cannot pass the bridge at Düben till to-morrow, 13th (when the Guard will have already passed); he can easily be at Taucha in the evening of the 13th.

[1] 20,757 to 20,761. [2] *Corr.* 20,764. [3] *Corr.* 20,765.
[4] *Corr.* 20,768. [5] *Corr.* 20,772.

"Latour Maubourg, being at Kemberg, will have no more difficulty.

"The Duke of Tarentum will only receive orders at 3 P.M.; if he has passed the Elbe, he will require the night to recross; he can only be at Düben to-morrow, 13th; during the day of the 14th he will march on Taucha.

"General Reynier, marching on Rosslau, can only get to Wittenberg this night and reach Taucha on the 15th. He can come by Eilenburg.

"It is the same for General Sebastiani.

"As for the Dukes of Treviso (Mortier) and Reggio (Oudinot) and the reserve of the Guard, all that will pass the Düben bridge to-day and reach Taucha early to-morrow.

"The King (of Naples) is to-day at Cröbern, to-morrow he will be at Leipzig and Taucha, where I shall have arrived to-morrow with Curial, the Old and Young Guard, and the Duke of Rugusa, nearly 40,000 men, which, with the king's 50,000, will make nearly 90,000. These 90,000 will be reinforced during to-morrow (13th), when the enemy necessarily cannot attack, by Ney, Bertrand, and Latour-Maubourg. The 15th our whole army will be united. To-morrow (13th) the enemy arrives at Cröbern. He will know that the Grand Army has arrived. He will spend the 14th in placing himself for battle. I have, therefore, the 13th and 14th for concentration. I say more; if all my army were at Düben, it could not arrive earlier, unless it had five or six issues."

Then he recapitulates the situation.

"The King of Naples is at Cröbern on the 12th, Marshal Marmont at Lindenhain; they can be to-morrow, 13th, at Taucha, a good position; my Guard, to-day at Düben and Eilenburg, will easily be to-morrow at Taucha; Oudinot and Mortier will be to-day at Düben with Ornano, Walther, and Latour-Maubourg.

"To-morrow all this will be at Taucha.

"I shall then have to-morrow at Taucha.

"In the first line, the King of Naples' 50,000 men, inclusive of the garrison of Leipzig, which will remain

BERNADOTTE AND BLÜCHER

there; Marmont, 20,000 infantry, 2000 cavalry; the Guard, 30,000 infantry, 8000 cavalry; Latour-Maubourg, 3000 cavalry; total, nearly 120,000 men, at Taucha to-morrow.

"In second line, the Duke of Tarentum, to-night at Kemberg, to-morrow at Düben; the Prince of the Moskowa, to-night at Gräfenhainchen, to-morrow at Düben; Bertrand, to-morrow at Düben; Sebastiani, to-morrow at Düben; Dombrowski and Reynier, to-morrow half-way to Düben.

"On the 14th all can join me; Tarentum, 20,000 infantry, 2000 cavalry; Moskowa, 12,000 infantry, 2000 cavalry; Bertrand, 10,000 men; Sebastiani, 3000 men; Dombrowski and Reynier, 20,000 men. Thus: First line, nearly 120,000 men; second line, 70,000 men; total, about 190,000 men."[1]

Here is, once more, a complete change of plan. The idea of the passage of the Elbe and the pursuit of Blücher is abandoned in favour of concentration for battle at Taucha.[2]

Odeleben's famous description of the Emperor at Düben, sitting idly drawing Gothic characters on a sheet of paper, is not quite consistent with the actual outturn of correspondence. Still, all accounts represent him as a very different person from the ceaseless worker of former times. He talked for five hours in the night of the 11th-12th to Marmont, who says: "One no longer recognises Napoleon again during this campaign."[3] Fain says: "He remains almost constantly shut up in his room, to which his bed and his maps have been moved."[4]

In proof of the irresolution and uncertainty which mastered him at Düben, it is only necessary to look back

---

[1] The totals, according to the Emperor's details, come to, 1st line, 113,000; 2nd line, 69,000; total, 182,000. But he apparently does not include artillery and engineers, and as he generally uses round figures, the arithmetical difference is more apparent than real.

[2] "My intention being to give battle there (at Taucha) with all my forces united" (*Corr.* 20,771).

[3] *Mém.* v. 271.

[4] *MSS. de* 1813, ii. 372.

over the correspondence which we have quoted or described. On the 10th he proposes to go to the right bank of the Elbe if Murat could not keep Leipzig; the same afternoon he talks of only driving Blücher and Bernadotte over the Elbe, and keeping them there by destroying their bridges. Then he would return to Leipzig. On the 11th he is in great uncertainty as to Blücher's and Bernadotte's whereabouts, and reverts to the idea of going to the right bank and leaving them stranded on the left. Then he finds out that they are not, as he had fancied, towards Dessau, but towards Halle. On the 12th he has changed his plans entirely, and proposes fighting a great battle at Taucha. All this is very different from the quick grasp of the situation and the immediate decision as to his course of action which characterise his earlier campaigns.

There is no mention of Bernadotte in the correspondence of the 12th till 3 P.M., when the Emperor writes to Marmont[1] that he has seized the enemy's bridges on the Elbe, and that the army of Berlin has gone to the right bank.

On this subject, Marmont says[2] he reported to the Emperor, in the evening of the 11th, that he had made certain that the whole of the enemy's army was on the hither side of the Elbe. If he is correct, the Emperor's letter of the 12th is only one of many instances of the way in which he now chose to believe what would suit him.[3]

Let us see now what had really been happening whilst Napoleon sat in doubt and hesitation, very unusual in him, in the "schloss" at Düben. Blücher had marched to his right on the morning of the 9th October, just as Napoleon was beginning his advance down the Mulde on Düben. He was making for the Saale towards Halle, as arranged with Bernadotte. His movements on the 9th, and the escape of Sacken by Raguhn have already been described. Bernadotte went to Rothenburg, but he left Tauenzien behind at Dessau to cover the bridges at Rosslau and Acken.

[1] *Corr.* 20,775.   [2] *Mém.* iv. 270.   [3] For positions, Map I., inset (*d*).

BERNADOTTE AND BLÜCHER 315

On the 11th Tauenzien heard that Reynier had crossed the Elbe at Wittenberg on the previous day, and had driven the blockading force on Coswig; also that Macdonald was following Reynier. He, therefore, himself crossed to Rosslau on the 12th, leaving one division at Dessau, which was dispersed with the loss of some 2000 prisoners on that day.

On the same day (12th) Bernadotte was still at Rothenburg, whilst Blücher had reached Halle and occupied Merseburg. He had thus passed with the Silesian army from Bernadotte's left to his right.

That same night Napoleon was still hesitating as to whether he would himself go to Leipzig or not. At 8 P.M. he wrote to Murat, estimating the latter's force at 60,000, and adding that Marmont will be "to-night" only ten miles from Leipzig. "If I do not decide to go there (Leipzig) myself, I will send him to you, which will give you 85,000 to 90,000 men; with that you ought to be able to gain some days."[1] The Emperor still believed that Bernadotte had retired to the right bank of the Elbe; for Ney, in reporting his action with Tauenzien's division at Dessau, mentioned that he had seen immense baggage columns and packs marching up the right bank from Acken. Reynier and Dombrowski, the Emperor also says, had passed Coswig and were marching on Rosslau.[2]

At 5 A.M. on the 13th Napoleon was decided to concentrate on Leipzig, but thought there was still time for Reynier to march to Acken, in which operation Ney could support him by a diversion from the left bank.[3] As soon as that was done, Ney must hurry back to Düben. An hour later [4] Napoleon ascertained that Reynier had been fighting, on the previous day, only with Thümen and Tauenzien, whom he had driven to a hurried and somewhat disorderly retreat on Berlin. Bernadotte's headquarters had been at Bernburg on the 11th; he had not re-crossed the Elbe, but, on the contrary, was with Blücher behind the Saale.

[1] *Corr.* 20,781.   [2] *Corr.* 20,783.   [3] *Corr.* 20,789.   [4] *Corr.* 20,790.

Macdonald and Reynier were called back on Düben.

There was no advantage now in operating on the right bank of the Elbe, where there was no enemy of importance left. Even Thümen and Tauenzien were off to Berlin in such a hurry that there was no probability of their returning at present.

Leaving Napoleon to his concentration on Leipzig, we turn back to bring up to date the events in the south.

When Napoleon left Dresden, Colloredo and Bennigsen began their advance from Teplitz on Dresden by the now well-known route. On the 8th Colloredo's advanced guard was at Zehista. On the same day, Bubna who, it will be remembered, was left by Blücher to watch Dresden on the right bank of the Elbe, took the bridge head opposite Pirna. The garrison retired to Dresden, taking their boats with them.

On the 10th Bennigsen, after making a reconnaissance on Dresden, left Osterman to observe it with 20,000 men, and himself marched by Colditz for Leipzig with 30,000. Chasteler was left behind at Teplitz with 10,000 men to guard Bohemia.

Murat's movements had been as follows:—

On the 8th he was at Mittweida. Poniatowski drove the Austrians from Penig.

On the 9th Klenau recaptured Penig, and, threatening Poniatowski's left, compelled him to fall back towards Murat at Rochlitz.

On the 10th Murat retired northwards, on learning that Wittgenstein was moving on Borna.

On the 11th he took post at Wachau and Liebertwolkwitz[1] with the II., V., and VIII. corps, and 5th cavalry corps. His outposts were on the line Threna-Gross Pösna-Naunhof.

It was this move which alarmed Napoleon, and induced him to propose sending 20,000 men to support Murat.

Schwarzenberg's headquarters had been on the 8th at Chemnitz. On the 11th they were at Altenberg. Wittgenstein, Kleist, and Klenau were about Borna.

[1] Map IV. (d).

BERNADOTTE AND BLÜCHER

On the 12th Augereau (IX. corps) reached Leipzig.

Schwarzenberg was more intent on getting into communication with the northern armies than on fighting a battle with Murat.

Napoleon, in his bulletin of the 15th October, says that he gave up the project of operating on the right bank of the Elbe, because, on the 13th, he learnt of the defection of Bavaria, and feared that of other German states. That is certainly an afterthought, since (1) the Convention of Ried, by which Bavaria joined the allies, was not ratified till the 14th; (2) Napoleon himself writes to Murat, "in the evening" of the 13th, that he has seen the Austrian, Krafft, who had been captured with papers showing the positions of Blücher and Bernadotte, and the terms of peace the allies would grant. From this man he had learnt that there was nothing definite about Bavaria.

Napoleon's orders for the 14th were issued at 3 A.M.[1]

His own headquarters would be at the gates of Leipzig.

Ney was expected to pass the Düben bridge that evening, so as to be at Leipzig on the 15th.

Macdonald was believed to be at Kemberg on the 13th, and to be able to pass at Düben in good time on the 14th, so as to make room for Ney to pass at night.

Reynier was supposed to be at Wittenberg on the night of the 13th. He would be near Düben on the 14th.

Sebastiani to hurry up past Macdonald, and reach Leipzig as soon as possible.

Latour-Maubourg also to hurry forward on the right, reconnoitring towards Delitzsch.

Oudinot and Mortier, the Guard cavalry, and Old Guard to approach within two and a half miles of Leipzig.

Curial and Lefebvre-Desnoettes to march on Eilenburg and Taucha at daybreak, accompanied by the King of Saxony, who would be sent on with an escort to Leipzig.

General Durrieu to guard Eilenburg, where he would collect parks, etc., on the left bank of the Mulde.

[1] *Corr.* 20,799.

Bertrand to leave Düben at 9 A.M., and to be within two and a half miles of Leipzig by evening.

In writing to Macdonald at 7 A.M., the Emperor says: "There can be no doubt that to-morrow, 15th, we shall be attacked by the army of Bohemia and by the army of Silesia. March then in all haste, and if you hear a cannonade, march to its fire."[1]

Napoleon left Düben some time after 7 A.M., reaching Leipzig about midday. He had intended staying there, but went on to Reudnitz after riding through Leipzig. To the south, as he rode towards Reudnitz, he could hear plainly, and even see the artillery of the action then proceeding between Murat and the Bohemian army.

The positions of Murat's forces on the morning of the 14th were[2]:—

	Infantry.	Cavalry.	Guns.	
VIII. corps	5400	600	30	Markkleeberg, Dölitz, Lösnig and Connewitz
4th cavalry corps	—	1800	?	Main body behind Markkleeberg, with detachments beyond the Pleisse.
II. corps	15,000	—	58	On heights between Wachau and Markkleeberg, the former being strongly held.
V. corps	12,000	700	53	About Probstheida.
5th cavalry corps and Berkheim's division of the 1st	—	4,000	?	Just west of Liebertwolkwitz.
A division of the Guard cavalry	—	2,700	?	In reserve at Holzhausen.

In all 32,400 infantry, 9,800 cavalry, and 156 guns.

Early in the morning Pahlen, with Wittgenstein's advanced guard, moved forward by Cröbern. He had 1800 Russian cavalry and Cossacks, 1000 Prussian cavalry, and 20 guns.

The Cossacks came to a standstill in face of the great cavalry masses in front of Wachau and Markkleeberg.

[1] *Corr.* 20,801.   [2] Map IV. (*d*).

Pahlen was first reinforced by 6 squadrons, and then by 14 more, with 16 guns, under Röder, sent by Kleist from the Prussian reserve cavalry.

Eugen of Wurtemberg, reconnoitring in front of Guldengössa, denied Diebitsch's assumption, according to which there was only a French rearguard. He succeeded in convincing Diebitsch, who went off for more cavalry. Pahlen, however, advanced as soon as the Prussian reserve cavalry began to come up. The cavalry combat which ensued in this direction swayed backwards and forwards with varying success. On the whole, the French got a little the worst of it.

About 2 P.M. Klenau attacked Liebertwolkwitz and took the whole of it, except the church, in which the enemy obstinately held out. Counter attacks failed to dislodge Klenau, but there was a long fight, and in the evening he evacuated the village.

There were more cavalry combats in the afternoon in the centre, when again the French got rather the worst of it. In one of the charges here, Murat, leading in person, narrowly escaped capture. He was easily recognised by the extravagance of his costume.

About Markkleeberg the French cavalry, at first victorious, were in the end driven back.

The upshot of the whole affair was that both sides remained in their original positions.

The battle was the greatest cavalry contest of the war. Friederich considers there were faults in leading on both sides. The allies attacked piecemeal, instead of in masses, whilst Murat kept his cavalry so closely massed that, once they were shaken, it was impossible to prevent their getting into confusion. Neither side could hope for a decisive victory, and Murat caused his cavalry unnecessary loss, when he should have preserved it for the battles of the following days. Pajol's in particular was so knocked about as to be quite unserviceable in the evening. All that Murat required to do was to keep the Liebertwolkwitz-Wachau line of heights, and prevent the enemy from seeing into his position behind them. That he could have done by using his infantry more freely, and sparing his cavalry.

The allies, on the other hand, had not enough troops up for decisive success. What they wanted was (1) to get a view of the positions behind Murat's front, in which they succeeded to some extent, and (2) to ascertain if he really meant to hold it. The latter they could infer from the resistance encountered.

On the morning of the 15th October Murat came to headquarters to report the events of the previous day. After a long conversation with the Emperor, both rode to the heights between Liebertwolkwitz and Wachau. Here Napoleon remained for several hours in conversation with Berthier, Murat, and others. Thence he went, after noon, to the position occupied by Poniatowski, who had his right on Dölitz and Markkleeberg. Here he gave much attention to the ground beyond the Pleisse, to the possible points of passage, and to the marshes interfering with the movement of troops. Then he rode to Reudnitz along the front by Holzhausen and Zweinaundorf.

The published correspondence of the 15th is very scanty.

At 8 A.M. the Emperor writes [1] to Macdonald, saying it is not known yet what has become of Murat's opponents of the day before. He tells Macdonald at Lindenhain to report when he will be at Taucha, but not to cross the bridge there over the Partha, in case it should be necessary to send him by Naunhof. Then follows an important passage:—

"All reports are that, by a manœuvre which I cannot understand, the Prince of Sweden has passed the Saale, and is marching on Merseburg, so that the Duke of Ragusa can have nothing but cavalry in front of him."

This, he thought, was folly on Bernadotte's part, as it would leave him (Napoleon) time to destroy the Bohemian army.

This passage seems to show that the Emperor believed the Silesian and Northern armies to be united under Bernadotte, towards Merseburg. In another letter of 10 P.M.[2] he

[1] *Corr.* 20,807. [2] *Corr.* 20,812.

tells Marmont, who was towards Breitenfelde in the direction of Halle, that many camp fires had been seen at Markranstädt, which seemed to indicate that the enemy was to be expected, not by the Halle road, but by that from Weissenfels, on which he would have his right connected, by Zwenkau or Pegau, with the left of the army of Bohemia.

Four hours earlier Napoleon had sent orders to Macdonald that he was to start from Taucha at daybreak, to march on Holzhausen and Seifertshain, where he would receive orders for turning the enemy's right, that is, the right of the army of Bohemia.

These conclusions were erroneous; for Blücher had advanced from Halle towards Leipzig, and was already facing east with his right about Schkeuditz. The Emperor had good reason for regretting, in his letter to Marmont, that the latter had not pushed his reconnaissances as far as Schkeuditz.

Bernadotte was not at Merseburg, but far away on the the line Wettin-Zorbig. The fires which were seen at Markranstädt were those of the left wing of the Bohemian army, which extended thence by Cröbern and Guldengössa. Napoleon believed it to extend only from Cröbern [to Naunhof.

The French corps stood this evening thus :—

Bertrand at Eutritzsch.

Marmont at Lindenthal facing towards Halle.

Poniatowski at Markkleeberg and Dösen, with his right thrown back along the Pleisse as far as Connewitz.

Victor at Wachau.

Lauriston—Liebertwolkwitz.

Polish cavalry (Kellermann) at Dösen.

Latour-Maubourg—Zweinaundorf.

Pajol at Holzhausen.

Augereau—Zuckelhausen.

Guard—Reudnitz and Crottendorf, as general reserve.

Souham—Two divisions at Mockau, the third behind, on the road from Düben.

Macdonald—Taucha.

x

Sebastiani—Marching on Taucha.

Reynier—Düben.

We have already referred sufficiently to the indecisions of Napoleon. There is only one story on which we need say a word further, that which pretends that Napoleon gave up his plan of crossing the Elbe under pressure from a deputation of his own marshals and generals. Friederich shows that the evidence of this is very slight, and the probabilities strongly against it. In this connection the German critic mentions that there was an idea that Napoleon might cross the Elbe at Wittenberg, march behind it to Magdeburg and recross there to retreat in safety by Wesel, picking up Davout as he went. Friederich seems to think that if the Emperor ever really contemplated abandoning the left bank in order to pass to the right, it would have been with this object, rather than with the intention of operating eastwards, or across the line of the allies' communications.

Of the allies, Bernadotte was at this time as shifty as ever. Blücher's scheme for posting him in front of Halle, whilst he himself faced south on the right bank of the Saale, did not suit the Crown Prince at all; for it put him in the forefront of the battle, exposed to Napoleon's first attack. Seeing that Bernadotte and Blücher together were only about equal in numbers to Napoleon, it seems doubtful whether the plan was not too risky.

As for Schwarzenberg, von Caemmerer is very severe on him. Starting with 160,000 men, he had taken 17 days to march 70 miles, though he had nothing to stop him except the 45,000 [1] men under Murat, a mere handful in comparison with his host, not enough to do more than watch him. "Schwarzenberg's operations in western Saxony can only be characterised as a most defective piece of generalship, which was also diametrically opposed to any reasonable interpretation of the Reichenbach agreement." [2] Such is von Caemmerer's general verdict. He goes on to point out that, had

---

[1] When Napoleon, on the 10th October, estimates Murat's strength at 60,000, he had been reinforced by Augereau and Arrighi with 22,000 men.

[2] *Die Befreiungskriege*, 1813-1815, p. 73.

Schwarzenberg used his cavalry as he had seen Napoleon do, he should have known at once the weakness of the enemy opposed to him. By the 9th October he knew that Napoleon could not at once support Murat, and that Blücher was in great danger. Had he had the decision to attack Murat at Borna on the 10th, he could have decisively defeated him, have seized Leipzig next day, and have cut off Augereau, who had only reached Weissenfels on the 10th. He had still great opportunities even up to the 14th. "The battle against the King of Naples, south of Leipzig, which he missed, is a grave reproach against the commander of the allies, for which he alone must bear the responsibility."[1]

[1] *Ibid.*

CHAPTER XIX

THE BATTLES ROUND LEIPZIG ON THE 16TH OCTOBER[1]

LEIPZIG, like Dresden, has increased in population from about 30,000 in 1813 to over half a million. Like Dresden, too, it was no longer a fortress in 1813, and, though the old wall still stood in a rather dilapidated condition, the suburbs had spread out some distance on all sides of it. Since then they have absorbed large areas, which were then open country dotted with villages, the names of which now represent areas of closely-built city.

The suburbs of 1813 contained numerous open spaces, and were separated from the old fortified city (an irregular quadrilateral of 800 or 900 yards) by the open ring on the site of the old glacis, which is now represented by the Ross Platz, and other open gardens and boulevards.

The principal entrances to the city were by the four gates, Halle in the north, Grimma east, Peters south, and Rannstadt north-west. These were all suitable for wheeled traffic, and there were several others for foot passengers only. The southern and eastern suburbs were the best built, full of substantial houses, with garden walls and other readily adaptable means of defence. The northern and western were poorer quarters, with narrow, crooked streets.

The western side of Leipzig rested on the Pleisse and the ramifications of that river and the Elster, which unite here, and the former is absorbed in the latter. Both rivers arrive from points only a very few degrees east and west of south. The space between them is a network of channels, with

[1] Maps I. and IV. (*d*).

woods, marshes, and gardens between them, a very difficult country in which to move troops. After passing Leipzig, the Elster turns almost at right angles to its former course, and makes for the Saale above Halle. South of this part of its course is the Luppe, which seems to be really a branch of the Elster. Between the two is a strip similar to that between the Elster and the Pleisse above Leipzig. The channels between the Elster and the Pleisse are so numerous that it is almost impossible to say which belongs to which river. The road from the north-west gate of Leipzig was carried to Lindenau on an embankment, which had five stone and several wooden bridges over the numerous channels in a distance of about a mile and a half. The principal bridge, one destined to gain a terrible notoriety, was just outside the Rannstadt gate.

The Partha, rising south of Grimma, flows north-west to beyond Taucha, where it turns suddenly to the south-west to join the Pleisse just north of Leipzig. Though a small stream, it was very tortuous, with steep or marshy banks, which made it a serious obstacle to troops. The Rietschke brook, flowing past Eutritzsch to join the Elster near Gohlis, was also a lesser obstacle.

The circle round Leipzig is divided by the Elster, the Pleisse, and the Partha into three main segments, with a fourth in the shape of the marshy ground between the two first named. The western segment lies between the upper Elster and the Luppe, the northern between the lower Elster and the Partha, the southern between the Partha and the Pleisse.

The southern area is marked by a succession of low ridges, like waves flowing outwards from Leipzig. The ridges, low though they are, formed good positions for troops defending Leipzig, whilst the hollows behind them served to conceal reserves. At the same time, the country was very open and well suited to cavalry, which was only obstructed by the marshes and ponds in the hollows. The highest point on this side was the Galgenberg, between Wachau and Liebertwolkwitz. A feature to be noticed is the low, flat hill called the Kolm Berg, half a mile east of Liebertwolkwitz, crowned by the remains of an old Swedish redoubt, a relic of the days of Gustavus Adolphus. A marshy brook flowed round its western and northern sides.

The western segment is an almost level plain. Two slight elevations west of Lindenau alone afforded some command for artillery.

The plateau of the northern segment is less undulating than that of the south, though perhaps the descent to the Rietschke brook is rather steeper than the southern slopes.

The villages surrounding Leipzig were generally well built (least so in the west), with broad streets, massive churches, and clay or brick garden and cemetery walls.

Napoleon had caused the existing means of defence in the suburbs, such as garden walls, ditches, and tanks, to be improved by loopholing, palisading, and excavation. Round Lindenau he had constructed several small works, besides palisades, chevaux de frise, etc.

The road over the causeway to Lindenau was the only one left for the French retreat, and the allies were threatening to close that. The Emperor himself had contributed to the difficulties of a retreat by Lützen, for, in order to render the bad ground between the rivers a better protection to his flank, he had destroyed nearly all the bridges of the Pleisse and Elster, except those of the causeway.

The only paved roads to the south and east were those leading to Borna, Grimma, and Wurzen, and even these were only in good repair within municipal limits. From the north of Leipzig one more such road issued, dividing outside into the roads to Halle, Landsberg, Delitzsch, Düben, and Eilenburg. With these exceptions, there were nothing but very bad country roads.

Schwarzenberg's first orders for battle on the 16th contemplated the following operations :—

(1) Blücher, with the Silesian army, to advance by the Merseburg road on Leipzig, through Günthersdorf, maintaining at the same time his communications with Halle.

(2) Gyulai, with Moritz, Lichtenstein, and Thielmann, to concentrate at Markranstädt and advance direct on

THE BATTLES ROUND LEIPZIG

Leipzig. For the day he was to be under Blücher's orders.

(3) Meerveldt's corps, with the Austrian reserve and the Russian Guard, to assemble at Zwenkau and move on Leipzig, between the Elster and the Pleisse.

(4) Wittgenstein, Kleist, and Klenau, to attack on the right bank of the Pleisse, and drive the enemy northwards on Leipzig. All attacks to begin at 7 A.M.

These orders came to this: that Wittgenstein, Kleist, and Klenau, with 72,000 men, were to attack Napoleon, who was assumed to be concentrated south of Leipzig, in front. Meerveldt, with 52,000, to attack his right and rear about Connewitz, through the difficult tract between the Elster and the Pleisse. Gyulai and Blücher to attack Leipzig in the western segment, between the upper and the lower Elster; with 73,000 men. These were to stop the Lindenau outlet.

The lesson of Dresden had been forgotten; the army was to be split by the marshy valley of the Elster and Pleisse, as at Dresden it had been split by the Plauen gorge.

Blücher, Gyulai, and Meerveldt, with two-thirds of the army, were set an almost impossible task, against a point which Napoleon had satisfied himself could be defended by comparatively small forces. Meanwhile, he would be able to fall with greatly superior forces on the 72,000 on the south of Leipzig.

Toll,[1] Jomini, and others protested against this, and finally appealed to the Tsar. Even he could not convince Schwarzenberg, and, in the end, he was forced to tell the Commander-in-Chief that he could please himself about his Austrians, but that the Russians must come to the right bank of the Pleisse.

Then Schwarzenberg at last gave way, and issued fresh orders :—

(1) Blücher to remain as he was, on the right bank of the lower Elster, attacking, not Lindenau, but the north side of Leipzig.

(2) Gyulai to attack Lindenau.

[1] *Danilewski*, pp. 233-235.

(3) Meerveldt's force was reduced to 28,000 Austrians only.

(4) 24,000 of the Russian Guard and cuirassiers, withdrawn from Meerveldt, were ordered to Rötha, five miles behind Wittgenstein.

Napoleon had hoped to be able to attack the army of Bohemia on the 15th of October, but was prevented by the absence of Macdonald's and Souham's corps.

On the morning of the 16th October he had available round Leipzig, or approaching it, these forces :—

	Men.	Guns.
(1) South of Leipzig	138,600	488
(2) At Lindenau	3,200	16
(3) North of Leipzig, including Delmas' 4,800 men still marching from Düben	49,500	186
Total	191,300	690

The number was really not quite so great, as no deduction has been made for the losses in Murat's battle of the 14th. The only other troops to come up were Reynier's 14,000, who could not arrive from Düben till the next day. Against these the allies had :—

I. South of Leipzig—

	Men.	Guns.
(1) On the line Fuchshain, Gross Pösna, Guldengössa, Cröbern	62,000	181
(2) Reserve at Grühna	10,500	34
(3) Marching on Rötha	24,000	243
Total	96,500	458
II. Between the Pleisse and Elster	30,000	90
III. Opposite Lindenau	19,000	58
IV. At Schkeuditz (Blücher)	54,500	310
Grand total	200,000	916

THE BATTLES ROUND LEIPZIG

Including Cossacks, etc., they had, in round figures, 205,000 men and 916 guns, against Napoleon's 191,000 men and 690 guns. They already had an immense superiority in guns, though many of them never came into action. Of cavalry they had on the 16th about 40,000, against 30,000 of Napoleon. Still, except in artillery, it cannot be said they had any marked superiority; certainly not sufficient to compensate for the superiority of Napoleon as a commander.

But when we come to look at what the two opponents could bring on to the field between the 16th and the 19th, it is different. Napoleon could only expect another 14,000 men with Reynier, raising his total to 205,000, with about 700 guns.

The allies had to be joined by the 18th by :—

	Men.	Guns.
(1) Bernadotte	61,000	226
(2) Beningsen	31,000	134
(3) Colloredo	19,000	106
Total	111,000	466
Grand total, including those available on the 16th	316,000	1,382

Even to this number must be added 5000 Cossacks with Bernadotte's army. The whole of the allied cavalry (exclusive of 8500 Cossacks) would be roughly 60,000 against 30,000. Briefly, in the whole of the battles round Leipzig the allies had a superiority of about 130,000 men.

The troops on either side on the southern battlefield were disposed thus at the commencement :—

I. FRENCH

(1) On the line Connewitz-Lösnig-Dölitz-Markkleeberg,

Lefol's small French division,[1] the VIII. corps (Poniatowski) and the Polish cavalry.[2]

(2) Victor behind, and on both sides of Wachau.

(3) Lauriston between Wachau and Liebertwolkwitz, with the Young Guard and Curial's division of Old Guard behind him.

(4) Augereau (IX. corps) behind Zuckelhausen.

(5) Macdonald and the 2nd cavalry corps marching on Holzhausen.

(6) In reserve about Probstheida, Friant's Old Guard division, and the mass of the cavalry (1st corps, Guard cavalry, and 5th corps).

II. Allies

(1) Between the Pleisse and the Elster, about 15,000 men each at Gautzsch and between Zobigker and Prödel.

(2) Kleist advancing on Markkleeberg.

(3) Eugen of Wurtemberg on Wachau from the south.

(4) Pahlen's cavalry linking Eugen to Gortchakow.

(5) Gortchakow, moving on the south side of Liebertwolkwitz.

(6) Klenau and Ziethen on the east side of the same village.

(7) Reserve at Grühna. Russian grenadiers and cuirassiers.

(8) Russian and Prussian Guards, marching on Rötha from between the rivers, under the second set of orders.

Of the allied troops elsewhere than on the south we need only say, for the present, that Gyulai was at Markranstädt; Blücher about Schkeuditz, opposed to Marmont about Lindenthal and Breitenfeld.

Of the French, Bertrand was at Eutritzsch; Brayer's and Ricard's divisions (III. corps) marching on Mockau; and Delmas' of the same corps convoying the trains from Düben. Dombrowski's division was at Plaussig; Arrighi (Governor of Leipzig) with the small force at Lindenau.

---

[1] Consisting of portions of his " regiments de marche " newly arrived, and not yet distributed to their units.

[2] Commanded by Sokolnicki in the absence of Kellermann—sick.

THE BATTLES ROUND LEIPZIG

The first act of the "battle of the nations," that which was played on the 16th October, comprises three distinct actions.

(1) The attack on the south, generally known as the battle of Wachau, with its flank attack between the Pleisse and the Elster.

(2) Gyulai's attack on Lindenau.

(3) Blücher's attack on the north.

These we will describe in the order given.

(1) WACHAU [1]

1st period, 9 A.M. *to* 11 A.M.—The chief command of the frontal attack in the south was vested in Barclay, with Wittgenstein in executive command under him.

Wittgenstein decided to attack in five columns.

(1) Klenau on the right, with about 33,000 men and 80 guns, to assemble between Fuchshain and the Ober Holz, and to attack Liebertwolkwitz from the east.

(2) Gortchakow, 9000 men and 20 guns, to march from between the Ober Holz and Störmthal, against the south side of Liebertwolkwitz.

(3) Eugen of Wurtemberg, 11,000 men and 31 guns, to assemble at Guldengössa for an attack on the south-east of Wachau.

(4) Kleist, 8400 men and 26 guns, to start from south of Cröbern, advancing through it on the space between Wachau and Markkleeberg.

(5) Pahlen, with 5400 cavalry, was to move from Guldengössa on the heights between Wachau and Liebertwolkwitz,

---

[1] *Danilewski* (p. 237) gives Schwarzenberg's proclamation to his troops before the battle of the 16th October. It is a palpable, and by no means bad, imitation of Napoleon's proclamations of happier days. It runs thus :—

"Brave soldiers! The most important epoch of this holy war is at hand. The decisive hour is striking. Prepare yourselves for battle! The bond which unites the mighty nations in one great enterprise will be drawn closer and tighter on the battlefield. Russians! Prussians! Austrians! you fight for a cause! You fight for the independence of Europe, for the freedom of your sons, for the immortality of your name! All for one! one for all! With this sublime, manly cry, enter upon the sacred battle. Remain ever constant and victory is yours."

thus linking the attacks of Gortchakow and Eugen of Wurtemberg.

In reserve, the Russian grenadiers and cuirassiers, 10,500 men and 34 guns, on the high road south of Grühna.

The 24,000 men and 243 guns, withdrawn by the second set of orders from Meerveldt, were at Audigast on the night of the 15th. They were to march at 1 A.M. on Rötha.

Wittgenstein's five columns were spread over a front of some six miles, unable to see one another. There was, therefore, little hope of simultaneous action. Napoleon's positions have already been described.

The morning of Saturday, October 16, broke cold and rainy, with a thick mist shutting out the view. Attack at 7 A.M. was out of the question, and the allies only began to move an hour later, as a west wind sprang up and cleared away the mist and smoke.

Napoleon reached the battlefield shortly after 9 A.M. At the Galgenberg he was met by Murat, who had been observing from the château at Wachau. The Emperor made a long and careful study of the battlefield through his glass. He saw that the enemy had anticipated the attack he himself intended, and that his own corps were by no means all up. Accordingly he sent reinforcements to the points most threatened.

The Tsar, arriving about the same hour on the height south of Guldengössa, saw the weakness of Wittgenstein's attack in widely separated columns, and that it must fail, unless supported. He immediately ordered up the Russian grenadiers and cuirassiers, from Grühna and Magdeborn, to Auenhain, directed the Russian and Prussian guards from beyond the Pleisse on Cröbern and Guldengössa, and sent to request Schwarzenberg, who was with Meerveldt's force, to send the Austrian reserve over the Pleisse.

Eugen of Wurtemberg, the first of the allies to advance, easily got possession of Wachau, but could not get beyond it, owing to heavy artillery fire. Napoleon had sent the artillery of the Young Guard to this part of the field. It was 9.30 when Eugen got into Wachau. For the next hour, a furious hand-to-hand fight raged in the village which, after changing hands several times, was finally recaptured by the French by 11 A.M. Eugen's men took shelter in a fold of the ground south of Wachau, on which they kept up a continuous fire. Eugen held on pluckily, for he felt that his defeat would mean ruin for the rest of the army.

On Eugen's left, Kleist had got possession of Markkleeburg, and he managed to hold on there, though he could not get forward in face of the French artillery. He still held it at 11 A.M., though he had suffered heavily, especially in an attempt to support Eugen by an attack on the west side of Wachau.

Gortchakow's column, on Eugen's right, had advanced on Liebertwolkwitz without waiting for Klenau's attack from the east. Crushed by the French artillery, it fell back towards the Nieder Holz, thus making a gap between Gortchakow and Eugen, which the latter had to fill with Pirch's brigade from his second line. Pahlen's cavalry had equally been unable to face the French artillery.

Klenau had not begun his advance from Gross Pösna till 10 A.M. The Kolmberg was found unoccupied, and Klenau sent two battalions and 12 guns on to it, supported by Schäfer's brigade in rear. At the same time, he sent 5 battalions, 4 squadrons, and 14 guns against Liebertwolkwitz, which had been almost reduced to ruins on the 14th, except the church, in which the French now held out after they had lost the rest of the village.

From the Kolmberg Klenau had marked the advance of heavy French columns between Baalsdorf and Holzhausen. He, therefore, appealed to Pahlen for help in cavalry, and received 14 squadrons. At 11 A.M. his left was fighting in Liebertwolkwitz, and he held the Kolmberg, the garrison of which was supported by Schäfer's brigade, having Pahlen's 14 squadrons on its left. Abele's and Ziethen's brigades were between Fuchshain and Gross Pösna.

Whilst all this was going on east of the Pleisse, Meerveldt had found insuperable obstacles to his attack on Napoleon's right. He could not bring up his artillery in the bad ground, all the bridges over the channels and the Pleisse were gone, except one which was barricaded, and flanked by artillery. By 11 A.M. all his attacks had failed, with the solitary exception of that on the "schloss" at Dölitz, on the hither side of the Pleisse. He was reduced to the defensive against the French counter-attacks.

It was about this time that Wolzogen, carrying the Tsar's message to Schwarzenberg, found him and Radetzky at Gautzsch. Both were very depressed, saying Meerveldt had already lost 4000 men and had no hope of crossing the Pleisse. It was not till noon that Schwarzenberg could be persuaded to part with the Austrian reserve. At that hour Bianchi's and Weissenwolf's brigades, preceded by Nostitz's cavalry, started viâ Gaschwitz and Deuben.

Napoleon, meanwhile, had reinforced his weakest points by sending Augereau to support Poniatowski on the line Dösen-Wachau. Letort's division of Guard cavalry also supported the Poles. Four divisions of Young Guard, and Curial's of Old Guard, were placed behind Liebertwolkwitz when Klenau attacked it, and Friant's was moved forward from Probstheida to the Meusdorf farm. Oudinot was sent to behind Wachau when that place first fell.

The Emperor had no reason for dissatisfaction with this first defensive period of the battle. Macdonald was now deploying between Holzhausen and Liebertwolkwitz, with Sebastiani's cavalry on his left, marching on Seifertshain. The attack on Napoleon's right had failed, as he could now see, since the weather had quite cleared up.

2nd period, from 11 A.M. *till* 2 P.M.—Napoleon now prepared to pass from the defensive to the offensive. He expected presently to be strengthened by Marmont from the north, as well as by Souham (III. corps). He had obstinately maintained, notwithstanding Marmont's reports to the contrary, that there was nothing of importance on the Halle road, and that the enemy was to be expected rather by that of Merseburg. He wished Marmont to come south across the Partha, to halfway between Leipzig and Liebertwolkwitz, whence he would be in a position to support the Emperor, or, in the improbable event of a strong force approaching from Halle, to assist Bertrand in that direction.[1] It suffices here to record the fact that Napoleon's hopes were disappointed, and that, of all these expected reinforcements, only two divisions of the III. corps arrived, and they too late for a decisive stroke. The reasons for this will appear later.

In the meanwhile, Macdonald was ordered to storm the Kolmberg and push thence on Seifertshain, turning the right flank of the allies. When this movement was complete, the Emperor proposed to advance all along his line. Victor and Oudinot would advance on Auenhain, Lauriston on Guldengössa, Mortier with two divisions of Young Guard on the Nieder Holz, the attack being supported, and the enemy's centre shattered by the fire of a great battery, to be collected by Drouot between Victor's left and Lauriston's right.

Having thus driven a great wedge into the centre of the allies, the Emperor hoped to drive their left into the Pleisse, their right eastwards off its communications with Dresden. It was to give the finishing touch to this great movement that he wanted Marmont and Souham.

Macdonald himself went with Charpentier's division against the Kolmberg, whilst Gérard's division moved on Klein Pösna, and Ledru's on Seifertshain. Marchand in reserve. There was a moment's hesitation before the artillery fire from the Kolmberg, then it was carried with a rush, four guns being taken in the Swedish redoubt. Klenau narrowly escaped capture, his horse being killed. Schäfer's reserve brigade, led forward by Toll, broke and fled when only one battalion had come into action. It made for Fuchshain. The only redeeming point was a gallant charge by four squadrons of Ziethen's cavalry, which recaptured three guns taken by the French at the southern foot of the knoll. Sebastiani's cavalry came near to making an end of Schäfer's fugitives, but their leader's heart failed him on the arrival of

[1] *Corr.* 20,814, dated 16th October, 7 A.M.

Pahlen's 14 squadrons and a few of the dreaded Cossacks, whose shouts were more effective than their charge. During this fight Lauriston drove the Austrians in Liebertwolkwitz back on Gross Pösna. Farther west, Klenau's repulse compelled Gortchakow to retire to the line Guldengössa - University Wood.[1] Pahlen followed suit; Kleist had been forced back, leaving only a detachment desperately holding out in Markkleeberg. Eugen of Wurtemberg alone, though two-thirds of his force had been killed or wounded, obstinately held his place. A confused cavalry fight on Kleist's left had eventually ended in the repulse of the allies.

Then Kleist, receiving a fresh impulse from the advance of Rajewski's grenadiers, pushed forward again to the heights between Wachau and Markkleeberg, whence meeting Poniatowski and Augereau, he was again slowly forced back towards Cröbern. His detachment still clung desperately to the southern part of Markkleeberg.

Between the Pleisse and the Elster, Meerveldt made no progress during this period.

Napoleon had remained on the Galgenberg, watching the progress of the battle. When Macdonald had stormed the Kolmberg, and Lauriston had retaken Liebertwolkwitz, he wrote to the King of Saxony that "all is going well, and we have occupied the heights and villages." He also ordered all the bells of Leipzig to be rung, to announce his victory.

At 2 P.M. all the attacking columns of the allies had been driven back to their starting points.

3rd period. After 2 *P.M.*—During Macdonald's turning movement, Napoleon had been preparing for the general attack. The 1st cavalry corps and the Guard cavalry were massed at Meusdorf. Victor formed columns of attack, with Oudinot's two divisions of Young Guard on his left; Lauriston did likewise, with Mortier's two divisions behind him. Friant's division of Old Guard moved up towards Wachau.

When Napoleon gave the signal for the general advance,

---
[1] The Ober and Nieder Holz.

he still anxiously expected the arrival of Marmont, though he knew Bertrand had already been sent to Lindenau.

Victor and Oudinot advanced on Auenhain farm, Lauriston on Guldengössa, Mortier on the University Wood, Macdonald on Seifertshain.

Kleist was in desperate straits as he fell back before Poniatowski and Augereau on Cröbern. At this juncture Nostitz's cavalry arrived from beyond the Pleisse, just as Letort's French Guard cavalry and Berkheim, with ten more squadrons, reached the plain north of Cröbern. Nostitz sent two regiments against Letort and two against Berkheim. In each case the French were driven back, but the Austrians, suffering severely from the fire from infantry squares, and meeting more cavalry, were driven back to Cröbern. In support of the general advance, which had commenced just after 2 P.M., Drouot had collected a battery of 84 guns on the plateau in front of the Galgenberg.

Behind the guns was the 1st cavalry corps, now commanded by Doumerc, since Latour-Maubourg had lost a leg by a round shot. It was about 2.30 P.M., whilst the cavalry fight on the right was still in progress, when Doumerc sent forward Bordesoulle with his cuirassier division of 18 squadrons, 2500 men at most.[1] Sending 4 squadrons of Saxons against the battery on his right, Bordesoulle charged straight ahead with the rest, starting from a point on the right of Drouot's great battery. One of the battalions of Eugen of Wurtemberg, still holding on in their old position, was carried away, and, though another had time to form square, Bordesoulle gained possession of 26 guns. Hewing down the enemy right and left as they passed, the cuirassiers arrived at some ponds in front of the Wachtberg, on which were Alexander and the King of Prussia. The position of

[1] Pelet represents this cavalry charge as made by 111 squadrons, 12,000 men. His story is disposed of by a letter from Bordesoulle to the *Spectateur militaire*, dated 23rd March 1827. His narrative, which bears the stamp of truth, shows that only his own division charged. It is confirmed, not only by the omission of mention of this charge in the regimental histories of the regiments of the other divisions, but also by the fact that he was beaten off in the end by 13 allied squadrons, a fate which could hardly have fallen on 111 squadrons.

Y

the sovereigns was analogous to that of Napoleon at Eylau after Augereau's repulse. But the French charge was nearly spent. As they struggled to get forward between the ponds, they were charged by the Cossack escort, and, on their left flank, by 13 squadrons of Russian cuirassiers. The French horses being blown, and their riders exhausted, the whole division was driven back in confusion behind Drouot, whose grape fire finally brought the pursuit to an end. It was 3.30 P.M. when the last of Bordesoulle's horsemen disappeared behind the guns, and the artillery fire, which had been partially suspended during their charge, broke out with renewed violence. During this cavalry action Napoleon's infantry had pressed steadily on. Victor and Augereau on the right drove Kleist back on Cröbern, from which Bianchi, at the head of the Austrian reserves, began to debouch at 4 P.M.

Eugen of Wurtemberg had been forced back to the line Auenhain-Guldengössa, with Rajewski's grenadiers behind him.

The Prussian Guards were now marching on Guldengössa, where there was a battery of 94 Russian guns.

Klein Pösna had been occupied by Gérard and Sebastiani ; Macdonald was advancing with Ledru's division to the attack (4 P.M.) of Seifertshain, and Charpentier's against the University Wood. At 5 P.M. Seifertshain had been stormed and retaken several times. As darkness fell, Gérard retired on Fuchshain, Ledru towards Marchand on the Kolmberg. Charpentier, after driving the Austrians from the Nieder Holz, and failing to take Gross Pösna from Ziethen, still held the Nieder Holz when darkness stopped the fighting.

Mortier, meanwhile, after assisting Charpentier's attack on the Nieder Holz, failed to make his way into the Ober Holz.

Maison, leading Lauriston's advance on Guldengössa, got into the village, but was driven out by reinforcements and compelled to retire in such disorder to the heights that nothing more could be done. He was himself badly wounded.

THE BATTLES ROUND LEIPZIG

Victor, at 4 P.M., had got possession of Auenhain, except the Manor House, which the Russians held. Presently Augereau, on Victor's right, was forced back from before Cröbern by Bianchi, with Kleist on his right, a movement which compelled Victor to retire from Auenhain.

Weissenwolf had now come up, and enabled Bianchi to get forward again to Markkleeberg and towards Dölitz.

The French right was now in a critical position, as Meerveldt, relieved by Bianchi's advance, had at last got across the Pleisse. At 5.30 he even got into Dölitz. But Napoleon had now sent Curial's Old Guard division, and Ricard's of Souham's corps, which was at last up, to strengthen his right. This resulted in the stoppage of Bianchi's advance, and the driving of Meerveldt's troops back over the Pleisse. Meerveldt himself, being shortsighted, rode into the midst of some Saxons and Poles, whom he mistook for Hungarians, and was taken prisoner.

At nightfall Bianchi was still between Dölitz and Markkleeberg, the former, including its "schloss," having been recaptured by the French. As a whole, the battle had been a drawn one: the gains of the allies on their left towards Markkleeberg were counteracted by the advance of the French on the other wing to Klein Pösna, to in front of Gross Pösna, and into the Nieder Holz.

Artillery fire continued into the night after darkness had stopped other fighting.

The ensuing night was spent by the allied sovereigns in Rötha, Borna, and Grüna. Napoleon was in the centre of Friant's division of the Old Guard.

(2) LINDENAU

Gyulai's attack on Lindenau can be described more briefly than the battle about Wachau. His task was to form a connecting link between the Austrians on the left bank of the upper Pleisse and Blücher on the right bank of the Elster below Leipzig; also, by his attack on Lindenau, to lighten the task of the allies on his right and left. Any real success against Lindenau, which Napoleon had fortified, or any turning of the defile behind it, was not to be looked for. Therefore, Gyulai resolved merely to demonstrate, in order to withdraw as many as possible of the allies' opponents north and south of Leipzig. At 8 A.M. his look-out, on the church tower of Markranstädt, reported heavy fighting south of Leipzig, and Gyulai began his advance.

It was 10.30 when the Austrians, approaching Lindenau, saw the French drawn up in two lines across the Lützen road in front of the line Lindenau-Plagwitz, their artillery in three redoubts, and their cavalry (6 squadrons) advancing from their left wing.

Whilst Gyulai's artillery was bombarding the French position, and especially Lindenau, from both sides of the road, his 10 squadrons drove the French cavalry back behind their guns. At the same time, Austrian infantry moved on Klein Zschocher, seeking to drive the French on Lindenau. The only reserves were 3 battalions on the Markranstädt road, and two at Schönau. Cavalry escorted the guns.

Klein Zschocher was taken after a desperate struggle with the French garrison, which retired on Plagwitz. All attacks on the latter place failed, as it was strongly held, and was flanked by artillery beyond the Elster.

On the Austrian left, Leutzsch was taken by the Hessen-Homburg division. Beyond it the Austrians found themselves in a network of ditches and branches of the Luppe,[1] flanked by the fire of batteries beyond the stream. With great courage and patience they succeeded at last in approaching Lindenau, only to find the near side closed by walls and other defences. On the Leipzig side it was open, but was defended by artillery on the causeway leading to the city. Nevertheless, the Austrians succeeded in getting into Lindenau, which they had almost immediately to leave under the storm of artillery fire. In a second attack they captured two guns, which, however, they had to abandon, after spiking them, as they were once more forced from the village.

[1] The southern branch of the lower Elster.

THE BATTLES ROUND LEIPZIG 341

At 10 A.M. Ney had directed Bertrand (instead of Marmont, whom it was impossible to send owing to the development of affairs on his front) to proceed to the south of Leipzig. The commander of the IV. corps was on his way when he received an urgent appeal for help from Arrighi at Lindenau, who saw himself threatened by the advance of Gyulai's vastly superior force. Bertrand, accordingly, turned towards Lindenau with the whole of his corps. The position was really so strong that a brigade would have enabled Arrighi to hold it easily, and he would probably have done without any help. But it was the sole line of retreat of the French army to the Rhine, and must be held at all costs. Bertrand had joined Arrighi with Morand's and Fontanelli's divisions when the Austrians were finally ejected from Lindenau. The Hessen-Homburg division now retired to the heights west of Leutzsch, but, by placing skirmishers in the meadows along the Luppe, kept the French in apprehension of a fresh attack.

After the bells of Leipzig had announced the Emperor's apparent victory in the south, Bertrand began to advance towards Klein Zschocher, covered by a furious artillery fire from beyond the river. Twice he attacked the village, but each time was repulsed by Czöllich's brigade, reinforced by a battalion and some Cossacks. After this, the action was confined to artillery fire till evening, when Gyulai, withdrawing his main body to Markranstädt, still kept advanced posts in Klein Zschocher, Schönau, and Leutzsch.

(3) MÖCKERN

Perhaps the most important of the three battles fought on the 16th October was that on the north of Leipzig, between Marmont and Blücher.

It will be remembered that Marmont had been ordered to seek out a position north of Leipzig, covering it in the directions of Halle and Landsberg. He selected one at Lindenthal and Breitenfeld, the very ground on which

Gustavus Adolphus had defeated Tilly on September 7th, 1631.[1]

The Emperor approved the position, but said some field fortifications were required. Marmont had reported the position good, though too extensive for defence by his corps alone. He required 24,000 to 30,000 men in order to be able to hold it for twenty-fours against Blücher. Napoleon promised that he should be supported by the III. corps if attacked by Blücher. That quite satisfied Marmont, who set to work at his fortifications, setting up many abattis in the wood which still stands between Lindenthal and Radefeld, and which he made almost into a fortress. He also threw up some redoubts. His advanced guard held Radefeld. On the 15th, Marmont felt more than ever secure, as the III. and IV. corps stopped behind him at Eutritzsch. That evening some French sappers, who had been captured two days before, escaped from Halle, and reported to Marmont that Blücher was about to march from Halle on Leipzig, a report which was passed on to the Emperor at Reudnitz. At 10 P.M. Marmont, mounted on the church tower at Lindenthal, saw the whole sky towards Halle illuminated by the enemy's camp fires, and again reported to Napoleon, saying he required the aid of the III. corps. That night he received a letter from Berthier saying, "In case the enemy appears before you in great force, your corps, that of General Bertrand, and that of the Prince of the Moskowa are destined to be opposed to him." All seemed to be well, when a thunderbolt fell on Marmont in the shape of the Emperor's letter of the 16th at 7 A.M.,[2] ordering him to the south of Leipzig, his own place being taken by Bertrand, and asserting the Emperor's belief, in the face of all Marmont's reports, that there was no enemy of importance towards Halle. "Thence (from between

---

[1] Napoleon had already drawn comparisons between his battle of Lützen and that in which Gustavus Adolphus lost his life in the moment of victory. As a matter of fact, the scene of Gustavus Adolphus' battle is on the opposite side of Lützen to that of the battle of 1813. Napoleon now sent Marmont an account of the battle of Breitenfeld to assist him (*Corr.* 20,805).

[2] *Corr.* 20,814.

THE BATTLES ROUND LEIPZIG 343

Leipzig and Liebertwolkwitz)," writes Napoleon, "you can march on Lindenau if the enemy attacks seriously on that side, which seems to me absurd to suppose."

There was nothing for it but for Marmont to obey, since the Emperor had fallen deliberately into his error as to Blücher's movement, with all the information before him. His doing so is a remarkable instance of Napoleon's growing habit of making the wish father to the thought.

Scarcely had Marmont begun his movement towards Leipzig, when the enemy appeared and occupied Radefeld with a strong advanced guard.

Blücher, at Schkeuditz, having succeeded in getting Schwarzenberg's first orders changed, prepared for his march on Leipzig. Believing that the enemy would fight either at Lindenthal and Breitenfeld, or on the line Podelwitz-Hohenössig,[1] he thought he had two alternatives open, either to march direct on Leipzig, leaving the enemy on his left, or else to attack him. Of assistance from Bernadotte he had no hope; for the British Commissioner, Colonel Stewart, had brought a message from the Crown Prince, saying he could only reach Landsberg on the 16th, but on the 17th he could support Blücher with 8000 or 10,000 cavalry and light artillery.

Blücher decided on attacking Marmont, and issued orders accordingly. Langeron, on the left, followed by Sacken as reserve, was to attack Freiroda and then Radefeld.[2] Yorck turning leftwards from the Leipzig road at Lützschena, and leaving his advanced guard on the road, would move on Lindenthal. St Priest, on arrival, to follow Langeron and Sacken.

Blücher's intention was to gain the heights of Radefeld, and there decide, according to what he saw of the enemy's position, what was to be done next. Stewart was sent back to Bernadotte to urge him on.

It was 10 A.M. before Blücher's troops left their bivouacs

[1] That is on the Düben-Leipzig road facing west.
[2] Radefeld is on the Landsberg-Leipzig road, just beyond the limit of Map IV. (*d*), and Freiroda about half a mile from Radefeld towards Schkeuditz.

Langeron reached Radefeld without opposition, and drove Cœhorn's rearguard from it. Blücher, who was with Langeron, was surprised to see the French retiring on Lindenthal, but, still fearing an attack from Hohenössig, he left Langeron to watch it from Breitenfeld.

Yorck, meanwhile, had driven Normann's cavalry and 16 guns from Lindenthal, whilst his advanced guard had moved forward by the main road on Möckern, compelling the French to evacuate Stahmeln and Wahren.

It was 2 P.M. when Blücher discovered the error of his assumption that the French would defend the Hohenössig-Podelwitz plateau. Yorck, also realising this, wheeled to his right on Horn's brigade at Lindenthal. But he still had to keep in touch with Langeron on his left, and this resulted in the formation of a gap between Horn's brigade and Hunerbein's on its left, with a still larger gap between Horn and the advanced guard on the main road.

Blücher now ordered Langeron to clear Wiederitzsch. Being still afraid of an attack on his left by some of Napoleon's corps marching from Düben, he kept Sacken's and part of Langeron's troops in that direction.

Marmont, meanwhile, had seen without surprise that it was impossible for him to comply with Napoleon's order to go to the south of Leipzig. He took up a position with his left in the long village of Möckern on the right bank of the Elster, his right resting on the marshy Rietzschke brook towards Eutritzsch. The barracks of the present day stand much where his centre was. Beyond the brook, Gross and Klein Wiederitzsch were occupied by Dombrowski's Poles and Fournier's cavalry, all that Ney had been able to leave for Marmont's support, though, when he took post, the latter understood that Souham's two divisions (Ricard's and Brayer's) were still available.

The VI. corps was perhaps the best in the army, for it consisted largely of old soldiers. The artillery (84 guns), posted on the highest point of the front, flanked by 12 guns the approach to Möckern which, Marmont argued, must be the side to be attacked, since the French right was thrown

THE BATTLES ROUND LEIPZIG 345

back, and an attack on it would be endangered by Dombrowski's advanced position beyond the brook.

Yorck, too, saw matters in the same light, not daring to advance with his left in front, so long as Wiederitzsch was held against him. At 2 P.M. his advanced guard went forward against Möckern, supported on its left by Prince Charles of Mecklenburg's brigade.

The two first attacks on Möckern were repulsed. Then ensued one of the most desperate struggles of the war for the possession of this village. It was partially taken and retaken again and again. Reinforcements were sent in by both sides.

Almost simultaneously with the first attack on Möckern, Langeron sent his advanced guard and Kapzewitch's division against the Poles in Wiederitzsch. Here, too, the fighting between the Poles and their hereditary enemies was of the most desperate character. It was about 3 P.M. when Dombrowski had been driven back on Eutritzch. Then Fournier's cavalry, with half of De France's division of cavalry, charged, and Kapzewitch was ejected from Wiederitzsch by the rallied Poles. Again he took it, and had driven the Poles in disorder on Eutritzsch, when there appeared Delmas' division escorting the parks and baggage by the road from Eilenburg. Though he had only 4700 men, Kapzewitch took him for a whole corps, on account of the trains accompanying him, and retired to the birch wood north-east of Wiederitzsch, whilst Olsuview deployed against Delmas. A detachment, sent by the latter to cover his right, took the wood, but was driven out again with the loss of a standard. Then Delmas, finding his line split in two, retired over the Partha, losing many wagons to the pursuing cavalry.

Yorck, meanwhile, after the failure of his first attacks on Möckern, had made up his mind to attack the centre of the French position, as well as the village, where the fight still swayed backwards and forwards with varying success.

Mecklenburg's attack with the bayonet on the French batteries was driven off with great slaughter; the French were already preparing to complete their victory when the explosion of several ammunition wagons spread confusion in their ranks. The gunners, with their own shells bursting amongst them, abandoned their pieces, which the Prussians rushed forward to take. But Compans' infantry fell on their left, and they were driven back in disorder till the enemy was again checked by grape from the Prussian artillery. Hunerbein's and Horn's brigades were now west of the Lindenthal-Leipzig road, but Steinmetz's brigade was the only one still intact and in action.

It was 5 P.M. when Steinmetz went forward with his right on Möckern, into which the right hand regiment of each line turned as it got to the cross road through its centre. The Prussian artillery had now been brought up to within 700 yards of the French. Steinmetz's first line was within 100 yards of the enemy when, overwhelmed by artillery and musketry, it hesitated, turned, and fled. Marmont ordered Normann to charge with his cavalry and complete the victory. He refused, probably treacherously,[1] as Marmont alleges. He did charge at a later stage, but the golden opportunity, on this occasion, was lost. Had he charged home then, Steinmetz's first line would probably have broken his second, which, as it was, held firm.

In Möckern things had gone better for the Prussians who had at last driven the defenders out, though they had the greatest difficulty in maintaining themselves in the village.

The crisis of the battle had arrived. Marmont was leading forward his infantry to complete the ruin of Steinmetz, when Yorck sent sent forward the only reserve within reach. Breaking through the intervals of the infantry, the whole of his cavalry charged furiously on the advancing French infantry. Two battalions were ridden over, Normann's and Lorge's cavalry were swept away, and the Prussian first echelon was in the midst of Marmont's guns. The fight which ensued is indescribable; all arms were inextricably mixed up; cavalry, infantry, gunners fought in desperate personal encounter with swords, bayonets, clubbed muskets,

---

[1] We say this having regard to his subsequent conduct on the 18th.

gun rammers, anything that came to hand. Then the French yielded, falling back in the greatest disorder, leaving behind 35 guns, 8 ammunition wagons, 2 standards, and 400 prisoners.

Marmont's left, now that Möckern was lost, could hold no longer. All he could do was to cover his retreat with his still unbroken right. This, too, attacked now by Horn's and Hunerbein's brigades, was soon forced to retreat, though still maintaining good order.

When Marmont was across the brook he left 300 Wurtembergers to guard the crossing at Gohlis, whilst he reorganised his broken left behind it. His right fell back on Eutritzsch.

That night the Prussians bivouacked with their right south of Möckern, left in front of Eutritzsch.

Blücher, always obsessed by the fear of an attack from the direction of Düben, had remained with Langeron beyond Lindenthal. It was only at 5 P.M. that he could make up his mind to call Sacken up. It was then too late for him to cover the four miles to the battlefield before all was over. St Priest had been sent forward earlier, but only one of his brigades fought at Wiederitzsch. To Yorck alone belonged the glory of the victory; on his corps fell the heaviest loss Going into action 21,779 strong, it lost 7969 men, more than one-third. His infantry lost 7120 out of 16,120 Langeron lost about 1500 men.

Marmont puts his losses at 6000 or 7000, but they were probably greater. Two of his divisional generals, Compans and Friederichs, were wounded, as well as himself.

Yorck captured 2000 prisoners, one eagle, two standards, and 40 guns; Langeron, one standard, 13 guns, and some hundreds of prisoners. Many ammunition wagons, Marmont's as well as Delmas', fell into the enemy's hands.

The battle ended dramatically; for, as the fighting ceased, the victorious Prussians joined in a vast chorus of the hymn of thanksgiving, "Nun danket alle Gott."

Here we pause to take a general survey of the results of

the battles of the 16th October, and to call attention to the faults and merits of the combatants.

That Wachau was not a great defeat for the allied right was probably due to the Tsar and his advisers, especially Jomini and Toll. But for his pressure on Schwarzenberg, 52,000 men would have been left between the Pleisse and the Elster, to attempt a task which was perhaps more difficult for them than for the 28,000 who eventually undertook it, and failed. Napoleon knew the strength of his right wing, due to the difficulties of moving troops, and especially guns, through the intricate space between the rivers. Again, Blücher would have been brought, against his will, across the lower Elster, only in all probability to fail, as Gyulai failed, against the defenders of Lindenau, reinforced by Bertrand, and, if necessary, by Marmont. Napoleon would have had nothing to care for on the Halle road, and very little to fear either at Lindenau or on the side of Connewitz. He would have had his hands free to throw at least 100,000 men on the 72,000 whom the allies would have had between Gross Pösna and the Pleisse. There he would probably have gained a decisive victory, and would have been free next day to turn with a large portion of his army on the forces cooped up between the rivers, and on Blücher in the western segment.

To the Tsar, again, was due the hurrying forward of the reserves to support Wittgenstein's disjointed attack in widely separated columns, and the withdrawal of yet more troops from Meerveldt, in the Austrian reserves which Schwarzenberg so reluctantly parted with. Without these reinforcements the results of the day would still probably have been defeat on the right bank of the Pleisse, failure everywhere, except at Möckern.

Napoleon was not ready when he was attacked, and had to resort to expedients, such as using his Guard to reinforce weak places at the very beginning of the battle, which he was not accustomed to. The fact that Macdonald was not up, and that Reynier could not arrive on the 16th at all, were the result of the late date at which the latter was kept

THE BATTLES ROUND LEIPZIG 349

on the right bank of the Elbe, in pursuit of what Napoleon believed to be the army of the north, and only discovered too late to be nothing but Tauenzien and Thümen.

The Emperor's position south of Leipzig was an extremely strong one on the right, and to a less extent in the centre, but his left was in the air. The allies might well have occupied the Kolmberg overnight, in which case Klenau's attack on Liebertwolkwitz would have come off at least an hour earlier, and, with Macdonald not yet up, the French position there would have been critical. As it was, Gortchakow and Klenau did not support one another.

Napoleon, on the other hand, was tactically surprised before he was ready, and had to act on the defensive till after 11 A.M. Macdonald's late arrival has not yet been explained. Owing to it, Napoleon's scheme for turning the right of the allies was a failure, indeed it could hardly succeed in any case without reinforcements from the north, especially as the Emperor had to strengthen his right more than he anticipated, owing to the strenuous attack of Kleist on Markkleeberg, and of Eugen of Wurtemburg on Wachau.

It would seem that Napoleon would have done better to advance with his reinforced right at 11 A.M. instead of at 2 P.M. He would then probably have defeated Kleist and Eugen before Schwarzenberg had started off Bianchi, Weissenwolf and Nostitz, and before even the Russian and Prussian Guards were up. He could have sent Victor, Lauriston, and the whole of the Young Guard at 11 A.M. on Guldengössa and Auenhain against Kleist, Eugen, and Gortchakow, whilst Macdonald kept Klenau and Pahlen in play. These three columns of the allies would have been driven back, and would probably have involved the reserve in their ruin.

It would have been well, too, when the Emperor did advance at 2 P.M., if he had used the whole of the 111 squadrons, of whom Pelet and Thiers speak. Looking to what Bordesoulle actually effected with only 18, it seems possible that the larger force might have gained a very real success. Gyulai's attack at Lindenau was too late to effect anything. The French force, at first, was so weak (4 battalions and 6 squadrons) that he might, in the early morning, have captured Lindenau and blocked up Napoleon's only line of retreat. When he did attack, Bertrand was up with about 7000 more men, and success was hopeless. Gyulai did very little good; for all he managed was, with his 19,000 men, to prevent 8000 or 9000 French from joining Napoleon.

The Emperor wrongly reckoned on Marmont's being able to come south. For this his own obstinacy, in refusing to believe what Marmont had seen and reported to him, was largely to blame. It was quite impossible for Marmont, with his own corps only, to defend the Breitenfeld line against Blücher's army, and he rightly decided for that of Möckern-Eutritzsch. Even here, he had little hope, if Blücher brought his whole force into action. But the Prussian general employed only a small portion, owing to his apprehensions as to his left flank. Though they were as a matter of fact unfounded, Blücher was not unreasonable in entertaining them. He had every reason to suppose that a considerable part of Napoleon's army was still on the march from the north. He knew that, on the night of the 15th, there were still considerable French forces at Düben, and some of these might well intervene as they marched south. Indeed, there was serious danger from Reynier's corps, had that general marched direct from Düben, instead of going, as he decided at the last moment, up the right bank of the Mulde, and across at Eilenburg.

Yorck's corps, as matters stood, very narrowly escaped defeat, and was only saved by its commander's prompt and decided employment of all his cavalry at the crisis of the battle.

The result of Marmont's defeat was to shut Napoleon completely in on the north of Leipzig; for Marmont's lost position could easily be held against Leipzig by a comparatively small force.

The general result of the fighting on the 16th was a

serious defeat of the French at Möckern; a successful defence at Lindenau, and a drawn battle at Wachau. In Napoleon's then position, nothing short of a decisive victory at Wachau was of any use to him. Without that, he must be reduced to the defensive against the still increasing forces of the allies. There can be no possible doubt that the evening of the 16th should have found him hard at work arranging and commencing the retreat on the Rhine, which he was compelled to carry out on the 19th. He could still escape by Lindenau, for Gyulai could easily have been brushed aside from Markränstadt, as was done later. Had he been in full retreat on the 17th, Napoleon would probably have reached the Rhine with at least 50,000 men more than he actually did, and the army would have been in a far less disorganised condition. Who can guess what would then have happened in 1814?

CHAPTER XX

THE BATTLE OF LEIPZIG—18TH OCTOBER

WHAT the night of the 16-17th October was like on the southern battlefield is best described in the words, quoted by Friederich, of a Hessian diarist of Marchand's division which bivouacked on the Kolmberg. "It was the worst bivouac that the division had in this campaign. The weather was raw and damp, there was neither food, nor water, nor wood. Broken wheels, musket stocks, and saddles served for firing; the rain water, standing in puddles, into which men and horses had bled, had to be used for cooking. Numerous patrols were sent out, many piquets posted, so that half the men had to be under arms by turns."

Napoleon's tents were pitched " in the bed of a dried-up pond near the old tile factory, a short distance from the road leading to Rochlitz."[1] The Old Guard surrounded them.

Before they were pitched, Meerveldt was brought in as a prisoner. Napoleon, who knew him before, spoke affably with him for some time, and again sent for him later in the evening. Meerveldt has left a full account of the conversation. The most important point in it, from Napoleon's point of view, was the definite announcement that Wrede had joined the Austrians opposed to him on the Inn, and was about to march against the French communications at Frankfort and Mayence. That really convinced Napoleon that retreat was inevitable, though he still wanted to put it off. He then sent Meerveldt back to the Emperor of Austria, in the vain hope of opening negotiations which

[1] Odeleben, ii. 23.

THE BATTLE OF LEIPZIG 353

might, at least, give him more time. Needless to say, nothing came of Meerveldt's mission.

During the night, news of events at Lindenau and Möckern came in. Bad though the news was in general, the Emperor could not make up his mind for immediate retreat. Even allowing for the losses of the day, whilst adding in the 14,000 men of Reynier to be expected on the 17th, the Emperor could still have made good his retreat with at least 150,000 men. But the Emperor Napoleon was now, to a great extent, the master of General Bonaparte, and the Emperor could not bear to yield what practically meant his dominion in Germany, though the General doubtless saw that to do so was the only hope. At any rate, he would hold the battlefield for another day, which might impress on France the fact that he had not yet been beaten.

Early on the 17th Murat came over from Wachau, where he had spent the night, with consoling accounts of the enormous losses suffered by the enemy. Yet Napoleon must have known that his own losses had been equally great, and, what was worse, that ammunition would scarcely last for a repetition of yesterday's battle. He had really decided for retreat, though he meant to stay till the 18th. He had open to him three roads :—

(1) By Merseburg, Freiburg, and Buttelstädt, to Erfurt.
(2) By Weissenfels, Kösen, and Weimar, to Erfurt.
(3) By Zeitz, Jena, and Schweinfurt.

The orders, issued at 7 P.M., directed Bertrand to secure the passages of the Saale and the Unstrut at Merseburg, Freiburg, Weissenfels, and Kösen. Mortier would replace Bertrand at Lindenau.

But why, if Napoleon meant to retreat by the west side of Leipzig with a great army, did he leave himself with a single difficult issue over the long causeway to Lindenau? Why were not numerous bridges built over the Pleisse and the Elster above the causeway? It is certain none were constructed, and, so far, no orders for them have ever been

z

discovered. If none were given, was it because the Emperor feared the moral effect of advertising his intention to his own men, or the value of such information to the enemy?

Before he actually retreated through Leipzig, he decided to take up a fresh position on a smaller circumference round the city. At 2 A.M., on the 18th, in pouring rain, the troops left their bivouacs for their new positions on the line Connewitz - Dölitz - Probstheida - Zuckelhausen - Holzhausen - Zweinaundorf - Paunsdorf. Thence the line extended, through Schönefeld, along the left bank of the Partha to Pfaffendorf, whence it went to Gohlis. In detail the positions were these:—

I. Right Wing, under Murat

Lefol on the Pleisse; Poniatowski on the line Connewitz-Lösnig; Augereau in support of these two; 4th cavalry corps behind Poniatowski.

Victor on the right of Probstheida, with the 5th cavalry corps behind him.

Guard, with 1st cavalry corps behind, between Stötteritz and Probstheida.

II. Centre—Macdonald

Macdonald at Zuckelhausen, Holzhausen, and behind.

Lauriston in reserve behind Macdonald, with part of his corps in Zweinaundorf and Molkau.

Also Walther's Guard cavalry, with Nansouty left of him.

III. Left Wing—Ney

Reynier—Saxon division in Paunsdorf with an advanced post at Heiterer Blick farm; Durutte's division left of Paunsdorf.

Marmont—From Durutte's left to Schönefeld.

De France's cavalry division (less Quenette's brigade with Bertrand) behind Paunsdorf.

Fournier's cavalry behind Schönefeld.

Souham in reserve between Schönefeld and Volkmarsdorf.

IV. IN LEIPZIG, HALLE SUBURB, AND ALONG THE
PLEISSE TO GOHLIS

Dombrowski (infantry and cavalry) and Lorge's cavalry.

V. AT LINDENAU

Mortier, with two divisions of Young Guard.

After the departure of Bertrand, and allowing for losses on the one hand and for Reynier's arrival on the other, Napoleon still had about 160,000 men in and around Leipzig. Against these, when Bernadotte, Colloredo, and Bennigsen were in the field, the allies could bring about 295,000.

After the battle on the 16th, Schwarzenberg's orders of that evening required his troops to hold on where they were.

Colloredo was expected at Magdeborn at 6 A.M., as reserve to the right wing; Bianchi and Weissenwolf at Cröbern would occupy the same position towards the left. Gyulai would form the link with Blücher by the west of Leipzig. Bennigsen to come up by Grimma and Naunhof from Colditz. A French attack in the morning of the 17th was expected, and during the night Colloredo was directed to halt behind Magdeborn, near the Leipzig road.

Nothing happened up to 10 A.M. on the 17th, when the sound of guns north of Leipzig gave rise to the belief that Napoleon was attacking Blücher. Accordingly, an attack from the south, in three columns, was ordered, the right on Liebertwolkwitz and Holzhausen, centre also on Liebertwolkwitz, left along the right bank of the Pleisse. Gyulai, and Meerveldt's corps, now commanded by Lederer, were also to attack, all at 2 P.M.

At that hour a council of war was held on the heights of Guldengössa. Firing in the north had then ceased. Colloredo had arrived at 10 A.M., but his men were dead beat. Bennigsen was present in person, but his army was still behind. The attack was put off till next day. Gyulai had at first been ordered over to Cröbern, but, just as he started, he was ordered to wait till he was relieved by St

Priest, who, as we know, had long been with Blücher. Then he began to demonstrate towards Lindenau, not being able to tell, in the wind and rain, whether the main army was engaged or not. Darkness finally stopped all but a little skirmishing.

During the night of the 16th-17th Blücher brought Sacken on the right, and St Priest on the left, into 1st line. Marmont had now retired across the Partha, leaving Delmas' division, and part of the 3rd cavalry corps between the Partha and the brook. He held Gohlis and Eutritzsch; Dombrowski was at the Gerber gate of Leipzig.

Yorck's four brigades were now amalgamated by Blücher into two, owing to their reduction by the losses of the 16th.

Blücher, desiring to clear the country north of the Partha, sent Sacken, at 9.30 A.M., against Gohlis, Langeron against Eutritzsch. This brought Ney on to the field, who replaced the one and a half Wurtemberg battalions at Gohlis by Dombrowski, and ordered Delmas to the slopes between Gohlis and Schönefeld.

The Russian cavalry now drove Fournier and Lorge back into Leipzig, taking 5 guns and 500 prisoners. It also charged Delmas' infantry, who, however, repulsed them and went back to the Halle suburb. It was only after his retirement that the Poles evacuated Gohlis, going partly to the Rosenthal, partly to the Pfaffendorf farm. By 10 A.M. there were no French north of the Partha in this direction.

The stream here was so marshy that a crossing in face of the French was out of the question. At first, Blücher thought of sending Langeron round by the left, whilst St Priest and Sacken held the French in front. Then hearing the main army was not engaged, he postponed his attack till next day.

Meanwhile, Reynier coming from Eilenburg, reached Taucha, where he beat off a small attack by Winzingerode's cavalry. Then, after some hours' rest, he marched for the Heiterer Blick farm. Here he was compelled, by the flight of Arrighi's cavalry already mentioned, to take post facing Schönefeld. When, however, he was not attacked, he sent

THE BATTLE OF LEIPZIG

the Saxon division to Paunsdorf, Durutte's French between it and Schönefeld; Saxon cavalry at Heiterer Blick. In the evening, under orders from Napoleon, Guilleminot's division went to Lindenau.

Schwarzenberg's orders for the 18th are not forthcoming, but can easily be inferred from the actual formation and movements of the troops. The attack was in six columns.

I. The Hereditary Prince of Hessen-Homburg, with the 1st and 2nd "abteilungs" of the Austrian army, the Reserve divisions of Bianchi and Weissenwolf, and Nostitz's cavalry division, to attack by Markkleeberg-Lösnig, with a detachment beyond the Pleisse helping when it could.

II. Barclay—Corps of Kleist and Wittgenstein, Russian and Prussian Guards, and Reserves. To take Wachau and Liebertwolkwitz, and then move on Probstheida.

III. Bennigsen — Polish reserve army, Bubna's (2nd) Austrian light division, Klenau's corps, Ziethen's brigade, and Platow's Cossacks, to envelop the enemy's left, moving from Fuchshain and Seifertshain on Zuckelhausen and Holzhausen.

IV. Bernadotte—Such parts of the northern army as were up, Langeron's and St Priest's corps (given over by Blücher)[1]

[1] Blücher had, throughout, infinite trouble with the unreliable Bernadotte, who was always playing for his own hand. The Crown Prince had compelled him to go behind the Saale, when the old Prussian was for fighting Napoleon on the right bank. Then Bernadotte had laid claim to the command of the united Northern and Silesian armies, a claim which Blücher had quietly ignored. Bernadotte continued to hang back, and had only promised a reinforcement of 10,000 cavalry even on the 17th. Colonel Stewart had to keep him up to the mark with hints of a stoppage of the British subsidy.

When the two armies crossed the Saale, Blücher, in the post of danger nearest Napoleon, had passed south of Bernadotte, thus becoming the right of the two armies, instead of the left as hitherto. Bernadotte wanted him to revert to the former order of battle for the 18th. This was absurd, especially as Blücher's position before Leipzig was too small for more than 30,000 men. In the end, Bernadotte could only be induced to join in the battle of the 18th on condition that Blücher placed the larger part of his army under the Crown Prince. With true patriotism, Blücher agreed, but he resolved to go himself with Langeron and St Priest, so that they should not be frittered away, or left to do nothing, by Bernadotte. It is difficult to condemn too strongly Bernadotte's conduct in the whole of this campaign, or to praise too highly Blücher's honesty and devotion to the general cause.

to cross the Partha and form the link between Blücher and the main army.

V. Blücher, with the rest of the Silesian army, to advance against the north-east side of Leipzig.

VI. Gyulai, with the 3rd Austrian "abteilung," Moritz Lichtenstein's light division (1st), and the detachments of Mensdorf and Thielmann, to attack Lindenau from Klein Zschocher.

The strengths of the various forces are estimated by Friederich, after allowing for losses on the 16th, as follows :—

	Men.	Guns.
Main army	115,000	716
Polish army	30,000	134
Colloredo	20,000	50
Bubna	6,500	18
Silesian army	42,000	310
North army	65,000	226
Cossacks	16,500	12
Total	295,000	1,466

They had a superiority of 135,000 over Napoleon, and more than double his guns.

The battle up to 2 P.M.—Monday, the 18th October, broke dull and cloudy after a wet night. By 8 A.M. it had cleared and the sun was shining brilliantly. Meerveldt had reached the allies' camp in the early morning, bringing Napoleon's proposals. There was no place for negotiations now short of the Rhine, unless in the very improbable event of a great French victory.

Napoleon's troops had been already five hours on the move when the allies began to advance at 7 A.M. He had moved his headquarters to Stötteritz on the previous evening; at 2 A.M. he went to Probstheida, the key of his battlefield, to superintend the movements. As it was too dark to see anything, he adjourned to Ney's headquarters at Reudnitz till 5 A.M., when he went into Leipzig,

THE BATTLE OT LEIPZIG 359

met Bertrand, and gave him his instructions for the march to the Saale, which was not to commence without a special order. Then, after visiting Lindenau, the Emperor returned to Stötteritz at 8 A.M. At 9, hearing of the enemy's movement, he sent orders, from the tobacco factory near Probstheida, to which he had now moved, to Bertrand to start for Weissenfels.

The battle up to 2 P.M. can be briefly described.

The allies soon found that Napoleon was gone from his position of the 16th, where they seem to have expected to find him still. Their left column, under the Prince of Hessen-Homburg, had some severe fighting at Dölitz, Dösen, and Lösnig, all of which, as well as Meusdorf, were taken and re-taken, but eventually remained in the hands of the allies. The Prince of Hessen-Homburg, being wounded, was succeeded in command of this column by Colloredo. By noon it was in front of the French main position, with Lederer's detachment, between the rivers, in front of Connewitz. The fight after this was restricted to an artillery duel. Up to 2 P.M. the French on this side had merely been driven on to their main position.

Barclay, with the next column on the right, got within cannon shot of Probstheida, where he waited for the columns on his left and right to come up. He stood just in front of the elevation since known as the Monarchen Hügel, on to which the Tsar and the King of Prussia moved from the Galgenberg, as their troops advanced. By 2 P.M. this second column was thus in front of Probstheida, but unable to attack it, pending the arrival of the third. Here again the allies' artillery was busy preparing the way for attack.

Bennigsen, charged with the envelopment of the French left, had farthest to go. From Machern, at 3 A.M., he sent Platow by Hirschfeld and Althen to get into communication with Bernadotte's army. Platow's unexpected appearance created considerable confusion amongst Macdonald's trains, which were still at Sommerfeld, Engelsdorf, and Molkau. The rest of Bennigsen's army was assembled at Fuchshain by 6 A.M., waiting for Bubna, who only got across the Partha from Machern by Beucha at 8 A.M. He was delayed by the bridge at Beucha having been carried away.

As soon as Bennigsen heard that Bubna was marching on Klein Pösna, he advanced on that village, where he believed the French left to be. Another column went by Seifertshain towards the Kolmberg to attack it, with a third advancing from the south, whilst Ziethen with the fourth was to clear the Nieder Holz and move on between the Kolmberg and Liebertwolkwitz, in touch with Barclay's right. On Bennigsen's extreme right, Platow and Bubna were to seek to gain the Leipzig-Wurzen road by Engelsdorf and Sommerfeld. As the French had retired, Bennigsen met with no opposition before 10 A.M., when Ziethen was before Zuckelhausen; Hohenlohe before Holzhausen; Doctorow and the advanced guard east of Baalsdorf; Bubna between Engelsdorf and Sommerfeld. There was no sign of Bernadotte. The roar of artillery fire was heard on the entire circle round Leipzig, except in the gap between Bennigsen's right and Langeron's left, where Bernadotte should have been.

It was important for Klenau and Ziethen to take Zuckelhausen and Holzhausen from Marchand and Charpentier respectively, in order to protect the right of an attack on Probstheida. About 1 P.M. Charpentier, attacked from the south and east by very superior forces, had to retreat in some disorder from Holzhausen. This compelled Marchand, who had hitherto maintained himself in Zuckelhausen, to retire also, though in good order. As the Austrians and Russians advanced on either side of Holzhausen, which was on fire, they were charged by Sebastiani and Walther's Guard cavalry, who were driven off by the allied cavalry. Gérard, behind Holzhausen, had now to retire, and another cavalry combat ensued in which Pahlen was not so successful, owing to momentary delay caused by his horse being killed and himself stunned. Macdonald had now fallen back to between Zweinaundorf and Paunsdorf, where he was heavily fired on by Austrian artillery established on the Steinberg, west of Holzhausen.

THE BATTLE OF LEIPZIG 361

Doctorow and Bennigsen's advanced guard stood opposite the line Zweinaundorf-Molkau. On his extreme right Bubna, after bombarding Paunsdorf for two hours, ventured on an assault at noon. His first attack failed but the second sent Reynier back on Sellerhausen. Then Reynier, coming down on Bubna's left, compelled him to evacuate Paunsdorf again.

About this time Platow, near Heiterer Blick farm, more or less got between Normann's Saxon cavalry and the French. Normann solved the difficulty by going over to the allies, though he said he could not fight against the French without orders from the King of Saxony.[1] Some other bodies of Saxons and Westphalians had already changed sides.

At 2 P.M., then, Bennigsen had driven the French from some of their advanced posts, but they still held Zweinaundorf, Molkau, and Paunsdorf. Bennigsen dared not advance farther till he received the long expected support of Bernadotte.

That astute but unreliable personage, after his arrangement with Blücher, had ordered

(1) Bülow to march on Taucha, to force the passage of the Partha there, and to watch with detachments towards Wurzen.

(2) Winzingerode to follow Bülow's movement on Taucha, sending cavalry towards Eilenburg and Wurzen to protect his left.

(3) Langeron to search out all passages of the Partha between his present position and Taucha, to throw bridges, and pass the stream below Taucha in touch with Winzingerode's right.

(4) The Swedes to cross between Langeron and Winzingerode.

[1] Normann and several other commanding officers were afterwards cashiered for their conduct on this day, and banished from Saxony; the regiments concerned were disbanded. Whatever may be thought of Napoleon's tyranny in Germany, there is no excuse for this desertion on the field of battle. Normann, who, it will be remembered, had behaved badly at Möckern, died in 1822, fighting for the independence of the Greeks.

(5) If the enemy should attack the northern and Silesian armies, all to take post on the heights of Plaussig.

Bülow, marching at 9 A.M., was by 2 P.M. nearly up to the line Plaussig-Heiterer Blick, facing west.

The rest of the North army was slowly approaching by Taucha, but it was not till 4 P.M. that the Swedes crossed the Partha at Plaussig. Some Cossacks, sent by Bülow to try and seize Napoleon's trains at Eilenburg, failed, as the Bavarian, Saxon, and Hessian escort remained faithful. The trains retired to Torgau.

Blücher, notwithstanding Bernadotte's orders, would not allow Langeron to go far towards Taucha, away from himself. He ordered him to cover Bülow's march at Mockau and Plaussig, only forcing the Partha when the North army should be engaged on its left bank. Nevertheless, part of Langeron's corps was across between Mockau and Plösen before Bülow was up, and had driven Marmont back towards Schönefeld.

Sacken, attacking with Blücher's right at Gohlis, had not succeeded in getting into the Halle suburb or the Rosenthal, in the face of a strenuous resistance by the Poles. At 1 P.M. Yorck had to be called up in support.

On the French side, Ney, seeing threats from Paunsdorf, Mockau, and Thekla, had drawn Marmont back to between Schönefeld and Paunsdorf. The VII. corps (Saxons) was between Paunsdorf and Stüntz; Souham (III.) in reserve at Volkmarsdorf. When Normann's cavalry had gone over they were soon followed by Von Fabrice's Saxon cavalry.

Between 1 and 2 P.M. Langeron's artillery opened on Schönefeld, and he presently received orders from Bernadotte saying that, as most of the north army was across the Partha, he was to attack the village.

Meanwhile, Bertrand, bursting out impetuously from Lindenau, had completely defeated Gyulai, driving most of his forces across the upper Elster, part across the Luppe, and capturing many prisoners at Klein and Gross Zschocher. Bertrand was now marching on Weissenfels with three

THE BATTLE OF LEIPZIG 363

divisions,[1] and Quenette's cavalry brigade. The line of retreat on Weissenfels had been re-opened for Napoleon.

To sum up, by 2 P.M. the allies had gained no substantial success, though they had driven the French from Dölitz, Dösen, Zuckelhausen, Holzhausen, and Baalsdorf. Napoleon still held Lösnig, Probstheida, Molkau, Zweinaundorf, Paunsdorf, and Schönefeld; his main position was intact. Sacken in the north had been repulsed.

After 2 P.M —On the left of the allies, towards Dölitz and Dösen, the French now again took the offensive. It was with the utmost difficulty that Bianchi and Colloredo kept their position, and were eventually able to return to the offensive. The fighting was furious, and it was only after repeated failures that the allies at last captured Lösnig. From Connewitz they were repulsed by Augereau and Poniatowski, the latter now reduced to 2500 Poles.

The attack on Probstheida fell to Barclay's column. This was the key of Napoleon's position, the loss of which must result in the collapse of the whole. Barclay would have waited for the advance of the columns on either side of him, but the Tsar insisted on an immediate attack.

The first attack was by two Prussian brigades, supported by the 2nd Russian infantry corps. They bravely faced an overwhelming rain of projectiles, and got partly into the south of the place, whence they were driven again with awful loss by Victor's reserves. On the east, where there was a gap in the wall surrounding the village, the Prussians made more progress at first. Then, coming under the fire of a 15-gun battery and charged by cavalry, they fell back. Again they advanced, this time right up to the centre of the village; again they were driven by infantry from the village, this time in disorder, notwithstanding reinforcements sent up by Ziethen from Zuckelhausen.

It was after 5 P.M. when Eugen of Wurtemberg with 1400 men, all that he had left, made another attempt on Probstheida from the south. But Napoleon had now replaced Victor's exhausted troops by those of Lauriston, and

[1] Including Guilleminot's, the French division of the VII. corps.

these were sent forward. Eugen's feeble force was driven off in disorder. Any further attack on Probstheida was forbidden by the allied monarchs, who had now received good news of the progress of the battle on their right. Barclay remained on the defensive, easily stopping Victor's attempts to break out. The struggle for Probstheida had been an heroic one on both sides. Vial had been killed at the head of his brigade of Victor's corps, which lost three-fourths of its numbers: Rochambeau and many of his staff, fighting with equal valour, were killed. The Prussians and Russians had behaved with equal gallantry. So terrible was the artillery fire that, next day, Kleist found no less than 30 disabled guns in and about Probstheida.

We now return to Bennigsen, and to the army of the North. It was 2.30 P.M. before Bülow's leading troops were really up. Then it was decided, in consultation with Bernadotte, that Bennigsen's right should not extend beyond Paunsdorf, whence the North army would take post up to the Partha. This enabled Bennigsen to close up his divided columns and act in greater force against Zweinaundorf and Molkau.

On the French side, Reynier's Saxons had been posted in front of Sellerhausen, to support Paunsdorf.

The Prussians now advanced on Paunsdorf, supported by a tremendous artillery fire and by that of Bogue's rocket brigade.[1] The then recently-invented Congreve rockets had a

[1] The English rocket brigade, commanded by Captain Richard Bogue, had been attached to Bernadotte's bodyguard, on the understanding that, on days of battle, it was to be more freely used than the rest of the bodyguard. Congreve rockets had been used for the first time in war on the 16th September, when Davout's detachment under Pecheux was destroyed at Görda (*supra*, p. 287). As the French left Paunsdorf, Bogue charged at the head of the squadron of dragoons escorting his brigade, and was killed soon after by a musket ball. His grave is now to be seen at Paunsdorf. He was succeeded by Fox-Strangways, who, curiously enough, it is said, was the first officer killed at Inkerman, fighting against his former allies the Russians. It is also said that, in acknowledgment of his gallant leading of the rocket battery, Fox-Strangways was decorated by the Tsar with the badge of the Order of St Anne, which he himself was wearing at the time.

The rocket brigade afterwards distinguished itself at Waterloo.

(For this subject see *Progs R.A. Institution*, vol. xxiv.; also Kinglake's

THE BATTLE OF LEIPZIG 365

specially demoralising effect on the defenders, as the village was stormed. From the position to which they were driven back they were again forced, largely by rocket fire, to retire on Sellerhausen.

The two Saxon brigades chose this moment to abandon their French allies and pass over to the enemy. It appears that the Saxon officers had in the morning decided on this step. They informed General von Zeschau (the Saxon commander-in-chief). An adjutant was then sent to inform the king of this proposal. He returned at 2 P.M. saying the king looked to Von Zeschau to keep his men to their allegiance. The officers held this answer to be ambiguous; moreover, they said, the king was not a free agent. The French had lost the campaign, and now, when Durutte's French had enough on their hands to occupy them, without thinking of keeping their Saxon comrades in order, was the best opportunity, perhaps the last, they would have to go over. When Reynier ordered the Saxon 12-pounder battery back, it marched off to the enemy, followed by the two infantry brigades. De France's cavalry, thinking they were going to attack the Prussians, cheered them as they passed. Von Zeschau made an attempt to induce them to remain, but his personal authority only sufficed to recall 24 officers and 593 men. Napoleon himself, in his bulletin,[1] attributed his defeat largely to the Saxon desertion. Some French writers have followed him, but Friederich shows that the total strength of the Saxon division on the 17th October was only 4544 and 22 guns. Allowing for losses and those who remained true to the French, on one side, and adding Normann's cavalry on the other, the total defection probably did not exceed 4000 men and 20 guns. That is hardly a loss which could vitally affect the course of a battle of such

---

Invasion of the Crimea (cabinet edition, vol. vi. p. 518), where Fox-Strangways is shown as killed at Inkerman. The story about the Order of St Anne, as well as about Fox-Strangways generally, was told to the author by Colonel Shea, Royal Artillery, who was responsible for looking after the repairs to Bogue's grave at Pannsdorf.)

[1] *Corr.* 20,830.

proportions, though it may be admitted to have had a demoralising effect.

Bennigsen's column could not venture on any general advance before the greater part of Bernadotte's army was on the field, and that was not till about 5 P.M. It was a little before that hour that the Saxons had changed sides, and then Nansouty, with the French Guard cavalry, issuing from between Stüntz and Stötteritz, made an attack on the gap between Bubna and the rest of Bennigsen's army. The attack never got beyond the line Paunsdorf-Zweinaundorf.

At this moment, Bennigsen, seeing that the North army was at last up, moved forward. Klenau, after getting into Zweinaundorf and being again expelled, finally took the village. Bubna stormed Molkau. There was another cavalry combat, as Klenau issued from Zweinaundorf, between the Russians and Sebastiani and Walther, who eventually retired before the fire of 24 guns and a Jäger brigade north of Zweinaundorf. Klenau now failed in an attack on Stötteritz, which was strongly defended by walls and ditches, and flanked by artillery from Probstheida. A counter-attack by the French on Zweinaundorf was repulsed before darkness brought the fighting here to an end. Bennigsen, like the commanders on his left, had gained no decisive success.

On his right, after Durutte's flight from Paunsdorf, Sellerhausen was stormed, but the captors were unable to get beyond it. Durutte and Delmas retired to the fork of the roads to Wurzen and Taucha. Durutte's retirement had exposed the flank of Marmont, who wheeled his right back till he stood on the line Sellerhausen-Schönefeld. He would still have been in danger, had not Ney sent Durutte to retake Sellerhausen, in which he was successful. Occupying it, Durutte was linked by Delmas to Marmont's right.

As the rest of the North army came up, it took post with its left on Paunsdorf, and its right touching Langeron, who continued the line to the Partha.

We left Langeron at 2 P.M., preparing for his attack on Schönefeld. The place was very strong, the marshes of

THE BATTLE OF LEIPZIG 367

the Partha prevented its being turned, the few entrances to it had been barricaded, and, as at Probstheida, there were numerous ditches, walls, and other obstacles. Marmont in person superintended the defence, which was entrusted to Lagrange's division (3000 men), with that of Friederichs on his right. Nevertheless, the Russians managed to force a way into it and up to the centre of the village. Thence the French counter attack drove them back to the outskirts. Just at this time Durutte's retreat had rendered possible an attack on the right flank of the village, which was to be executed by St Priest, whilst Kapzewitch reinforced the frontal attack. Marmont's guns were silenced by an overwhelming force, and he felt compelled to withdraw Lagrange and Friederichs to Reudnitz about 4.30 P.M.

Ney had now in reserve only about 7000 men and 40 guns of the divisions of Brayer and Ricard, who were ordered to retake Schönefeld. At this time both Ney and Souham were wounded as they reconnoitred the place.

Langeron's artillery ammunition having given out, he had again to retire, and the French, bursting into Schönefeld, became once more masters of it. Then the tide turned as Bernadotte replaced Langeron's guns by 60 of Winzingerode's and 20 of the Swedish corps. Brayer was wounded and his men had to fall back in disorder on Reudnitz along with Ricard. They occupied a position between Reudnitz and Schönefeld till 9 P.M., when they were once more driven back to the brook in front of Reudnitz. The North army, considering its great superiority of numbers, had done remarkably little.

On the north of Leipzig, Sacken, renewing his attacks on the Rosenthal and the Pfaffendorf farm, had again failed.

When, towards evening, Blücher heard that the enemy was retreating, apparently on Merseburg and Weissenfels, he ordered Yorck to occupy the passages of the Saale at Merseburg and Halle. Yorck started at 8 P.M., and, by 7 A.M. on the 19th, had the reserve cavalry and Horn's brigade at Halle, Hunerbein's at Burg Liebenau.[1]

[1] On the Elster, north-east of Merseburg.

As early as 2 P.M., Gyulai had orders to watch the French retreat. At 3 P.M. he reported Bertrand on the Lützen road. An Austrian detachment, too weak to maintain itself at Weissenfels, destroyed the bridge and retired on Zeitz.

Napoleon had ordered the retreat to begin at 11 A.M., and at once there commenced a continuous stream across the Lindenau causeway of everything that was not actually required on the battlefield. At 4 P.M. the 1st cavalry corps, followed by the 3rd and 5th, was sent to the slight elevations beyond Lindenau.

Napoleon had spent the morning at the tobacco factory. There is no record of his orders, or of what he said. At noon he had paid a short visit to Probstheida, and went there again at 2 P.M., when he was in the thick of the fire, encouraging his troops in their defence of the village. When he heard of the Saxon defection he went to the left and had a long conversation with Ney. Here he personally ordered the attack by Nansouty's cavalry. At 4 P.M. he had ordered the cavalry corps to Lindenau, and directed the whole artillery park to follow, after replenishing the ammunition supplies at the front, and destroying part of the empty wagons.

At 5 P.M., exhausted by a sleepless night, he slept calmly at the tobacco factory, sitting on a wooden bench, until he was waked by a round shot scattering the fire close by him. Whilst he slept, his staff stood silent and dejected around him.

Waking, he calmly dictated orders for the retreat of the troops next day. Up to the present these orders have not been found. According to Pelet, part of the artillery and parks was to go first, then, starting before daybreak, the rest were to follow in this order: Old Guard, Oudinot's two divisions of Young Guard, 4th cavalry corps, IX. and II. corps, 2nd cavalry corps. The rest were to defend Leipzig and cover the retreat.

At 6.30 P.M., finding his tents had gone on, the Emperor betook himself to the Hotel de Prusse, which still stands in the Ross Platz. Strange coincidence that he should spend

THE BATTLE OF LEIPZIG 369

this night in a hostel bearing the name of the nation which had taken the principal part in his overthrow! The roads were so encumbered with the wreckage of his army that it was long before he got there.

The allied monarchs had spent most of the day on the Monarchen Hügel, where the Tsar and Frederick William remained till 8 P.M. The story that they knelt and publicly thanked the Almighty for their victory is devoid, Friederich says, of historical foundation. The allies bivouacked thus: Colloredo behind the line Lösnig-Dölitz-Dösen; Barclay in front of Dösen and Probstheida, and in Zuckelhausen; Bennigsen on the line Zuckelhausen-Zweinaundorf-Molkau; Bernadotte about Stüntz, Sellerhausen, Paunsdorf, and Abtnaundorf; Langeron at Schönefeld; Sacken between Gohlis and the Partha. The French line ran from Connewitz to Probstheida, Stötteritz, Crottendorf, Reudnitz, and the Halle suburb of Leipzig. The outposts of the opposing forces were so close as to be able to distinguish one another's orders. We may appropriately close this account of what was certainly the greatest battle, so far, of modern war, with a quotation from Danilewski describing the scene on the battlefield that night:—

"Night fell; the sky glowed red, Stötteritz, Schönefeld, Dölitz, and one of the suburbs of Leipzig were in flames. Whilst with us (the allies) all were intoxicated with joy, and messengers of victory sped in every direction, indescribable confusion reigned in the enemy's army. Their baggage, their artillery, their broken regiments, the soldiers of which had been for days without food, were stopped for want of bridges over the streams round Leipzig. In the narrow streets resounded the cries of woe of innumerable wounded, as our shot and shell fell upon them. Over the battlefield, so recently filled with the thunder of 2000 guns, there reigned the stillness of the grave. The silence ensuing after a battle has something terrible in it which inspires the soul with an unspeakable feeling."[1]

The first remark to be made about the battle of the 18th

[1] *Danilewski*, pp. 259-60.

is that, from the point of view of Napoleon's interests, it should never have taken place at all, at least, not on the scale or in the position in which it did. There can be no possible doubt that, after the negative result of the 16th, the Emperor's hope of success was gone, and he should, from a military point of view, have set about preparing for retreat on the 17th, starting that same night. Had he done so, he could have had the greater part of his army beyond the Elster by the morning of the 18th. The allies would probably have advanced cautiously on Leipzig; for, as it was, they were not aware of his evacuation of his forward position of the 16th. Leipzig lent itself to the fighting of a rearguard action to gain more time for the French army to pass behind the Saale. The Emperor could have built more bridges on the 17th for the rapid passage of his army, and these, as well as that at the head of the causeway, would have been destroyed as his rearguard left Leipzig on the 18th. But his invincible obstinacy, based mainly on political grounds, in holding on to Leipzig, ruined the Emperor. Knowing that Bernadotte, Bennigsen, and Colloredo were coming up, he could hardly fail to realise the enormous superiority of the allies on the 18th.

The position which he chose for what was practically a purely defensive battle was, no doubt, an admirable one for that purpose; but there were no facilities for the offensive, if he had been able to contemplate it. On the defensive, the circumscription of the circle occupied facilitated the rapid movement of reserves to threatened points.

The allies played into the Emperor's hands by distributing their forces all round the circle instead of concentrating great strength against his most sensitive point. The blame for the failure to make an end of Napoleon there and then lies chiefly at Bernadotte's door. For days past he had been hanging back; even on the 18th he might easily have been up three or four hours before he was. Then there would have been an overwhelming force against Napoleon's left on the Partha. Even when he did arrive, Bernadotte acted very feebly. His Swedes did practically nothing, and the

THE BATTLE OF LEIPZIG 371

real success in this quarter was gained by Langeron in the capture of Schönefield, which cost him 3700 men.

When Bertrand issued from Lindenau, Gyulai was actually recalled across the Pleisse, though the order was countermanded before he reached the river. There has always been a suspicion that the allies in this intended to leave open a road for retreat to the French. Friederich says, however, that there is no evidence of this to be found in the archives of Berlin, Vienna, or St Petersburg. The fear of Napoleon on the Continent was still so great that it cannot but seem far from improbable that the allies would have felt relieved to find him gone, even at the expense of a failure to destroy his army. Eighteenth century ideas were still powerful in the allied camp.

The allies were fully aware of their great numerical superiority, for Meerveldt told Napoleon that they had 350,000 men, and believed him to have only 120,000. That was an exaggeration of the disproportion, but still it seems strange that, when Bertrand drove Gyulai across the Elster, the Austrian was not reinforced, instead of being at first told to withdraw farther. Much must probably be attributed to distrust of Bernadotte, who might still fail to appear in his full strength. As it was, he made an unnecessary circuit to cross the Partha at Taucha. He might perfectly well have saved hours by crossing where Langeron did.

There seems to have been a fear amongst the allies that Napoleon would endeavour to break out towards Taucha, between Bennigsen and Bernadotte. When it is remembered that in doing so he would have had Bernadotte and Blücher on his left, Bennigsen on his right, the idea seems absurd. Nothing but a remnant of the French army could hope to get through to Torgau.

Had Bernadotte been earlier on the field, the superiority of the allies in his direction would have been so enormous that Napoleon would have had to use all his reserves there. What, then, would have become of Probetheida, which in any case must have fallen if Bennigsen held Stötteritz and Stüntz, with Bernadotte in force on his right.

There was no commander on the side of the allies great enough to take full advantage of their splendid opportunities. To realise this, it is only necessary to think what Napoleon himself would have made of the situation had it been reversed.

That the French troops fought magnificently is admitted by all, and the credit due to them is all the greater when it is remembered how much they had suffered from almost superhuman exertions, from deficiency of food, and from privations of all sorts. If the rank and file could not realise the desperate position they were in, the knowledge of it probably extended far down in the ranks of their commanders. We have already shown that the attempt to throw the blame on the defection of 4000 or 5000 German allies will not hold water.

CHAPTER XXI

THE STORMING OF LEIPZIG

SCHWARZENBERG'S orders to the generals assembled on the Monarchen Hügel on the evening of the 18th were very short and simple "All parts of the army must be ready in battle order at daybreak to renew the battle. In case of the enemy's retreat, the army will advance, as on the 18th, in five columns concentrically on Leipzig, since only on the capture of the city can the victory be deemed decisive."

The following orders issued in the night:—

(1) Colloredo, now commanding the 1st column, to send Nostitz with three cavalry brigades to reach Pegau at 7 A.M.

(2) Lederer (left of the Pleisse) also to reach Pegau at 7 A.M. Alois Lichtenstein's division also to go thither.

(3) Bubna to march on Pegau, as soon as his troops were sufficiently rested.

Thus Schwarzenberg had already ordered 40,000 men from the battlefield to follow the enemy, and 20,000 more to be ready to move with the same object next day.

An order, sent through Nostitz at midnight, cancelled (1) and (2) above. It said the enemy's retreat was not yet certain. In reality there could be no doubt, and it is not clear why Schwarzenberg gave this counter order.

The night was dark and misty, the French outpost service very good, so it was difficult to get any knowledge of their actual movements.

At 2 A.M. they began evacuating Connewitz, Probstheida, and Stötteritz, and drawing off to Leipzig, leaving rearguards in these places, and numerous camp fires burning.

Only at 5 A.M. did the allies' patrols bring positive news of the French withdrawal.

Napoleon, as soon as he reached the Hotel de Prusse with Berthier and Murat, began issuing orders for the retreat, which he now recognised as inevitable. First, orders were sent to all the marshals to expedite the march during the night of troops, artillery, and all wounded fit to be moved.

Bertrand, with the IV. corps, Guilleminot's division, Quenette's cavalry brigade, and the French part of Margaron's troops were already gone, as well as Mortier with two Young Guard divisions, and two divisions of light cavalry of the Guard.

On the march to Lindenau were the 1st, 3rd, and 5th cavalry corps.

The order of march prescribed was :—(1) Old Guard, except the allied brigade of Rottenbourg; (2) Oudinot's two divisions of Young Guards; (3) the 4th cavalry corps; (4) Augereau and Victor; (5) Sebastiani's 2nd cavalry corps.

For the defence of Leipzig the troops were thus posted :—

Durutte's division, all that remained of the VII. corps after the Saxon defection, in the Halle suburb.

Marmont (VI.), and one division of the III. corps, were to hold the section from the Partha to the Grimma gate.

Souham (less one division) on Marmont's right, right of Souham, the V. corps, then the XI., and finally the VIII., the last resting its right on the Pleisse.

These corps to march away as soon as circumstances permitted.

Macdonald was to command the rearguard, consisting of the VII., VIII., and XI. corps, and, if possible, to hold Leipzig for twenty-four hours longer.

The bridge leading over the Elster to the Lindenau causeway was to be mined at once, and blown up as soon as Macdonald was over.

Having issued these orders, the Emperor looked farther ahead. Bertrand, who should have reached Weissenfels on

THE STORMING OF LEIPZIG

the evening of the 18th, was to spread over the country between Kösen and Merseburg, watching the passages of the Saale and occupying Freiburg. He was also to arrange for the collection of supplies at Erfurt, and other convenient points.

The despatch rider who took these orders to Bertrand was to go on to Kellermann at Mayence, with orders to recall thither all recruits on the march to Erfurt and Würzberg. Also, Kellermann received orders regarding the calling out of the National Guard, and the defence of France. Erfurt and Würzburg were to be provisioned at once. To St Cyr, at Dresden, orders were sent to escape as best he could. Torgau and Wittenberg could capitulate, on condition of free exit for all troops, including sick and wounded.

The Emperor thought of everything, and it was only towards morning that he slept for a short time. Whilst he slept, Murat went to the King of Saxony to propose his going with Napoleon to Erfurt, the Emperor guaranteeing his security. This the king declined, saying he would await the arrival of the allies.

With the fall of darkness the troops began marching through Leipzig. Streams of them poured through each gate into the streets, which no one had thought of arranging to light. Naturally, confusion ensued, columns crossing columns, broken-down wagons barring the roads, and, still worse, the cavalry and artillery recklessly pushing past and through the infantry. Towards morning there was a feeble moonlight, which rendered less difficult the march of the II., IX., and V. corps.

Everywhere in the streets wounded men lay in agony, hungry and unattended. Many of them met an ignominious death by being ridden or driven over in the darkness.

Stragglers who had sought safety in houses came out and joined whatever troops happened to be passing, thus adding to the confusion of the columns.

At 2 A.M. the troops told off for the defence of Leipzig began to withdraw from their advanced positions to the suburbs. As day dawned, strenuous efforts were made everywhere to improve the defences of the place. There were massive houses, brick or clay garden walls, plank fences, hedges, ditches, every sort of defence likely to be found in an open town. But, as Napoleon had selected for the defence of the city just those corps which were nearest the enemy, and would have him following close on their heels, there was necessarily little time left for improvising defences, or for studying the situation. The French soldier, with his inborn genius for the defence of localities, might be trusted to make the best of matters, but some places were insufficiently occupied, others were overcrowded. The gates and smaller entrances were closed, hedges and fences embanked, palisades set up as far as possible Batteries were placed at the ends of streets, and the reserves collected on the open places.

When the allies began their attack, the defenders, under Marmont, Macdonald, and Poniatowski, were thus placed :—

(1) In the Halle (northern) suburb, Durutte's division and the special garrison of Leipzig. Behind him, two divisions III. corps.

(2) On Durutte's right, as far as the Hintertor, Ricard's division of the III. corps, with the 22nd division (VI. corps) behind.

(3) From the Blindentor to the outer Grimmator, the other two divisions of the VI. corps.

(4) From the Grimmator to the Windmill gate, Ledru's and Gérard's divisions of the XI. corps, with Charpentier's and Marchand's in reserve. Of Marchand's men, the Baden brigade was on the right, the Hessian brigade before the inner Grimma gate.

(5) From the Windmill to the Munz gate, near the Pleisse, was Rottenbourg's foreign division of Old Guard (only two battalions) and Poniatowski's corps. Dombrowski's division in reserve behind.

In the inner city, within the old wall, the Badener Count von Hochberg had succeeded Arrighi as governor. He had two Baden battalions and one Italian. The 1200 Saxons who had not deserted were left in front of the king's quarters in the Market Platz.

Altogether, Leipzig was defended by about 30,000 men on a perimeter of about 6500 paces; four to five men to the pace.

Day broke on Tuesday, October 19th, into a beautiful sunny autumn morning. The Tsar and the King of Prussia, with their headquarters, were early on the battlefield. The French, indications of whose movement had appeared in the night, were found to have retired on the suburbs. Even now, when there could no longer be any possible doubt of the French retreat, there was no serious idea at the allied headquarters of attempting to disturb it on the west of Leipzig. At 7 A.M. the allies began to advance on the city.

The battle up to 10 A.M. :—

The whole allied army advanced concentrically on Leipzig; Colloredo, nearest the Pleisse, and Barclay against the south side; Bennigsen on the south-east; the North army on the east; Blücher on the north. Only on the west was there nothing.

Friedrich has given as full a description as is possible of the details of the storming of Leipzig; but there is not much military interest in details of an affair of this sort, and all we propose is to give a general outline of it.

Blücher, on the allied right, was the only general who had any choice of directions, and he decided to make his principal attack with Langeron direct across the Partha on the Halle suburb, whilst a secondary attack, to the right across the Pleisse, was made by Sacken.

Bülow began the advance of the North army about 8 A.M., driving the French from Reudnitz and the other villages which they still held. By 10 A.M. he stood outside the eastern suburbs, with Borstell on his right and the Hessen-Homburg division on his left. At that hour the French had abandoned everything they held outside the suburbs all round Leipzig. The allies stood ready for the attack on the suburbs.

Then there ensued a pause in the action, ordered by the Tsar with a view to negotiations for the surrender of the city. He had been approached by a deputation of the magistracy, who had really been urged to that course by Napoleon in order to gain time. At this time Alexander and Frederick William were at Napoleon's headquarters of the day before, at the tobacco factory. Soon after this deputation, an emissary from the King of Saxony also arrived. Neither he nor the deputation had any military authority. Nevertheless, they proposed to negotiate for the surrender of the city on the basis of an unhindered withdrawal of the French garrison. The two monarchs, anxious to spare Leipzig the horrors of a storm, were willing to agree, and sent Natzmer to say so. Into the details of this negotation which, as might be expected, came to nought, we need not enter.

Napoleon, meanwhile, had been relieved to learn that the allies were making no serious attempt to cut off his retreat by the left bank of the Elster. He had also heard at 7 A.M. from Bertrand, that the Saale bridge at Weissenfels was restored. He at once sent orders for the construction of more bridges there. Bertrand was to occupy the defile of Kösen, and, if possible, Merseburg.

About 9 A.M. the Emperor mounted and went off with Murat to bid adieu to the King of Saxony. Even then he could not make up his mind to speak the truth; for he appears to have assured the king that he would be back again in a few days. The king had, before this, believed he was rid of the French for good, and, as he assured the emissary of the Tsar, it was in this belief that he had already sent his proposals for negotiations.

After a visit of half an hour, Napoleon left his ally and started for the Rannstädt Gate, leading to the causeway to Lindenau. The narrow gate and the causeway were so crowded with the retreating troops that the Emperor and his staff had literally to abandon themselves to the human stream and drift along with it. It was not till 11 A.M. that he dismounted at the Lindenau mill, after giving orders for officers to be posted to direct stragglers to their corps.

Odeleben and others say that he bore the look of a ruined man. Knowing what we do of the calmness which he showed in the midst of the horrors of the retreat from Moscow, it seems safer to believe the evidence of an eye-witness who says, " In his countenance there was nothing which could be read as betraying fear or anxiety."[1] He had schooled himself too well to allow his feelings to be read from his face.

After dictating orders for the defence of Leipzig, he yielded to exhausted nature and slept calmly in the mill.

Second period, from 10 A.M.—Soon after 10.30, when the negotiations had broken down, the attack recommenced. By 11.30 the French had everywhere been driven from the suburbs into the inner city. So far, all had behaved splendidly; now the thought uppermost in the minds of all was of escape. Where men stood to resist, they did so generally because the way behind them was blocked. The left wing was nearest to the bridge, the VII. corps and the XI. were farthest, and in danger of being completely cut from it, as the allies got forward from north and south.

At the Grimma Gate, in the east, the fighting was more desperate than anywhere, for the French, driven by Bülow against the gate, found it shut against them by the Baden troops, who had instructions to allow no one to pass. The massacre was horrible, till at last the gate gave way. Through it the French poured, and, as they got through, the Badeners again closed and barricaded it.

Durutte, meanwhile, had held out beyond the Partha till the advance of Bülow's right, threatening his retreat, compelled him to retire. The bridge over the Partha was stormed by Langeron with fearful loss on both sides. Some of Durutte's men surrendered, the rest made for the Elster bridge.

The awful struggle at the Grimma Gate had continued

[1] Huszell, *Leipzig während die Schreckentage*, p. 68.

with unabated fury, but now the defenders were turned, and the Hessians who held the gate surrendered. It was about 12.30 P.M. On the south, Poniatowski and his companions fought fiercely, but in vain, against overwhelming numbers.

Bülow's troops were pushing westwards through the city; Blücher was struggling forward from the north; the French cause was lost, and the troops had no hope save in reaching the bridge and the Lindenau causeway, now covered by a struggling crowd of desperate fugitives. Even this hope was soon taken from them.

Shortly before 1 P.M. Napoleon, sleeping calmly in the Lindenau mill, undisturbed by the roar of cannon, was at last awakened by a far louder and more awful explosion. As will be remembered, the bridge at the Leipzig end of the long causeway had been mined by Napoleon's orders. The mine was only to be fired when the last of the French had quitted the city. Colonel Montfort of the engineers was in charge of it. In vain he inquired of many passing generals which corps was to be the last over. No one knew. Then he went off to Lindenau to inquire of Berthier. In charge of the bridge he left a corporal of sappers named Lafontaine, with instructions not to fire the mine unless it appeared that the enemy was on the point of mastering it.

Montfort was carried along with the stream of fugitives to Lindenau, but getting back against the stream he found to be impossible. Meanwhile, some of Sacken's skirmishers had got forward into the meadows north of the causeway, whence they began firing at the fugitives. The unfortunate corporal, seeing these men, and seeing no French troops to drive them off, believed the time had come to blow up the bridge and lighted the train. As the fire reached the mine, it exploded with appalling effect. The air was filled with flying fragments of the bridge, with broken parts of waggons, and with the limbs of horses and men, which descended in a ghastly shower on the whole neighbourhood.

As the smoke cleared off, the unhappy soldiers on the Leipzig side of the stream found themselves with no alternative but surrender or a desperate endeavour to escape by

THE STORMING OF LEIPZIG

swimming. Thousands surrendered, others tried swimming; some succeeded, many were drowned.

Macdonald, plunging into the Elster on his horse, succeeded in getting over; Poniatowski and Dumoustier were drowned in the attempt.

Towards the north-west corner of the city another fearful struggle had been taking place as the French and Dombrowski's Poles found themselves between Blücher's troops on the north and Bülow's on the east. Here the slaughter was so awful that, in places, the Pleisse was choked by a gruesome dam of dead men and horses, across which their comrades found a means of escape to the gardens beyond, only to be surrounded there and forced to surrender.

At 1 P.M. the fighting in the city was practically over, and the French troops still on that side had yielded themselves prisoners.

About that hour the Tsar and the King of Prussia, with Schwarzenberg and their staffs, rode into Leipzig by the Grimma Gate to the market-place. Troops lined the streets, bands played, and even the French prisoners, whom there had been no time to disarm, presented arms. The inhabitants, filling the windows and covering the roofs, cheered vehemently, forgetting the horrors of the moment in the prospect of a brighter future. In the market-place the sovereigns met Bernadotte and Bennigsen coming from the presence of the King of Saxony. A little later came Blücher and Gneisenau from the Rannstädt Gate.

Passing the residence of the King of Saxony, who in vain awaited a visit from them, the monarchs tried to go to the Rannstädt Gate, but were prevented by the blockage of the streets, and by the shells which Marmont was throwing from beyond the river to prevent the issue of the enemy. They returned by the Grimma Gate to meet the Emperor of Austria, then arriving from Rötha, whither he soon returned. The Tsar and the King of Prussia then, at Bernadotte's request, went to inspect the Swedes at Reudnitz.

In the midst of the excitement, Blücher alone thought of

pursuit. He would have sent Langeron after Yorck in the morning, had he not required him to support Sacken. He had to rest content with despatching the cavalry of both corps, which crossed the Elster at Schkeuditz at 11 A.M. When the bridge was blown up Blücher, seeing that there were already ample troops in Leipzig, stopped Sacken and Langeron and ordered both on Schkeuditz, which they reached early on the 20th.

In the evening Bennigsen's cavalry crossed the Elster by swimming, whilst Paskiewitch's infantry got across by an extemporised bridge. This brought to an end the French bombardment which had continued all day.

Sappers worked all night at constructing bridges for the allies. The rest of the troops bivouacked in the meadows round Leipzig.

What the losses were on both sides in the four days, 16th-19th October, will probably never be known with any accuracy. All attempts to distribute them between the different days are useless.

The allies' losses have been calculated at from 40,000 to 70,000 killed and wounded, both of which Friederich considers extreme figures. He estimates them roughly as follows, for the four days by nationalities:—

I. Prussians

	Officers.	Men.	Total.
Yorck	176	5,467	5,643
Kleist	244	7,882	8,126
Bülow	78	2,186	2,264
	498	15,535	16,033

II. Russians

	Officers.	Men.	Total.
Main Army	512	11,411	11,923
Silesian Army	250	6,897	7,147
North Army	33	432	465
Polish Army	70	3,000	3,070
	865	21,740	22,605

THE STORMING OF LEIPZIG

III. AUSTRIANS

General Staff	10	...	...
1st Light Division	25	525	550
2nd Light Division	11	227	238
I. Army Abteilung	53	1,441	1,494
II. Army Abteilung	53	1,885	1,938
III. Army Abteilung	39	1,486	1,525
IV. Army Abteilung	99	3,900	3,999
Reserve Corps	130	5,074	5,204
	420	14,538	14,958

IV. SWEDES, ETC.

	9	169	178
Grand total	1,792	51,982	53,784

Other estimates are:—

	PLOTHO.		HOFMANN.		BEITZKE.
	Officers.	Men.	Officers.	Men.	
Prussians	522	14,950	620	13,550	16,430
Russians	576	21,740	800	20,000	22,604
Austrians	406	8,000	360	7,000	8,399
Swedes	10	300	10	300	103
	1,514	44,990	1,790	40,850	
	46,504		42,640		47,536

It is still more difficult to estimate the losses of the French.

Friederich takes them at—

Killed and wounded	38,000
Prisoners	15,000
Sick and wounded in hospitals	15,000
Germans gone over to allies	5,000
	73,000

Camille Rousset says Napoleon had 80,000 men left

after crossing the Rhine. Marmont reckons only 60,000 fit to fight.

The trophies taken by the allies were: 28 flags and eagles, 325 guns, 900 ammunition wagons, besides many burnt by the French before the retreat; 14,400 cwt. of powder, and 40,000 muskets.

Of well-known French generals there were—

Killed. — Poniatowski, Dumoustier, Vial, Rochambeau, Friedrichs, and Delmas.

Wounded.—Ney, Macdonald, Marmont, Reynier, Lauriston, Souham, Latour-Maubourg, Pajol, Sebastiani, Compans, Gérard, Maison.

Prisoners. — Thirty-six generals, including Lauriston, Reynier, Charpentier, Pino, Count Hochberg, and Prince Emil of Hesse.

The most illustrious of the prisoners was the King of Saxony. After waiting in vain all day for a visit of the allied sovereigns, he sent Von Zeschau to request an interview with the King of Prussia and the Emperor of Austria. They referred him to the Tsar. But already the Russian Privy Councillor, Anstett, had informed the king, in the Tsar's name, that he was to be sent to Berlin, where all suitable arrangements would be made for his comfort. Nevertheless, he was a prisoner of war, guarded by a company of Russian Grenadiers. He left for Berlin on the 23rd October.

"The greatest general of the age would have found no retreat from his chosen position unless the enemy had allowed it. It did not depend on him that Sedan was not merely a repetition."[1] No attempt was made by the allies to forestall Bertrand, to occupy Freiburg, Kösen, and Naumburg, or to destroy the bridges at those places. Some allowance must be made for the exhaustion of the allied troops on the night of the 18th, but still it seems more might have been done. With the great superiority of the allies in the east, they might apparently have reinforced Blücher, so as to enable him to interfere with the retreat by way of

[1] Quistorp, *Geschichte der Nord Armée im Jahre* 1813, ii. 307.

THE STORMING OF LEIPZIG 385

Schkeuditz. There was a quantity of cavalry which had done very little on the 18th, and might have been sent to Pegau during the night, and thence, on the 19th, against the line of retreat. The fact is that Schwarzenberg was not of a sufficient calibre as a general. To this may perhaps be added the mortal dread in which Napoleon's genius was held, and the fear that he might have some surprise in reserve against any bold movement. If the allies desired to cut off the retreat of the garrison of Leipzig, their attack should have been directed in greatest force against the French right and left near the rivers, rather than against their centre in the east, where they required to be "fixed." There was a good deal of confusion in the allies' attack, which was unnecessarily deferred. Columns crossed, got in one another's way, and put one another out of action. This was especially the case in the southern attack.

Napoleon's fault was in his neglect of details, which he appears to have left largely to his subordinates, with the result that, whilst his attention was fixed farther west, there was no unity of command in Leipzig. He had hitherto saved his subordinates practically all of the thinking, and now they still looked to him to arrange everything. The greatest fault of all was the reliance for the retreat of a great army on a single bridge. The Elster and the Pleisse are not great rivers like the Elbe, or even the Mulde. Even during the night of the 18th-19th, temporary bridges might have been built. But for this there has as yet been found no order of the Emperor, and, under his system of command, no initiative was to be expected from subordinates.

The premature explosion of the mine at the bridge probably cost the Emperor from 10,000 to 15,000 troops cut off in Leipzig. It appears to have been due to insufficient instructions given to the officer in charge. He, too, must bear some share of the blame for his conduct in leaving the mine in charge of an ignorant corporal, whilst he himself went off to get more definite orders.

CHAPTER XXII

THE PURSUIT AFTER LEIPZIG AND THE BATTLE OF HANAU

GYULAI and Lederer joined Nostitz's cavalry on the 19th October, and were about to march on Naumburg when Schwarzenberg's counter-order stopped them. At 2 P.M. a fresh order reached them, directing them to proceed at once to Teuchern, and to reach Naumberg next day. Later came news that Thielmann already held Naumberg. Yorck reached Halle at 10 A.M. on the 19th, and the reserve cavalry passed through. Yorck, who had noticed little progress in the battle before he left on the 18th, thought that, though Napoleon would probably be beaten, he would yet be able to retreat in good order, and that it would, therefore, be dangerous to risk attacking him. It was only at 6 P.M. on the 19th that he heard of the fall of Leipzig and the march of Blücher on Schkeuditz. The positions of the allies in pursuit on the evening of the 19th October were:—

Gyulai, M. Lichtenstein and Nostitz,—Dobergast.[1]
Murray's detachment—Zeitz.
Thielmann, Mensdorf, etc.—Naumburg.
Yorck—Halle.
Sacken and Langeron—towards Schkeuditz.
Russian and Prussian Guards and reserve—Pegau.

On the 20th the French main body passed the Saale at Weissenfels, protected by Marmont with the III., VI., and VII. corps, facing towards Merseburg. Oudinot had left Lindenau only at daybreak, and was not at Weissenfels till late in the evening.

---

[1] Three miles south-west of Pegau.

THE BATTLE OF HANAU

That evening the advanced troops of the allies were :—
Gyulai, etc.—Naumburg.
Russian and Prussian Guard, etc.—Teuchern.[1]
Kleist and Wittgenstein—Pegau.
Bennigsen—Schönau.
Yorck—Gross Kaina.

On the 21st Gyulai's corps came up with Bertrand's rearguard at Kösen, standing on the heights of the left bank of the Saale, on to which Davout had marched on the 14th October 1806 to the battle of Auerstädt.

The first object of the allies was to prevent the destruction of the bridge. At first they not only got across, but succeeded in nearly reaching the top of the heights. Then they were driven down again and pursued across the bridge. Gyulai, putting himself at the head of a strong force, again turned the scale, repassed the bridge, and captured Neu Kösen on the left bank below the heights. It was not till 10 P.M. that Bertrand retreated. The losses were about 1000 killed and wounded on each side, but the French lost also 649 prisoners.

Yorck attacked the French rearguard at Freiburg on this day, as the army was passing the Unstrut. He was, in the end, compelled to retire, leaving the enemy to complete his passage unmolested.

Napoleon reached Erfurt on the 23rd with, even at the highest estimates, 90,000 or 100,000 demoralised men, quite unfit to face the great armies behind them. At Erfurt he remained till the morning of the 25th when he started again. On the 26th there was a fight with Hunerbein's brigade of Yorck's corps at the Horselberg, before reaching Eisenach. Yorck's cavalry, at the eastern end of the ridge, drove some French skirmishers on to it, and themselves got there, but found it impossible to descend by its south side to the road. They had, therefore, to rest content with shelling the French camp at the east end of the defile, thereby expediting the movements of its occupants. Then they tried to go round to the west end, but were prevented by marshy

[1] Half-way from Pegau to Naumberg.

ground. There was another fight at the west end, where Hunerbein arrived in sight of the camp of two divisions of the Young Guard, amongst whom his shells at first created much alarm. Then, however, a sharp fight developed, which eventually compelled Hunerbein to retire to the hills in his rear.

The line of the French retreat showed very unmistakable traces of the demoralisation of the army. "The roads on which the French retreated," says Plotho, "showed the most unmistakable traces of the disorganisation of the enemy's army. The numbers of corpses and dead horses increased every day. Thousands of soldiers, sinking from hunger and fatigue, remained behind, unable to reach a hospital. The woods for several miles round were full of stragglers and worn out and sick soldiers. Guns and wagons were found everywhere."[1] The allies pursuing Napoleon moved in several columns, the distribution of which need scarcely be dealt with here. They concern more closely the history of the subsequent campaign in France.

But, in addition to the direct pursuit, Napoleon was now threatened by the advance of Wrede with the united Austrians and Bavarians who had recently stood as enemies on the Inn.

THE BATTLE OF HANAU.[2]

It is curious to find Wrede, who certainly owed his military advancement as well as his title of Count to Napoleon, now becoming the bitterest enemy, after Blücher, of the man he had followed since 1805. Even German writers seem to look rather askance at his conduct.

It was perhaps due to his well-known favour with Napoleon that he had earned a reputation in Austria which led to his being appointed to the chief command of the army, with which he moved, south of the Main, to intercept

---

[1] *Der Krieg in Deutschland und Frankreich*, ii. 440.
[2] Map IV. (*e*).

THE BATTLE OF HANAU

such of the beaten French army as might be making for Frankfort and Mayence. With the details of his march we are not concerned.

On the 27th October, he was under the impression that he had only to deal with a flank column of 18,000 or 20,000 men, and that Napoleon was farther north on the road to Coblence. With some trifling successes on the 28th and 29th, Wrede became still more confident. He was at Hanau by 2 P.M. on the 29th with all his troops, except Rechberg's division, which he sent ahead to occupy Frankfort. His army had dwindled, owing to hard marching and detachments, including one he had to leave before Würzburg, which he had failed to take. He had at Hanau about 30,000 men and 58 guns.

Hanau, then a town of some 15,000 inhabitants, stands in the angle between the Main and the Kinzig, a tributary reaching it from the north-east. The town was still surrounded by a wet ditch, though the fortifications had fallen into disrepair. The Kinzig, which flows in a semicircle round the northern side of the town, was, especially in the rainy autumn of 1813, a serious obstacle, passable for all arms only at the bridge north-west of Hanau, and at that a mile or so to the east, near the Lamboi forest. The forest comes down to within a mile of Hanau on the eastern and northern sides. The main road from Erfurt to Mayence passes north of the town, without crossing the Kinzig.

Still under the impression that Napoleon was far away, Wrede, on the morning of the 30th October, posted his army east of Hanau and across the great road, to bar the retreat of the French. His left was astride of the road, facing its issue from the forest. This wing consisted chiefly of cavalry, and of 28 guns. A few squadrons watched northwards on the Friedberg road. The centre stretched from the road to the Kinzig (which was behind it) at the Lamboi bridge. The right was south of the Lamboi bridge. The position was so bad as to justify Napoleon's remark that he had been able to make Wrede a count, but not a general. The separation of the front by the Kinzig, the position of the centre with its retreat barred by that stream, and the facilities offered by the forest to the approach of the French, were the chief defects of the position. If the enemy could seize the Lamboi bridge, the right would be hopelessly separated, and the ruin of the centre and left was almost certain. Napoleon had but 16,000 or 17,000 men available for the moment, but they were sufficient, under him, against Wrede with nearly double that strength.

By noon, after some fighting with the Bavarian advanced troops in the forest, Victor, supported by Macdonald, was at the outer edge of the wood opposite Wrede's centre. Even then Wrede had only just realised that he was opposed to the Emperor. He now called over a brigade from his right to protect the Lamboi bridge. Napoleon had decided to attack in superior force against Wrede's left. Drouot had reported the feasibility for artillery of a track he had discovered through the forest north of the road. The wood opposite Wrede's left was cleared about 3 P.M. by two battalions of Old Guard, and Drouot gradually collected a battery of 50 guns in that direction, whilst the 2nd cavalry corps and the Guard heavy cavalry assembled behind him. Wrede's 28 guns were soon mastered, and then the French cavalry charged that of Wrede's left, who were carried away and driven off the field. Wrede's centre, hard pressed by Drouot's guns, and with the French cavalry now descending on it from the left, held out for a time, but was presently compelled to retreat. With the Kinzig barring direct retreat, it had to move to its left, an operation in which it naturally suffered heavily. The last three battalions were cut off and driven into the Kinzig, where several hundreds were drowned. The remains of Wrede's centre and left assembled at Gross Auenheim.

When Wrede saw the danger to his left and centre, he tried to bring help from his right across the Lamboi bridge. The first brigade, called over earlier, was already retreating

THE BATTLE OF HANAU

when the second succeeded, for the moment, in driving the pursuers back to the wood. Then the tide turned again, and both brigades were pushed in confusion on to the bridge, which was insufficient for their passage. Here again several hundreds were drowned in the Kinzig.

That night Wrede bivouacked with his right on the Lamboi bridge, his centre and left along the Aschaffenburg road and holding Hanau.

Napoleon, having driven Wrede across the Kinzig, had no desire to pursue him. He continued his retreat on Frankfort, leaving a rearguard to keep Wrede from interfering with the remainder of the army still behind.

At 2 A.M. on the 31st Hanau was bombarded, and presently Wrede evacuated it, leaving it to be occupied without resistance by Bertrand when he arrived at 8 A.M.

With Bertrand in Hanau, and Marmont preventing his issue over the Lamboi bridge, Wrede could do nothing against Napoleon's troops passing along the road beyond. By 3 P.M. all had passed and Marmont followed with the III. and VI. corps, still leaving Bertrand with the IV. to cover the retreat.

When Wrede again advanced he completely failed in his attack on the Lamboi bridge. In storming Hanau itself, he was badly wounded. An attack on the Kinzig bridge beyond the town, to which the French retired, failed, and there was now no further obstacle to Napoleon's retreat to Mayence through Frankfort, which had been evacuated by Rechberg as the French approached.

In the four days, 28th to 31st October, Wrede lost about 9250 officers and men. The French loss in killed and wounded was probably less, but during this period there fell into the hands of the enemy, in small detachments or as stragglers, 5 generals, 280 officers, and about 10,000 men.

There is not much to be said about the battle of Hanau. The position taken up by Wrede was hopelessly bad, and he suffered the penalty of taking it. He seems to have realised what was coming when he learnt that he was in the presence of his late master, for he remarked that he was bound to fight, and that he and his men must just do their best. On the whole, he might consider himself fortunate in saving any part of his centre and left, which had to pass round the northward bend of the Kinzig before reaching a passage at the bridge of the branch road joining Hanau to the main road.

Napoleon had, with unerring instinct, instantly seized the features of the battlefield and the weaknesses of Wrede's position. He could not avoid fighting. He was probably not anxious for another battle, though he felt satisfaction in reading Wrede, who after all had treated him with considerable ingratitude, a severe lesson.

Here we close the history of this campaign, for it is unnecessary to follow the course of the operations of the allies against the fortresses still held by Napoleon's garrisons in Germany. A few words may, however, be said about the fate of Dresden and St Cyr. It has already been told how Napoleon, after deciding to take St Cyr north with him and to abandon Dresden, made that fatal change which deprived him of the I. and XIV. corps, which he so badly needed at Leipzig. Not only that, but he also insisted on keeping Magdeburg, Torgau, and Wittenberg, the garrisons of which and of Dresden would have given him at least 50,000 more men at Leipzig, and might even have changed the result of the battle of the 16th.

St Cyr at Dresden, blockaded by Russians and Austrians after Leipzig, made some ineffectual attempts to escape down the right bank of the Elbe. Then, the garrison and the inhabitants being reduced to the greatest straits by starvation, he accepted a capitulation under which the garrison was to be sent back to France under promise not to serve again in the war. The capitulation was signed on the 11th November, and the garrison was already on the march to France, when it was announced that Schwarzenburg had refused to ratify it. Though the allies offered to replace St Cyr in Dresden in exactly the same position, as to arms, provisions, etc., as he held when the capitulation was signed, he considered it useless to return, and he and his army became prisoners of war.

Under all the circumstances, the conduct of the allies in this matter seems open to censure.

INDEX

ALBERT (French General), 129, 132, 255
Alexander I. (Tsar of Russia), 5, 58, 59, 83, 122-124, 130, 134, 145, 153, 181, 193, 203, 217, 233, 237, 238, 249, 327, 332, 337, 348, 359, 363, 377, 378, 381
Armistice of Poischwitz, 156-159
Army (French)—Losses in Russia, 9; organization in 1813, 10; cohorts, 10, 11; levy of four classes, 11; Municipal Guards, 11; levies of conscripts, 10-12; National Guard, 10; elements available, 12; quality of recruits, 13; marine artillery, 11; infantry, 13, 14; provisional corps, 14; cavalry, 15; its quality, 19; village fighting, 20; Eugène's organization, 32, 33
—— (Prussian) — Limitation in 1807, 21; "old" army, 21, 22; "Krumper" system, 22; general reforms, 22; artillery, 21; material, 21, 22, 24; "free" corps, 23; "Volunteer Jägers," 23; compulsory service, 23; "landwehr," 24; strength of army in August 1813, 25; its spirit, 25
—— (Russian), 26
—— (Austrian), 27, 28
—— (Swedish), 28
—— (Other allies), 28, 29
Arrighi (Duke of Padua), 300, 341, 356, 376
Aster (Saxon writer), 202, 206
Augereau (Marshal), 36, 286, 300, 317, 337, 338, 339, 363
Austria (policy, etc.), 5-7, 30, 62, 153, 168
—— (Emperor of), 4, 155, 233, 237, 381

BARCLAY DE TOLLY (Russian general), 30, 46, 100; attack on Lauriston, 112-114; at Bautzen, 120, 121, 128, 129, 132; appointed commander-in-chief, 145; sees danger on 2nd June, 150; plan of campaign, 180; at Dresden, 193, 217, 228, 229; at Priesten, 237; in Bohemia, 279; at Leipzig, 359, 363, 377
Barrois (French general), 131, 133, 134, 203
Bautzen (battle of)—Description of field, 116, 117; fortifications, 118; allies' mistaken assumptions, 119; their strength, 119; dispositions, 120; Napoleon decides to attack on 20th May, 121; action of Oudinot, Macdonald, and Marmont, 121, 122; Napoleon's design, 122; Soult's action, 123, 124; Ney approaches, 123; battle of 21st May, 1st period, Oudinot and Macdonald, 127; Soult, 127, 128; Ney, 128-130; 2nd period, French centre, 131; Soult's advance, 131; Blücher falls back, 131; Ney at Preititz, 132; 3rd period, attack on Blücher, 133, 134; Ney's and Soult's corps clubbed, 134; retreat of allies, 135, 136; remarks, 136-141
Bavaria, political attitude, 55, 317
Beaumont (French general), 105, 106, 259
Benkendorf (Russian general), 34
Bennigsen (Russian general), 289, 292, 294, 316, 355, 359, 360, 361, 364, 366, 376, 381, 382
Berg (Prussian general), 59, 77
Berkheim (French general), 337
Berlin, 34-38, 44, 45, 176, 178
Bernadotte (Crown Prince of Sweden)—Position in 1812-13, 6; and Swedish army, 28; after armistice, 176, 180, 181; at Gross Beeren, 260, 263; at Dennewitz, 271, 277; in September, 291, 292, 299; with Blücher, 306, 307, 308, 314, 315, 321, 322; at Leipzig, 343, 357, 361, 364, 366, 371, 381
Bertrand (French general), 50, 52, 54, 55, 64; at Lützen, 81, 83, 87, 95; at Bautzen, 113, 121, 127,

395

133, 134, 138; 145, 148; at Gross Beeren, 259, 260; at Dennewitz, 272-275; at Wartenburg, 297-299; at Leipzig, 362, 387; at Hanau, 391
Bessières, Marshal, 50, 53, 63
Bianchi (Austrian general), 206, 339, 355, 363
Blankenfelde, action at, 259, 260
Blücher (Prussian general), 30, 33, 36, 37, 44, 46, 57-61, 66; at Lützen, 73, 75, 77; at Bautzen, 120, 121, 129, 131-134; in retreat after Bautzen, 145, 151; after armistice, 168; retires before Napoleon, 187; at the Katzbach, 250, 251, 254, 256; again retires before Napoleon, 271; in September, 290, 291, 292, 294; at Wartenburg, 298, 299; and Bernadotte, 306-308, 314, 315, 321, 322; at Möckern, 341-344; at Leipzig, 356, 357, 362, 367, 377, 381, 382
—— (Prussian colonel), 237, 284
Bogue, Colonel, 364
Bonnet (French general), 63, 77, 82, 83, 123
Bordesoulle (French general), 220, 337, 338
Borstell (Prussian general), 260, 261, 274, 377
Brayer (French general), 367
Bremen, taken by Tettenborn, 287
Brennier (French general), 77
Breslau, 36, 150, 156, 185
Briesnitz, passage of Elbe at, 98
British troops, 29, 364
Bubna, Count, 153, 154, 294, 359-361
Bülow (Prussian general), 33, 91, 151; at Gross Beeren, 260-262, 264; at Dennewitz, 271, 273-275, 278; in September, 291; at Leipzig, 362, 364, 377, 379, 381

CASSEL, raid on, 287
Caulaincourt, Duke of Vicenza, 155, 207
Charles of Mecklenburg, Prince, 298, 299
Charpentier (French general), 82, 335, 338, 362, 376
Chasteler (Austrian general), 212, 316
Clausewitz, 60
Colloredo (Austrian general), 212, 233, 316, 359, 363, 376

Commanders (French), 17, 18
—— (allied), 30, 31
Commissariat, 90, 165-167, 289
Communications, line of (French), 102
—— —— (allied), 94
Compans (French general), 63, 77, 82, 121, 346
Constantine, Grand Duke, 119
Corbineau (French general), 211, 222, 230, 235
Corswant (Prussian general), 135
Curial (French general), 339
Czernitchew (Russian general), 34, 35, 45, 152, 264, 287
Czöllich (Austrian general), 220, 228

DANILEWSKI (Russian historian), 65, 78, 130, 217, 233, 331, 369
Danzig, 32, 47, 48
Davout, Marshal, 18, 39, 41-43, 45, 53 n., 152, 264
Decouz (French general), 202, 207, 214
De France (French general), 259, 274, 275, 345
Delmas (French general), 129, 132, 133, 345, 356, 366
Dennewitz (battle of)—Description of field, 272; Bertrand's fight with Tauenzien, 273; Reynier and Oudinot arrive, 274; Ney ruins battle, 275; defeat of French, 275; retreat, 276; losses, 276; criticisms, 276-278
Diebitsch (Russian general), 235, 319
Discipline, 95
Doctorow (Russian general), 361
Dolffs (Prussian general), 78, 81, 148
Dombrowski (French general), 300, 344, 345, 356, 376, 381
Doumerc (French general), 337
Dresden, 4, 38, 42-44, 46, 47, 48, 53, 57, 59, 60, 96, 98, 102, 160, 163-164, 192, 193, 194-196; battle at, 200-226; surrender of, 392, 393
Dresden (battle of)—Description of field, 194-197; positions of both sides, 25th-26th August, 197-198; allied plan of attack, 198, 199; Russian and Prussian attack, 200, 201; Austrian attack, 201; Napoleon arrives, 201, 202; French reinforcements, 202, 203; hesitation of allies, 203, 204; renewal of battle, 204; progress

INDEX 397

of allies, 204-206; spirit of French, 206, 207; French counterattack, 207-209; results of battle of 26th August, 209; rain sets in, 210; French troops arrive during night, 210; forces available for 27th, 210; despondency of allies, 210, 211; Vandamme's operations of 26th, 211; positions on morning 27th, 211-214; advance of French left, 214-216; Napoleon reaches left, 216, 217; death of Moreau, 217; affairs in centre, 218; French attack beyond Wesseritz, 218, 219; breaking of Austrian line, 219; captures by French cavalry, 219, 220; ruin of Czöllich's brigade, 221; Austrian left destroyed, 221, 222; Vandamme's operations of 27th, 222; Napoleon's return to Dresden, 223; losses of allies, 223; criticisms, 223-226

Drouot (French general), 82, 98, 337, 390

Du Casse ("Le général Vandammé"), 232 n., 246

Dumonçeau (French general), 230, 284

Dumoustier (French general), 57, 209, 381

Dunesne (French general), 239, 241

Durosnel (French general), 102, 110

Durutte (French general), 41, 43, 44, 92, 260, 261, 366, 376, 379

ELBE—Army of, 50, 51, 53, 55, 57, 63, 101

Erfurt, 33, 47, 50, 52, 53, 56, 387

Eugen of Wurtemberg (Prince)—At Lützen, 81; between Lützen and Bautzen, 91, 99; at Bautzen, 115, 135; in retreat, 142; about Pirna, 211, 218; from Pirna to Kulm, 230, 234, 235, 236; at Leipzig, 332, 333, 337, 338, 363

Eugène Beauharnais (Viceroy of Italy)—Commands in Germany, 32; position and troops, 33; retires to Frankfort-on-Oder, 34; to Berlin, 36, 38; behind Elbe, 39; decides to defend lower Elbe, 40; recrosses Elbe and fights at Möckern, 45; retires again, 45; at Lützen, 82, 89; in pursuit after Lützen, 93; sent to Italy, 101

FONTANELLI (French general), 260, 273, 299

Fortifications—At Bautzen, 118; at Dresden, 163, 164, 193, 195, 196, 200, 201; Magdeburg, Torgau, etc., 162; Hamburg, 164; on the Bober, 189; at Leipzig, 326, 376

Fortresses, 162-165

Foucart (French historian), 109 n., 136

Fournier (French general), 262, 344, 345, 356

Fox-Strangways, 364 n.

Frankfort-on-Oder, 34

Franquemont (French general), 50, 54, 57, 131, 298

Frederick William, King of Prussia, 5, 6, 37, 58, 83, 124, 130, 181, 203, 204, 227, 233, 237, 238, 249, 292, 337, 359, 377, 378, 381

Free Corps, 23, 34, 35, 54, 152, 287, 288

Freiburg, action at, 387

Friederich (Prussian historian), 21, 179, 182, 184, 211, 241, 244, 246, 277, 299, 309, 310, 319, 352, 365, 377

Friederichs (French general), 123

GÉRARD (French general), 27, 39, 253, 256, 335, 338, 376

Girard (French general), 39, 63, 76, 77, 80, 264

Glashütte, action at, 237

Glogau, 33, 35, 44, 47, 149, 150

Gneisenau (Prussian general), 30, 84, 119, 145, 381

Gobrecht (French general), 231

Görda, action at, 287

Gortchakow (Russian general), 120, 121, 333, 336

Gourgaud (French general), 193

Grenier (French general), 34, 39

Grosser Garten, 195, 196, 200, 201, 204, 208, 214

Gross Beeren (battle of)—Bertrand at Blankenfelde, 259, 260; Reynier at Gross Beeren, 260-262; cavalry fight in evening, 262; criticisms, 263, 264

Gross Görschen, battle of (see Lützen, battle of),

Grouard (French writer), 179, 246

Grouchy (French colonel), 111, 112

Guilleminot (French general), 262

Gustavus Adolphus, 70, 342

Gyulai (Austrian general), 339-341, 355, 362, 368, 386, 387

HAGELBERG, action at, 264
Halle, 56, 57, 59, 61, 91, 386
Hamburg, 39, 44, 152, 164, 165
Hanau, battle of, 388-392
Harz mountains, 51
Havelberg, 45, 47, 48
Haxo (French general), 241
Hellendorf, 230, 231
Helwig (Prussian colonel), 54
Hessen-Homburg division, 261, 273, 377
Hessen-Homburg, Prince of, 359
Hirschfeld (Prussian general), 264, 271
Hochkirch, 117, 133, 271
Holland, 39, 41
Horn (Prussian general), 134, 298, 346, 347, 367, 387
Hörselberg, action at, 387
Hospitals, 167
Hotel de Prusse (at Leipzig), 368, 374
Hoyerswerda, action at, 151
Hunerbein (Prussian general), 298, 346, 347, 367, 387
Huszell (Saxon writer), 379

ITALY, Corps of Observation of, 14, 52, 53, 54, 56

JENA, 53, 56
—— Manœuvre of, 51-53
Jerome Bonaparte, King of Westphalia, 7, 287
Jomini (general and writer), 30, 66, 107, 111, 127, 129, 133, 138, 153, 203, 217, 227, 233, 327

KALISCH, Convention of, 37, 48
Kapzewitch (Russian general), 345, 367
Katzbach (battle on)—Description of field, 251; Blücher's orders, 251; Macdonald's orders, 252; allies evacuate Kroitzsch, 252; confusion among French, 253; Lauriston and Langeron, 253, 255; battle on plateau, 254; defeat of French, 254; repulse of Albert and Ricard, 255; night after the battle, 256; losses, 256; criticisms, 256
Kellermann (French general), 113, 123, 128, 330 n.
Kirgener (French general), 143
Kleist (Prussian general), 56, 61; at Lützen, 73, 74, 83; in retreat, 91; at Bautzen, 132, 133; at Dresden, 204, 217; in retreat and at Kulm, 229, 237, 238, 239, 240, 249; in advance on Leipzig, 316; at Leipzig, 333, 336-339
Klenau (Austrian general), at Dresden, 222, 225, 228; in September, 279, 282, 300, 316; at Leipzig, 333, 335, 336, 360, 366
Klüx (Prussian general), 76, 77, 134
Knesebeck (Austrian general), 30, 181
Königstein, 39, 162
Königswartha, action at, 113
Konowintzin (Russian general), 81
Köpenick, 36
Kösen, action at, 387
Krafft (Prussian general), 261
Krapowitzki (Russian general), 235
Kudaschew (Russian general), 286, 287
Kulm, battles at, 233; description of field, 234; battle of 29th August, 234, 235; 30th, 239-241; action of 17th September, 285
Küstrin, 33-35
Kutusow (Russian general), 4, 33, 35, 37, 38, 44, 46, 58

LAFONTAINE, Corporal, 380
Lagrange (French general), 34, 132
Langeron (Russian general), 113, 251, 252, 253, 258, 344, 345, 362, 366, 367, 379, 382
Lanrezac (French writer), 15, 17, 19, 23, 36, 39, 41, 48, 55, 62, 68, 86, 89, 90, 138
Lanskoi (Russian general), 61, 123, 128
Lapoype (French general), 46
Latour-Maubourg (French general), 89, 91, 121, 122, 127, 142, 203, 271
Lauriston (French general), 35, 39, 56, 61; at Lützen, 74; in pursuit, 91, 93, 94, 110, 111, 112, 114; at Bautzen, 124, 128, 129, 132, 133, 142; at the Katzbach, 252, 253, in September, 300; at Leipzig, 336, 338, 363, 384
Lecoq (French general), 260, 261
Lederer (Austrian general), 212
Ledru (French general), 252, 257, 335, 338, 359, 376
Lefebvre-Desnoettes (French general), 281, 286, 287
Lefol (French general), 330
Leipzig, 44, 47, 59-61, 64, 66, 152
Leipzig, battle of (see also Wachau, Lindenau, Möckern)—Description of field, 324-326; positions

INDEX 399

morning of 18th October, 354, 355; allies' plan, 357, 358; strength of forces, 358; battle up to 2 P.M., 358-363; allies' failure against Probstheida, 363, 364; advance of allied right, 364; defection of Saxons, 365; Bennigsen's advance, 366; Paunsdorf stormed and retaken, 366; fighting at Schönefeld, 367; failure of allies in north, 367; Gyulai watches retreat, 368; end of battle, 369; remarks, 369-372

Leipzig, storming of, Schwarzenberg's orders, 373; French retire, 373; Napoleon's orders for retreat, 374; orders to Bertrand and Kellermann, 374, 375; Leipzig at night, 375; measures of defence, 376; French positions, 376; advance of allies, 377; Blücher, 377; Bülow, 377; pause for negotiations, 378; Napoleon goes to Lindenau, 378; attack on suburbs, 379; the Grimma Gate, 379; explosion of mine, 380; last combats, 381; losses, 382-384; comments, 384, 385

Letort (French general), 337
L'Heritier (French general), 192
Lichtenstein, A. (Austrian general), 220, 228, 279, 282
Lichtenstein, M. (Austrian general), 228
Liebertwolkwitz, Murat's action at, 318, 319
Lilienstein, 162
Lindenau, action at, 339; Gyulai's advance, 340; Bertrand arrives, 341; repulse of Austrians, 341
Lobau (French general), 79, 284, 285
Loewenberg, 187, 189, 190
Lorencez (French general), 121, 127
Lorge (French general), 259, 286, 356
Losses in battles in Russia, 9; at Lützen, 89; at Bautzen, 136; at Dresden, 221, 223; at Kulm, 236, 241; at Katzbach, 256; at Gross Beeren, 262; at Dennewitz, 276; at Wartenburg, 299; at Leipzig, 382-384; at Hanau, 391
Lübeck, 152
Luckau, action at, 152
Lützen (battle of)—Wittgenstein's plan and orders, 66-68; description of field, 69, 70; Napoleon's orders, 71-73; Kleist and Lauriston, 75; Prussian attack, 75, 76; cavalry at Starsiedel, 76; Ney returns to Kaja, 77; Napoleon arrives, 78; Kaja taken and recovered, 79; Blücher wounded, 79; arrival of Russian reserves, 79; struggle for the villages, 79-81; Bertrand, Marchand and Macdonald arrive, 81; allies driven back, 83; Prussian cavalry charge, 83; end of battle and criticisms, 83-90; losses, 89

MACDONALD, Marshal, 5; at Lützen, 81; in pursuit, 105; at Bautzen, 121, 122, 127, 130; after Bautzen, 145, 148; left on Bober, 187, 189, 190; at Katzbach, 250, 251, 253, 254, 256-258; in September, 270, 271; at Leipzig, 334, 335, 337, 338, 359, 360, 376; at Hanau, 390
Magdeburg, 35, 39, 41-44, 47, 48, 52, 60, 162
Main, Army of the, 49-51, 53, 55, 56, 57, 63
Maison (French general), 74, 128, 129, 132, 147, 148, 338
Marchand (French general), 55, 57, 81, 82, 189, 335, 360, 376
Marmont, Marshal, 50, 53; at Lützen, 76, 77, 78, 83; at Bautzen, 121, 122, 131, 133, 146, 148; between Bautzen and Dresden, 176, 178, 187; at Dresden, 218, 227, 229, 232; pursuit after Dresden, 232, 237, 241, 248, 250; in September, 270, 289, 300, 301; at Möckern, 341-347; at Leipzig, 367, 376; at Hanau, 391
Mayence, 54, 56
Mecklenburg, Prince Charles of, 298, 345
Meerveldt (Austrian general), 333, 334, 339, 354, 371
Mensdorf (Austrian general), 287
Merseburg, 57, 61, 320, 321
Messery (Austrian general), 219
Meszko (Austrian general), 206, 219-221
Metternich, 233
Michelsdorf, action at, 147, 148
Miloradowich (Russian general), 33, 38, 46, 57, 60, 61, 64, 81, 86, 88, 91, 93, 99, 105, 120, 127, 130, 217

Mine, explosion at Leipzig, 380
Möckern (near Magdeburg), 44, 45
—— (Leipzig), battle of, 341; Marmont's first position, 341; his views and orders, 342; retires to new position, 343; Blücher's plans, 343; his advance, 344; Yorck's movements, 344; Marmont's plans, 344; failure of attack on Möckern, 345; affairs at Wiederitzech, 345; arrival of Delmas, 345; Yorck attacks French centre, 345, 346; crisis of battle, 346; defeat of Marmont, 346, 347; losses, 347; criticisms, 350
Montfort, Colonel, 380
Morand, Count (French general), 54, 57, 63, 71, 81, 131, 273, 298, 299
Morand (French general), 35, 39, 44
Moreau, 30, 193, 203, 217
Mortier, Marshal, 50, 106, 208, 214, 215, 289, 337
Mouton (see Lobau)
Mouton-Duvernet (French general), 194, 223, 230
Müffling (Prussian general), 30, 70, 134
Mumb (Austrian general), 219-221
Murat (King of Naples), 5, 32, 192; at Dresden, 202, 218, 220, 224; in pursuit, 232, 236; in September, 270, 289; sent against Schwarzenberg, 300, 301, 316; battle at Liebertwolkwitz, 318-320; at Leipzig, 374, 375, 378

Nansouty (French general), 215, 366
Napoleon—Returns from Russia, 1; political situation, 2, 7, 8; organises new army, 9-20; evils of system of command, 17; correspondence with Eugène, 36, 38, 40, 42; first scheme for spring campaign, 47-49; revised plan, 49-52; orders of 28th-29th March, 52; explains views, 52, 53; leaves for front, 54; his use of the Saale, 56; decision to advance, 62; orders before Lützen, 71-73; orders at noon, 74, 75; reaches battlefield, 78; arranges decisive attack, 82; in pursuit after Lützen, 91, 96; and King of Saxony, 96, 97; orders to Ney, 97; crosses Elbe at Briesnitz, 98; prepares further advance, 100, 101; dissolves army of Elbe, 101; rearranges communications, 102; his doubts, 103, 104; orders advance on Bautzen, 106-109; leaves Dresden, 109; orders to Durosnel and Ney, 110; plan for Bautzen, 124; orders to Ney for 21st May, 125-127, 129; during battle, 127, 130, 131, 135; his views on tactics, 140; criticisms, 137-141; his remark on result, 141; and Duroc, 143; pursuit after Bautzen, 142-145, 146, 150; negotiations, 153-156; why he accepted armistice, 156-159; returns to Dresden, 160; plans for autumn campaign, 161; prepares Elbe base, 162; fortresses, 162-165; commissariat, 165-167; hospitals, 167; reconnaissances, 167, 168; his assumptions regarding enemy, 168-170; plan of campaign, 170-180; leaves Dresden, 185; view of situation, 185, 186; moves against Blücher, 187, 188; order for Army of the Bober, 189; scheme for movement by Pirna, 190, 191; decides to move on Dresden, 193; arrives there, 194, 202; his arrangement of troops, 203, 204; prepares for counter-attack, 206; return to Palace, 209; arrangements for 27th August, 210, 213; on morning of 27th, 215; goes to left, 216; directs battery which killed Moreau, 217; return to Palace, 223; criticisms, 223-226; orders for pursuit, 227, 229, 230; goes to Pirna, 231; returns to Dresden, 231; orders to Vandamme, 232; conduct of pursuit and responsibility for Kulm, 241-248; alleged illness, 248; how far responsible for Katzbach, 258; for Gross Beeren, 264; his note of 30th August, 265-268; orders to Ney, 269; changes plans, 269; drives Blücher back, 270, 271; returns to Dresden, 271; position of affairs, 6th September, 279; joins St Cyr, 280; hears of Dennewitz, 281; drives enemy to Bohemia, 281-284; returns to Pirna, 285; goes south again, 285; back to Pirna, operations against "free" corps, 286; inactivity at Pirna, 288, 289;

INDEX

orders of 21st September, 290;
third advance against Blücher,
290, 291; decides to abandon
right bank of Elbe, 291; orders
for this, 293; orders regarding
Rhine fortresses, 294; remarks
on his indecision, 295, 296; sends
Murat against Schwarzenberg,
300; scheme for destruction of
Bernadotte and Blücher, 300, 301;
question of holding Dresden, 302-
305; note of 7th October, 303,
304; views and orders, 9th
October, 306, 307; advance, 9th
October, 308, 309; vacillation
at Düben, 309-314; decides to
concentrate on Leipzig, 315;
defection of Bavaria, 317; orders
for 14th October, 317; leaves
Düben for Leipzig, 318; meets
Murat, 320; correspondence of
15th October, 320, 321; alleged
influence of Marshals, 322;
reaches battlefield of Wachau,
332; reinforces weak points, 334;
passes to offensive, 334, 335;
announces victory, 336; prepares general attack, 336; at
night, 339; interview with Meerveldt, 352; hesitates to retreat,
352, 353; failure to provide
bridges, 353; retires to new
position, 354; personal movements on 18th October, 358, 368,
369; mistake of delayed retreat,
370; orders for retreat, 374; to
Bertrand and Kellermann, 374,
375; on 19th October, 378-380;
reaches Erfurt, 387; at Hanau,
390-392
Ney, Marshal, 49, 52, 53, 63; faults
at Lützen, 72, 73, 76, 77, 85, 86;
from Lützen to Bautzen, 92, 94,
96, 97, 107, 114, 121-123; at
Bautzen, 125-129, 132-134, 137-
139, 146, 149, 187, 190; at
Dresden, 203, 207-209, 215, 250;
at Dennewitz, 270, 271-277; in
September, 299, 300; at Leipzig,
356, 362, 367
Normann (Saxon general), 346, 361
Norvins, M. de (quoted), 304 n.
Nostitz (Austrian general), 337, 386

ODELEBEN (quoted), 20, 248, 283,
291, 379
Oder, R., 35-37, 47, 49
Olsuview (Russian general), 345

Osterman Tolstoi (Russian general),
211, 230, 233-235, 316
Oudinot, Marshal, 92; at Bautzen,
121-123, 127, 130; against Bülow,
151, 152; ordered on Berlin, 179,
180; at Gross Beeren, 258, 259,
262, 267; at Dennewitz, 271, 272,
274, 275, 277; his corps dissolved,
289; at Leipzig, 337

PACTHOD (French general), 54, 127
Pajol (French general), 192, 202,
203, 209, 218, 220
Petri (Prussian mappist), 125, 167 n.
Peyri (French general), 54, 57, 63,
113
Philippon (French general), 222,
230, 235
Plagwitz, action at, 258
Platow (Cossack Ataman), 300, 359-
361
Poniatowski (French general and
Marshal), 6, 9, 33, 35, 47, 270,
316, 337, 363, 376, 380, 381
Positions on various dates:—
(French), 19th February, 35;
25th April, 56; 30th April, 57;
1st May, 63; 4th May, 93; 5th
May, 94; 8th May, 96; 11th May,
103; 18th May, 108; 19th May,
110; 20th May, 123, 124; 21st
May (evening), 136; 22nd May,
143; 23rd May, 144; 25th May,
144; 27th May, 148; 30th May,
149; 31st May, 150; after
armistice, 172; at Dresden, 26th
August, 197; 27th August, 212,
213; 29th-30th August, 236, 237;
Macdonald, 24th August, 250;
Ney, 5th September, 272; 5th
September, 293, 294; end of
September, 294; 7th October,
305, 306, and Map 1 inset (c);
9th October, 309; evening, 11th
October, 314, and Map 1 inset (d);
evening, 15th October, 321, 322;
16th October, 329, 330; morning,
18th October, 354, 355; 19th
October, 376
(Allies), 19th February, 35;
26th April, 59; 1st May, 64;
19th May, 120; evening, 21st
May, 135, 136; 23rd May, 144;
27th May, 149; 4th June, 151;
26th August at Dresden, 197;
27th August, 211, 212; 29th-
30th August, 236; end of
September, 294; 3rd October,

300; 7th October, 306; 16th October, 330, 331; morning, 18th October, 355; night, 18th October, 369; evening, 19th October, 386; 20th October, 387
Prague, Congress of, 160
Prussia, 5, 34, 35, 37, 49
Puthod (French general), 92, 124, 148, 252, 257, 258

Quiot (French general), 230, 231, 239
Quistorp (Prussian writer), 384

Radetzky (Austrian general), 30, 180, 228, 292, 293, 334
Raglowich (Bavarian general), 50, 54, 259, 275
Raids, 35, 54, 152, 287, 288
Rajewski (Russian general), 113, 336, 338
Rechberg (Bavarian general), 37, 39, 41
Reichenbach, combat at, 142
Reiset (French general), 121
Reuss, Prince, 231, 233
Reynier (French general), 6, 33, 35, 42, 43, 96, 108, 132, 142, 259, 260-262, 272, 274, 275, 356, 361, 364, 365
Rhenish Confederation, 7, 62
Rhine, R., 41, 42, 162
Ricard (French general), 77, 129, 132, 255, 367, 376
Ried, Convention of, 317
Rochambeau (French general), 132, 364
Rockets (Congreve), 364
Röder (Prussian general), 68, 77, 132, 134
Roguet (French general), 39, 43, 57, 202, 203, 214, 215
Roth (Russian general), 200, 214, 216
Rousset, Camille (French writer), 9 n., 15-17

Saale, R., 42, 43, 45, 50, 56, 57, 162, 307, 322, 387
Sacken (Russian general), 35, 251-255, 347, 356, 362, 367, 382
St Cyr, Carra (French general), 39, 44
St Cyr, Marshal Gouvion, 13, 18, 34, 35, 36, 41, 63 n., 140, 167, 178, 180, 188, 189, 191-193, 202, 215, 224, 227, 229, 232, 241, 280-285, 301, 375, 392, 393

St Priest (Russian general), 81, 252, 347, 356, 367
Saxony, King of, 46, 96, 97, 98, 361, 365, 375, 378, 381, 384
Schäfer (Prussian general), 333, 335, 387
Scharnhorst (Prussian general), 44, 58, 60, 80
Schuler (Prussian colonel), 237, 238
Schwarzenberg (Austrian general), 6, 30, 33, 34, 35, 47, 191, 192, 197, 198, 204, 227, 237, 279, 282, 292, 316, 317, 322, 323, 326, 327, 328, 331, 332, 334, 355, 375, 381, 392
Schweidnitz, 146, 149
Sebastiani (French general), 92, 108, 252, 253, 256, 270, 335, 338, 360
Sehr (Saxon general), 260, 261
Serrurier (French general), 204
Sokolnicki (French general), 330 n.
Souham (French general), 61, 63, 64, 77, 129, 132, 251, 256, 258, 339
Soult, Marshal, 18, 121, 123, 127
Spandau, 33-35, 46
Stadion, Count, 153, 154
Stedingk (Swedish general), 271
Steinmetz (Prussian general), 93, 133, 134, 346
Stettin, 33, 35, 38, 47, 48, 49
Stewart (Colonel), 343
Strengths on various dates:—
  (French) 19th February, 35; 10th March, 39; beginning of April, 49; 12th April, 53; 25th April, 55; 15th May, 101; 21st May, 136; after armistice, 169, 170; at Dresden, 197, 199, 210; end of September, 296; 7th October, 306; Murat on 10th October, 310; morning, 16th October, 328; 18th October, 358, in Leipzig, 19th October, 377
  (Allies) 18th February, 35; 15th March, 38; 1st May, 65; 15th May, 101; 19th May, 119; after armistice, 169, 170; at Dresden, 198, 199; at Blankenfelde, 259; at Gross Beeren, 263; 16th October, 328; 16th to 19th October, 329; 18th October, 358
Striegau, 149
Sweden, 6, 7

Tangermunde, 45
Tauenzien (Prussian general), 259, 260, 271, 273, 314, 315, 316
Tauroggen, Convention of, 6

INDEX 403

Tchichagow (Russian general), 32, 33, 34
Teste (French general), 202, 203, 209, 218
Thielmann (Saxon general), 46, 96, 97, 98, 287
Thorn, 34, 46, 100
Thümen (Prussian general), 273, 274, 299, 314-316
Toll (Russian general), 30, 58, 59, 60, 180, 181, 228, 327, 335
Torgau, 39, 92, 96, 98, 162, 299
Tormassow (Russian general), 58, 59, 61
Trachenberg, protocol of, 181-183; modified, 183-184, 271
Tschaplitz (Russian general), 113, 123, 128, 132

VANDAMME (French general), 194, 211, 218, 222, 224, 229, 230-232, 234, 235, 237, 238-241
Victor, Marshal, 39, 92, 108, 147, 149, 218-222, 284, 337-339, 363, 390
von Boyen (Prussian general), 21, 260
von Caemmerer (Prussian writer), 68, 73, 75, 88, 89, 112, 124, 125, 137, 169, 223, 295, 322, 323
von Hochberg, 376
von Zeschau (Saxon general), 365

WACHAU (battle of)—Description of field, 324-326; Schwarzenberg's orders, 326-328; positions of troops, 329, 330; Wittgenstein's plan of attack, 331; Schwarzenberg's proclamation, 331 n.; Tsar tries to correct faults, 332; Eugen of Wurtemberg's attack on Wachau, 332, 333; Kleist's on Markkleeberg, 333; Gortchakow, Pahlen and Klenau, 333; Meerveldt, 333, 334; Napoleon reinforces weak points, 334; Macdonald takes Kolm Berg, 335; Lauriston retakes Liebertwolkwitz, 336; fight at Wachau and Markkleeberg, 336; Meerveldt's failure, 336; Napoleon anticipates victory, 336; prepares general attack, 336, 337; advance of Victor, Oudinot, Poniatowski, and Augereau, 337; cavalry fight of Letort and Berkheim, 337; Drouot's battery, 337; Bordesoulle's cavalry charge, 337, 338; French left advance, 338; Maison at Guldengössa, 338; Victor at Auenhain, 339; critical position of French right, 339; Meerveldt crosses Pleisse but is driven back and taken, 339; positions at night, 339; criticisms, 348-350
Walmoden (Swedish general), 152, 287
Wartenburg, passage of Elbe at, description of field, 297; Mecklenburg's attack, 298; Steinmetz, Horn, and Hunerbein, 298; Blücher arrives, 298; Franquemont's retreat, 298; retreat of French, 299; losses, 299
Weissenwolf (Austrian general), 220, 339, 355
Winzingerode (Russian general), 37, 76, 81, 271, 367
Wittenberg, 92, 96, 162
Wittgenstein (Russian general), 33, 37, 38, 44, 46, 58, 60, 61, 112, 119, 123, 124, 130, 145, 191, 193, 208, 214, 229, 281, 316, 331, 332
Wobeser (Prussian general), 299
Wolkonski (Russian general), 59, 61, 78
Wolzogen (Russian general), 230, 234, 334
Woronzow (Russian general), 152
Wrede (Bavarian general), defeated at Hanau, 388-392

YERMOLOW (Russian general), 134, 230, 235
Yorck (Prussian general), 5, 33, 35, 120, 251-255, 298, 344, 345, 346, 387
Yorck von Wartenburg (Prussian writer), 47, 80, 82, 113, 126, 131, 133, 134, 151, 165, 177, 244, 291, 356, 362, 367, 387

ZIETHEN (Prussian general), 134, 147, 148, 239, 240, 335, 338, 360

EXPLANATION.

GENERAL FOR ALL MAPS.

※※ Leafy wood.	Gr.	Gross.		■ ■	French Troops (Infantry, Cavalry, Artillery.
♣♣♣ Pine wood.	K).	Klein.		□ □	Allied Troops (Infantry, Cavalry, Artillery.
▨ Lake or pond.	df. (termination)	dorf.			Earlier positions of French
	bg.		berg or burg		Troops where two sets of positions are shown
≈≈ Marsh or marshy meadows	S (after a name)	Berg in case of a hill: Bach in case of a stream.	⊙ ⊙	on same Map.
▦▦ Redoubts, etc.	Sm. (termination)	bauen.	⚬ ⚬	Earlier positions of Allied Troops where two sets of positions are shown on same Map.

Map Sheet I.
GENERAL MAP OF THEATRE OF WAR.

Positions marked in Eastern portion are those of 1st June, 1813. The numbers of French Corps are shown by Roman figures in brackets.

G. Imperial Guard.   M. Marchand's Division, III. Corps.

INSET (a)
The French march to concentrate on the Saale in April, 1813.
Positions shown are those of Corps, etc., on the 29th April. Numbers of Corps shown in Roman figures in brackets. Those along the Lines of March are in the order of March.

G. Imperial Guard.   Ba. Bavarian Division.
Wa. Westphalian Division.   E. Army of the Elbe.
Bs. Baden Division.

INSET (b)
Positions of both sides on the 30th April (see general explanations above) and 1st May.
Numbers of French Corps in Roman figures.

V. Four Battalions, V. Corps at Halle.   G. Guard Infantry.
A. Durutte's Division, VII. Corps.   IV1. Franquemont's Württemberg Division of IV. Corps.
(T) 1st Cavalry Corps.   V1. Friederich's Division, VI. Corps.
G.C. Guard Cavalry.

ALLIES.
Y. Yorck's Corps.   W. Winzingerode's Corps.
B. Blücher's Corps.   RG. Russian Guard and Grenadiers.
Bg. Berg's Corps.   M. Miloradowich's Corps.

INSET (c)
Diagram of general positions, evening of 7th October :—
FRENCH.
G. Guard, Macdonald and Sebastiani.
A. Arrighi (Garrison of Leipzig).
Other Corps shown by Roman numerals.
Murat's Army not shown – farther South.

ALLIES.
Be. Bernadotte.
Bl. Blücher.
Bohemian Army not shown – farther South facing Murat.
Also Bennigsen and Bubna not shown.

INSET (d)
Diagram of general positions, evening of 15th October, 1813 :—
French Corps marked as usual.
M. Murat, G. Guard and Napoleon.

ALLIES.
Te. Tettenborn and Thielman.   W. Wobeser – watching Torgau.
Be. Bernadotte – North Army.   Bl. Blücher – Army of Silesia.
Sw. Schwarzenberg's Army.   Bn. Bennigsen – Reserve Army.
Bu. Bubna – watching Dresden – right bank of Elbe.

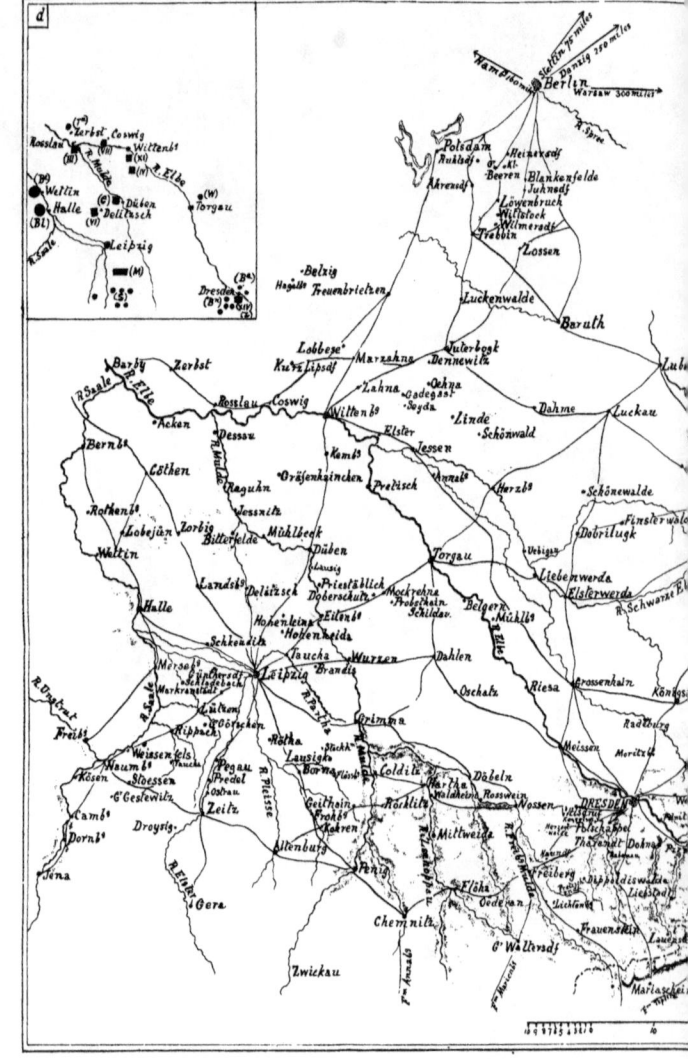

Map Sheet II.

(a) THE BATTLE OF LÜTZEN.

Positions of Troops about 11 a.m. (☐ ○ &c.) and 6 p.m. (■ ● &c.).
Figures on Map are approximate heights in feet above contour

FRENCH.

G.	Guard Infantry.	Br.	Brennier's Division, III. Corps.
G.C.	Guard Cavalry.	M.	Marchand's ,, ,,
Y.G.	Young Guard.	S.	Souham's ,, ,,
O.G.	Old Guard.	Gi.	Girard's ,, ,,
N.	Ney with remains of Four Divisions, III. Corps.	Ma.	Marmont's VI. Corps.
		Mo.	Morand's Division, IV. Corps.
Md.	Macdonald XI. Corps.	Pi.	Peyri's ,, ,,
L.M.	Latour-Maubourg 1st Cavalry Corps.	Dt.	Drouot's 80-gun Battery.
R.	Ricard's Division, III. Corps.		

ALLIES.

Bl.	Blücher's Corps.	R.	Reserve.
Y.	Yorck's ,,	R.G.	Russian Guard and Grenadiers.
Bg.	Berg's ,,	Kn.	Konownitzin's two Divisions, Russian Grenadiers.
E.	Prince Eugen of Wurtemberg (Winzingerode's Infantry).	G.	Gallitzin—Russian Guard Cavalry.
D.	Dolff's Prussian Reserve Cavalry.	Sz.	Steinmetz's Division, Yorck's Corps.
W.	Winzingerode's Corps.		

(b) THE BATTLE ON THE KATZBACH.

Positions about 2 p.m.

FRENCH.

Si.	Sebastiani's Cavalry.	La.	Lauriston, V. Corps.
Xl.	Gerard, XI. Corps.	A.R.	Albert's and Ricard's Division, III. Corps.
S.	Souham, One Division III. Corps.		

ALLIES.

Y.	Yorck.	Ln.	Langeron.
Sn.	Sacken.		

(c) BATTLE OF GROSS BEEREN.

Positions about 3.30 p.m.

FRENCH.

S.	Saxons of VII. Corps.	L.	Lorge's Cavalry.
D.	Durutte's Division, VII. Corps.	Bd.	Bertrand retiring from Blankenfeld.

ALLIES.

Be.	Bernadotte, with Russians and Swedes.	Bl.	Borstell's Corps.
H.	Hessen-Homburg's Division.	Tn.	Tauenzien's Corps at Blankenfeld.
K.	Krafft's Division.		

(d) BATTLE OF DENNEWITZ.

Positions about 3.30 p.m.

FRENCH.

S.	Saxons of VII. Corps.	Sg.	Spitzenberg.
Def.	Defrance's Cavalry.	G.	Guilleminot's Division, XII. Corps.
De.	Durutte's Division, VII. Corps.	P.	Pacthod's ,, ,,
M.	Morand's ,, IV. Corps.	R.	Raglowich's ,, ,,
Fl.	Fontanelli's ,, ,,	Fr.	Fournier's Cavalry.
Ft.	Franquemont's ,, ,,		

ALLIES.

O.	Oppen's Cavalry.	Thn.	Thümen's Division (Bülow's Corps).
Bl.	Borstell's Corps.	Tn.	Tauenzien's Corps.
K.	Krafft's Division (Bülow's Corps).	K.	Kleist's Detachment from Juterbogk.
H.	Hessen-Homburg's Division (Bülow's Corps).	Be	Bernadotte, with Russians and Swedes.

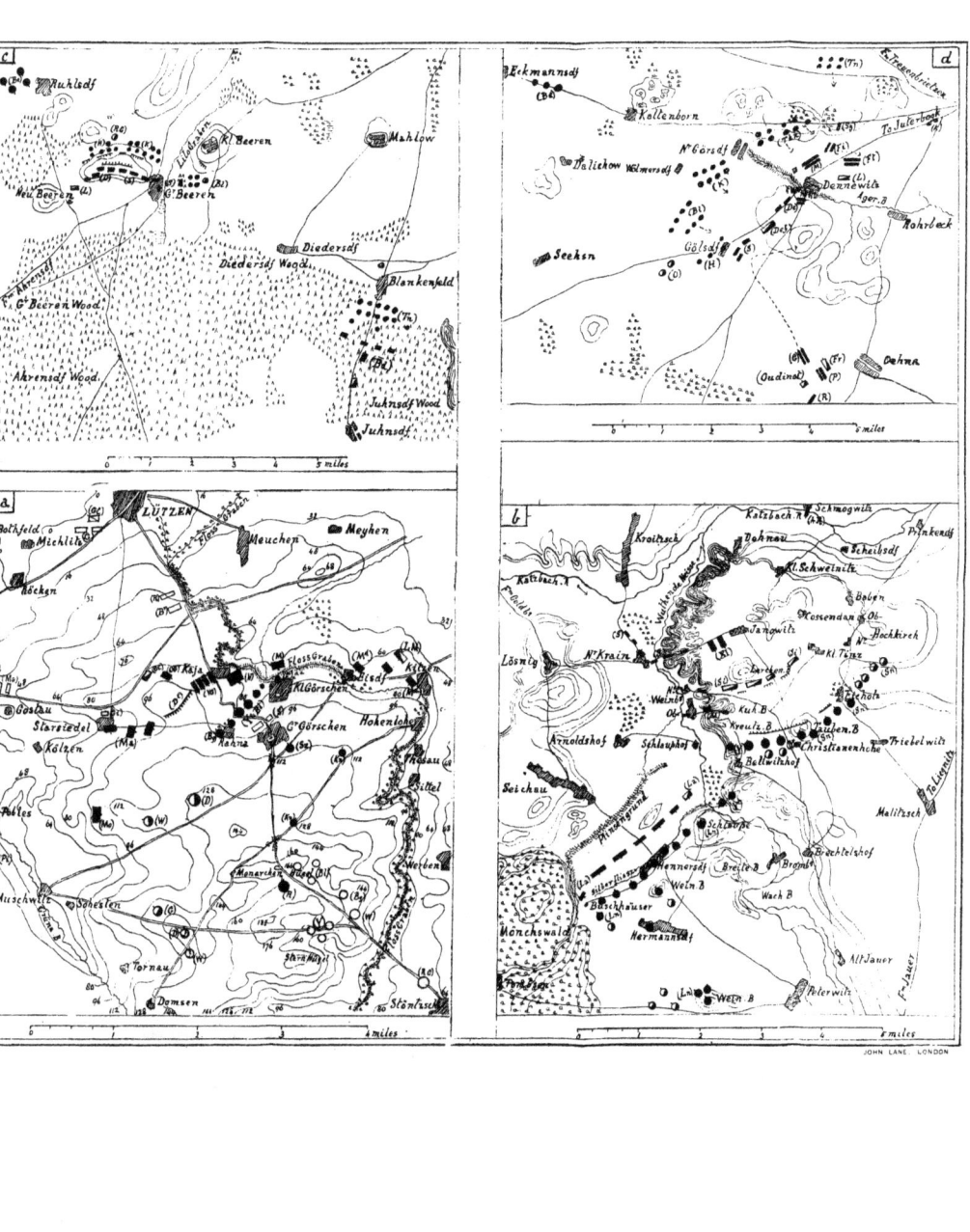

Map Sheet III.

THE BATTLE OF BAUTZEN.

Positions about 11 a.m. on 21st May, 1813.

Figures on Map represent approximate heights in feet above the River Spree where it leaves Map in North.

FRENCH.

XII.	Oudinot's Corps.	P.	Puthod's Division, V. Corps.
XI.	Macdonald's Corps.	Md	Marchand's Division, III. Corps.
G C.	Guard Cavalry.	A.&R	Albert's and Ricard's Divisions, III. Corps
1st.	Latour-Maubourg 1st Cavalry Corps.	D.	Delmas' Division, III. Corps.
G.	Guard Infantry.	S.	Souham's Division, III. Corps.
VI.	Marmont's Corps.	K.	Kellerman's Advanced Guard.
B.	Two Regiments of Barrois' Guard Division.	L.	Lauriston, with Lagrange's Division, V. Corps.
IV.	Bertrand's Corps.		
Mn.	Maison's Division, V. Corps.	R.	Rochambeau's Division, V. Corps.

ALLIES.

Tz.	Tschaplitz's Advanced Guard.	Y	Yorck's Corps.
By.	Barclay's Corps.	Co.	Grand Duke Constantine.
R.	Röder's Brigade.	Bg	Berg's Corps.
Kl.	Kleist's Corps.	E.	Eugen of Würtemberg.
R.C.	Prussian Reserve Cavalry.	M.	Miloradowich.
Bl.	Blücher's Corps.		

INSET (a)

The French march from Lützen to Bautzen, and positions evening of 19th May.
Corps numbers given in Roman figures in brackets in positions and on routes of March.

FRENCH.

(1)	1st Cavalry Corps.	P	Puthod's Division, V. Corps.
(2)	2nd "		

ALLIES.

B.	Barclay, followed by Yorck, retreating.	A.	Main position.

INSET (b)

General disposition of forces of both sides, middle of August.
The approximate strengths of the corps are shown by figures in brackets.

The distances in Marches between the several French group centres are approximately as follows:—

Hamburg to Luckau	12	Marches.	Bautzen to Görlitz	2	Marches.
Luckau to Berlin	8	"	Bautzen to Zittau	1½	"
Luckau to Bautzen	3½	"	Görlitz to Zittau	1	"
Bautzen to Dresden	1½	"	Görlitz to Bunzlau	2	"
Dresden to Teplitz	2	"	Bunzlau to Liegnitz	2	"

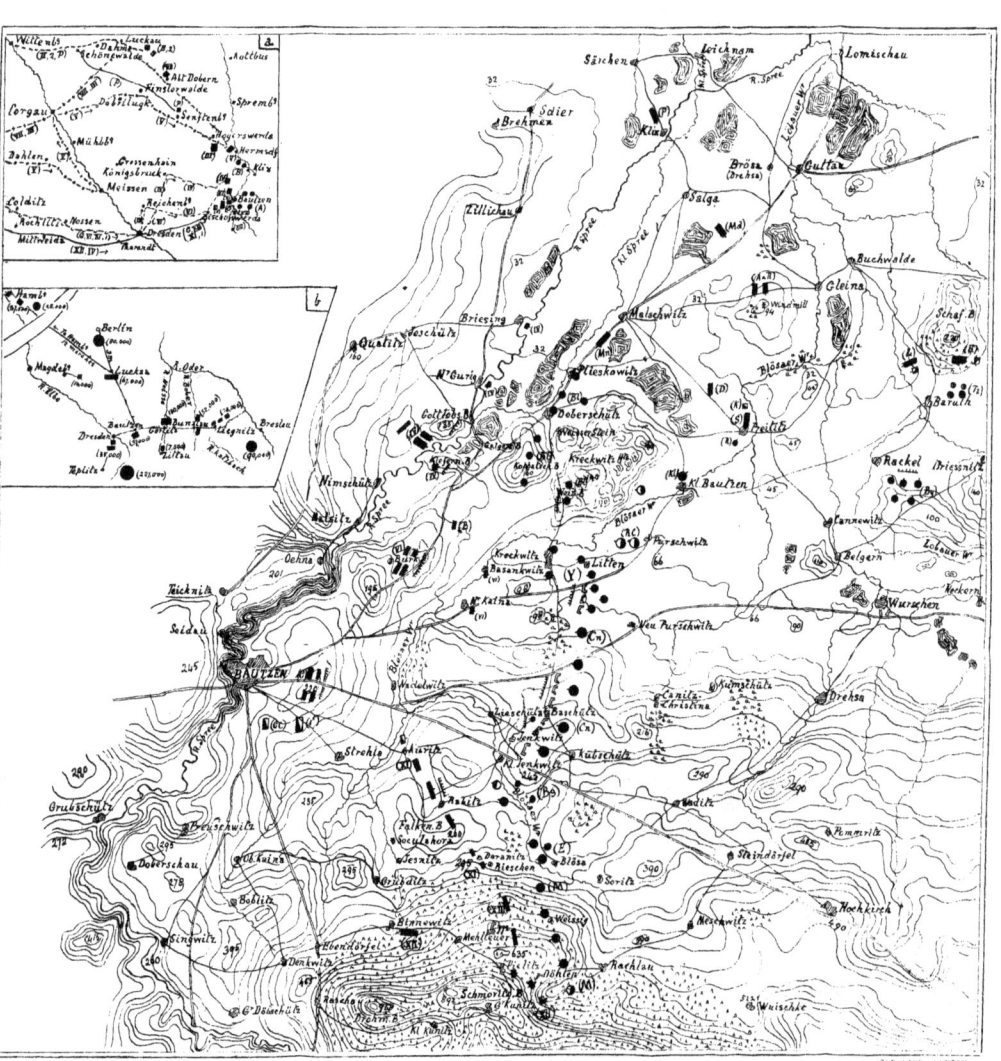

Map Sheet IV.

(a) THE BATTLE OF DRESDEN.

I.V.	French redoubts round Altstadt.	*x.*	Flèche.
a.	Stone bridge.	*5b.*	Boat and raft bridges.

Dresden suburbs not named on Map:—*c.* Ziegel Schlag.   *d.* Rammischer Schlag.   *e.* Lobtau Schlag.

Figures on Map show approximate heights in feet above level of Altstadt.

  —o—o—o Extreme limit of Allies' advance on 26th August.
  —+—+— French Outpost Line, night of 26th and 27th August.
  —×—×— French Outpost Line, night of 27th and 28th August

Troop positions at beginning of Battle of 27th August:—

FRENCH.

Mu.	Murat's Cavalry.		*O.G.*	Old Guard (Reserve).
T.	Teste's Division.		*St.C*	St. Cyr's Corps (XIV.).
P.	Pajol's Cavalry.		*N.*	Ney (Young Guard).
V.	Victor's Corps (II.).		*Mo.*	Mortier (Young Guard).
Ma.	Marmont's Corps (VI.).		*Ny.*	Nansouty's Cavalry.

ALLIES.

Rh.	Roth's Advanced Guard.		*Ch*	Chasteler's Division.
P.R.C.	Prussian Reserve Cavalry.		*Ch G.*	Chastek's Grenadiers.
Wn.	Wittgenstein's Corps.		*Bi.*	Bianchi's Division.
P.	Prussians (Kleist, etc.).		*Wf.*	Weissenwolf's Division.
Zn.	Ziethen's Advanced Guard.		*Sch*	Schuler's Cavalry.
Ph.	Pirch's Division.		*Cz.*	Czöllich's Brigade.
P.A.	Prince August (Prussian Reserves).		*A.L*	Aloïs Lichtenstein's Brigade.
Mi.	Miloradowich.		*Mo.*	Meszko's Division.
Co.	Colloredo's Division.		*Mb*	Mumb's Brigade.
M.L.	Moritz Lichtenstein's Cavalry.		*My*	Messery's Brigade.
Nz.	Nostitz's Cavalry.			

(b) COUNTRY SOUTH OF DRESDEN. BATTLE OF KULM.

Figures on Map show approximate heights in feet above sea level.
Troop positions at Kulm about 10.30 a.m., 30th August, as Kleist reached **Tellnitz**:—

A-A.	Original Line of French, left and centre, in early morning.
B-B.	Kleist's Line of March, Furstenwalde to Nollendorf.
Z.	Ziethen's rearguard.
Kl.	Kleist's main body.

(c) PASSAGE OF THE ELBE, AND ACTION AT WARTENBURG, 3RD OCTOBER.

FRENCH.

M.	Morand's Division, IV. Corps.		*A-A.*	Line of Franquemont's retreat.
F.	Fontanelli's ,, ,,		*B-B.*	,, Morand's ,,
Fr.	Franquemont's ,, ,,		*C-C.*	,, Fontanelli's ,,

ALLIES.

S.	Steinmetz's Brigade.		*D-D.*	Prince Charles of Mecklenburg's movement to turn Wartenburg.
H.	Horn's and Hunerbein's Brigades.			
Mg.	Prince Charles of Mecklenburg's Advanced Guard.		*a*	Prussian Bridges over Elbe.

(d) THE BATTLES ROUND LEIPZIG, 16TH—18TH OCTOBER.

Figures on Map show approximate heights in feet above the level of the Rosen Thal.
References in Leipzig to places which there is not space to name on Map:—*a.* Halle suburb.   *b.* Hinter Gate.   *c.* Grimma Gate.   *d.* Sand Gate.   *e.* Peters Gate.   *f* Ranstadt Gate and Bridge leading to Lindenau.

  ———— French fronts at beginning of Battles of the 16th October.
  — — — French fronts at end of Battles of 16th October.
  —o—o— French front morning of 18th October.
  —+—+— French front evening of 18th October.

(e) THE BATTLE OF HANAU.

  ■ 2 -- French positions at the time of decisive attack.
  ● Q --- Wrede's positions at same time.
  ◌ Q   Wrede's positions after the Battle.

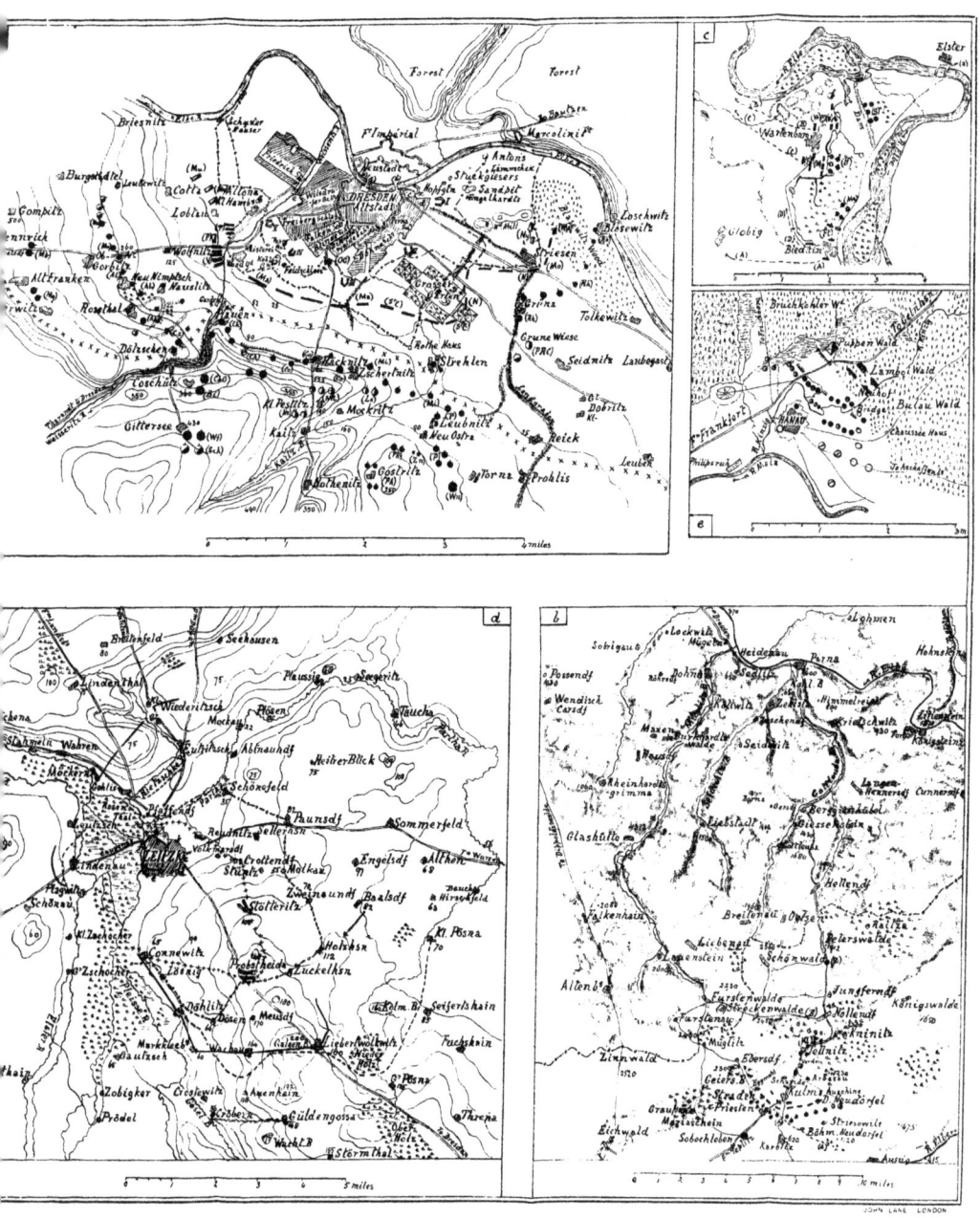

www.ingramcontent.com/pod-product-compliance
Lightning Source LLC
Chambersburg PA
CBHW070957160426
43193CB00012B/1819